D0867036

THE
AMBIVALENCE
OF
PROGRESS

THE AMBIVALENCE OF PROGRESS

ESSAYS ON HISTORICAL ANTHROPOLOGY

Carl Friedrich von Weizsäcker

PARAGON HOUSE
New York

First English translation, 1988

Published in the United States by
Paragon House Publishers
90 Fifth Avenue
New York, New York 10011

Copyright © 1988 by Paragon House Publishers

All rights reserved. No part of this book
may be reproduced, in any form, without written
permission from the publisher, unless by a reviewer
who wishes to quote brief passages.

Originally published in German under the title Der Garten des Menschlichen.
Copyright © 1977 by Carl Hanser Verlag München Wien.

Library of Congress Cataloging-in-Publication Data

Weizsäcker, Carl Friedrich, Freiherr von, 1912–
   The ambivalence of progress.
   Translation of: Der Garten des Menschlichen.
   Includes index.
   I. Title.
AC35.W4413   1988   083'.1   87-22202
ISBN 0-913729-92-2

Manufactured in the United States of America

Contents

THE
AMBIVALENCE
OF
PROGRESS

Self-Portrait

This self-portrait, instead of presenting the author's philosophic positions *in abstracto*, attempts to throw light on the path that has led him to these philosophic positions. Is it that we learn, that we find, philosophy, or is it that we recognize it as that which somehow we have always known?

A. Preparation

For my twelfth birthday, in June 1924, I wished for and got a rotating celestial chart that could be adjusted to the day and hour. Shortly after that, we left Basel, where my father was German consul, for our summer vacation. We went to a secluded pension, Mont Crossin, in the Jura Mountains near Berne. The Swiss Independence Day was celebrated there, as usual, with fireworks on the evening of August 1. There was an outdoor ball for pension guests that began with a long polonaise. At one point the long line of dancers separated, and I managed to lose the young lady I was dancing with. I escaped from the crowd into the magical, warm, starry night with my celestial chart. The experience of such a night cannot be described in words; I can only give the residual thoughts after the memory has faded. God was present, somehow, in the indescribable magnificence of that starry night. Concurrently, I was aware that stars are balls of gas consisting of atoms and obeying the laws of physics. The tension between these two truths must not be unresolvable. But how could they be reconciled? Is it possible to find the reflection of the glory of God also in the laws of physics?

I had begun, perhaps a year earlier, to read the New Testament. The truth of the Sermon on the Mount had deeply affected and disturbed me. If it was true, my life was false; perhaps all our lives were false. During a long talk with my mother I defended to the verge of tears the duty to refuse military service because of the commandment "Thou shalt not kill." During a night of intense religious experience, I had vowed to devote my life to the service of God. I cautiously added "If He should call me." I could only image becoming a minister as service to God, and yet I wanted to become an astronomer. My situation could perhaps best be described as "the moral law above me and the starry heaven within me." I still had to learn that once we begin to listen God is always calling; and later, that God is neither above nor within but that I am in God.

My family comes from Württemberg. My father became a naval officer in 1900, and switched to the diplomatic corps in 1920, two professions that serve the state beyond its borders. My mother, as a young girl, had rather imagined herself doing social work, not being a diplomat's wife; she fulfilled the requirements of his career *sans peur et sans reproche* with a humanity that is not always customary in that profession. Afterwards, during the twenty-three years of widowhood to the present, she cared for the old and sick in the family and stayed young by making excessive demands upon herself. There are ministers, scholars, civil servants, and military officers among my ancestors. The Weizsäckers were millers in Hohenlohe and, later, theologians. My grandfather Carl Weizsäcker, a jurist, was the last minister-president of the Kingdom of Württemburg. On August 1, 1914, he said to his family, "This war will end with a revolution." He supposedly also said, "My fortune is lost." The fortune had been accumulated through decades of saving from modest civil-servant salaries to provide security for children and grandchildren. His prophecies proved accurate. After World War I, the corpulent, and rather short-tempered, old man took me, a little boy, for walks in the forests around Stuttgart. We gathered mushrooms for the family table, and he would occasionally stop to make some witty and worldly remark, something about parliaments on the occasion of finding "a parliament of mushrooms."

My father also liked to go on walks with me and talk about history and politics. In school, I was absorbed in history and indoctrinated my younger brothers and sisters. I thought about the best form of government and decided it would be a constitutional monarchy. In my fantasy land my friends and family were given roles, and there was foreign policy and war; the leading statesman resembled, although contrary to my father's taste, Mussolini (of whom I knew hardly more than that he existed).

As I grew older, two of my uncles played very important roles. My father's brother Viktor, the philosophical doctor whose anthropological medicine is still not understood today, opened for me essentially important horizons. For decades, I worried about certain remarks by him, such as, "I believe the law of causality is a neurosis." My mother's brother, Fritz von Graevenitz followed the family tradition, first as an officer, but after the war as a sculptor in accordance with his nature. He was a man who was newly enraptured each day by the magic and deep laws of beauty.

In Copenhagen, at fourteen years of age, I believed I could perceive the secret of life in nature around me, virtually down to spinning atoms. I began to think about the relationship between truth and beauty. For a while, the phrase, "beauty is subjective truth and truth objective beauty," was helpful to me. Taking long, tiresome walks through the city during the damp, dark, and cold autumn, I thought that since truth was everywhere, I should be able, with the right subjective attitude, to also find beauty everywhere. I discovered beauty in a spot of sunlight on a green copper roof, beauty in the smell of fish in a basement grocery store. On an excursion to Lund on a magnificently bright, clear, sunny December day, I realized that the natural laws that are valid for atoms are not those that are valid for visible bodies, but that the one must be the consequence of the other.

A few days later, my mother invited to our house the twenty-five-year-old Werner Heisenberg. She had met him during a music evening where he played piano and amicably argued with her about the youth movement. This visit determined my direction in life. I was not only fascinated by the almost mad brilliance of the recent fundamental discoveries, which the rather shy, unassuming, blond young man radiated; his superiority in every field, including skiing and chess, was healthy and sobering for my enormous ambition and arrogance. He advised me and tested my mathematical ability, finding it barely adequate. I was soon convinced that theoretical physics was the science where I could find the answers to my questions about astronomy. When I discovered, in my final *gymnasium* year, that the field that actually attracted me most was called philosophy, I was tempted to study that. He advised that to practice philosophy relevant to the twentieth century one had to know physics, that one learns physics only by practicing it, and that one succeeds best in physics before thirty and best in philosophy after fifty. I followed his advice, studied theoretical physics, and have never regretted it.

A few months after Heisenberg's first visit to our house, my father was assigned to Berlin. I was waiting there for the beginning of the school year when, in April 1927, Heisenberg sent me a postcard saying that he was traveling through Berlin to Munich in a few days and that I could meet him at Stettiner station in Berlin and accompany him in a taxi to Anhalter station. In that taxi he told me of his yet-to-be-published uncertainty principle. Then he boarded the train and was gone. The following days were spent walking around Berlin thinking about it. I had a continual dispute with my mother who upheld that freedom of will was a moral postulate to be defended against physically defined determinism. I could never seriously consider the postulate of separating nature and the person. I saw that they could be united in a manner still mysterious to me. But I first had to understand physics. I thought, "If I would now run into Einstein on the street, I would recognize him and, overcoming my shyness, address him and ask him what he thought about Heisenberg's theories." But he must have walked other streets, and I never met him.

Some time later I suddenly realized with a brief but profound shock that I was no longer tied to the religious faith of my childhood. The previous conflict between church and science now seemed less important to me. For example, in the debate about miracles, on the one hand one could apply the psychology of eye-witness accounts to reports of miracles, while on the other hand empirically verifiable natural laws are discovered under certain experimental conditions. In the presence of someone divinely inspired, still other laws could prevail. Finally, the tendency of confirming religious truth through breaches in the divine order of nature appeared rather impious to me. Historical criticism went much deeper. To have been raised a Lutheran is not an argument for the correctness of Lutheranism; to have been baptised a Christian is not proof of the falsity of Oriental religions; to have come from a religious tradition is not proof of the truth of religion. It still amazes me that there are educated, religious people who have not completed this simple thought process and are therefore helpless when confronted with the convenient arguments of antireligious rationalism. I was now in the difficult situation of having to regain and redefine the religious experience for myself.

This sketch of my development, of what I attribute to the circumstances of birth and upbringing, ends here. I will now pursue general problems, leaving aside much of my private life.

B. Philosophical Physics

That I studied physics in order to philosophically understand the quantum theory in a philosophical manner was obvious. My limited mathematical ability made the technical more difficult for me than for most theoretical physicists, and at first I failed. Philosophical problems of physics did occupy the minds of physicists, but I learned, step by step, that neither they nor contemporary philosophers really understood them. For twenty-five years I escaped into unphilosophical, concrete physics, while continuing a quiet meditation on the quantum theory and depressing myself with self-reproach. But physics, like good bread, was nourishing and invigorating, and although it is not really the theme of this book, I would like to dedicate a brief retrospective to it.

Theoretical nuclear physics became possible in 1932 with the discovery of the neutron. I was there, in 1932, when Heisenberg grasped the idea that atomic nuclei consisted not of protons and electrons, but of protons and neutrons that interact through interchanging forces. I chose nuclear physics as my specialty, succeeded in doing some satisfactory work (on the partially empirical theory of nuclear masses, on nuclear isomerics, and on dual β-disintegration), and wrote a textbook on atomic nuclei that I unfortunately did not later republish because of other preoccupations. Because of my old love, I chose astronomy as the third subject, after physics and mathematics, for my doctoral examination. While writing the book, I realized that the knowledge of nuclear reaction now permitted an assault on Eddington's problem of the energy sources of stars. I thought out the carbon cycle that Bethe found simultaneously, and which he worked out more thoroughly. This lead to the question of the historical development of stars and to the drafting of a theory on the evolution of the planetary system that gratified me. I later recognized it as an application of Kant's theory, using modern methods. I had to learn hydrodynamics to be able to deal with these problems more throughly, and to devise a theory of spectrum turbulence. This took place during and just after the war, and later it turned out that Kolmogoroff and Onsager had developed the same theory a few years earlier. For several years, occasionally as a guest at American observatories, I pursued the general theory of the evolution of stars and galaxies. In Göttingen I pursued these problems in a small study group that met in a garret, and out of which came some of today's mul-timillion-dollar-budget administrators like Lüst and Häfele. The next necessary step in physics was the introduction of plasma physics. I have not participated in this because I returned to my central quest by devoting myself to philosophical physics (since 1954) and by accepting a professorship in philosophy (in 1957).

All of my work in concrete physics suffers from deficiencies. It was not intention or carelessness, but weakness, of which I was always conscious. I would recommend that no one follow my example. But I was still a physicist among physicists, and if I find myself again in that circle, it is like coming home.

Now, on to philosophical physics. In January 1932, when I was nineteen years old, Heisenberg took me to his teacher Niels Bohr. I witnessed there a three-hour-long discussion between them about philosophical problems of the quantum theory. Afterwards I wrote, "I have seen a physicist for the first time," quite unfair toward Heisenberg and many others, but meaning, "Here is a person who practices physics as it must be done." Bohr was the only physicist in whom one sensed, with every word, how he suffered from thinking. Perhaps, he suffered mainly from speaking. In his later years, he said, "We are trapped in language. One must talk, one can do nothing else but talk, but saying what one should say, this one cannot do." For months, during long walks, I tried to understand what he had awakened in me. Then I wrote a note that began with the phrase "Consciousness is an unconscious act." With a youth's focus, I believed that I now had the insight around which I could construct "my" philosophy. I found out much later that the phrase came from William James, whom Bohr was reading at the time. A clever aperçu of a great psychologist had entered my unconscious and had emerged as a seed for crystallization. I was unable to construct on it anything consistent.

I slowly acquired fragments of actual philosophy. The positivism of the Vienna Circle initially appealed to the physicist in me. I have felt, ever since, that if one did not at least understand the technique, practiced there, of inquiring into the meaning of statements, one could not participate in the dialogue. However, it soon became apparent that this school never even approached the problems of physics as Bohr saw them. It employed an uncritical concept of experience in which everything was assumed that should have been explained. Only in Kant could I find the possibility of this kind of criticism. My friend Georg Picht gradually introduced me to Kant, Aristotle, and Plato. I came to know Heidegger personally and experienced his incredible power of questioning into the core of the respective problem. But I could confront the philosophers only after I had taken some direct steps on my own in philosophical physics.

My attempt to understand the explanation of thermodynamic irreversibility through statistics seemed initially to be merely a secondary occupation. I self-imposed, for years, the intellectual exercise of imagining for each incident its chronological mirror image and then saying precisely why it was impossible (for example, why there are train accidents where a train quickly comes to a complete stop, but why there are no "train good fortunes" where a train just as quickly reaches top speed after having stood still). In an essay published in 1939, I reached the conclusion that the concept of probability is applicable only to future incidents because the future is still possible while the past is already fact. With that idea I thought to have solved an almost trivial problem, trivial especially for someone who understood positivist conceptual criticism. To my amazement, I found that even Heisenberg could follow me there only with difficulty, and that physicists and theoretical scientists in general still do not realize that a problem of which they had not been fully aware had been recognized and solved here. I began to realize slowly that understanding the structure of time is seminal to the understanding of physics, and that precisely because of that, like all fundamental problems, it was in great danger of being repressed.

During the second half of the thirties, Heisenberg was thinking about whether the physics of elementary particles required the introduction of an elementary length, thus a modification of geometry on a small scale. I had dealt some with the paradoxes of set theory and with intuitionism, and I formed the idea that it was not physics that had to be changed here, but the mathematics of the continuum itself. The potential concept of the infinite contains the concept of possibility of which I had become aware in my analysis of time. But possibility is quantified in physics as probability. Could it occur that the attempt to either identify or differentiate two points, like any measuring of an observable in the quantum theory, produces with a certain probability the one result p, and with some probability the opposite result $1-p$? I thus wanted to introduce quantum theory into the fundamentals of analysis the way Einstein introduced gavity into the fundamentals of geometry.

I had the sure instinct that, with this reversal of the hierarchy of science,

I would not commit a philosophical mistake. But again my strength failed me in its execution. I could certainly see where I was blocked. A modification of mathematics through the concept of possibility would probably also require a modification of logic and perhaps the introduction of modal logical concepts into the fundamentals of mathematics. Only ten years later, while staying at a spa in Wildungen during the fall of 1954, did I dare to approach this problem. I was inspired by an essay by Picht on the fundamentals of logic and now tried to develop the nonclassical logic that is immanent in quantum theory. Luckily, I only later read the old treatise on this subject by Birkhoff and Neumann since it would have distracted me from the main issue, the introduction of "complex truth values" as I called them. The philosophical problem, whether it was a matter of logic or only a formalism constructed with classical logic, was clear in my mind. The Rhodus of this leap was to apply this logic to itself. First I outlined the logic of the single alternative. Its quantum states form a two-dimensional complex vector space. The question, "Which quantum state exists?" is then itself an infinite alternative. I awoke early one morning with the answer: The quantum theory of this alternative is the Schrödinger theory of a free particle in a three-dimensional space. The self-application of quantum logic is what is formally called a multiple quantization, and the three-dimensional space itself is a structure of all quantum objects that can be defined from single alternatives through multiple quantization. For the last twenty years now, I have been working on, clarifying, and elaborating this idea. I am not finished. A complete publication of the many thoughts I have had on this subject has not yet been issued. I would never have thought that it would take so long.

I got mathematical help from Scheibe and from Süssman, and in 1958 we published a first version of the theory. My professorship on the Hamburg philosophic faculty gave me the opportunity to study the fundamentals of mathematical logic for a few years, particularly the thoughts of Lorenzen. I realized that quantum logic is a special version of a logic of temporal statements in which the difference between the possible and the actual is formalized. Then I studied the fundamentals of probability calculus and understood that the definition of probability as an expectation factor of relative frequency results in stages of statistic totalities (a collective) piled one upon the other, and that multiple quantization is nothing else but a quantum-theoretical form of this sequence of stages. This suggested the attempt to axiomatically construct quantum theory as a nonclassical theory of probability with only one nonclassical axiom—if possible—that would express indeterminism (the open future). Drieschner did this in his Hamburg dissertation in 1968.

Besides the conceptual clarification of the meaning of multiple quantization, there had to be its concrete realization, the actual construction of physical space from the quantum theory of the single alternative. This is the equivalent of the construction of all physical objects in space from many uniformly simple alternatives, which I called "origin-alternatives." This theory has to be simultaneously a theory of the most simple observable objects, the elementary particles, and of outer space, thus cosmology. It is perhaps excusable that I have not advanced any faster in these incomplete chapters of physics than others.

By 1972, I was ready to give up, and merely to publish all my thoughts on the subject. With this intention, I again studied the fundamentals of logic and thereby became confirmed in my conviction that the logic of temporal propositions is, in a certain sense, also the base of mathematical logic, namely, as a theory of operation, which itself takes place in time. Concurrently, this gave me a new impulse in the fundamentals of physics. The effect was that the book was not written, and the exploration of physics was reopened with new zeal. The result remains to be seen.

In the last section of this self-portrait I will discuss what this undertaking might mean philosophically. In the meantime, I would like to present some political reflections.

C. Politics

I have actually never been interested in political theory for the sake of theory, but only for the sake of politics. My theoretical interest directed itself spontaneously to physics and metaphysics rather than to the structures of state and society. My political thinking was sustained through political will. This might be excusable in a man who by nature is interested in nature, but who, by tradition and also by ambition in his youth, is a *homo politicus*. But in this individual reaction, a truth might also be discerned. The fact that theory is even possible is almost wondrous; but that it is possible in as entangled a phenomenon as history is by no means self-evident. The natural scientist searches for the lost key in the reflection of a street light, not because he lost it there but because he can see something there; only the memory that the key was lost somewhere else makes us go out into the darkness. In physics, too, one must have the experiences one wants to theorize about; to pursue the theory of science without practical research is a hopeless endeavor. This applies even more to politics where practical decisions are also ethical decisions. Who could make a law theoretically without obeying it oneself? I may have often given the impression of expressing my political thoughts freely, but often my own ethical self-criticism has kept my mouth shut. Can one advise politicians without having assumed political responsibility oneself? Can one postulate the elimination of violence and social injustices while leading a comfortable bourgeois life in a social class *secured* through violence? Can this argument even be publicly expressed without the very act of expression making it into a reactionary ideology?

My father brought about my political consciousness. I could only agree with his attempts to avoid future wars through an intelligent foreign policy, "to watch a tree grow" as Moltke said. My father forever determined one aspect of my political thought. But I belonged to another generation, and perhaps to another intellectual world. Once, during a boring history class in my last year in *Gymnasium*, during a snowstorm, I had two daydreams. First, I saw the endless marching armies of nations and princes, of whose hopes and suffering we know little, and then I saw the snow outside falling on ruins. When I drove into Berlin one morning after a devastating air raid, in 1943, I knew: This is exactly the way I had seen it back then.

Why did I think so? When I first became conscious, as a child, there was war. I did not see it, but I was absorbed into all its phases through the worries of adults. The world is full of murder. Later, in the innocence of a twelve-year-old, the Sermon on the Mount shook my belief in the legitimacy of the bourgeois society, and I could never completely restore it. Nevertheless, as an instinctive conformist, I continued to live in it and hid my feelings.

Then came domination by National Socialism. I must speak somewhat personally about this because not to do so would be an example of cowardice, the cowardice that since then has constructed dangerous repressive barriers in German political consciousness. I am one of those Germans who have never overcome the reality of National Socialism, but have survived it. More precisely, I belong to that social class that detested the Nazis wholeheartedly but nevertheless cooperated with them once they were in power. We cooperated with the system for the sake of preserving the existing order while hoping for change. A few from this class did decide upon active resistance making the ultimate sacrifice. I knew and highly respected some of them, but I did not join them.

The attitude of this class as a whole has subsequently been judged more severely than it deserved, as having contributed to the catastrophe. This should be expressed publicly, for moral clarification. The capacity for reluctant conformism is, in all societies, a means of survival. Many who acted this way without self-delusion cannot be blamed except by themselves in their moral sensitivity. But it also belongs to moral clarification that we admit that there are situations in which the insufficiency of customary political morality is not only evident to those who are aware, but finally manifests itself to everyone in its terrible consequences. In the Adenauer era there existed, not just through the guilt of one man, the exactly opposite attitude. There was moral obscurity concerning the past, an obscurity that can at best be excused as a healing sleep under the protection of repression. The same people now controlled the government and economy who had previously cooperated reluctantly or willingly with conformism. To acknowledge this fact freely was, unfortunately but understandably, a taboo. There was a tacit understanding of having acted then as now correctly, whereas self-criticism would have been beneficial. Criticism was left to opponents of the system, where it remained shrill and ineffective.

I did survive in reluctant conformism; but much more was at work in my consciousness. My father had a morally simpler position. He had always detested Hitler and his supporters, but he remained in office to try to prevent the war he saw coming and, later perhaps, to find a chance to end it less disastrously. This was the task he took upon himself, one at which he failed. I had never seen him as desperate as in the summer of 1939 when he saw no way to avoid disaster. It was a terrible mistake to condemn him later as a "war criminal," and it can only be explained as the inability, often inherent in the idealism of Americans, to understand political conditions in systems different from their own. But my father made, especially in the beginning, the mistake of underestimating Hitler, as did many like-minded people. That irrational and unscrupulous charlatan just could not last long in power! That this proved to be true only after twelve years instead of two or four, made all initial reactions to him political mistakes.

My mistake was different. Until 1933, I likewise underestimated Hitler; I detested him. My disbelief in the legitimacy of the bourgeois system, very widely held in my generation, and an unclear chiliastic expectation made me, a twenty-year-old, receptive to the spiritual process that an astute social critic called the pseudo effusion of the Holy Ghost of 1933. Mindless slogans impressed me not at all. It was the fact that so many people who had been despondent and desperate now felt a common purpose in life—which adherents of the movement called their idealism. Behind the liturgy of parades, the fascination with power, the ecstasies of the Führer, I believed I felt the possibility of a higher, hidden purpose. My father's warning and my friendship with Jews saved me from the temptation to join the movement. In 1945 I emerged with an undeserved clean record. Whereas my father had to accept a high rank in the SS, I was not even a plain member of the party or the SA. I was right, though, when I said to my resistance friends, who looked for years for ways to eliminate Hitler, their plans neglected to take into account any actions of Hitler himself. The resistance, morally so admirable, was based mostly on the belief in the unbroken validity of political, religious, and cultural thought systems, whose shakiness had become obvious through Hitler's successes.

I owe the fact of my marriage to those troubled times. Gundalena Wille, whose family was as politically responsive as mine, was a Swiss journalist in Berlin in 1933–34. My father had become the German ambassador to Switzerland and advised her to ask me about the German Labor Service. Our first appointment for June 30, 1934, never occurred because of the assassinations of Röhm and Schleicher. I do not know how I would have since then endured the tensions of a life in the shadow of politics without her.

During the Christmas holidays in 1938 I was living and working in Dahlem. Otto Hahn, in whose institute I had previously worked for half a year, called and asked me whether I could imagine radium behaving in every chemical reaction like barium. He had discovered uranium fission. Two months later, worried and terrified, I visited Picht to discuss with him the modification of the world through the possibility of an atom bomb. Throughout the war, I collaborated in the "uranium project." But we were spared the decision of whether or not to construct atom bombs for Hitler. After little more than a year, we realized that this was far beyond our capabilities, and we concentrated on working on a reactor model. Knowing what I know today, I would not take the same risk. Would the usual reluctant conformism of the physicist have sufficed to prevent construction of the bomb if the bomb had been possible for us? Heisenberg, Wirtz, and I worked together to learn the technical possibilities in order to decide for ourselves *what* we wanted to tell and *to whom*. Heisenberg was concerned about the survival of German science in the period after the certain loss of the war. I dreamed for a while about influencing events, a dream that, luckily for me, did not come true. Heisenberg attempted, in vain, to discuss these problems with Bohr. The international family of nuclear physicists was no longer in agreement. We have no reason for seeking praise for our morality. But I can say that in our small circle we thought much more about preventing the construction of atom bombs than about building one.

We were interned at the end of the war for nearly one year, mostly in England, which for me was a time of self-examination and work. Even before the end of the war, I wrote, just for myself, an essay entitled "Attempt at Historical Construction": Reinhold Schneider had deeply impressed my generation. In Strasbourg I learned much about the Middle Ages from Hermann Heimpel. The self-contradiction of modern dynamics seemed to be fulfilling itself before our eyes. According to my calculations, there would be several more World Wars between America, Russia, and China. I attempted to describe the history of Europe as the result of three forces that I called nature, Christianity, and reality. Nature is the human being as he finds himself (in the Middle Ages, the feudal world of aristocrats and peasants). Christianity is a constant attack on nature (the effect of the Sermon on the Mount, wherever one believes in it). Modern revolutions are the heirs of the permanent revolution that is Christianity. All revolutions fail. And through their failure the transformation of the world proceeds towards a rational and functional structure with neutral values, called "reality," constructed upon the ruins of nature.

The conclusion read: "History is not destined to be the place where Christians triumph. Its work will not have been in vain on that day that will illuminate, like lightning, the beginning and the end." In a second version, which I rewrote from memory while interned in England, I omitted an eschatological quotation by Jesus, because it seemed to me like an arrow shot into the unknown and in its certainty like a *sacrificium intel-*

lectus. However, this omission meant being silent on the core of the matter, for the sake of conversations with enlightened intellectuals, just as Ibsen changed Nora's final words, for performances, from a departure to a return.

Like our entire nation, I had a need for rediscovering the common sense of the Enlightenment.

The political experience of the postwar years was the strength of the liberal social order. I had not previously understood that, although I descended from it. Let me convey some of the theory of liberalism.

I begin with the economic liberalism that was the cause of the German *Wirtschaftwunder* and that, in my opinion, remains in less of a crisis today than in most of its history of two hundred years. The prognosis today is of rigorous survival. Liberalism's intellectual father, Adam Smith, stated a paradoxical thesis. The entire previous Western political theory proceeded from the assumption that the community of humankind can only exist if general welfare is placed before individual self-interest. Recognition of what the general welfare requires is difficult, more difficult than ever in today's mobil functionalized world. The old theory, then, is that those who rule must be those who recognize this. From that comes the ideology that every system of domination uses to justify its power. Here, as everywhere else, the unmasking of an ideology is far from being a solution of the problem. Smith gave a powerful hope to the egalitarian movement of the late Enlightenment. At least for his basic needs, therefore in economics, every individual is capable of recognizing one's self-interest; and the mechanism of a transparent market with free exchange relationships assures that the general welfare is well served precisely because everyone is pursuing his own interest. This is the "invisible hand," concealed to the individual free-market participant but obvious to the theorist, that guides the process. The state must only provide three things: defense from the outside, legal order inside, and operation of certain not-for-profit services.

The moral pathos of this thesis is trust in the freedom of the individual. The Marxist criticism, that the fundamental inequality of the division of goods is not eliminated through a liberal economy, is empirically true. The Marxist prognosis of the continual descent of the masses into misery was false, at least for fully industrialized societies. It therefore becomes at least questionable to what degree and in which sense the continuous inequality deserves to be termed a class society. I assume that a selection-theory analysis would reach the conclusion that in free competition a "limited inequality" would result. There would be neither equality nor extreme inequalities such as exist in transitional phases or in stabilized power systems. Equality, where it does succeed, is always the result of a continual, explicit effort. It is certain that the competitive system is full of cruelties against humans and nature and that it teaches us to tolerate these cruelties. It is also certain that the state today has to solve problems that not only the early liberals but also their absolutist opponents never could have imagined. Who determines the actions of the state, and how can it be done?

It is here that the real core of liberal theory begins: its political part. I would like to reduce it to a tension between two equally unassailable theses:

1. Factual politics is only possible with knowledge of the true circumstances.

2. Nobody must dogmatically claim to be in possession of the truth.

One can also express it more pointedly and say, with justification, "Truth must be intolerant because it is essential to life, but truth must be defended tolerantly because it can only be found in free discussion." May I ever concede, for the sake of tolerance, that two times two also equals five? But can I still convince anyone that two times two equals four if I force the other to acknowledge this statement politically? The condition for the existence of truth in time is freedom; the freedom of others, and the truth, are limitations of my freedom. One can learn this last sentence from Kant.

The people of the Federal Republic of Germany opted for political and economic liberalism. They joined both with a clear decision on foreign policy for the West. I agree with all three decisions. They convinced me. They certainly coincided with the stable, conservative-bourgeois instincts of my background after the catastrophe of National Socialism and the confrontation with the terrifying image of Stalinist communism. I viewed myself, for two decades, as a conservative who wants reform to defend the always threatened essence of humanity. It also satisfied my intellect to think out the progressive-liberal theory that I have just outlined. Its realization could be observed not only in small protected European states like Denmark and Switzerland, which I had already known well, but also in England and America, under the burden of great power politics. The core of my thinking is not political but scientific and religious, which I can perhaps conclude from the fact that in physics and religion it has never been difficult for me to think differently from my surroundings, whereas in politics, though critical and open, I have followed the tendencies of my time.

My political attitude encountered difficulties when two systems collided. My religious-ethical motivation and my scientific expertise forced me to criticize the prevailing politics in regard to nuclear weapons. In America, I met Quakers and began to read Gandhi. Here I found for the first time a true way of life where the Sermon on the Mount was taken seriously. I saw incomparable happiness radiating from it. My Quaker friend Douglas Steere quoted with a gentle voice "A Christian is three things: absolutely fearless, always in trouble, and immensely happy." I was not fearless enough to be always in trouble and to be immensely happy. I also saw something that the Quakers perhaps did not see as clearly. The threat of nuclear war continually hangs over us. I knew that nations and their governments were not capable of the fearlessness of violence-free politics. They did not even think of this possibility. Was it not meaningful that liberal governments should formulate a policy, one they really wanted and could maintain, that could prevent or postpone this danger? I was aware that it was precisely the growing size of the weapons that diminished the danger of war, without however, abolishing it. Could it be the task of our era to find a solution to the ancient hope of eliminating war through a rational construction? I studied the idea of a nuclear world agency and a federated world government, saw its functional rationality, and saw the hopelessness of its realization by the sovereign superpowers.

In the late fall of 1956, the appointment of F. J. Strauss as minister of defense was a signal to German nuclear physicists for the planning for nuclear armament of the West Germany military. The Arbeitskreis Kernphysik (nuclear-physics group), an advisory committee of the atomic ministry, knew *Straus* from his time as an efficient and dynamic atomic minister. We discussed the situation and discovered that despite different political positions we unanimously opposed German nuclear armament, such as the French were already preparing. We wanted to state this publicly, but for the sake of fairness we first wanted to inform the government. We wrote a letter to Strauss, which was followed by a memorable meeting with him. In the first fifteen minutes, he tore apart all of our arguments. Then for the next two and a half hours, he demonstrated with expert and detailed knowledge that our arguments were aimed at the wrong goals; America would eventually withdraw from Europe, and then Western Europe (and just the Federal Republic of Germany) will need nuclear forces equal to those of the Soviet Union. Afterwards we found ourselves confused and without a concept for a public statement. Later, a careless statement by Adenauer, that tactical nuclear weapons were only an extension of the artillery, helped us to a new formulation. Our text contained two central statements: "We do not feel competent to make concrete proposals for the politics of the superpowers. We believe that for a small country like the Federal Republic of Germany, world peace and self-defense are best served if it explicitly and voluntarily renounces the possession of nuclear weapons of any kind. In any case, not one of the undersigned would be willing to participate in any way in the production, testing, or use of nuclear weapons." Publication of the statement caused great public turmoil. Adenauer invited a delegation of us to Bonn for a one-day meeting that he conducted in sovereign style. Naturally we did not reach a real agreement. At least between Adenauer and myself positions were almost the opposite of what the public saw. Adenauer said that to avoid another World War, disarmament was necessary and would eventually be achieved (I believed he was sincere in his wishful thinking, and he even seemed troubled in his last years because of it), and we should not enter into negotiations with advance concessions. I, however, did not believe there would ever be disarmament and that we would only find ourselves stuck with nuclear weapons that in a crisis would provoke a fatal strike from our enemy. A few days later, a brief illness affected my ears, and ever since I do not hear well on the right side.

I had taken it upon myself to advise the nation concerning a vital question. Now I had to acquire facility not only with foreign policy, which I had already, but also with the effects of weapons and with strategy, to be capable of discussions with experts. The American nuclear physicists had practice with this situation for more than a decade. I was probably the first to introduce the teachings of the American arms-control school to Germany. H. Afheldt, who had worked with me since 1962, had made essential contributions to their immanent critique. The conversations in America stimulated my old friendship with Edward Teller and a new one with Leo Szilard. I have too often publicly described the results to repeat them here. They are not at all comforting on the issue of preserving peace on a long-term basis. It was for this reason that I was led to more and more complex political questions and finally to the founding of my present institute. This institute is not devoted to the propagation of the known but to the search for the truth in difficult questions.

The tension between religion and politics, which I so vividly experienced myself, encouraged me to resume, from the end of the war, my studies in the philosophy of history. I saw the history of the Christian era advanced by people who subjectively hoped for nothing but the end of history. During my years in Göttingen, Gogarten taught me to understand what I previously called "reality" as ambivalent secularization of Christian contents. The secularization is ambivalent: It makes real the meaning of Christian faith and simultaneously isolates it from its source. I attempted to describe the process in the Gifford Lectures in Glasgow on the significance of science. The tension was not resolved in this manner, only intensified, although intensified in a promising way by having become conceivable.

According to an old tradition, the age of fifty-six brings an experience of death. We had discussed, with our Czech friends, that the only way to the so implausibly promoted reunification of Germany would be a "reunification" of Europe as a way of overcoming international political differences. On August 21, 1968, when I heard on the radio the news of the long-expected Russian occupation of Czechoslovakia, my first though was "Now World War III is inevitable, not necessarily today, but sometime in the next thirty years." I had reacted the same way to the news of Hitler's withdrawal from the League of Nations in October 1933. The powers are too weak to allow a free development, so they use force as their means, leading to well-known consequences. Basically, I have always known this. The particular event did not have a causal but a revealing function. Since then, the politics of Kissinger achieved probably the most reasonable equilibrium possible in this world, and it would be immoral to imperil the small chance of a lasting equilibrium with disastrous predictions. It is possible, after all, that it will work.

The years 1967–68 opened a new learning process to me, one whose beginning, even though I welcomed it, was also something like a death experience; it was the revolt of leftist students. Before 1952, I was occupied with university reform, not from personal impulse but upon request. I abandoned it after I realized that the professors and ministries were blocking reform and that students and elected government officials were not interested in it. When I became a member of the faculty in 1957, the first faculty meetings confirmed my decision not to pursue university reform along while already overexerting myself with research, teaching, and nuclear politics. I abandoned, so I felt, the old university system, from which I came and which I loved, to its foreseeable decline. I did not expect, though, that this would happen only ten years later, and not through the state but through students. In retrospect, I have only myself to blame, in this case as in others, that I did not express my warnings loud enough. I should have said it as clearly as I was convinced I saw it.

The student revolt did not just concern the university, but the entire society. I have never seen myself as a leftist, but I have received political support mostly from left of center, that being the group to whom I have addressed my concerns. Now the leftist movement found me at a time when I had almost lost hope for stabilization of peace through foreign policy. The latter had always been a rational problem for me. It led to the hope of achieving through societal changes what foreign policy was unable to achieve. But it was accompanied by two intensely uncomfortable feelings. The first was typical for my generation: Although I personally welcomed what the young called "basic democracy," and though I willingly participated mentally in the experiment, I needed the utmost self-constraint to remain calm. The second was my concern for the young people: It soon became obvious that the movement was politically doomed to fail. But at this point I began to reap the theoretical benefits of these efforts. I owe it to discussions into which I was forced by the left that my eyes were opened to what was happening socially in the world. I finally learned to assimilate Marx. Jürgen Habermas, whom I convinced to become codirector at my institute, explained to me this method of thinking in the terminology of liberalism which I could understand. But despite all my readiness to learn, I have remained a critic of the left, and I think that only a deeply disillusioned leftist would find comfort in conversing with me. I offer not optimism but hope. I have just finished an essay entitled "The Human Species Today, Observed from the Outside," containing arguments I will not repeat here. They conclude with mistrust of the chances of capitalism and of socialism for solving the problems created by modern civilization and with the admonition that we look at humankind from the inside. This leads us back to philosophy.

D. Philosophy

I again begin from the beginning. Accordingly, I shall describe here the philosophical movements, not in a real dialogue with a partner, or through a literary intercourse with the dominant opinions of our time, but rather in conversation with the person I encountered in myself far back in the mistiness of childhood recollection, and with whom I still walk hand in hand, the one who I am. Who is it that says "I" here?

I have been intellectually involved in four fields. I listed them above as physics, politics, religion, and classical philosophy. The first three can alternatively be termed structure, history, and self-perception. Fourth is the Platonic undertaking of reflecting upon the unity of the other three. One can also designate this as skeptical theology, paraphrasing the Greek words *scepsis*, *theos*, and *logos* as "looking," "the One," and "rational speech." The first three fields came naturally to me. I have learned the fourth as one learns a new language in a good school. I speak the language with an accent, but I know that I could not converse lucidly on the other three fields if I had not learned that language; perhaps I know something about it that the native speakers do not know.

I came to physics, as I described earlier, through astronomy and the quantum theory. Astronomy was, to me, the knowledge of the universe, of the whole, a childish concept of philosophy. My highly respected Latin and Greek tutor Hilmer, at the German St. Petri *Gymnasium* in Copenhagen, said to me, after an outburst of my enthusiasm about the vastness of the universe during one of these sessions: "Certainly, the universe is vast and wonderful. But never forget that your mind is greater than the universe; it is capable of conceiving of the universe." I only reluctantly agreed with that. Knowledge was, for me, forever subjective after that awareness. But it seemed rather arrogant to me to connect a mind that can conceive of the universe to my person with the possessive pronoun "your." At the same time, if I had not been pious and cowardly, I perhaps would have left my confirmation class after the minister stated that, as Christians, we should not believe in the animal ancestry of the human race because humans, in contrast to animals, had souls. I hope he meant the immortal soul, but I was not aware of this nuance and it would have only further confused me. With deep indignation I asked myself how the minister would feel at the Last Judgment if he had to appear before God together with a horse. Despite my partiality, I felt that science was subjectively blind. The quantum theory promised to bring some light to this darkness, reminding us, as Bohr said so emphatically, that we are as much participants as spectators in the drama of existence.

The first twenty-five years of my work in physics gave me a clearer scientific model of the way we are participants under the heading of the history of nature. My work on the evolution of the solar system confronted me with the ancient theological debate in which some (including the great Newton) wanted to justify a belief in creation based on gaps in science. During my years in Dahlem, 1936–42, my good fortune led to introductions by the best German biologists and biochemists into the problems of the theory of evolution, and the new field of molecular biology. I understood the exact analogy of the motives behind the old rejection of the mechanical theories on the origin of the solar system and the recent rejection of the theory of human evolution, particularly of Darwin's causal explanation of evolution through natural selection. I quickly convinced myself that such rearguard actions are always lost, and felt myself in agreement with the young Kant, in his prologue to the *Allgemeine Naturgeschichte und Theorie des Himmels* (Universal History of Nature and Theory of Heaven), that they arise from a theology of disbelief. Everything that occurs in history does occur somehow, and the causal theories are nothing but statements of how it could have happened. I thought that whoever could not meet God, the soul, and life with positive knowledge of the exact sciences, would try in vain to find them in the gaps between these sciences.

But the intellectual task lay not in these popular philosophical debates, rather in comprehending how "chance" can create both order and diversity. My analysis of the second law of thermodynamics helped me here. We call events chance that comply with the laws of probability calculus. These laws define possibilities, and precisely because they are possibilities it remains to be seen which of them will occur. It became plausible to me that the increase in entropy and the growing differentiation of forms was a consequence of the same structure of time. I can say, in agreement with a later formulation of Picht: The past does not pass; therefore, the quantity of facts increases; the present of the future is its possibility based on facts; therefore, the quantity of possibilities increases.

Darwinism, intellectually indebted to the early capitalist theories of Smith and Malthus, has been mainly rejected because of the cruelty of its enthusiastic belief in progress. We, the survivors, are certainly heirs to the victors in the struggle for existence. War helped me see the other side. Creatures, coming about through the very struggle for existence, are sentenced to death and, if they have subjective perceptions of the kind known to us, also are sentenced to suffering. Perhaps no one saw this great reality more clearly than Buddha. Only by experiencing this suffering can one begin to comprehend what the great religions are about. Their departure point is not a naive belief in harmony but the most extreme experiences of suffering, guilt, and a sense of meaninglessness.

The path of science has not reached its end with this piece of natural history. Transition to the religious experience is still a giant step. A cybernetic mode of thinking emerged after the war. We discussed, in Göttingen, the cybernetic models of life and intelligence. We learned much from Konrad Lorenz and Erich von Holst. The formulation of the question was obviously legitimate, but limited on two sides. The cybernetic models describe life with the objective methods of classical physics; the introduction of the subject in quantum theory that had already occurred was not included in these models. An even greater difficulty was that nobody had a clear image of the thinking functions in question when these proceeded beyond the relatively simple levels of perception of form and the capacity to act. What is the operative structure of language, concept, and reflection? Chomsky and Piaget, who became famous a decade later, believed in classical logic, probably more than it deserves. We cannot further analyze our role as participants when we have not yet dealt with our role as spectators.

Thus we return to the core of philosophical physics. In my opinion, this only becomes comprehensible if two problems (they appear to be strictly separate to the prevailing methods of consciousness) are comprehended as belonging together, even identical: the interpretation of the contents of physics, particularly the quantum theory, and the question about the essense of empirical exact science. Either of these questions, taken alone, leads to aporias that are, in my opinion, a consequence of the separation.

Let us confront cybernetics with the quantum theory. Darwinism, behavioral science, and cybernetics treat the subject as a thing appearing in space and time. They give a physical model of the empirical subject. To whom this thing appears, or the method of appearance in space and time, is generally not a theme. The quantum theory now destroys the ontology that is postulated here. Becoming most evident in the composition of objects, this manifests itself in the "paradox" of Einstein, Rosen, and Podolsky: That a whole object can be reduced to partial objects does not mean that partial objects exist, as long as the whole object is not factually reduced to them. Now every object must be strictly understood as part of greater objects. Objects designate facticity. But facts are facts only because of the possibilities included in them. The only irreducible whole object could, at most, be the universe. Yet it is not even an object, because to whom could it be an object? In so speaking, I am using a stenographic abbreviation of my own conceptual analysis, so far only partially published. Otherwise I would have to write a book on the matter instead of essays concerning its reflection in my consciousness. The quantum theory thus introduces objects as objects for subjects. But it does not describe the subjects. In order to avoid this obligation, it replaces them, wherever possible, with measuring instruments. However, the fact that these instruments are not just objects, but objects suitable for measuring, preserves their subjectivity (therefore, according to Bohr, they have to be called "classical"). Cybernetics knows, in Kant's terminology, only the empirical subject, not as the "I," but as an existing thing. But the quantum theory knows only the transcendental subject, and without reflection on the unity of apperception.

Philosophers in the dominant German tradition going back to Kant and idealism have used these limitations of science to understand the subject to reject the competence of science in these questions. Even as a student I reacted to this school philosophy as an epigonic mistake and a misunderstanding of the Kantian question. In order to be able to state this, I had to study philosophy—not only because of this, but because philosophy had become most important to me.

I began with positivism. Mach's idea not to begin with the subject-object division but to talk about elements, termed "perceptions," whose valid relationships are designated, for purposes of simplication, as things and egos, seemed brilliant to me. But neither he nor others were successful in implementing it. What are laws? They regulate possibilities. What does possibility mean? From where does one know the laws? From experience? How can experience establish laws? —laws that, once discovered, can be formulated in clear simplicity on half a page, laws that perpetuate their future validity a millionfold. Like Kant I could say that it was the memory of David Hume that awakened me from dogmatic slumber: How can one ever logically conclude from the facts of the past the necessities of the future? At some point I realized that Hume's epistemological problem used exactly the same structure of time that I recognized as the substantial basis of thermodynamics, and of the quantum theory. Then it became obvious to me that epistemology and physics can only be understood together.

In view of these problems, I paid only peripheral attention to the empirical theory of science that developed in my lifetime. It was uninteresting to me as long as it had not recognized that Hume's problem remains unsolvable in this context. Popper also only scratched the surface of problems that were obvious to Einstein and Bohr, for example, that the concepts in which we formulate simple empiric statements, are meaninful only in the context of a theory. In my opinion, the most important breakthrough was achieved by Th.S. Kuhn; in the one conversation I had with him, I found myself in spontaneous agreement on Galileo, Einstein, and Bohr. I would like to interpret his view of the history of science as follows: If empirical scientific theory is itself science, then it must establish its concept of empirical science empirically, meaning historically and descriptively. But it was Heisenberg with his concept of closed theories, not Kuhn with his own highly informative concept of paradigms, who defined the core of "scientific revolutions" ten years earlier. Common to both is the recognition that there are a series of plateaus in historical development on which "normal science" can develop, until the next crisis. Kuhn rightly compares these plateaus to species in Darwin's theory of evolution. Here the structural identity of theoretic scientific knowledge and direct scientific knowledge becomes again apparent. Species are plateaus because they are adapted to an ecological niche. The ecological niche of a closed theory is what is called truth in direct speech. And so again, as before, the essential question is, "What is truth?"

Here I must express my thanks to the classical philosophers. It was my incomparably good fortune that I had to teach them in Hamburg as my civic duty. I thank also all my students and others in Hamburg that they wanted to hear what I had to say. Even though I also studied Aristotle, Descartes, Hegel, Heidegger, and the modern logicians, it took an entire decade to study just two philosophers thoroughly: first Kant, and then Plato. I had already read both as a young student. Nevertheless, as is usual with a rereading of philosophers after much study, I was often brought to exclaim, "So that is what was actually meant here!" This is the way it must be if the truth is the whole. The first sentence in the *Critique of Pure Reason*, or an ironic adjective in a question by Socrates, can only be understood by someone who has meditated on the entire philosophy of Kant, including his religious writings, or who has ascended to the sight of the One. Can a reasonable person, when thinking about it, expect anything else? I know I still have far to go to reach a thorough and adequate understanding of Kant and Plato, but I believe if I were to meet them in the meadows of Hades they would appreciate conversing with me.

The four semesters in the seminar on the critique of pure reason, 1960–62, were probably the height of shared philosophizing, especially because I had to learn everything myself. My unforgettable student Peter Plaas afterwards taught me about the severity of the systematic demands of the Kantian theory of science. I cannot interpret Kant here, but want the severity of the demand in the context of the possibilities of contemporary science. There is (in the multiple layers in which exact science generally exists) only *one* solution to Humes's problem, namely the Kantian. Validity of natural laws requires necessity, otherwise they are not valid for the future. One cannot not prove unconditional necessity of the natural laws, neither through special experience nor through metaphysics. But their conditional necessity can be understood, namely, that it has to be valid if experience is to be possible at all. I define experience with regard to the structure of time: to learn possibilities from facts, to learn the future from the past.

Kant failed with the problem of special laws of nature. But in unified physics, such as is being developed now, there are no special laws. Quantum theory as a universal theory of nondeterministic probabilities for determinable alternatives is still a probably preliminary formulation of the only laws that are generally valid. In this sense, space itself is a form of simultaneousness defined through the quantum theory of alternatives.

This idea must be formulated with such explicitness because it only then makes obvious that the fundamental problem of empiricism, the justification of special laws through special experience, does not exist. Here one must differentiate the problems *quid facti* and *quid juris*. Factually, special laws are obviously found through special experience. Hume's problem was only the strict justification of laws found accordingly. This justification can happen only conditionally, not universally. It can happen in physics that justifies itself only through the expectation of the possibility of experience. In this sense, the theory of science and basic physics are identical.

The so proposed unified physics, the final goal upon which I concentrate my conscious ambition, would again be a historical plateau. What might occur beyond that plateau can only be hinted at. (A central law of historical philosophy must be: We philosophize *now*.) The concept of experience is, as Kant has seen, only defined through laws and concepts and only meaningful within those laws. In this theory it is reduced to verifiable prognoses for constructable alternatives, namely, formulable possibilities. Such possibilities exist for subjects. How are the subjects themselves to be thought of? We could begin by asking science.

The theory intends to include simultaneously physics and operative logic and mathematics. Since Gödel, one knows that, to say it rather generally, recognizable possibilities can never be completely formalized. Therefore, in a certain sense, a complete theory of possibilities is at no time possible; the number of possibilities increases. But what is the operative meaning of "knowing" and "knowable?" Here a cybernetics of reflection would have to be developed. It would be an objectifying theory of empirical subjects, with the inclusion of the immanent limits of objectivization, a reflecting theory of reflection. I think I can precisely visualize these possible theories, but to make them real exceeds my strength, and convincing others of carrying on this task has thus far exceeded my ability.

But what is the empirical subject? Who says "I" here?

Descartes' problem of the duality of substances disappears in this proposal. If humans develop from molecules, then molecules are *virtualiter cogitantia*, potentially conscious. But the transition from the abstract potential that is recognized only in retrospect to the actual potential needs billions of years to be realized. One who is aware that we do not even understand our parents and teachers should not be surprised at the inability to empathize with such distant ancestors; Freud's concepts of the unconscious, the id, might make such empathy easier for the contemporary intellectual. "Matter" means that which obeys the laws of physics. If these laws merely formulate what can be experienced unambiguously, there is no reason not to consider that which simultaneously makes experiences and can be experienced as a consciously experiencing ego and an experiencing matter. A scientific theory is then confronted by the central problem of a structural differentiation between self-consciousness and other kinds of quasi subjectivity. Facts and possibilities in one context belong to this, as well as reflection that understands them as facts, as possibilities, as the connection (the "I think" must be able to accompany all my thoughts). This is the transcendental model of the finite subject. Whoever thinks it thinks a unity that is more than the unity of the finite subject. It is also more than society and human history. It appears here as the unity of time. How finite subjectivity originates in it becomes a discussible problem, and as little as there are ultimate objects, one may expect that the description of a finite subject is the final word. On this path I was accompanied only by Georg Picht, if not always on the same side of the stream, at least always toward the same source.

Why this monism? I think I say here, with the hindsight of an old man, what I believed as a child. But I see no other speculative possibility. Pluralism is never true. At most it is honest in its resignation to the task of thinking of the tacitly assumed connections. But two or more final principles are not final principles because their common principle is to be "final principles." On the other hand, a single principle seems to deny the fundamental experience of our existence, of our being derelicts in the finite: suffering, guilt, meaninglessness. Philosophy cannot stop with such paradoxes. It must ask, "How do these questions arise that can lead to such answers?" It is already obvious on this level that time is an infinite principle of finiteness. It is, respectively, an always different presence, consisting of these facts and no others, of these possibilities and no others, and possibility means that there is this choice or that choice, but not both simultaneously.

With the question of unity we enter Platonic territory. Plato is—if it is not too presumptuous of me to say this—the only philosopher with whom I have felt at home. I have also felt that way with Goethe since my school days, especially with his later lyrics. But Plato thinks what Goethe says and witholds, and he sees more than Goethe. Politics and ethics, art and passion, mathematical science, logic, ontology, and mysticism: They all refer back to him. I have tried to visualize his philosophy, following the cave allegory, as a system of ascents and descents. The ascent is what takes us there. It is what one generally knows about Plato, the differentiation of idea from sense perception. When I began to lecture on Plato, I initially sought to use new examples to make the ascent accessible to modern consciousness. For example, the greylag goose, defined through its adapation to its ecological niche, is really the idea of the greylag goose. It follows that ideas are the only things that one can know. I pragmatically modified the adequation theory in that I translated adequation as adaptation, or acting according to circumstances. Thus I could reconcile behavioral research and Kuhn's theory of science; and the structure of reality, which is the ecological niche of the concept, proved itself to be an idea. The ascent to the higher ideas permits a view of what makes the pragmatic possible and leads to the characteristics of the idea as idea: being and truth, which originate in the one, which is the good. The actual philosophy is the descent that leads back to the shadows on the wall, to Mach's perceptions that now will be understood through that which makes the shadows. The sense-objects are also ideas. This is a modern mirror image of Plato, and if I had another six years, I could probably work out an even more contemporary and more grandiose image of his philosophy. But to achieve this is presumably not the lot I have drawn in this incarnation.

The One, as the *Parmenides* dialogue teaches, cannot be expressed without contradictions. The One tolerates no being and no saying next to it as the second, and the existing One as such is duality, and with that is infiniteness; this, then, is the descent. What is wonderful in this philosophy is that it does not draw the limit of rationality one step too early but develops it from a rational analysis of the conditions of the possibilities of rationality. The One is simultaneously the good. The good is the principle of movement. Every idea is good; it is the standard by which all things that share in it are measured. Accordingly, the idea is the principle of the intention, of the desire of enlightened love, and thus of movement. Intention and being are not opposites in this philosophy. Bad is the absense of being. Are these thoughts realizable for us, too, or are they mere ornaments?

In the thoughts about politics I left out the question of how I relate to the Christian church. When I was sixteen years old, I was inwardly no longer connected to it, but I came early to the conclusion that there is no sense in leaving the place where one has found oneself already; I have always been, and not unwillingly, a member of the Lutheran Church. But as much as the New Testament meant to me, the church meant little, or so it seemed to me to my disappointment. In those places where I looked, in ethics and mysticism, it did not challenge me; it expected of me neither the Sermon on the Mount nor the Gospel according to St. John. At the university, I heard Johannes Wach lecture on Asiatic religions. I read the Chinese classics in Wilhelm's translations, especially the short, gemlike texts of *Tshuang Tsis*, and the discourses of Buddha in K.E. Neumann's translation. One must read this so slowly that one breathes along with these teachings, "whose beginning soothes, whose middle soothes, and whose end soothes." Since then, I have felt more at home spiritually in Asia than in Europe, though fully aware of the deep cultural differences. I knew there are individuals there who see and who are.

The decisive religious influence by a living person came, for a long time, from Alastair, a highly gifted artist, a lover and mystic, a relentless self-examiner, and a man who always was in need of help. Today, sixty years after his brief fame, his drawings are again found on the art market. The way he played piano, sang, and danced, though, is lost to us. The countless translations, from which he tried for decades to make a living in flowered and tapestried pension rooms, are scattered like his own verse. I never met the challenge that this relationship with a man two decades older meant to me, and I have painfully learned from it what I could hardly have otherwise learned. Like many who were close to him I could never translate what I learned in his presense into thoughts or deeds, and thus I quote here influences that were of less importance but easier to translate than his own.

I was, in 1938, a guest at a retreat of the Lutheran Michael Brotherhood in Marburg. I saw that I could not belong to this community, but I am grateful for the week of experiencing their liturgically ordered routine. Liturgy and regularity impart something to the deep layers, not penetrated by willful intelligence, that is certainly as necessary for me as food and drink. I have lived, so far, without any permanent liturgical community because I have never found one connected to the modern consciousness I need. Nevertheless, I have adopted the general habit of daily morning meditation. I have never studied meditation formally because I never met a teacher who challenged my intelligence enough, and perhaps because of my urge for independence. This is against the rules, dangerous and not recommended to others. I have never attempted to go to extremes in meditation, but rather have let come whatever came. Yet, I could not live without this regular retreat into quietness. The often held opinion that meditation is narcissism and exists in opposition to involvement with other people is an error whose existence is difficult to understand. There are also, though rarely, contemplative ways of living that do more good to others through inaction or even without human contact than through any activities.

My relationship to the church normalized itself only after the war, when I learned how to appreciate everyday life. I am grateful to the American Christians, who were immediatey prepared to help our country, for that decisive step. Scientific colleagues abroad, old friends, initially investigated (with the exception of Teller) whether our relationship to the Nazis made us worthy of a new partnership; and who could blame them for this? But the Christians knew that "we are all sinners," and were there without hesitation. Love creates love, exactly because it is undeserved. But I owe my relationship to theology almost exclusively to one man, who was not an academically trained theologian: the mathematician Günther Howe, whom I had met in Marburg in 1938. He talked to me about the relationship between the thoughts of Bohr and Barth and organized, for ten years after the war, conversations between physicists and theologians. Here I learned the language of theology. Howe expected more from the church than I and thus suffered more from it; I learned from his suffering what it is all about. The scholarship of the Old Testament, the most believable aspect of learned theological work that I know, now opened to me a thousand-year-long history that, especially in the penitent sermons of the prophets, still concerns us directly. It helped me to understand the historical situation of Christianity. I needed this when I sat with Howe in two ecclesiastical commissions, an ecumenical and a German, about the ethics and politics of nuclear weapons. I learned to understand the judgments and attitudes of the church through the situation of its representatives. I learned to make reasonable political use of the good will of a church that distanced itself from the general corruption and conflicts of interest. And it became easier for me to let quotations from the teachings of Jesus, always so vivid in my mind, slip into a conversation in such a way that they suited the concrete situation.

I could now also interpret the Sermon on the Mount a little better, meaning I could connect it with my modern consciousness. It contains at least three layers of reality. The outermost is the universal ethic of the golden rule. This has certainly never been thought out more precisely than in the practical philosophy of Kant. It does not impose this or that commandment, but the form of the universitality of commandments: "Let your behavior be guided by principles that you would want to be the guiding principles of all humankind." The Sermon on the Mount can be understood everywhere because it appeals to what makes people human. The second layer is the revelation of convictions as the place of ethical decisions. That I do not actually murder my brother is not the fulfillment of the commandment, but that I love him. This "but I say unto you" reveals our reality and its contrast even to the commandments consciously accepted by us. We humans avoid again and again this unbearable tension. The specific danger of the church is eagerness for good works, also the good work of having the correct faith. Luther recognized the escapist aspect of this eagerness. The works also cover deviations from literalism, from the strictness of the universal commandment. The scientific view of humans finally tends to side with his causally understandable psychic reality against the commandment. But the commandment is the condition for the existence of human society; it is the truth, whose embodiment is peace. History is a chain of deserved suffering for disobeying the commandment. And the experience that the church calls penance could teach us, just as does the experience of psychoanalysis, that healing is not possible if we accept our psychological compulsions as our nature, if we do not distinguish ourselves from them and do not acknowledge the guilt as our own. Healing is possible; with this we come to the third and real layer: the Beatitudes. Without the imperative of behavior no society is possible, without the imperative of convictions no maturity of the person. But the world of the imperative is merciless, it drives the sensitive to desperation. The imperative is permitted only because there is reality, "Blessed are the peacemakers, for they shall be called the sons of God. Blessed are the pure in heart, for they shall see God."

I learned to talk and think more about this. But until my fortieth year, there was "the moral law above me." I knew what was demanded of me but did not do it. I knew that humankind was driven towards catastrophe, and that only those who followed this way could help. I reacted with depression to being unable to become a "pillar of society." A personal crisis, where I became guilty toward people, liberated me. All of a sudden I saw the personal ambition in the claim for perfection, in the postulate of helping the world. I experienced that there is an inner voice that teaches unmistakably and directly, if we only ask it with complete renunciation of our own will; it demands where it hurts the most, and it consoles where we would not have expected it. I limited my obligations to the narrowest circle of duties and sacrificed my ambitions of knowledge and of politics. And then came the first breakthrough to philosophical physics and political effectiveness.

I put this report about the church and Christianity near the end of this essay because it contains experiences that answer previous questions. The last question was whether Plato's philosophy of the good can still have meaning to us. The message of the Beatitudes can be interpreted to mean that being and intention come together and that the bad is the absense of being. The church tradition had accordingly incorporated Platonism and has presumably seen deeper than modern Protestant theology. But the consideration of Plato itself originated from the question of a doctrine of the subject in historical nature that simultaneously understands that the nature we know is nature for subjects. One could call the empirical side of this science anthropology. However, an anthropology that does not know the experiences about which I have just tried to report is certainly not a science. It can only be a registering of the more superficial contents of the consciousness of our era, inevitably connected with the wrong causal theories. Therefore, the anthropological relevance of art in modern times is so much greater than science, especially if the art is not "committed," that is, not inundated with well-intended contents of consciousness.

This report about experiences must therefore be taken one step further. Twenty years ago, somebody visiting me in Göttingen said I should seek contact with certain Indian sages, for the sake of an essential connection between Eastern wisdom and Western science. I spontaneously replied that I was not yet ready for that and I was not able to force myself to get into contact. I was convinced that the Indians taught truth, and that if their teachings were truth the deeper self would make the move when the time was right. I held to this attitude for a long time. Martin Steinke, or Tao Chun, a German who became a Buddhist monk in China, personified to me the brilliant wisdom of Zen. He became a mature friend. I owe my meeting with Professor Mahadevan from Madras to Queen Friederike of Greece. He explained the Advaita teachings of the Vedanta to me. I immediately saw its closeness to, if not identity with, Plato's theory of the One. This world of things, of multiplicity, exists only for finite subjects; They, as parts of the world of multiplicity, exist only for each other and for themselves; in a truth that alone experiences the meditative enlightenment there is only one self. "This is you, O Svetaketu," as Hilmer addressed me in Copenhagen. At the beginning of 1968, the pandit Gopi Krishna from Cashmere visited me in Hamburg. In a split second I realized this was one to whom I could listen. I do not want to repeat what I wrote a few years later in the introduction to his book *Biological Basis of Religious Experience*. He was self-taught in yoga and certainly in Western thought, but an eyewitness. His kundalini experience concerns especially the physical realm, and it is painful that Western medicine has not yet taken notice of this. I assume that for today's science to be able to recognize what is experienced here it has to take the detour of physics.

In 1969 I took a position in the German program of aid to underdeveloped countries and used the opportunity for numerous week-long fact-finding trips to India. I could report much on the misery and the developmental work, and also about the fact that these poor have a much greater capacity for happiness than we rich. Actually I was there for the sake of one particular experience. I met Gopi Krishna again, spent twenty-four hours in the ashram of the highly venerated saint Anandamayi Ma in Vrindaban and one day at the *Aurobindo* ashram in Pondicherry. Mahadevan took me, with the kind support of the German General Consul Dr. Pfauter, to Kanchipuram to meet the head of the second largest Hindu community, the Shaivas (worshipers of Shiva). How might a high dignitary of the Indian church look? In a simple bamboo hut on a suburban street a little man with white hair sat on the floor and silently looked at us for a few minutes with powerful eyes; that was the audience with him. The utter cultural foreignness and the unquestioning human proximity were seldom so evident to me as in that moment.

Mahadevan's master had been Sri Ramana Maharshi. The latter, when he was sixteen years old—the son of a Brahman, and a student at an American missionary school—had an experience of death. It became clear to him that "Whatever is dying now is not I." A few months later, he fled to the old temple city of Tiruvannamalai, got rid of all possessions, lived only on what compassionate passersby and, later, venerators gave him, and remained in complete silence alone with the self whose presence he was. Eventually, he returned to an external routine, to regular eating and talking, and an ashram evolved around him at the foot of a holy mountain. He transmitted his inner blissful happiness silently, smilingly, and by asking questions. To those who questioned him because they saw God's presense in him he taught to ask, "Who is it then who asks 'Who am I?,' " in order to lead them where they could see the same presence in themselves. He died in 1959, twenty years before my visit. I knew all this when I drove to Tiruvannamalai with Mahadevan.

The reader must excuse the fact that I do not actually describe what is indescribable, and yet speak about it; if I did not at least try, I could not have begun this autobiographical report. When I had taken off my shoes and stood before the grave of Maharshi, I knew in a flash: "Yes, this is it." Actually all questions were already answered. We sat in an amiable circle as a delicious meal was served on large green leafs. Afterwards I sat on the stone floor next to the grave. The knowledge was there, and within half an hour everything had happened. I still perceived my surroundings, my hard seat, the buzzing mosquitos, the light upon the stones. But the layers had already been swiftly penetrated, the layers of which words can only give a hint: "You"—"I"—"Yes." Tears of bliss. Bliss without tears.

The experience brought me back to earth very gently. I now knew which love held the meaning of earthly love. I knew all dangers, all terrors, but they were not terrors in this experience. Should I now stay here forever? I saw myself like a metal ball that falls onto a polished metal surface and, after a moment's touch, bounces back to where it came from. But I now had become somebody completely different: the one I always had been. A younger German member of the ashram led me into a room where three older Indians sat. We greeted each other with a glance and sat together silently for an hour. My German friend made coffee for me in his room. Mahadevan came, we walked through the great temple section of the city. I slept in the very simple guest house at the ashram, and in the morning my friend accompanied me to a cave in the mountain, under large trees, where the Maharshi had lived for years, and where sometimes he settled the wars of the monkey kings in the trees above him. Then we traveled on. The experience left with me incredible gentleness during the next days and weeks. Its substance remained within me. Without it, I might not have survived the suffocating experiences of those years.

My account comes to an end here. Obviously not because the theoretical questions are answered, even if the reader realizes that their formulation has already aimed at the last experience just described. My account comes to an end because it is an interim report from a way station. Where does the bouncing ball go now? I may perhaps be allowed to say on what theories I would still like to work.

I have promised a presentation of my thoughts on physics, and I still hope to do it with collaborators. Then I hope still to break through as far as elementary particle physics is concerned. If my approach is not wrong, this is the line where logic, epistemology, and ontology converge, and therefore the basis for an encounter with traditional religious metaphysics. The belief that one philosopher develops one philosophic system, and the other another, is representative of a past plateau of the history of philosophy. There is only one philosophy, and this is inseparable from concrete science, and many people work on its history. How far one's own contributation extends is difficult to foresee.

The pragmatic demand now comes from a completely different side: to state, if possible, which road the policies of the coming years should take in our country and around the world. The difficulty here is that a penetrating insight must be critical toward all existing practices and programs. It is a possible role to do nothing but express this criticism and exemplify it through one's own way of life, a difficult role if one takes it seriously. I have instead tried to propose practical policies, while aware of criticism, and I should give even more concrete and extensive advice in the future, from what my institute has taught me and continues to teach me. I also have a very strong desire at least to outline a critical and therefore constructive theory.

This critical theory needs as its foundation the outline of a historical anthropology. It approaches from the pragmatic side the same field that theoretical work is striving for. I will not be able to accomplish more than to indicate that field and to encourage those who want to work in it without ignoring scientific biology, leftist social theory, and religious experience. A few interpretations of Kant should be included, and it would be good to give another lecture on Plato.

All this is the consequence of the theory, and should be done. We are only hiding if we do not think the thinkable. But we will all still pass through other doors. This theory, too, is probably only one of the great historical plateaus. One cannot think what one does not do. The external actions exist under the uncertainty of the political future. The inner work is to become receptive to new perception. Here the deed is to let it happen.

Introduction: What Is Historical Anthropology?

The present book offers contributions to historical anthropology. Historical anthropology, in this book, is the name of anthropology as pursued in a certain manner, thus it is not one branch of anthropology; it is an anthropology in its entirety. Generally one translates anthropology as the science of people. "Person" in the singular is the true subject of this science. One can also say "the human," that which constitutes a person. Historical anthropology tries to understand humans as historical beings. It has been said many times that the human being is the animal that has a history. To the evolutionary biologist, of course, animals have a history, too, an unconscious one. But history does not create a system. History creates a multitude of beings living together. Thus historical anthropology cannot present itself concretely in a system of humanity; rather, it works, let us say, in humanity's garden.

Should historical anthropology be labeled a philosophy, or a positive, empirical science? Let us accept the reasonable assumption that anthropology is a philosophy. To philosophize means to keep questioning. To philosophize means, above all, to keep asking for answers to one's own questions. What, after all, does science mean? What does philosophy mean? We know how difficult it is to answer these questions with precise definitions. Certain is that we know science and philosophy as socially organized processes that interpret themselves as forms of the search for knowledge. The emergence of these specific forms of the search for knowledge in European culture is known to us at least in outline. Which field of knowledge have we entered with this thought? We are talking about historically evolved forms of the search for knowledge, about the social constitution of present human culture—we are in the field of historical anthropology. Whoever asks, "What is historical anthropology?" is already practicing historical anthropology. Whoever asks, "What is philosophy?" is already philosophizing.

What is the present historical perspective of the relationship between science and philosophy? When answering this question, let our perspective be, as much as possible, from the side of science. In the last decades it has become common to see science as a historical phenomenon. Th. S. Kuhn[1] discovered the structure in scientific history that will be seen in Part I of this book as generally the structure of evolution. He differentiates normal science, which solves individual problems in a fixed paradigm, from scientific revolutions, which change the paradigm. Normal science is essentially nonphilosophical because it does not question its own paradigm. A scientific revolution, however, just as the initial search of a science for its first paradigm, philosophizes implicitly and often consciously.

A practical application of this thought to our question is the conclusion that a governing paradigm for a comprehensive scientific anthropology does not yet exist. There have been separate scientific disciplines formulating fragmentary anthropological questions. By asking questions about a comprehensive anthropology we have already begun to philosophize. But our intention is to bring different scientific paradigms into contact and communication with each other. And we must not be shy about posing questions about the human condition that are currently, or generally, not considered to be scientific questions. How can we systematically structure these methods of interpretation? For an answer, let us return, this time with more depth, to the question of history.

The first known attempt by humankind at self-explanation occurred within the framework of *religion*. Humans learned to see themselves in the light of the gods, already an example of truth through distance. Up to the present, there has been a treasure trove of religious knowledge: in the form of doctrine as theology; in the form of practice as the ecclesiastical, religious, ethical life; in the form of self-experience in meditation.

The inner history of religion is itself a history of plateaus and crises. The higher religions have evolved historically. They are also, but not exclusively, the result of rational progress. Evolving mostly out of conflict with previous systems of domination, they, in turn, created new systems of domination. And, with the attempt to become rational and reasonable, the higher religions have been confronted in the course of history with the trend to present a new image of humankind. We call this the *Enlightenment*, a name that originated in the modern period of European history.

The Enlightenment recreates new structures in the course of its own plateaus and crises. The ancient Greek Enlightenment led to that great body of thought that linked together the truths of the newly discovered rationality (led by the paradigm of mathematics and the practice of secularly pursued politics) with the newly conceived fundamental truth of religion to *philosophy*. The European modern era finds philosophy as an already existing paradigm of comprehensive thought. It resumes, in the fervor of having emancipated itself from religious and philosophical domination, both themes of ancient Greek rationality. In the spirit of mathematics, it develops *natural science*. This, especially with the development of medicine and biology, makes humankind an *object* of causal cognition. Scientific anthropology is a consequence of the Enlightenment. It becomes historical anthropology insofar as it thinks in evolutionary terms. On the other hand, the individual who practices science sees himself as a powerful *subject*. The line of political emancipation, which also originates in the Enlightenment, sees the existing social order as an injustice to humankind. It is driven by a strong moral pathos, a fervor for political and moral freedom. It develops a *critical social theory* that acknowledges that history is made by humans and can be improved by humans. It implicitly presupposes a historical anthropology that judges history as the work of humankind. Finally, there is *human psychology*—perhaps the most direct anthropological science— which finds itself torn between all its various schools. Such a brief summary of a few of the major motifs is, of course, neither comprehensive nor systematic.

In this book the anthropological themes have been divided into the triad of religious, scientific, and socially critical perspectives, leaving to philosophy the task of examining their interrelationship. My personal experience has been that since childhood I spontaneously have found all three methods of thinking to be totally plausible. From experience I have learned that most people who follow one of these three ways of thinking look at the other two with suspicion, even with loathing. The traditional religious critic considers scientific anthropology as a reduction of the higher to the lower, irrelevant when staying within its limits, criminal when transgressing them. He considers socially critical anthropology as a human revolt against the divine order. The average scientific critic considers religious anthropology as the world being turned upside down, and he considers the opinions of socially critical anthropology as the heedless disregard for the biological facts of heredity. The committed social critic considers religious anthropology as an intrigue of priests to keep humankind under their domination, and he considers scientific anthropology as the ideology of racists and technocrats; he already suspects the very term "anthropology" to be a diversion to prevent a critical examination of social structures. When I learned of these six critical judgments, I could not help feeling that all six have the known ideological function of ideological criticism. Each of them protects its believers' prejudices by placing the blame on the adversary; thus they confirm each other in their antagonism.

This book tries, instead, to examine explicitly the relationship between the three approaches. One could begin this systematically as follows: Each of the three methods has developed its own language for observing certain human phenomena, with which to make these phenomena immediately comprehensible to its adherents. A preliminary attempt at an integral understanding consists of articulating in each respective language the other two methods of thinking to see how they are perceived by the other. This book, however, can only be a preliminary study of such first systematic steps, let alone of a conceivably more systematic philosophical anthropology.

Part I of this book assumes an almost naive socially critical attitude. It proceeds from phenomena of the present culture, which feels threatened in its political and cultural reflections, and it raises the question of the anthropological background. *Part II* sees with the eyes and speaks in the language of scientific anthropology. Similarly, *Part IV* sees with the eyes and speaks in the language of contemporary Christian theology, including, however, an openness for the Asiatic meditative experience. A chapter that would assume the eye and language of socially critical theory is missing; I felt I still had too much to learn to dare to apply here what I had learned so far. *Part III* consists of philosophical reflections, reflections on some of the problems of the great tradition of European philosophy. Philosophically seen this book remains a propaedeutic.

The book emerged mainly from lectures and essays for specific audiences and occasions. However, I had already chosen the themes of these essays for some time and in such a way that they would be suitable for collection in a volume on anthropological questions. In addition, I included several new essays that were specifically written for this book.

Part I
PLATEAUS AND CRISES

1. The Problem
   of Peace

A. Analysis

Peace has become the conscious duty of humankind in this century. The reasons are technological development and the altered self-consciousness that humankind now has of itself. Both are the offspring of the maturing of modern civilization. The unlimited growth of this determined and intellectual culture has prepared the means and revealed obligations that were previously in the domain of unmodifiable fate. It has also destroyed defenses in external nature and in human relationships that previously functioned by themselves. This did not only occur objectively but has penetrated step-by-step into our consciousness. We find ourselves confronted with duties and dangers of which there are no previous examples. We are confronted with the demand to find solutions to problems that heretofor never existed. The ancient institutions and the scourge of war are affected by the undertow of this changed thinking.

The problem of peace is, in the narrow sense, the problem of the prevention or restriction of war. The problem of peace in the larger sense results from this: the question of the powers and institutions that make authentic peace possible.

Reflections about the problem of peace lead us into four aspects of human relationships: military, foreign policy, social structure, and the psychological structure of the individual. The analysis that begins this essay joins broad reflections concerning these four thematic areas. The duty of securing peace proves itself to be authentically unsolvable in each of these regions. Thus, a basic discussion of the problem of peace in the larger sense has been included under the title "Peace and Truth."

Military. There has been no war since 1945 on the actual territory of the superpowers, nor in the politically stable part of their military alliances. At the same time, the problem of the prevention of war remains unresolved in two respects: First, in the rest of the world, usually called the Third World, wars are being constantly waged, and their continuation is to be expected. Secondly, in the zones of the superpowers that have been free from direct military conflict for thirty years, future wars, including a Third World War fought with nuclear weapons, can in no way be ruled out.

The prevention of war through even more powerful weaponry is unreliable. Next to the danger of either technical or personnel failure, there exists above all else the imminent law of growth that has brought us to the present state of armament. It will not be the weapons themselves, but only an equally enormous consciousness, that can preserve the peace.

The first attempt at this, on the military level, is the strategy of deterrence through the second-strike capacity. It is this to which we are indebted for the present period of peace and reduced tensions. But this strategy has three weaknesses, militarily: It is not reliable for the prevention of limited conflicts because the burden of preventing war that is based on this threat of escalation contains the danger of actual escalation. Weapons systems, including the second-strike capacity, become obsolete. And World War III could someday be started by that side that has made a sober calculation of its chances to survive and win.

That the military cannot permanently preserve peace is an old truth. *Si vis pacem, para bellum* is a proverb in a world in which war is an obvious institution. Weapons can prevent some wars, but not all of them. They will definitely not prevent what will be the last war for a superpower because it loses it. And at the same time, the enormous destructive powers make a continuation of the institution of large wars unacceptable. The military thus has been given a problem that it cannot solve with its own means.

Foreign Policy. The classical foreign policy concerns the arrangement of the interests of sovereign powers. Diplomacy and international law have developed means to the peaceful resolution of foreign-policy conflicts. But they have, up to now, never prevailed over the institution of war. The historical experience shows only two ways to stability in a system of sovereign powers, the concert of the powers or the hegemony that, however, either leads back to the concert or leads consequently to an imperium that replaces the system of sovereign powers. The concert of powers (mostly as pentarchy) has, throughout history, always needed periodic wars as a regulator.

It is important to recognize that a system of sovereign powers cannot simply through an act of good will be changed into a peaceful world of continual sovereign partnership. What must be overcome is the structure of power in order to accomplish change. In a power structure, the only reliable protection is power (only the less powerful are given the chance of renunciation of the competition through alliances, neutrality, or geographical situation).

But power can be accumulated practically without limit. Therefore the necessary corollary for every partner requiring protection through its own power leads with objective necessity to arms races. It is not the evil will of the politicians and military that makes the problem of peace permanently unresolvable through foreign power, but rather the structure of power.

There is no reason to believe that the present militarily bipolar, economically and politically somewhat pentarchically structured concert is not subject to this law. A stable hegemony would be reachable, as far as we can see, only through a world war and would, with frightful casualties, presumably lead to the creation of a world state. This could prevent future wars only as long as it remains stable. Its internal problems will not be mentioned here.

Social Structure. The members of a traditional power structure are states whose internal social structure is stabilized through domination. The relationship between the external power politics and the interests of the government is easily recognizable, not only to the degree that its policies are aggressive, but also to the degree that they are defensive. Since the European Enlightenment, there is a social movement that has as its goal the checking or the overcoming of domination. Accordingly, there is an understandable hope that by changing the social system the causes of war can be eliminated. Given the imprecise boundaries, one can differentiate between perhaps four political tendencies or systems: the preliberal order mostly known as feudalism, liberalism, socialism, and technocracy. As the means and motives of domination, one can separate three elements: hierarchy, function, and power. Feudalism accepts domination and sees it justified through hierarchy. Liberalism rests, at least in the economic sphere, in the selfish self-interest of the individual and attempts to limit the necessary sovereign acts of government to offices and functionaries, guided by free discussion, accordingly by the relationship between the discovery of truth and freedom. Socialism recognizes the continuation of the economically based system of domination in the liberal system and hopes to overcome this through nationalization of the means of production. Technocracy, which is less a doctrine than a practice, accepts domination insofar as it is a legitimate power that has the capacity to make intelligent decisions.

The struggle between social systems is not over. It ranks high today in the public consciousness as the cause of present and future wars. Could the worldwide victory of one of the competing systems assure world peace? The historical experience does not justify this expectation except if this were to be accompanied by the simultaneous establishment of a world state so that the structural elimination of foreign policy can succeed. Sovereign powers of similar social systems have previously bent to the imperatives of power competition as much as those of opposing social systems. Naturally the expectations of subduing state conflicts through the liberal world economy, through democratic reason, through socialistic morality, and through the elimination of the state based on domination, are not invalidated by historical parallels. The skepticism that opposes these expectations is perhaps depicted best through quotations from the sharpest criticism that each is accustomed to exercising against the others. The conservatives see in the three "progressive" systems the contemporary lack of moderation at work. The liberals miss in the other three systems the curtailment of domination at the decisive place, the free discourse of individuals in pursuit of truth. The socialists recognize in the idealistic claims of the other three the ideological superstructure of dominant economic interests. Technocracy sees in conservative, liberal, and socialist thought the general constriction of intelligence by ideology.

Individual and Group Behavior. One way or another the standard criticisms are examples of an almost always present pattern: criticism of the other for egotism and egocentricity. It appears that conflicts are contests among particular interests, no matter in which psychological guise they may present themselves to their adherents. What one means by the appeal to reason is the hope that the opponents in a conflict will be able to discern their real common interest. This, certainly in the widespread liberal expectation, seeks the origin of the lack of peace in irrational psychological occurrences that perhaps were produced or reinforced by erroneous education.

Aggression is conflict-seeking emotional disturbance. The important question, if a peaceful release is possible through educational and social changes, is controversial. The practical problem is not how to avoid aggression, but rather how to check it so that humankind has the capacity to live together socially. The social order is usually disrupted by aggressive warlike behavior that can be attributed to anxiety. Anxiety is the most important theme of the psychology of peace. One can differentiate in the anxiety complex between the fear of recognizable danger and the deep-rooted, consciously almost incomprehensible, remaining components. Fear is an emotionally excited mode of perceiving reality. The perceptions of danger causing fear are, in so far as they originate in other people or groups of people, deeply rooted in their own ways of relating, and consequently originate in their own anxious condition. The world of conflicts and anxiety proves to be a self-stabilizing system. This is the psychological version of the analysis of the power system.

B. Peace and Truth

The four regions of human behavior refer to each other and stabilize each other. In a world of conflict, the behavior that maintains and continues its conflict-generating structure is certainly rational for the individual or individual groups. At the same time, throughout history, a limited peace has always been possible for individuals or individual groups. Without that prospect it would not have been possible for anyone, because of resource limitations, to have continually carried on conflicts. How is peace possible? If it is possible, why is it so difficult?

In a symbolic manner of speaking, one can say that peace is the embodiment of truth. Peace is meant here as the possibility of living without conflicts that endanger existence. Peace can be the peace of an individual with oneself or with society, and the peace of a society with itself or with its environment. Truth, in this sentence, is understood as the perception of reality; exactly that reality which the possibility of existence is dependent upon, therefore reality itself and the environment. Perception can be either abstract or concrete, or it can be a combination of both. Embodiment means the reality of the behavior that is controlled by this perception and that always renews itself. The indefinite article in "a" peace, "a" truth, means that the whole of reality can never be perceived. Peace is possible only to the extent that the existing reality permits it. History is a conflict of different realities. Therefore, every historical peace was the result of conflict. Its preservation was the result of conflict. Its prospect is to be lost in new struggles to make possible a new peaceful interlude based on a new comprehension of reality.

The problem of contemporary humankind is world peace. This no longer means just the peace between sovereign powers that has been concluded through foreign policy and stabilized through periodic wars, but the "inner world" peace of humankind with itself. It will not be a peace without conflicts. Its reality will be adequate insofar as its perception protects humankind from itself and preserves the environment.

But why is peace so difficult? Why, if truth is the spirit of peace, is history the struggle between different realities? The systematic basis of self-stabilization through conflict is power. Let us, therefore, try to sketch an anthropology of power.

Struggle is inherent in all organic life. Power is a human condition. Everything that lives is threatened. In organic life, certain goods are always scarce because evolution makes them scarce. Fear presumes the capacity to recognize danger. Now there are ways to deal with danger. Power begins with the capacity of real recognition of these ways and means. Due to this recognition, the means of providing protection from certain dangers can be accumulated generally in animal life within fixed limits: food, tools, hunting weapons. This accumulation reaches its reasonable limit where its continuation cannot further eliminate the danger. Now when the danger itself originates in humans, it can continually increase through accumulated ways and means. In the competition between people, unlimited accumulation of these means serves a "rational" purpose, and power is based upon it. The most obvious economic manifestation of accumulated power is money. Power is essentially tragic because its step-by-step increase has the end effect of increasing danger.

The real accomplishment of peace between people is therefore the reasonable limitation of power. The struggle between the realities, accordingly the four above-mentioned concepts of society, is the struggle for the correct route to this limitation. The struggle itself can only be continued by way of power. Therefore, it depends upon the very law that it seeks to overcome. Consequently, the ever-repeated hope that the present struggle is the good war to end all wars has tragic overtones.

The possibility for peace begins when this tragic illusion is recognized, where the enemy, the opponent in the struggle between opposing realities, can be loved.

C. Politics of Peace

The politics of peace, like the problem of peace, can be discussed in a narrow or a broad sense. In a narrow sense it means political activities that have peace as a priority object. In a broad sense it means all activities that either create or protect the conditions of the possibility for peace. Let us proceed through the four regions once again, in reverse order, and by so doing proceed from the broad to the narrow sense of the politics of peace.

Human Behavior. Peace can only be made by one who is peaceful. One must live a truth whose materiality makes peace possible and not just phantasizes it. Education for peace consists of assisting everyone to live the truth that is accessible. This leads naturally to a struggle between different realities.

But it also leads to the strength to see this struggle itself in the light of the initially surmised higher reality. Anxiety is fear based on one's own incapacity for peace, and the inability to peacefully resolve conflicts sustains, through anxiety, this lack of peacefulness.

The politics of peace take place in the interests of everyone. The design must be such as to include the active participation of those whose growth process or whose experience of death has not allowed them to mature or fully mature. Given the limited means available to accomplish this participation, the continual and repeated failure of these efforts is to be expected. But attempts to achieve peace are useful even where they fail.

Social Behavior. In the struggle between different social systems, the politics of peace raises not just the question of ends but that of permissible means. Is physical violence justified? Is "structural violence" a meaningful concept? Which of these conceptualizations justifies which method of operation?

The question of power and powerlessness is not a question of the formal fulfillment of behavioral norms whose substance is neutral. It is itself a question of substance, of reality. The tragedy of power is intensified by the very application of power. Whoever uses force to assist his particular reality to victory will find it very difficult not to continue using force to repress new truths. But the renunciation of power can conceal a renunciation of the defense of truth that it is not considered sufficiently important to struggle for. "Nonviolence is better than violence, violence is better than cowardice," said Ghandi. The practical issue is the social reality of morality. The morality of the categorical imperative, the general lawful validity of one's own code of behavior, is applicable in its own way to everyone. I cannot desire the use of power if I do not desire that power will be used against me. The strict application of this assertion against one's own activities belongs to the process of personal development.

But the meaning of social rules that have been theoretically recognized as necessary is that by fulfilling their requirements we are relieved of the reality of our own weaknesses and dependencies. Therefore, the question of permissible means leads again to important questions concerning the appropriate social systems.

The politics of peace in the broad sense cannot for that reason refrain from being also social politics. Accordingly, the next step in these thoughts would show that it is necessary to ask radical questions about all four of the above-mentioned social concepts. Asking questions means having the ability to distinguish between their truths, without which they never would have been able to succeed in reality, and their falsehoods, through which they destroy peace rather than create it. On the surface this would be pointed out by quoting from their criticisms of each other. Of course the classical foreign and military policy would also be subject to the same kind of questioning.

Foreign Policy. Active politics of peace is necessary and possible. Its necessity can be formulated as follows: With every foreign-policy decision the first consideration must be that it serves world peace. This necessity has never adequately penetrated into general public consciousness and accordingly does not correspond with the practice of most governments. It can, however, be derived from the survival interest of each country if one reflects that catastrophical developments, including a Third World War fought with nuclear weapons, are not only possible but probable.

The possibility of politics of peace is hard to recognize. There is a repressive mechanism that shields our everyday political activity from recognizing a *necessity*, and this repressive mechanism is kept in effect by doubting the *possibility* of catastrophe. Does not the very analysis attempted here prove the very impossibility? This position must be answered in general and specifically.

In general the automatism of the power system tends as always toward warlike decisions. But the recognition of these dangers is greater now than ever before. The politics of peace can win time. It can permit worldwide structures to grow that could make possible, in a still not visible future, the replacement of the present system of sovereign powers through a world-wide order. The unity of humankind is, functionally observed, a new truth that pushes for a new body through which world peace can be realized. Absolutely indispensible for a conscious demand for this development is the recognition that world peace still does not exist.

The politics of détente of the seventies has in its details been replaced by a skepticism that lets one presume that many of its supporters and opponents were deceived about its meaning. Détente is a basic need of the people who feel the new truth of the unity of the human family and recognize that their fate is dependent upon the realization of this truth. It is also a name for a functionally practical agreement between sovereign governments. The realization of either version is a long-term, fluctuating, ongoing process. For the growth of the consciousness of humankind, such symbolic acts during the period of détente as Kissinger's first visit to Peking and Brandt's dropping to his knees in Warsaw are probably more important than all the agreements. For the world powers, détente is merely a diplomatic instrument that does not lie within the power of the two super-powers, but remains a sensible goal to strive for with peaceful decisions.

Reflections like these remain banal, and therefore ineffective, if they do not proceed to concrete details. For the research for peace as a contribution to the science of the politics of peace, the crucial points of the structural problem of peace are accordingly important.

Military. To the extent that public consciousness, as unclear as always, is concerned with the problem of peace, the role of the military shifts. In the developing countries, the military certainly continues to play its classical role in foreign and domestic policy as the base of power. Military dictatorship is there a version of the technocracy with feudal, capitalist, or socialist admixtures. But these military dictatorships almost always find it necessary to designate their power as transitional. They are the symptom of unresolved problems.

The participation of the military in the prevention of world war is brinkmanship. But it is necessary to be able to fight a war or to be able to threaten war in order not to have actually to fight or to be forced to surrender. This dilemma can be acceptable as long as we see it in the context of security measures in a transitional quasi balance of power.

2. Humankind in the Era of Science and Technology

The scientific-technological era was greeted with great and justified expectations. It fulfilled one important aspect of these expectations. It has, however, created new problems and new dangers.

The *expectations* were related to five areas of existence: economy, society, politics, culture, and consciousness. The original expectations, the problems, and the revised expectations in these five areas cover, to a certain extent, the entire human condition. The image that one has of oneself, the human image, will be dealt with under the title of consciousness.

I can quickly summarize the expectations.

Beginning with the *economy*, humankind was poor. Technology made it rich. Many people lived in hunger or with scarcity; the technological farm economy and modern methods of transportation made people satiated. They could clothe themselves better and live far away from their places of work. They had lived previously by the sweat from their brows and labored from morning to night. Their work became easier, their leisure time longer.

This had, however, consequences for the structure of *society*. All previous civilizations had been divided into different social classes. The minority owned the means of production and consumed the scarce goods that were produced. This minority also had the culturally most important product, leisure time. So it became the bearer of culture. If goods are no longer scarce, then such privileges are no longer functionally necessary. An egalitarian society should now become possible.

This transformation will also transform *politics*. Politics meant in previous civilizations domination and the struggle for domination. The classical stratification of forms of government as monarchy, aristocracy, and democracy indicates who ruled. If humankind presently evolves into democracies, it is a social consequence of a more egalitarian division of goods. Domination is, in such a society, perhaps no longer functionally necessary. On the horizon the expectation appears that perhaps power struggles between nations and wars will also eventually disappear.

The internal transformation of national *culture* also means that now all persons have the possibility of receiving a higher education. The first step, compulsory school and the proliferation of colleges and universities, has already taken place in the advanced industrial nations. As a consequence of this movement for universal, public education, a world culture is being created. The principal ingredient of this world culture, that which has actually made it possible, is scientific thought and its practical technical application.

A transformed culture means also a transformed *consciousness*. Consciousness is changed through knowledge. It becomes rational. Therefore, it becomes less dependent upon authority and rigid thought patterns. It becomes freer also from its own mental anxiety. It dares to think for itself, to become autonomous.

These are expectations of modern civilization. But what really happened?

Modern civilization evolved, seen from a distance, in wave movements. After a period of progress came crisis, after crisis came a new period of progress, to be followed by new crisis. Where are we today? First, I would like to give a brief, somewhat superficial survey.

The scientific-technological civilization had its origins in Europe and its greatest development in North America. In Europe one is aware that this modern civilization is built over an older independent civilization much more than one is in America. The European consciousness is much less completely identified with modernity than the American. The catastrophes from 1914 to 1945 meant for Central and Western Europe doubts in the belief in progress. The radical modernization of the world since 1945 also meant for Europe an economic, political, and cultural American domination that, at least from the military perspective, was accepted as the material condition for freedom.

In the world outside the European and North American cultural sphere, modernity was originally spread in the form of trade and colonialism. Japan shut itself off from the rest of the world in the seventeenth century, following the first European penetration, by strength of its own will and unity. This same strength of will and unity enabled Japan to open itself in the second half of the nineteenth century to modern civilization. Japan was determined to preserve not only its political independence, but also its cultural identity. Japan is the only country outside of the North Atlantic cultural sphere that has attained complete technical and economic modernization. Therefore, it is also the only non-North Atlantic country to receive its full share of the immanent problems of technological progress.

The economy of Japan and the North Atlantic sphere is organized as free enterprise capitalism. The Marxist expectation that capitalism would cause increasing misery through its ever-growing crises and therefore prepare the basis for socialism has so far not been fulfilled. Radical socialism has only achieved power in those economically backwards countries where it can serve as a means of modernization. The two old empires Russia and

China have combined socialism with the traditional structure of centralized governmental power. Russia is militarily the only world power next to America. Economically, though, the socialist countries have not reached the production level of the leading capitalist nations.

The so-called Third World is overwhelmingly and dependently integrated in the capitalist system. Its economic development is, in many regions, intense. The expectations that accompanied the deconstruction of the political colonial system have not been fulfilled. Development occurs in dependency upon the large capitalist centers, and these countries have not overcome the social differences but rather accentuated them. Over a billion humans are objectively suffering from malnutrition. If we include those who die from sicknesses resulting from malnutrition along with those who actually succumb to hunger, more people die annually from hunger than from war.

I would like next to name seven *apprehensions* about the future of humankind that many minds are currently preoccupied with. I have no solution to offer for any of them, although I am convinced that for each and every one of them a future solution will be found. The irrational in the rationality of modern civilization and the ambivalence of progress is actually the object of these questions.

Of the seven apprehensions, three are concrete or materially recognizable dangers. The other four concern structurally insupportable problems.

I do not see how, in the coming decades, a *hunger catastrophe* in the Third World can be avoided.

I do not see how, in the coming decades, the *arms race* of the superpowers and the danger of a *Third World War* can be avoided.

I do not see how, in the next fifty years, the *destruction of our natural environment* can be halted.

These are the first three concerns. The more structural concerns are the following.

It appears that in the capitalist societies the *class differences* will not disappear.

It appears that in the communist states the *civic freedoms* cannot be realized.

It appears that the world of modern civilization becomes ever more *ungovernable*. This leads to the attempt to rule with either the police or the military.

It appears that in the modern consciousness the feeling of *meaninglessness* becomes ever greater.

Trying to understand the basis of the structural concerns, I look at *society*, the persisting *class differences*, and the horrible reality of *hunger*. Now, the capitalist economy has been constantly expanding. This growth is certainly the hope of the modern world. It is the way to make poor people rich. When demands cannot be satisfied, why do they keep increasing?

The psychological reason is that the workers are aware of another class above them that certainly has no difficulty in satisfying its own demands. The modern capitalist economy has created a basic egalitarian expectation that did not previously exist. But the socialist states have also not been able to resolve the class problem. A new ruling class is firmly in control of the Soviet Union. According to Marxist theory the establishment of an adequate level of production must evolve into the classless society, which means that the present socialist societies will have to face the problems that currently concern the highly industrialized capitalist societies.

Hunger is the most direct evidence that world society is a class society. Compared with the Indian peasant or worker, an American or European belongs to the upper class. Hunger is the result of a vicious cycle. It is the result, despite the increase in productive capacity, of a population increase. This has been made possible by modern medicine and perpetuated by the traditional economic logic that for a poor family the more children there are, the more laborers there are to provide for the parents in their old age. Under modern conditions, poverty increases the growth of population and population growth increases poverty.

Under the heading of *politics* I join together two apparently unrelated themes: the absence of *civic freedoms* in the communist states and the danger of the *arms race* and a *World War*. Both are concerned with the unresolved problem of power. Competing powers often cause bloody struggle. One power alone causes the suppression of freedom.

Internally the liberal state has limited the struggle between interest groups by power sharing, by elections, and by arbitration. Thus, armed struggle has been curtailed. This is one of the greatest political advances that humankind has achieved. The socialist criticism that the power struggle and domination in the form of capitalist accumulation has not been overcome is correct. Communist states have eliminated this form of domination, only to replace it with domination by the Party, in turn suppressing the civic freedoms. They have repressed the very right to free discussion. If the specific danger of capitalism is cynicism, then the specific danger of socialism is the lie.

In foreign policy there exists until now no governing world body. Since the dawn of civilization, foreign-policy conflicts have led to war. It would be a terrible error to believe that nuclear weapons have freed us from this danger. What happened in Hiroshima and Nagasaki can happen again anywhere in the world.

A non-superpower is probably better protected from destruction by not possessing nuclear weapons than by possessing them. This is a position that I have long advocated in my own country.

Under the heading of *culture* I refer to the danger of *environmental destruction* and the threatening *ungovernability* of the world. Both are examples of contradictions of modern civilization.

The danger of the waste of natural resources and the destruction of the environment has been slowly entering the public consciousness. In the heavily populated areas one is very conscious of the destruction of the environment, be it Los Angeles or New York, the heavily industrialized Rhine or Tokyo. It is a situation in which a danger slowly accumulates, and after a certain point can no longer be brought under control. International cooperation is necessary to combat it. A precondition is that the damage that must be controlled in the national sphere must be effectively controlled. But international cooperation would require an organization that does not currently exist, and which eventually must institute controls that end the quantitative growth of world economy.

The dissatisfied youth of the world began a worldwide student rebellion in the nineteen sixties. It was unsuccessful and has died out for the present. But minorities have learned how to use violence and have forced the "silent majority" to approve of a police state. The world is becoming ungovernable.

With this we come to the core of the problem, the *consciousness* of humankind. The modern consciousness is, according to its own design, emancipated and rational. But it does not feel well with the world it has created. The naive result of this feeling of malaise is aggression. One does not look for the causes within one's self but rather in others. The guilty ones are the old order or the revolutionaries, the capitalists or the communists, the other races, the other generation, or society, anybody but ourselves, but I.

It is a giant step forward when one recognizes the failure in oneself. But that is still not the solution. What are the values that I neglect, that are missing in me? It is easy to be concerned with problems that are obvious causes of misery in the world, the feeding of the hungry and the liberation of the oppressed. But what about the higher values that give the saved life a sense of meaningful existence? The modern world is rife with the feeling of *meaninglessness*. There is a pervading, fundamental nihilism without which our irrational behavior would not be understandable.

With that we come to the question of *better understood expectations*. Modern economy is not only based on technology, but also upon the incentive to develop and use new technology. Historically, this incentive has been an integral part of the capitalist economic system. Capitalism's interpretation of itself is based on the market-economy theory formulated by Adam Smith and the classical economists who followed him. It is a theory of the freedom of the individual. The previous system, known as mercantilism, controlled the economy through state regulations. Smith reacted against this with the theory that when people are allowed to pursue their own selfish self-interests, free from state interference, the result is what is best for the entire commonwealth. The free market best protects the wealth of the entire commonwealth. The contemporary ambivalent reality of capitalism has already been commented upon. I assume that primarily because of capitalism's strongest organizations, the multinational corporations, the economic growth of the Third World will substantially increase while its dependency on the multinationals continues. But it will not be able to prevent hunger. And the problem of continued destruction of the environment, and the necessary limits of economic growth, probably lie beyond the range of private enterprise.

What does the theory of economic freedom mean for the *society*? It has a revolutionary character when compared with all of the old conceptions of a human society. The ethic of domination has always required of the master that he considers the well-being of his subjects. Or, stated differently, any system of domination that felt the necessity to justify its power has always done so with the justification that those with power were acting in accordance with the best interests of the entire society. On the contrary, the market theory, at least in its economic application, is based on the assumption that the interests of society are best served when each individual pursues his or her self-interest. This egalitarian turning-point of the modern era is based on a confidence in human reason, upon an intelligent egoism.

The actual realization of this new self-confidence is the task of political liberalism. Smith leaves those activities that remain outside the profit-making sphere to the state. They are protection of the nation from external enemies, preservation of internal law and order, and maintenance of what is known as the infrastructure. We must add to this list protection of the environment. Political liberalism is convinced that also the activities of the state are to be controlled through the free decisions of its citizens—not through an adjustment of their economic interests, but rather through intelligent dialogue.

Here we encounter the very core of modernity, a confidence in *reason*. The justification of political freedom is rooted in the correlation between freedom and reason. Reason understands truth. And truth can only be pursued in freedom. If I want to teach somebody that two times two is four, it does not help to give an order to repeat after me and believe it. Rather, the student must understand its truth. The student must only speak the sentence when its truth is convincingly obvious.

The political constitution of a state should be that which gives its citizens the best possibility to realize their welfare through the reasoned pursuit of truth. It is because of this ideal that I previously designated the liberal state as one of the greatest political advances of humankind.

The contradictions, though, of modernity itself threaten this very progress. If people are not able to solve their problems within the context of the liberal state, they will destroy this state. They will still not have solved their problems, but freedom will have been destroyed, and who knows when it will exist again.

The core of the problem, according to both the liberal and socialist interpretation, is the phenomenon of the need for *domination* of humans over other humans.

Modern civilization is ambivalent about this. Historically, it strives to overcome the phenomenon of domination. It has also given the phenomenon of domination access to greater technical and intellectual means than were ever possessed in previous historical epochs. To understand this ambivalence, we must first of all examine the components of the complex and unclear concept of domination. There are at least three components. They can be labeled hierarchy, function, and power.

Social *hierarchy* exists already in animals in almost all groups. Humans are the descendants of social apes, and it is highly probable that this instinct to organize in hierarchies is inherited. Humans strive towards a high place in the hierarchy and do not spontaneously question its existence. Natural science can certainly educate us about the origins of human society, but we are not compelled to blindly obey hereditary factors. All higher civilizations are created with instinct being used as a material that can also be justifiably repressed. Equality between people is not a natural state. In this regard Rousseau was completely wrong. But equality between us can be one of our highest social accomplishments. It exists when we consciously view each other as equal. That is the core of the golden rule that is taught by all the higher religions. The clearest modern formulation is Kant's categorical imperative, "Let your behavior be guided by principles that you would want to be the guiding principles of all humankind." The highest principle of a universal ethic does not command specific norms with regards to contents. It commands universality, consequently a reasonableness, to these norms.

In real human life equality can never be completely realized. The hierarchy that not even reason can abolish is the hierarchy of reason itself. The relationship between parents and dependent children, between teachers and students, between doctors and patients, even between those with knowledge and those without, cannot be symmetric. The balance is what religion calls "love." Those with knowledge treat those without knowledge basically as their equals. One loves even the partner who cannot or does not want to be proven equal. One loves even one's enemy. In modern civilization, exactly because of a belief in the autonomy of reason, there are few things more difficult than love. But without love, humankind in its community cannot survive.

The second element of domination is *function*. Higher cultures are dependent upon planned and directed social activities since the early history of river controls and irrigation systems on the Nile, Euphrates, Indus, and Yellow Rivers. Domination preserves itself through rational functions. Republican social orders have sought, even in antiquity, to separate the functions of hierarchy and personal power through the periodic change of official positions, following from the concept that the office itself is a function of domination. It is also the rational core of the modern concept of technocracy. Those who hold public office must change periodically, and they must be held accountable.

What the attempt to control domination really should overcome is the principle of *power*. Power in the narrow sense has no animal analogy. Power is specifically human. And just as with knowledge that is transmitted through language, it is virtually limitless. In a hierarchy one cannot be more than the highest. Power, though, can be unlimited. Weapons, followers, money, and information are unlimitedly increasable means of power. The ability of an opponent to increase his unlimited power brings about a compulsion to competition that can finally end only with victory or defeat. Capitalism, as Marx described it, with its compulsion to accumulate, is a typical example; the result is its accomplishments and its horrors, its growth and its crises. The competition must appear irrational when seen from a distance. What impulse will drive someone who has already made a million dollars to make another? The psychological answer is that only one who wants to earn the second million is capable of earning the first. Within the sphere of power, it is precisely this behavior that is rational. Only those who are more powerful can survive the struggle for power. At some time, though, every person succumbs to another. Power is essentially tragic. The ancient, unvanquished institution of war is the greatest manifestation of this tragedy.

Modern civilization with its belief in reason must assume that it can restrain power. But it is this requirement that has proven itself a contradiction.

Where does the contradiction come from? I attempt to find the origin when I differentiate between *intellect* and *reason*. Intellect is the result of the capacity for discursive knowledge through concepts. Reason is the perception of the whole. Modern culture makes use of will and intellect. Through will we can desire that which, through intellect, we can conjure. The intellect can come up with that which the will can accept. Intellect and will have been limited to finite obtainable goals. For this very reason, they are limitless: Goal can follow goal, concept can follow concept. Reason, as the perception of the whole, can limit this process, intellect and will alone cannot. Accordingly, we become the undeniable slaves of power, not the masters, and also accordingly, we cannot love.

It is a characteristic of this culture that the *beautiful*, and consequently the sense of the beautiful, is destroyed. Modern art and its esthetics for the sake of truth has even abandoned beauty as a goal of art. The sense of the beautiful is the capacity to perceive the whole. I am convinced that this is a life-preserving aspect of human nature.

This entire survey was just a description and critique of modern consciousness. Will the extraordinary expansion of the sphere of reason and intellect harmoniously enrich or impoverish humankind? That depends upon whether intellect, as a part of the new consciousness, can again find reason. Why should that not be possible? How does modern consciousness understand itself, and how should it understand itself?

There is no economy without technology and no technology without science. Science, natural science, is the hard core of modern civilization, its fundamental new discovery. True science does not exist without philosophy, nor philosophy without the essence of religion. With both of these statements, I go beyond the average understanding of modern science and, in fact, turn it around.

The relationship between science and philosophy is my personal sphere of work.

The American scientific theorist Kuhn has demonstrated that historically science has developed in two alternating phases, normal science and scientific revolution. Normal science solves individual problems according to proven paradigms. Scientific revolution finds a new paradigm. I maintain now that in normal science philosophy is not necessary, but that a great scientific revolution is impossible without philosophical thought. We remain on the brink of a fundamental revolution in physics in which the latter, I suspect, will be proven to be the theory of general conceptual knowledge. It will be the general science of understanding. The philosophy that thinks this, and without which this revolution cannot take place, is reason.

But what is the whole that this reason perceives? I suspect that it is consciousness itself. This consciousness cannot be the finite ego that is actually the subject of will and understanding. This ego is only a mode of appearance of that which a great tradition calls the self. But this is in a realm of experience that traditionally exists within the framework of religion. It was in this sense that I said that there is no philosophy without the essence of religion.

Modern culture has also completely changed our relationship to religion. It emancipates us undeniably from the known strictures and corresponding social orders of traditional religious communities. It makes one intellectually aware of the variety of the religious experiences of the world. We thus discover that in all of its different manifestations there are two things that all great religions have in common: *universal ethics* and the *meditative experience*. It is no accident that universal ethics, understood as social justice, and meditative experience become the desired goals of ever-growing circles of young intellectuals throughout the world. Use of drugs is a complete misunderstanding of the meditative quest. Today, Yoga and Zen are not simply the newest fad, although understandably they are also that.

What opens before us is a conscious consequence of the scientific-technological age, which already stands on the threshold of a new era.

3. The Ambivalence of Progress

A. The Concept of Ambivalence

A leitmotif of the preceding essay was the concept of ambivalence or, more precisely stated, the ambivalence of progress. This concept was used there as a means of analyzing many concrete phenomena. It now becomes the subject. What is the ambivalence of progress? Does it even exist? If so, what does it mean? Let us proceed from the perception that contemporary society has of itself.

The industrial societies approach the future with a shaken self-confidence and growing criticism from their own midst. While external progress in the form of continued economic growth remains a goal, and while the predominant futurology that extrapolates the changes and directions of this progress still exists, nevertheless, the perception and even certainty increases that the decisive questions are not even being touched upon. What then are the decisive questions?

Let us first of all choose as an example a problem that has been formulated in the technological sphere, the problem of the destruction or protection of the natural environment. By analyzing it, we find a kind of classification of the causalities.

The first category one can label as the scientific-technological. One finds certain phenomena, for example, smog or water pollution. One does not doubt that these phenomena are the consequence, and even the unintended "side effects," of technological processes.

The second category can be termed that of the immediate preventive measures. To the extent that the causality of the first category is known, then legal, political, educational preventive and corrective measures can be planned and in the political realm can be precisely formulated and enforced. What is involved here are social causalities that can be effectuated within a given social system.

The third category concerns the sociopolitical structures. In many cases the necessary, alleviating, preventive measures are known but either are not taken or fail. Here it is necessary to question the social and political structures that are responsible for these failures and examine the possibility of changing them. What is at issue are the very positions of society itself.

Although the difficulties in the first category involving the adequacy and reliability of the scientific analysis and prognosis are currently very great, one must still admit that the greatest source of difficulty is in the third category. The consequence of civilian technology, just as that of military technology, has made certain deficiencies of existing political and social systems obvious.

As I see it, science and technology have been less a primary causality than a radicalizing factor. They are not solely responsible for the improvement or for the deterioration of a situation, but because of the increased instrumental capacity and the prevailing tendency towards applying technology wherever possible, they have resulted in a radicalization of the risks and dangers.

Scientific-technological progress, at least in the realm of our recent historical experience, has actually been an irresistable force. It has consequently radicalized the problems of the society in which we live. It creates prosperity yet sustains social inequalities. It protects us from the forces of nature yet threatens the destruction of nature. It creates preconditions for freedom but stabilizes domination. It increases the destructiveness of wars, therefore making necessary the strident demand for elimination of war, and offers, as a means for this finally, a new order that contains within it the danger of the greatest tyranny.

One can explain much of this ambivalence through the illusory nature of the apparently neutral values of science and technology. That which understands itself as neutral in relation to existing values can be employed, and will work, in every system that allows its practical growth; consequently, the ideology of neutral values creates an artificial blindness to its own consequences.

But this critique, which I use as my own, must be careful not to fall, itself, into the "political syllogism" maintaining that the position of my opponent causes unhappiness and that therefore my position causes happiness. In reality, the positive political value judgments that are in conflict with each other are in practice analogously ambivalent. The core of this observation will therefore be the ambivalence of the political ideals as related in modern European history.

But first, a general observation about the concept of ambivalence: I use this concept descriptively, just as it has been used in the practical everyday world and in the course of historical observation. The platitude, "Everything has its good and its bad aspects," does not apply. Rather, we experience a frightening phenomenon I have so often seen: that a position, by presenting itself as radical, eventually destroys itself and creates its negation. With that almost always comes the first unconscious lies with which so many less prepared people are ready to deceive themselves. The resulting negation is actually the preferred position. The lie is the most profound barrier to healing, and the unconscious lie, the biggest barrier of all.

Those familiar with Marx and Engels will say that I am actually describing the dialectic here. I avoid, though, using the concept of the dialectic in order to avoid adopting a well-practiced conceptual apparatus before I have thoroughly experienced the phenomenon myself. I find, in the inclination to employ common dialectic thought that either justifies itself through the synthesis or retreats into the power of the negative, a false optimism of which even the founder of the dialectic, although certainly on a higher level, was guilty.

I will now attempt to discuss, with reference to modern political history, the concepts of absolutism, liberalism, and socialism. This has been the subject of many books. But in most, certain key concepts were used uncritically. I am going to refer to historical material that I used in formulating my critique of these three concepts, in the course of familiarizing myself with beliefs and their consequences.

B. The Ambivalence of Political Ideals in Modern European History

Absolutism. A historical examination of absolutism is necessary as background to an analysis of the present situation. It requires me to retreat to a historical examination of the preceding period. I limit myself to the major powers of continental Europe. Obviously, the historical and political concepts are rather inadequate abbreviations of many complex realities.

Absolutism historically occurred in those late-medieval-early-modern periods of very differentiated social systems that, to mention one aspect they had in common, did not really know the territorial state as such because there were so many different sovereign authorities and privileged enclaves mixed together that the best depiction of the political situation is through a varicolored map. One can perhaps best describe these social orders as the result of medievalism and domination by the landed aristocracy usually called feudalism. In the cities, however, the domination by the aristocracy was succeeded by that of the guilds from which the early capitalist patricians evolved. The landed aristocracy had limited rights and usually great financial problems. The peasants were in unremitting and continually increasing dependency. In a complicated way, the church shared political power with the aristocracy and the guilds. The pluralistic structure of this reality stood in contrast to an integrated political theory that combined the Christian idea of creation with the ancient concept of the theology of society. The appeal to these ideas was not entirely in vain, nor was it very effective. The tension between radical, world-transforming Christianity and conservative world government erupted in every century, resulting each time in a new compromise between the two opposing forces. The prosperity of the dominant class along with its relative education grew in every century; art was its highest manifestation, philosophy was a highly differentiated scholasticism, and humanism reintroduced the images of the ancient world while science prepared itself for its triumphant ascendency through a few of its major thinkers (Bacon, Galileo, Descartes) who were conscious of its future role.

Confronted with this richly variegated world and its mixture of misery, splendor, and partial efficiency, absolutism was one of the definitive strides into the modern era, even the absolutism of the church and the monarchs in the Counter-Reformation and their Protestant counterparts.

I would say that the most important value of absolutism was *unity*. I limit myself here to the domain of the profane. Political unity was an important value at the beginning of that period, and lapses of unity were experienced daily as a manifest evil. In terms of political power, the issue was the victorious struggle of monarchy against a powerful aristocracy. In general, the monarchs either were allied with the bourgeoisie or used it to their advantage. In reality, the creation of a unified political territory was an important precondition to economic growth. That was certainly the case where the large commercial centers were politically dependent upon the monarchy. The monarchy created an effective bureaucracy, reduced aristocratic privileges, created a uniform system of justice, and secured commercial traffic. The importance of these actions is apparent when one compares them with previous conditions. One can designate stable administration and equality before the law, in the best cases, as the gift of absolutism to the succeeding bourgeois social order.

The exception to this process of equalization was, of course, the monarchy itself. This is, however, in the self-interpretation of absolutism necessarily self-evident. The creation of a unified state serving the commonwealth is a problem of power, and only the monarchs had the power necessary to break the power of the aristocracy, the church, and countless enclaves of privilege, and make them submit in the interest of the whole. An unhesitating justification of absolutism, though, such as Hobbes wrote about, was certainly an exception. The practice of power needs justification, as does every other practice. It needs mythological consecration.

The formula "King by the grace of God" is, by itself, a form of humility: The king is neither God nor descended from God but exists only through the undeniable grace of God, who has set him upon his throne, and can topple him. In practice, however, God's approval is a justification of the monarchy, which often enough justifies actions in the name of God that, according to the universal understanding, could not please God. The fundamental lie of all struggles is, "My power is justified for its serves the good of all, therefore everything is justified that makes it stronger and preserves it." This lie finds "By the grace of God" a highly welcome formula. The unity of the political body finally breaks exactly at the site of its original inception, the relationship of the monarch to his subjects.

Liberalism. One must call *freedom* the most important value of liberalism; more precisely, freedom of the individual. Absolutism had established unity at the price of suppressing many ancient freedoms. Accordingly, in its late period lack of freedom was considered its greatest evil. The evil was perceived to increase the more the so-called gift of absolutism of the unified state administrative system was taken as self-evident and no longer considered an accomplishment. But the freedom of liberalism was not the return of preabsolutism freedoms even if that had often been the intention. The old freedoms belonged to the estates, or were locally conditioned privileges. This was one of the obvious weaknesses of the aristocracy. The new freedom had the radical intention of equal freedom for all individuals, and this was realized to a certain extent. Yet this was only possible because it had inherited the functioning state apparatus from absolutism. Consequently, it not only opposed but also continued what may be considered the progress accomplished by absolutism.

I consider the political theory of liberalism to be a high and never previously attained level of political consciousness. All political systems that are being examined here have in common the belief that a political order is, in the final analysis, based on truth.

The meaning of *truth* is a philosophical question raised throughout this book. This is just one example of the use of the word. The antiquity-Christianity theory of society that was the philosophical justification of the preabsolutist order is thoroughly grounded in the concept of truth. It presents a true role for every member of society. It is fulfilled, as far as is possible on earth and as much as it serves society, when every member plays his or her appointed role. The religious justification of the absolute monarchy is itself a justification of the highest known concept of truth, for God is truth. The functional understanding of absolutism is based on an entirely modern understanding of truth. Whoever has seen beyond the causal connections of the struggle for power and the appropriate division of goods knows also that power is delegated to one and must be rationally employed by that person. Liberalism also had its own relationship to truth, namely that truth must be freely accepted, not imposed by force but rather the result of free discussion and toleration. This interpretation, though, contains a fundamental criticism of all previous systems. These, of course, proceed from the assumption that those with power possess the truth. They must possess it in order to rule with it. This is the argument repeated as justification for religious compulsion and allows the necessity of religious wars, especially religious civil wars. The collapse of the absolutism of religious truth that gradually emerges in the principle of *cuius regio eius religio*—separating the order function of religion from its claim to truth, in the idea of the confessionally neutral natural law and the idea of tolerance—makes the intellectual world of the emerging liberalism possible. This does not recognize any master, and definitely no political group may claim the *possession* of truth by divine right. By freely communicating their ideas, the citizens will discuss the political problem of truth and elect their representatives.

If I defend liberalism as a matter of conviction, I defend it, above all, for the principle that I would like to summarize with the following, somewhat paradoxical formula: Good politics is only possible because of truth, and no one may claim to be the only one possessing the truth. Each of these two statements is valid only in conjunction with the other. Truth by itself is intolerant. Whoever knows that two times two equals four can remain silent, but cannot honestly maintain that it could be five. If the welfare of society is dependent upon the recognition that two times two equals four, then one must also fight for this recognition. But since the truth can only be recognized in freedom and not by force, tolerance is essentially the creation of the space necessary to discover the truth and recognize it as such. There is, therefore, no justification to the use of force to impose the truth that one possesses, even if one really does possess the truth. Certainly, in reality, this principle is often not realizable with external success; this dilemma is at play in the space between productive tension and failure. It is not accidental that liberalism, while operating in the secure space by the absolute state, makes use also of the police.

It is interesting to observe the conservative criticism of prevailing liberalism. Indifference towards the truth is a criticism of this tolerance that with the liberation of private initiative has resulted in the liberation of private interest, and which had as a consequence that the officials who serve the state were seen as "shopkeepers." The defeated party sees clearly the ambivalence in the behavior of the opposition which, for the moment, has emerged in the leading position. The triumph of liberalism is certainly the result of the liberation of the extraordinary dynamics that are based on the connection between unlimited private interest and the belief in progress.

This is nowhere more obvious than in the economy. Here the classical national economists (Adam Smith was a professor who associated with merchants) made their great discovery: That what must have appeared as chaos to the antiquity-Christianity concept of order as well as to the paternalistic-causalist concepts of absolutism, namely, free competition, can be the locomotive force of the wealth of nations. I do not defend this discovery with the same earnestness with which I defend the relationship between freedom and truth. I only defend it to the extent that one, sometimes impatiently, expects that intelligent people will also recognize the validity of this partial truth, the same intelligent people who are annoyed every day by the misuse and stupid application of this same partial truth.

A serious analysis establishes the partial nature of this truth. The market is endangered by monopoly that is the result of the Darwinian principle from which it arises. The market can be automatically effective only where statistically predictable reactions are adequate, not where the casual relationships must be grasped in detail. Similarly, the market successfully creates conditions for the continued redistribution of income, but not for equality. I believe that the coexistence of large and small units will prove to be by far the most favorable division in the economy, just as it is in biological populations in accordance with the theory of natural selection. The market, *de facto*, currently creates gross inequalities that sometimes are alleviated later through growth, but it always brings with it the merciless reality of the destruction of mature forms of life (this is one of the conservative critiques of liberalism). To the victims of this system, freedom appears often enough to be freedom of being chosen by sharks. The market is, in the final analysis, best in situations of real exponential growth; it often cannot deal with the problem of saturation, or if so, only with extraordinarily harsh side effects.

The central question concerning liberal economic philosophy that is equally raised by both the conservatives and the socialists, almost in unison, is, "What right does private interest have to claim that is supersedes the best public interest?" Exactly on this issue, though, the liberal theoreticians have a very important, if partial, defense. They can always say, "Show us a system claiming it serves the public welfare best that really has done that." We are perhaps cynical, but we do not lie about this point. Our success is deserved, for finally truthfulness proves usually to be the guide to the most frictionless course of events. "Lying is so complicated." It is certainly true that self-interest in the economic sphere is the most reliable motivator, and that the necessity to take care of oneself creates productive people.

This defense is full of ambivalence even in its claim of truthfulness. Cannot people be educated also by appealing to their conception of higher ideals? Is it not possible to assume that they understand what is the general welfare? Certainly this is requisite for the entire political doctrine of liberalism itself. But does not the successful economic liberalism, by its very nature, make us lose sight of the general welfare? The so-called self-interest is, in capitalist development, certainly no longer a vital interest. It belongs to secret human compulsions such as power, artistic creativity, knowledge, fashion, and sexual ritual. We will not be able to understand what actually happens in capitalism if we have no anthropological insight into these processes.

Socialism. I would like to label the most important value of socialism as solidarity. Yet another value is often recognized as most important, that of justice, more specifically social justice. This value is, in reality, vague. In the economic struggle it is reduced to the equal division of goods. This, seen in isolation, is nothing more than the equalization of economic egoism and exposes itself to the critiques above. This demand can only be justified when society is viewed as a moral solidarity.

It is perhaps not just arbitrary if one adds solidarity together with the two previously mentioned values to come up with the formula that together they form the *unity of freedom*. Again one sees here the effect of the continuity of opposites. The freedom of the bourgeoisie is only a freedom of a part of society, and in the growing functionalization of the capitalist-technical world, this freedom is becoming increasingly illusory and is continually reduced to that of the private life. Only a freedom of solidarity, a freedom in unity, is true freedom. Progress to full equality is possible, if at all, only in this way.

In its almost one and a half centuries of relating to the liberal world, socialism has divided itself. The Social Democrats have integrated themselves as a reform party in the liberal world. They have fully accepted the central value system of political liberalism and step by step partially accepted its economic value system.

It is due to their inner tension and resultant ambivalence that Social Democrats do not know if they represent a socially reforming variety of liberalism or the way to radical change. At the core of this ambivalence appears, above all, the question, the ambivalence, about the radical goal itself as it has been previously historically realized. The Social Democrats feel themselves, justifiably so in my opinion, horrified by the results that the competing branch, the revolutionary socialists, have produced up to now.

Communist parties and national revolutionary socialist movements have, up to now, only achieved power through internal means in those countries that were economically underdeveloped and did not have a real tradition of liberalism. (In the most obvious exceptions to this rule, East Germany and Czechoslovakia, the Communist domination was accomplished externally as the result of international political relationships.) In these countries the success of the Communist party must first of all be measured by the criterion of economic growth, which is the measure used by the Communists themselves. This success has actually not been as great as they depict in their own propaganda, but it has been noteworthy. If one seeks the reasons for this success, there are, I think, two: the possibility of closing a country to foreign capital, and the possibility of forcing a people to renounce consumption in favor of investments for the future.

In the early period of the great capitalist expansion, it was not necessary for the leading economic powers to close their borders to external capital. Other means, including mercantilist measures, were available to achieve the goal. A renunciation of consumption was compelled in early capitalism through the very economic power of the capitalists and the stability of their supporting state apparatus. Both of these means are, in general, not available in the contemporary developing countries where there is a "weak" and nonsocialist constitution. Another way to deal with the problem of the weak government is certainly through military dictatorship, which often gives itself a socialist interpretation in the contemporary Third World.

Seen from this detached point of view, the accomplishment of socialism has been to bring the advantages of absolutism to a still "feudal" society. This formulation certainly underplays the important role that socialism has played in developing a social consciousness in those countries, and therefore orientating the thinking of the country to the values of solidarity. Here, there is no king "by the grace of God," who then proceeds to reform the existing economic power relationships. Instead there is mostly a charismatic leader who, by remaining loyal to his own egalitarian teachings, has totally eliminated the old ruling class. The relationship between the four components that I call charisma, terror, bureaucracy, and self-determination is the problem with which all real developing socialist countries must struggle. The socialist doctrine, when employed positively, serves to instill the will to solidarity without which the conflicts would be self-destructive; or, stated negatively, it serves to conceal the radical contradiction between pretense and reality.

According to Marxist historical expectations, these developments initially appear to be paradoxical; and bourgeois critics of Marxism have often pointed out the contradictions between expectations and actual results. The countries that are here referred to should, according to Marxist theory, first go through the period of bourgeois development. I find it probable that these countries have, in accordance with their social development, a need for absolutism. On the other hand, we live in a modern world whose consciousnes is not that of absolutism, but rather of liberalism or socialism. Therefore, these countries must combine this need for a modern value system with a practical application of absolutism. They are still not ready for the liberal society. Where it formally exists (for example, in India), it has just made the necessary development more difficult. The avowal of socialism enables enactment of the necessary absolutist measures, but at the same time it corrupts the socialist doctrine. Russia is still, in one way or another, a czarist country whose intellectuals still demand the freedoms that we have realized. China struggles with the same problems.

What should we of the advanced industrial societies learn from this? The young leftists have often maintained in the last decade that the manifest evils of the present Eastern European socialist countries, while criticism of them is valid, can be fundamentally overcome, whereas the manifest evils of the capitalist system are the result of, and necessitated by, its very structure. The evils of the Soviet system are then either attributed to human failure or to the necessity of adopting a defensive position to counter capitalist imperialism. I find these arguments to be essentially short-sighted but nevertheless worthy of more thorough discussion.

From a historical perspective, I find the argument correct concerning human failure (the cult of the personality, bureaucracy), but actually it is just a manifestation of what I have designated as ambivalence. It is a naive political doctrine that holds to the illusion that it has found, for the first time, a resolution to the consequences of the failures we call the history of the world. A political system is rightly judged on the basis of its success in the struggle against human failure. The cult of the personality and bureaucracy must even be designated as two very special forms of absolutism, exactly that which is historically almost the necessary course of events in these countries. This makes it easier to comprehend such failures, but it also shows how little what is attempted as socialism in those countries can really be an adequate model for us.

That it has been necessary for the Soviet Union to develop under pressure from Western imperialism and for Maoist China to develop under pressure from American and Soviet imperialism cannot be denied. I only admit to the consideration that the conflict between the rival empires for world hegemony will be much more mystified than clarified through ideological differences.

I began this essay with the theme of how to prevail against international power politics, and I would be contradicting myself if I said that this goal is *a priori* unattainable. Here, under the title of the ambivalence of progress, is discussed why it is so difficult.

We encounter the paradox that the two main competitors for world hegemony today, the United States and the Soviet Union, must be indebted for their present political form to revolutions that had among their ideals the goal to eliminate international power politics. No world power ever has permitted itself to assume the role of world imperium so much against its will as the United States (even if it has always practiced economic imperialism against Latin America). The framers of the American Constitution had, as their ideal, renunciation of the power struggles of the European monarchies; this was due to their recognition of the close correlation between espousal of bourgeois freedoms and limitation of governmental power. The Russian revolutionaries hoped that world revolution would destroy the imperialist capitalist powers that were responsible for World War I and hoped for the eventual disappearance of the state; both of these expectations were a radicalization of tenets of the American revolution. Woodrow Wilson's war to end all wars and Stalin's socialism in one land were, however, compromises with reality, and the strength of this reality is my theme here.

I return now to the thesis that the elimination of evil is in principle impossible in the liberal system, but that it is in principle possible in the socialist system, regardless that it has not been successfully realized for the reasons I have mentioned. If one understands this to refer to the now existing capitalist and socialist established sytems, this thesis would be superficial and obviously false. Referring to the theoretical tenets of both systems rather than existing realities, both claim to be able to overcome the evil of the world. The question is which claim is more realistic. Now, when one compares the existing reality of a system, for example, that in which we live, with the ideals of a never realized other system, there is a natural and legitimate asymmetry between the evil reality and the ideal expectations. The thesis that I am attacking maintains as its theoretical basis that because the liberal-capitalist system fundamentally encourages the unrestricted pursuit of private interest and because the socialist system has as its priority the general welfare, the former is incapable and the latter capable of resolving the problem of general welfare.

On the theoretical level this is undoubtedly a distortion of liberal doctrine. This requires that the political mechanism of representative democracy be capable of solving the problems affecting the general welfare, and this doctrine has always been found, in principle, to be flexible enough to permit reform while adhering to the belief that the market mechanism operates best when governmental intervention has been kept to a minimum. Certainly this leads, also in theory, to periods of almost unendurable tension, since without such tension a majority consensus on the necessity of reform would not be reached. In practice, however, the present principal criticism against this system is that it is possible, through manipulation of public opinion and self-deception, to maintain that the conditions of this society are basically healthy and that this is the best of all possible worlds and there is no social tension. If just once conservatives criticized the chaos of public opinion, lack of resolution, and obvious scandal resulting from unbridled private egotism that seem inherent in the liberal state, a justifiable response would be that in an open society the scandals always come to public attention where they can be dealt with, whereas in an authoritarian system they are hidden from public view, causing a continual decay of the foundations. The criticism of the present liberal state, that it sweeps its dirt under the rug, though, is justifiable to a very large extent. This shows the ambivalence of progress in the liberal societies. Nevertheless, there should be a careful scrutiny of how socialism deals with these same problems.

In contrast to the reforming socialism whose weakness is often that it compromises, revolutionary socialism, when it found itself not in opposition to feudalism but rather to liberalism, has compelled adherence to a principle that has certainly produced ambivalent consequences. That is the return to dogmatism, meaning that a certain group, alone, is in possession of the truth. Just as did the classical churches and sects, dogmatic socialism divides humankind into true believers and infidels or heretics. The happy realization that one belongs to the believers greatly increases the power of the Party. The manifestly correct criticism that the liberal system does not give everyone an equal chance, and that it, too, has established a domination of interests and doctrines, serves the rejection of its fundamental values in the illusionary hope that now this bastion of power must also be stormed if we are finally to realize the free society. Now the principle comes into operation that the ends justify the means in the form of reproaching the opponent for his immoral conduct and behavior while the other side is justified in exactly that conduct and behavior in the name of revolutionary progress. This self-contradiction often assumes grotesque shapes in such a way that the extremely elitist-antielitist doctrine accuses the opposing majority of false consciousness.

Let us consider again an issue, briefly mentioned in the section on liberalism, concerning the tension between the political necessity of truth, and its lack, that also causes a rupture in the belief in expressed values. Recognized truth is intolerant. Where absolutism is the requirement of the times, the result of this recognition can be the historical imperative. But for us, the requirement of the times is a solidarity that does not sacrifice freedom. The issue here is not the freedom that we claim for ourselves but the freedom that we guarantee our fellow humans. These issues are dealt with today under the headings of democracy, democratization, and participatory democracy.

I would like to add here another thought that I believe is valid, namely, that majority democracy, taken by itself, is not freedom but rather domination by the largest group. Only in its early stages is the purpose of liberalism freedom of the many from the domination of the few. Such a struggle must be fought in new forms again and again, and the result is that as long as the struggle continues the majority experiences solidarity. But a victorious group is not necessarily less foolish just because it is larger. Minorities are often better protected under a self-confident enlightened conservative government than they are under militant democracy. In the victorious democracy, therefore, one of the most important exercises of liberal philosophy must be the protection of minority rights, above all the rights of those who have no chance of ever becoming the majority.

C. In Search of the Causes of Ambivalence

The word ambivalence has, like many of our words, a wide range of meanings and usages. I would like to propose, though, that the central meaning be defined as follows: Ambivalence is what we call achievement of a goal with realization that the struggle, not the goal itself, was what we perhaps really wanted. The phenomenon of ambivalence has been found in the full range of contemporary existence. We find it in technological progress, which has created not just security and prosperity but also weapons of mass destruction and destruction of the environment. We find it also in political movements whose goals were to eliminate the bases of human misery that were the result of the manifest ambivalence of existing social and political conditions. The efficient unity of the nation state was the success of absolutism realized through the division of society into monarch and subjects. The freedom of all citizens was the success of liberalism realized through the economic domination of the bourgeoisie. Solidarity, meaning freedom in unity, was the success of socialism realized through erection of an absolutist bureaucracy. The hope is that finally the way is open to healthy uninterrupted evolution. Stated differently, the next revolution will eliminate the basis of the previous ambivalence. This expectation seems rather naive in the light of what we have already learned: that exactly this expectation has been the driving force behind all of the previously ambivalent progress. We must ask deeper questions about the reason for this ambivalence. What is actually the structure and reality of ambivalence?

But this very question exists in the shadow of ambivalence. It contains within it the critical assumption that the question itself is a withdrawal from the requirement for action. I do not deny this danger and do not attempt to defend my own weaknesses. I can only respond under the *recognized* shadow of ambivalence. A great part of all human activity, even action that is the direct result of the moralistic impulse, happens without an awareness of this ambivalence. That is as it should be. The impulse to paralyze through reflective hesitation is furthermore mostly motivated by self-ambivalence, namely, the expression of unadmitted cowardice. But whoever acts without knowledge of ambivalence will have to experience ambivalence, and a large part of human unhappiness exists because most have not learned to look for the causes of ambivalence within themselves. Rather, they project the basis of their own ambivalence onto others. Consequently, someone else is always responsible for my failure. A morally solid character is what we term a person who has learned to look for the basis of ambivalence within, and who has not lost the readiness to act but, rather, has clarified this readiness.

The issue in these reflections is not immediate political action but a theory based on practice. Now, a theory that has not taken into consideration the consciousness of ambivalence seems to me positively dangerous and barbaric. It gives to people who believe in it a justification, even the apparent obligation, to repress ideologically the ambivalence in themselves and in their followers. Therefore, it is necessary to demand that a political theory explain its position on ambivalence.

One can easily recognize that in all of the above-mentioned examples of ambivalence, there is the commandment, in any case also violated, to "Love your neighbor as yourself." In technological planning, the victims of weapons and pollution are not viewed as fellow humans, not as "neighbors," but rather as a part of the functional relationship. In all of these political examples, there is a rule that privileges come with obligations, a rule that, in the more egalitarian political philosophies, is connected to the denial that its adherents ever act from egoistic furtherance of their own privileges. While under the pressure of this very natural egoism, the theory itself imperceptibly becomes a lie. The lie, though, is perhaps at the very core of ambivalence. The lie is admittedly difficult to eliminate, and the obligation to love the neighbor now stands in the shadow of ambivalence. Is this not a weak obligation, a meaningless appeal in the face of the power of the objective structures? Does not this obligation become merely the pious talk of those who cannot and do not want change?

The political theory must, nevertheless, ask, "What is the basis of the harshness of these structures?" This is the reason for the anthropological and philosophical turn of these reflections. Or to phrase it more loosely, one can look for reasons in three areas, nature, society, and oneself.

Whoever looks for reasons in *nature* sees the origins of egoism, anxiety, and aggression in the conditions of life of our animal ancestors. They belong to our instinctual inheritance. A social system that forces us to repress them, even to deny them, forces us to lie, with the resulting ambivalence.

Whoever looks for reasons in *society* can come to the conclusion that humankind had the capacity to sublimate its instinctual fragments through custom and insight and create culture. One can see the reason why the perpetuation of egoism, anxiety, and aggression, instead of their decrease through sublimation and civilization, is the result of a false social system. Because of this, humankind, instead of finding in itself what it really is, becomes alienated. This alienation is the reason for the ambivalence, and its denial belongs to the lies that cause the ambivalence.

Whoever looks for reasons in *oneself* does not need to lie about what has been said about society but will ask why a false social system has been erected and maintained. It is easy to see that it is preserved exactly by egoism, anxiety, and aggression. This point of view has three aspects. One can return to nature as the origin. That means finding the real reasons for social misery in unchangeable human nature. This, though, is a retreat to a position that was already dealt with in this analysis. One can stay in society and see the self-stabilization of the system through egoism, anxiety, and aggression as an error that can be corrected, and which need not reappear, by destroying the existing social order. This optimism is, at least until now, unjustifiable through history, yet it cannot be refuted as a future possibility. I would like to believe that this expectation will be fulfilled in the distant future. But it is completely naive, as long as it does not see the play of the mechanism with which the ego, above all in the so-called unconscious, creates and preserves ambivalences. Psychoanalysis says that if I have achieved the opposite of what I thought I wanted, something in me must have wanted this result; it is not false to say that I myself actually wanted this opposite, and healing results when I can recognize that the unconscious desire was the real desire. The ambivalence of the ego has certainly been morally recognized for a long time under the title of evil. It is not adequate to observe the social causes of this mechanism, no matter how important and necessary this step may be. The real issue is the fact that the ego contains within it the possibility of different ways of reacting.

Everything said here is, in substance, not a new discovery of this century. In the most ancient thinking, that of religion, above all the advanced religions, this has always been a theme. In order to simplify, let us remain within our own, the Judeo-Christian, tradition. Our natural instincts, the misuse of power and social injustice, and the evil within are the classical themes of religious ethics. In the concept of God is found the answer to the question and the power of healing. God is, at the same time, three things: the creator of nature, including mine, the lawgiver of society, and the partner of the ego in prayer, repentance, forbearance, and love. Therefore, the command to love your neighbor is the second part of the command to love God with all your heart and to love your neighbor as yourself. As one says in the language of religion, "Only through God can I love my neighbor."

Certainly religion, too, stands in the shadow of ambivalence, and it is just this that drives it forward in the movement of its inner history. Certainly it is nonsense to declare, as did certain extremes of the Enlightenment, that the entire teaching of religion was the result of a priest caste trying to maintain its domination. One cannot build a permanent system of domination on fictions. Religion expresses much more an immediate, repeatable, and, because of that, enduring human experience. It is not false, but it is itself ambivalent. Only a great truth can be used to stabilize a great falsehood. In the Bible the struggle for religious truth stands in the bright light of history from the prophet Amos to the crucifixion of Christ, and the history of the Christian church is a continuation of this struggle.

Along with this never-ending moral struggle continues the progress of profane knowledge in the course of history. Nature, society, and the ego are for the lively Greek thought already self-evident themes, and they are just as much for the steadily increasing strength of the isolated rationality of the modern era. Modern times have incorporated (secularized) the ancient themes of religion and thus realized, in a certain sense for the first time, their concerns; one can understand the themes of freedom, equality, and solidarity accordingly. But this realization causes, at the same time, a splintering of religion. The unity of nature, society, and the ego becomes, with the abstraction of the modern concept of God, just a figure of speech, and finally an unbelievable dream of the past.

The fragmentation of truth that occurs here and that results accordingly in an increase in ambivalence should not come as a surprise to us. In our previous reflections on the origin of ambivalence, we had to keep jumping back and forth between nature, society, and the ego. Now we have recognized knowledge in the form of science. We have, to a certain extent, a coherent science of nature (physics, biology, medicine), a rather incoherent science of society (with a deep factual gap between history and social science), and a highly controversial concept of the ego (all the schools of psychology and the fleeting morality of the individual). If the relationship between these areas is important in order to understand the role every one of them plays in our lives, then it is obvious that we do not understand the role of any of them in our present condition.

This situation is also not new. For example, in ancient Greece during the period of the Sophists, the progress of questioning and thinking caused a similar fragmentation of viewpoints. Then, just as now, the intellectual progressives knew that a return to the outdated naive unity of the previous religous consciousness was not possible. The answer was a heroic undertaking of philosophy, thus, the attempt to formulate a unity on the level of the new enlightenment and to establish this inquiry through an expressed body of thought.

This attempt was historically successful. The thoughts of the Greek philosophers served not only the late antiquity but above all the entire Christian epoch in order to have at least a minimal conceptual basis of the unity of reality. In opposition to the new fragmentation of the truth through science and the Enlightenment, the German philosophical tradition from Kant to Hegel was the last great revival of philosophical thought in its unifying function. If the past still has anything at all to say to us, then we find ourselves in a conversation with the previously formulated questions of this philosophy.

Accordingly, the themes of parts II, III, and IV of this book are devoted to biological anthropology, philosophical tradition, and the reality of religion. We can attempt our task of seeking the basis of ambivalence only in these subsequent parts. The body of knowledge about evolution offers us an apparent aid to orientation. We want first to take a quick look at this so that we can use it in all further reflections. It can best be designated through the pairing of opposites I have chosen as the title for Part I: plateaus and crises.

D. Plateaus and Crises

Evolution does not usually proceed linearly but rather in a succession of extended periods of stability, then with short, sometimes catastrophic, crises. This phenomenon is well known in biological evolution. It does not appear to be just related to the specific mechanism of organic evolution, but appears to be a much more general phenomenon. The phases of personality development described by Erik Erikson[2] and the phases of scientific development described by Th. S. Kuhn[3] are well-known examples. But even in inorganic nature, such as the development of stars, there are similar processes. At this point we should concern ourselves with two questions: Can the universality of the phenomenon of plateaus and crises be understood? And does an understanding of the phenomenon of plateaus and crises contain within it an understanding of the universality of the ambivalence of progress?

As to the first, one does not need to look for specific models for a phenomenon of high universality. The plateaus and crises are apparently a universal characteristic in the behavior of somewhat complex systems that change themselves with time. Let us take a simple example such as river flow and use it as a model. The cross section of the riverbed in rocky ground will be sometimes wide and sometimes narrow. Thus, if the river flows uniformly, if, therefore, through every cross section at all times the same amount of water flows, the water must flow through the narrow cross sections more rapidly and through the wide cross sections more slowly. Interior irregularities of the flow, such as eddies, definitely accentuate this phenomenon. In the quiet, stable eddies of the slow-moving rivers where the water along the banks often flows upstream, any objects being carried along can remain caught for hours, days, even weeks before the eddy vanishes.

The river is just a visible example. One can say abstractly that already in the one-dimensional flow a slow speed means slow progress. Where an object stops for a long time, one can frequently describe it with statistical means. This is a most primitive preliminary form of Darwin's principle of selection. In recent decades, the theory of multidimensional movement (where the dimensions of selected variable conditions can be described more than just spatially) has been thoroughly studied. If the movement is understood through a nonlinear differential equation (and that is generally the case), then it passes through the "space" of the possible states of "singular surfaces," at which the state cannot arrive (similar to the outer limit of the eddy in which the floating object swims). Between them comes the space of the "basin." The object must normally remain in the basin in which it is. The transfer out of the basin into another is only possible in exceptional circumstances or "catastrophes."

René Thom[4] has developed a mathematical theory of the catastrophes in order to describe these relationships. What in this book is called "plateau" or "level" is described in the mathematical model as "basin"; the comparison expresses the self-stabilization with the image of the raised borders of accessible space.

A nonlinear differential equation is already a valid model with a very high universality. The biology of evolution teaches us, in relation to that, a specialized model of the creation of self-stabilizing forms, the species and the individual. This procedure is more precisely explained in the first part of the essay on death, below. It is no accident that its depiction comes in the section about death. It explains at the same time how death is the work of evolution. Just as the individual is the most meaningful manifestation of the phenomenon of the plateau, so is the death of the individual the most meaningful manifestation of the phenomenon of the crisis without which plateaus would merely be the blind alleys of history.

The planned expiration of the plateaus and crises of organic life, including that of the individual, has tempted observers of the political and cultural antecedents in human history to describe this history in terms of biological comparison. One speaks about the birth, growth, and death of a culture, of a nation, of a movement. Names like Spengler and Toynbee come to mind here. It is obvious that the comparison of social development with that of the life of an individual is, for biological reasons, one of the worst methods of comparison one could choose. Individuals are biologically programed to be born, to grow, and to die so that the species remains constant, and can even develop further. Such programing does not exist for social processes. On the other hand, human history shows again and again a phenomenon that has been described through the concept of plateaus and crises, namely, that of the decline of a dominant and stable civilization. Accordingly, we should mention again that this phenomenon is the result of very general preconditions that are quite different from those to which the individual owes his or her existence. In the present social sciences, one likes to articulate this phenomenon with the concept of systems theory. By doing so, an abstract level is reached that approximately corresponds to the universality of the phenomenon. I must refrain in this book from also having an argument with the systems theory in the form presented by Luhmann. It is not difficult, though, to describe the phenomenon of plateaus and crises in that language.

Now to the second question—does an understanding of the phenomenon of plateaus and crises contain within it an understanding of the universality of the ambivalence of progress? The answer should be an ambivalent yes. Anyone who has learned to think in universal concepts cannot perceive anything other than the anticipated crises in every plateau. In periods of deep crises, one can even describe this reflection as courage, serving as invigorating consolation. The perception of crises is not simply the perception of the threatened decline. The negative, too, is ambivalent. In its perception we do not just perceive the currently finite plateau but also the future plateau with new possibilities. The perception of the negative is made much clearer through the tentative perception that the future waits beyond this negation. The danger is manifest, but there are also paths through this danger. Therefore, ambivalence belongs with progress, in-so-far as progress evolves through plateaus and crises.

But the explanatory value of these thoughts remains limited because they are quite general; thus the ambivalence of the previously expressed yes. We have no accomplishments for our real problems if we do not examine specifically the contents of the actual contemporary ambivalence.

A concrete manifestation of the fundamentally overwhelming ambivalence of progress can be discerned. We do not just live as the simple, passive victims of our own history; we accept the responsibility for our destiny, and we judge according to what should be in our moralistic thought. The fundamental ambivalence is consequently the *ambivalence of morality*.

4. The Scientist, Mediator between Civilization and Nature

A. The Cultural Role of Science

Nature is older than humankind. Humankind is older than science. In the world that existed before and which later was named nature, humankind created an artificial environment that we call civilization. The practical reflections about nature belong to the survival conditions of civilization. A definite method of the reflections that developed late in the history of civilization is what we call the scientific investigation of nature, natural science. Natural science is a cultural method of approaching a subject; the subject is nature.

The reality we know, the natural as well as the cultural, is historical. It has many forms. It changes and it evolves. It stabilizes itself in special plateaus of relationships, and goes through crises from plateau to plateau. The tempo of historical change is uneven. Civilization changes faster than nature. Individuals go through their short lives faster than their cultural background changes. The relative stability of the cultural background is necessary for life. Without it, there could be no precise forms of cultural life, and human individuality could not develop. There must be periods of stability. Otherwise life consumes itself in a state of permanent crisis, because crisis, even if it is a necessary step in moving from one plateau to the next, always means new dangers that threaten life itself. Therefore reflection seeks to find ever new forms of stability. Fixed concepts are the plateaus of reflection. The discovery of the historicity of reality is then itself first a production of the history of culture, of the progressive critique of its own concepts through scientific thought.

Certainly the great myths of the creation of the world and of human culture already express an awareness of this historical authenticity. But here one thinks mostly within the framework of heaven and earth and the institutions of civilization as having been created once and as now unchangeable. The conceptual thought of early philosophy and science only confirmed the unchangeableness of this framework. Now the recognition of historical change slowly succeeds because of the discovery that the apparently unchangeable structures were only the framework of a specific historical plateau.

A period of Western science saw civilization as historical but nature as essentially nonhistorical. In the nineteenth century, it is true, there already was the discovery of the history of nature through the evolution of organic life and through speculations about the evolution of the stars. But the idea of nonhistorical nature was preserved through the unshakable concept of mathematical laws of nature. The laws themselves do not change; occurrences change in accordance with the laws. The phrase "the geodetic surveyor as mediator between humankind and space" expresses precisely this manner of thinking. Historical humans live in nonhistorical space. Exactly because of this they need a mediator. It is a historical accomplishment to recognize mathematically the timeless structure of space, and it is a historically central accomplishment to divide the available space on earth through the application of the recognized laws for human existence: the apportionment of the earth, geodesy.

This image of the world of classical science itself had a cultural role that must be designated as a plateau of cultural history.

We have to make clear that mathematical science is not an essential part of a high civilization. The classical civilizations of the Middle East, India, and East Asia are older than the civilizations of the West and were equal, if not superior, to Western civilizations in political, economical, technical, artistic, ethical, and metaphysical development until just recently in the modern era. And these civilizations did not have mathematical science as a major body of thought, but only as a tool of wisdom or as a reflection of metaphysics or, to express it with a metaphor, as one of the many flowers blossoming in the garden of civilization. One can build the Chinese wall, the temples of India, and the bazaar of Baghdad, one can engage in world trade through caravan routes and sailboats, and one can determine the length of the year by observing the constellations without developing a mathematical image of the world. The mathematician, whatever his dream might be, remains just one of many contributing artists, and not one of the highest order.

In contrast, mathematical science has proven itself from century to century ever more to be the hard core of modern European civilization. When saying hard core, I do not mean that it was also the highest conscious and cared-for ideal. Europe has actively practiced its belief in reason at least in the sphere of politics and society. But for the dominant individualistic fulfillment of its work such as by the blind dynamic of its civilized progress, other forces have played a much more important role than reason. Hard core means here the product of this culture that is most capable of resistance, its steadily strengthening framework. The resistance against their own culture that has been carried on by believers, artists, conservatives, and most recently the ethically motivated radicals, has proven itself to be powerless against this skeleton of steel. Non-Western civilizations have been inferior to our own civilization with its technical strike force in the period of colonialism, and they are now preparing the unavoidable countermovement as they take over our own technological means. In the process it will be proven, where it still might seem unclear, that one cannot take over technology without taking over the method of thinking whose truth has made technology possible in the first place.

The ambivalence of progress certainly is at work. Is the scientist really the mediator between civilization and nature? Is he not rather the heir and executor of their ancient animosity? The glorification of the natural is a late cultural product with a historically relevant history. The primitive lives in the midst of the all-powerful nature in which there are good and evil forces resulting in an existence full of justifiable anxieties. Civilization meant first of all agriculture. The neolithic revolution changes the forest and steppe into farmland, therefore it tears away the earth from the powers to whom it previously belonged; the peasant has other gods than the hunter. The city creates new cultural boundaries with nature. The great kingdoms teach humankind to change a geographical area into a cultural area. Material techniques are developed along with social techniques. Civilization grows in the social form of domination. The enemies we fear the most are now not the forces of nature but other people. The instrument of unlimited accumulation of power is developed against others. If one cultural plateau must be succeeded by a new one, then during the catastrophe of the transitional crisis the now tamed nature is seen as the realm of eternal order on which falls the yearning glance of those who are trapped in the tragedy of their own history. Researchers of nature have always seen nature accordingly. Kepler who found himself involved in the absurdity of the dispute about the nature of the Eucharist calls out, "If only I could see God's work in humanity as clearly as I can recognize it in nature!" But the recognition of natural laws gives power over nature. Yes, they have in our sciences the very logical form of power, "Create this condition at the beginning, and this result will follow." Unlike humans, the impersonal nature cannot defend itself against exploitation. It reacts once in a while with the collapse of its structure. Since the beginning of agriculture, and culminating in our technical civilization, it seems that humankind has discovered too late how its quiet animosity towards nature has underminded the very foundations of civilization.

This process is not unusual. It has had many antecedents in organic evolution; every successful species that has increased too rapidly has created its environmental problems. But now the dimension is much greater. And the key figure within civilization is the scientist. Destruction of the environment, catastrophic famines, loss of freedom, war with suicidal weapons—is *science* guilty, without which these forms of disaster, these threats to life would not have come about?

Has science understood nature too well or not well enough? Is the scientist the mediator of nature or the enemy of nature? And who recognizes most correctly and sees the sharpest: the mediator or the enemy?

B. The Truth of Science

In answer to the question as to reasons for the historical success of science, I know no other answer except its truth. It owes its power to knowledge. Whoever has done scientific research cannot really explain to someone who has not how uncompromisingly this research for scientific truth is pursued. The scientist always is aware of how knowledge or lack of knowledge determines how successful research is. I only wish that social scientists had some idea of the depth of the gulf between knowledge and lack of knowledge. Or, expressed *ad hominem*, if one can manipulate an instrument on the surface of Mars about 250 million miles away, can this be explained in any other way than through knowledge of the laws of motion and of wave theory?

The basic discipline of contemporary physics, the theory of quantum mechanics, can be mathematically expressed on one piece of paper, at least in its fundamental principles. There have been today a billion isolated experiences that obey this principle. Not one of them has been proven to contradict it!

The power of science is based on its truth. But what is truth? Truth is a much debated philosophical concept. I will not attempt to answer the question of truth in science with a direct application of philosophical concepts; I will remain in the cultural and historical context. But I will allow myself at least an allusion to the philosophical justification of this process. A classical definition of the truth states, *Veritas est adaequatio intellectus et rei.* Truth is balance between mind and object. Stated another way, the scientist is the mediator between civilization and nature. Here nature means reality, the object. Mind is the culturally defined self-interpretation of humankind. Balance and mediator are two vague expressions with which the problem of the relationship between humankind and reality is more concealed than revealed.

Where is the origin of the world-transforming, unique role of the modern technological civilization? I said its hard core is science. And it comes from the Greeks. The decisive intellectual contribution of the Greeks was the creation of deductive mathematics. With this statement I am contradicting a thesis that has gained wide acceptance, namely, that the Greeks' enchantment with deductive science was an obstacle in the path of empirical research. But this thesis is based on a half-truth. The decisive Greek discovery was that general intellectual theories were possible. I have never perceived in any of the non-European cultures before this century—with the exception of the Arabic philosophers of the Middle Ages who were, however, working within this Greek tradition—another example of the transforming effect of this discovery. Whoever, though, has understood this discovery can now examine all experiences and all speculations with the tool of verifiability.

Apparently science began in the ancient civilizations of the Orient as practical geodesy, in the context of astrologically useful astronomy. But even in the advanced mathematical texts of the Babylonians one does not find any explicit reflection on the difference between empirical rule and necessary truth. With the Greeks the theory itself becomes a subject of reflection. And with this begins the distinction between mathematics and science. Mathematical truths are necessary. Whatever the philosophical meanings of these necessities, we submit to them. With that, though, the possibility of science becomes a problem. How can there be theories of mathematical science such as those of the movements of the planets? Do they necessarily represent truth? If they are not necessary, why are they considered valid? But if they are necessary, then their necessity must be proven by the evidence.

Questions concerning the philosophy of science are so difficult to answer that after a few centuries of ancient Greek and a few centuries of modern science, there is again a certain philosophical resignation when attempting to answer them. An always informative method of dealing with contemporary resignation in the face of systematic questions is to convert them into historical questions.

Kuhn has a historically based way of describing the progress made by science as the result of plateaus and crises. I am grateful to him for the contribution of his well-known method of historical analysis. He writes about the normal science that operates in a fixed successful paradigm for the resolution of separate problems as opposed to scientific revolutions that lead from one paradigm to a new one. The evolution of science follows structural laws similar to those of the evolution of culture as well as the evolution of natural life. One could say that the truth of the paradigm, meaning its structure of reality, is its ecological niche that makes its success possible for a certain period of time. Structures of reality become visible to us insofar as they allow us to act successfully. The concepts we use to describe them are at the same time the commands to use them successfully. Concepts are rules of conduct; they are functions, as Kant said.

The real problem of how successful science is possible at all is not solved by listing a historical record of its success. On the contrary, the issue would not even be raised. Kuhn is aware of this and mentions it on the last page of his book. Cabbage plants have an ecological niche, rabbits have another ecological niche, and foxes a third. All three are but parts of a comprehensive evolutionary plateau that we call organic life within which the ecological niches for species exist. Scientific paradigms have their niches in the great evolutionary plateaus that we call knowledge. Science has not only been successful but can also give an accounting of the reasons for its success. Its realization justifies its claims. Its supporting framework is the major theory, and this framework is knowledge itself. Heisenberg described before Kuhn the development of the physical fundamental theory as a result of the so-called closed theory. A closed theory is not a final theory. Heisenberg doubted that the final theories even existed. A closed theory is closed to further changes and could not be improved by any changes. Accordingly, the step to the next theory can by necessity only be a giant step, only a crisis, a revolution. Only the succeeding theory can give an accounting for the reasons of the successes of its predecessor. It contains or implies the previous theory as a borderline case that is valid in its immediate proximity. More magnanimous than most political revolutionaries, victorious scientific revolutionaries admit why and to what extent the previous system was valid. One can explain the basis of a truth only after one has also learned the extent of its falsity.

But how can a theory be established that cannot be improved by any further changes? This is possible if its basic postulates are very simple. Are these simple axioms, such as those of physical geometry, of classical mechanics, of the relativity theory, of the quantum theory, merely truth by chance? Can other axioms that contradict them be truth instead? This is something one cannot seriously imagine. But if these are examples of necessary truths, we would still like to understand why they are necessary. And with that, after centuries of experience, we must again return to the initial question of the Greeks. The fundamental questions are usually asked either at the beginning or at the end of a historical epoch. What, then, is the basis for the truth of science?

I will now depart from the security of the consensus of contemporary scientists when I speculate as to the answer to this question. An absolute necessity for the basic laws of physics cannot be shown, except for a perhaps relative necessity. Our science is empirical. Only insofar as experience is possible is science possible. Experience means that one can learn from the past for the future, from the actual for the possible. This can only happen if the law joins the possible together with the actual. I follow Kant with the speculation that the necessary laws of science are those that formulate the conditions of the possibility of experience.

It first of all concerns an axiom of the contemporary fundamental theory, namely, of the quantum theory. This is the most general theory of the law of probability for the prognosis of definitive alternatives. The mathematical structure of the space-time continuum, accordingly that of physical geometry as applied in geodesy, should be founded on the fundamental symmetrical group of the quantum theory of binary alternatives.

For the purposes of this essay, I do not need belief in the correctness of my special physical hypothesis. Apparently, science has already obtained a unity through all the diverse applications of its fundamental theories. Is the scientist who follows these theories then the mediator between civilization and nature, or is he the enemy of nature? Or am I asking the wrong questions?

I said one can recognize the extent of a truth after one has learned to see through the extent of its falsity. I have questioned the basis of the truth of science and therefore implicitly the extent of its falsity. What would be the case if the basis of its truth were that its axioms formulate the conditions of the possibility of experience? What is called experience in science is power-forming experience. It is the prognosis, based upon isolated facts, of the probability of the failure of other isolated alternative possibilities to take place. Our scientific judgment form is power-forming. It can think that there are possibilities in conditions other than they actually are, and it asks, "What would then happen?" The realism of this thought is that one can will things into another preconceived condition. Abstract understanding is in conformity with selection through the will.

Our scientific-technological civilization is a product of the fraternal co-operation of mind and will. The scientist mediates between the civilization of mind and will, and nature. Science teaches us how to behave in nature; it sees nature as it must be seen by a civilization based upon the mind and will. This is not an illusion, but neither is it the complete truth. The complete truth has not been discovered by any culture known to us. Every culture has its immanent perceptual conditions. If we can think beyond the boundaries of our own culture, it is only because this culture transcends its own designated preconditions by the very process of describing them.

The spontaneity of the fraternal forces of mind and will create a capacity that I would like to call perception. We children of nature cannot want, act, and think without a perception of our condition, our own and that of the world, even though perception may become conscious of itself only in the process of acting. I would like to call reason the fully articulated perception of the whole that itself serves the mind. The productive mental accomplishment of science would not be possible without a guiding reason. The whole that this reason perceives is certainly not made explicit in the statements of science. It can be perceived only implicitly. Normal science in the sense of Kuhn, science that works with established paradigms, does not need the expressiveness of guiding reason. Heidegger says about this science, justified in his choice of words, that "Science does not think." It is the mediator between civilization and nature in a closed and finite field. Outside this field it is blind. In crises, though, science becomes self-criticism, and thus thinks beyond itself.

How theoretical truth might appear *beyond* the paradigms of our contemporary science is a question I will not speculate about in this chapter. But we will still take a look at the practical role of science in the present and future world.

C. The Political Role of Science

Politics is an aspect of the self-formation of civilization. It is the permanent struggle about power and the reason of power. It is the permanent necessary struggle about the organizational framework of society, about necessary stability and necessary change, about the form of the plateaus, and about risks and survival of crises. Science is now a source of economic and military power, and thus of political power. Therefore, I will concentrate on the practical role it should play in our society and on its political role. Accordingly, I will not lose sight of the mediator relationship to nature because the economic and military conflicts within the civilization are linked to its natural existence. Politics is our future and, whether it knows it or not, is always, at the same time, environmentally, concerned.

Here I would like to add a personal recollection. Around 1932, I was a student of physics who had just advanced enough to be able to elect a special branch. Around that time, the theory of the atomic nucleus became possible, primarily due to the discovery of neutrons. So I chose nuclear physics as my specialty, meaning at the time basic research that was purely theoretical. I said to myself, "If society is seriously prepared to pay me for the rest of my life so that I can ride my own useless hobby-horse, then I certainly want to make the most of its generosity." Six years later, shortly before 1939, Hahn discovered, in what was similarly pure research, how to split the uranium atom. It is interesting to recall how his institute, the Kaiser-Wilhelm-Institut for Chemistry in Berlin-Dahlem, was financed at the time. Ninety percent of its budget came from I. G. Farben, the former German chemical trust, which expected no direct benefit from Hahns work, which was the chemistry of radioactive matter. It exercised no influence on work of the institute either. This money, though, was not paid as a cultural contribution but as an investment in the general scientific and technological competitiveness of Germany, which included its chemical industry.

The political effects of the discovery of the fission of the uranium atom were two-fold: the military use of the atom bomb only six years later, and long-term economical effects through the development of nuclear power plants. Both of these developments resulted in the necessary incorporation of the new power source into the existing power struggles. Of course, the individuals, the physicists and technicians, wanted a choice in working on either the atomic bomb or nuclear-reactor projects. But at the same time they found themselves working under the auspices of the existing political and economic powers. For anyone who is aware of the role of power in all previous civilizations and of its role in our own, this was self-evident. The scientists who had grown up in the spirit of bourgeois individualism had to realize this truth for the first time. And many of them understood almost immediately, as citizens of the state, that they had to share the responsibility for their work. In effect, the increase in power that resulted from science has lead humankind into one of its deepest crises, a crisis that must be understood as the unavoidable transition from one stable plateau of our civilization to a new one.

The atom bomb is the symbol of the foreign-policy and military aspects of this crisis. Without giving my reasons as to why I believe it, let me say that our worldwide political crisis, resulting from the discoveries of modern weapon technology, will not end before the system that has existed for almost 6,000 years—a civilization of sovereign and stable powers that were capable of fighting war and of justifying their power—has been replaced by a new form of political organization of humankind. The present phase of peaceful coexistence is not a solution but merely a pause while we catch our breath and contemplate with horror that both superpowers now can continue their conflict for world power and world hegemony with nuclear weapons. A solution is only possible with a radical change of the international political structure, which throughout history has always resorted to war to resolve its conflicts.

The concern about nuclear weapons is more susceptible now to the psychological repressive mechanism than it was three decades ago. One hopes, irrationally, that the stability of the existing international political division can be maintained. The present concern about nuclear power plants is perhaps the only anxiety that most people allow themselves to have when confronted with the unthinkable. This fear results from a repression of confrontation. I have conducted, in the last decade, a study about the dangers of technical failure in the peaceful use of nuclear energy and have come to the conclusion that remedies are technically possible, economically feasible, and, let's hope, politically realizable.

But dangers from human volition would still exist. They are terrorism, proliferation of nuclear weapons through worldwide technology of nuclear reactors, and destruction of reactors in a conventionally fought war. If this analysis should prove to be correct, then the solution to the possible dangers related to nuclear reactors would lie in the political field, most certainly internationally. We will not be able to survive the power tools of modern technology without the creation of a political structure that can control them. Today this structure does not exist.

What, then, should be the role of the scientist?

Technology: The twenty years following 1945 were perhaps the high point of the belief that material need could be eliminated through technological progress. To counter this simplistic belief in technology, various opposition groups formed more than a decade ago, even including technocracy itself in the prognoses of the Club of Rome, and, on the other extreme, the new left with its romantic fundamental critical opposition to technology. All of these protest movements express a still vague perception of the approaching crisis that cannot be avoided by returning to the cultural forms of the past, but can only be resolved through the conscious construction of a new cultural form.

Technology is a means to an end. In its period of unlimited growth, technology was fueling itself or it was the means of realizing particular goals of economic and military power. A culture cannot be stable if the technological means of achieving an end are stronger than any consciousness of what the end should be. It is necessary, but not adequate by itself, to base this goal consciousness on individual ethics. It is necessary to create political institutions as a forum for free discussion and for education toward responsible applications of technological means. This, of course, remains impossible without crisis, and it will only happen, if it happens at all, under the shock of continuing crises.

Applied research: The roots of technology in handicrafts, trade, and the organization of large political territories are older than science. The modern progress of technology has been based, to an ever-increasing degree, upon scientific research. Whoever wants technical prosperity must want practical research. Whoever sees the necessity of resolving crises caused by technology not through the renunciation of technology but through the reasonable application of technology, is dependent upon new research that is not just oriented toward practical application but has a specific socially conscious use. It would be self-deceiving to believe that applied research should provide the economic and political managers only with neutral applications. This ideology only serves for a lulling of the self-cricitism that is indispensible for the survival of technological civilization.

Basic research: The origins of basic research are older than those of applied research. It does not matter if one calls this the pursuit of truth or eternal, childlike curiosity, it is just part of human nature. Whoever wants applied research must also want basic research, otherwise, after a while, applied research does not know the difference between research and systematic operations. Basic research is, precisely, the origin of so many unforeseen applications because its goal was not originally application.

Applied research is similar to a pumping operation that comes to an end when the demand for what was pumped out no longer exists. Basic research is like a deep spring that continues to prove itself a source on its own and not in response to external pressure. This basic reality has been obscured and made more ideological because of the constantly growing cultural role of science and the accompanying increase in the number of scientists. Earlier, we scientists were something like a clever, arrogant family. Now we have become a significant section of society, almost a class by ourselves. In the pecking order of scientists, the basic researcher stands relatively high. Accordingly, much is claimed to be basic research that actually is not. Here we encounter not only the sociological problem of who it is that represents the interests of society in this now indispensible condition, but also the philosophically more profound problem of how far science can be carried in its basic research and how unlimited the apparently limitless progress actually is. This is a question of pure, basic research, a question of truth. The vitality of science, even in its self-criticism, lies in its spontaneous and unparalyzed quest for the truth. If we want our civilization to survive, then we must also want the truth.

5. The Moral Problem of the Left and the Moral Problem of Morality

A. The Moralization of Politics

We are witnessing a politicization of humankind. Never before has such a large percentage of people been concerned with politics. This is an aspect of the democratization of politics.

This process has also led directly to a moralization of politics. Politics is less the game of the powerful, is less the business of professionals, and is less perceived as fate. On the contrary, it is the theme of morally judged decisions in which everyone is required to participate. Whether politics has actually become more moral is certainly doubtful. However, it has become a moralizer. The appeal to moral values has become one of the most effective means of politics. The ancient tactic of lying to achieve one's ends and the process of self-serving justifications that were always an aspect of politics have taken on more and more the form of ideology. That means justification through reliance on a general, universally valid, moral principle. The moralization of politics is another example of the ambivalence of progress.

It was a concrete occurrence that aroused such strong emotions in me that I had to write the comment below. The writing resulted from the attempt to objectify these emotions by analyzing their origins in order to master them. This comment because of its emotionally motivated origins mirrors in a much franker way my true feelings about the phenomenon of "the Left," much more than my other, more controlled writings. This comment, though, at the same time touches on problems that appear to have a much greater significance than remarks that merely concern the history of the leftist movement in recent years. I wanted to give this comment to certain friends who, in their emotional makeup, are much more sympathetic to the Left than I am. But this comment is not just concerned with those emotions, it is more concerned with the question of how to overcome them in an attempt to clarify the ambivalence of progress.

B. Comment

The word "Left" or "leftists" is first of all used to designate those political tendencies that were dominant in the student movement in the nineteen-sixties and early nineteen-seventies in countries like our own. Liberal professors (similar to other liberals) have often had the following experience with these leftists: The professor concerned was a critic of many of the structures of the society in which he lived. He had greeted the beginnings of the student movement with sympathy and with great willingness to learn. He saw the intellectual force of a mostly Marxist-inspired global interpretation of society and its importance as a political-economic perspective. He was fascinated by the fixed positions, not without self-criticism, that he attributed to his own practical, bourgeois conformity. Most of all, his sympathy with the Left did not rest on theoretical agreement, because he found the leftist theories still too confused, but on the deep impression that the young people made upon him with their *moral* motivation. He easily overcame his first bourgeois shock caused by the loose manners, the sexual freedom, and similar breaks with moral traditional, even if he could not personally participate. He was aware of the morally motivated protest against the moral hypocrisy of the prevalent external forms. He offered the Left access to open conversation, free cooperation, and protection against repression by the dominant system. Not in every case, but in a significant number of cases, he experienced sooner or later that his trust was crudely and irreparably misused and abused. He came to see himself the victim of a conscious plot to seize power and realized that he had only been of interest to the leftists as long as they could use him.

He understood that he had been a "useful idiot." This is the currently unhealable trauma with which many liberals suffer in relation to the Left. It causes the previously progressive injured party to assume a reactionary stance that he himself would have sharply criticized a decade earlier. I assume, too, that this is the deepest reason, at least for the time being, for the lamentable failure of the leftist movement in all highly industrialized representational democracies. As justified as the criticisms of the system of domination is, the Left still could not win the support of even those nonintellectuals and workers who are not easily deceived in their moral judgments and whom the left sought to win over. The Left was unable to win large support in its criticism of an obviously corrupt system because its own morality usually shocked, even though the core of its critique, no matter how clumsily expressed, was fully justified. Even the highly motivated Left thus failed with its systematic assault on the prevailing morality.

It is obvious that my analysis is highly controversial. I would be prepared to enter into a discussion as to its correctness and, to prove my point, would be prepared to show examples in support of my thesis regarding this and other societies. We come to the question of how something like this can be explained. The moral problem of the Left leads then to the question of the moral problem of morality.

It deals first of all with the relationship between morality and society. Morality here is meant as an abbreviation of the so far highest form of the moralistic principle, the universal ethic. It exists in the old formulation as the golden rule, "Do unto others as you would have them do unto you." Its most thorough philosophical reflection is in Kant's categorical imperative: "Let your behavior be guided by principles that you would want to be the guiding principles of all humankind." There has existed in human history, for thousands of years, the phenomenon of domination, a manifest inequality of socially guaranteed rights. Most of the religiously based traditional moralities have found compromises between the recognition of this reality and the universal ethic. To it belongs the ethic of the higher duties of the dominant class, an ethic whose meaning is disdained by the contemporary leftist critics to a quite unrealistic extent. Another way out is the individual renunciation of participation in the system of dominance, and renunciation of material wealth, by becoming hermits and mendicant friars. But in both the core of the ethic of dutiful rule, and obviously in the ethic of renunciation, is concealed the conviction that I must require more from myself than I can expect from others. This attitude has been possible through its religious core, which believes that not an individually accomplished self-justice but rather the mercy of God, which is present in all our acts, is the basis for moral behavior. This religious experience is just as real as the uncontradictable validity of the universal ethic.

The radical European Enlightenment, in which tradition the present Left exists, attacks the very reality of domination. Its tendency is the abolition of domination in all its forms. I will not comment on whether this will someday be possible in a radical sense. However, in accordance with my anthropological judgment, I hold this to be fundamentally possible, although realizable only in the very distant future. There are problems that arise if one hopes to realize this directly, with the first attempt. The Left hopes to accomplish it either in a revolutionary advance or in the still unbelievably short step of a final "long march through the institutions." It directly criticizes the institution of domination itself from the perspective of morality and calls this a demand for justice.

The Left now encounters the old moral problem of ends and means. It recognizes the social dependence and the concealed ("ideological") ends of moralistic judgments. It is convinced that a change of the society that would abolish domination as the actual precondition of the social lie would make possible a genuine universal social ethic. Its adherents, therefore, feel justified to use a different morality against the supporters of the existing system, therefore acting in such a way as they themselves would not like to be treated. They repress the truth they themselves want to establish by their very own actions, and its more aware members cannot fail to see the treason. So they create their own moralistic discredit and lose their moral justification. They then find themselves, if they are aware of this contradiction, in a desperate situation. They known that the dominant system cannot be overthrown with other means. If the means fail, the system cannot be overthrown in the foreseeable future.

I am not talking about what might happen to the system in the long term, but rather about the moral problem of the Left. It is the result of the moral problem of morality itself. Morality, to a certain extent, can be radical insofar as it renounces social security, as do the above-mentioned religious groups. It must, however, be a genuine duty of the politically responsible to assure the creation of those social conditions that permit ordinary people, people who are not radical nonconformists, to also act in accordance with the demands of morality. How is this realizable if the existing powers can only be fought by acting against these same moral principles?

I maintain that there are many practical solutions when individual situations are considered, but in regard to plain morality no one is in possession of a general solution. By the concept of plain morality I understand a morality that can be based upon the golden rule or the categorical imperative, but which may be deeply rooted in what I have called the religious experience. This is the experience of grace, of the redeeming power of love, and, certainly, of the love, honor, and fear of that deepest self that is called God in the religious tradition. Without this experience there is no communion between unrealizable rigor and lazy compromise. Both of these positions lead an intelligent and sensitive person to self-hate. The result is eventual hatred of others because of the psychological mechanism of projection. This hatred is the real basis for the moral failure of the Left. I believe that one can observe in this train of thought the "dialectic" of leftist morality. It is exactly *because* the Left is first of all morally motivated that it ends up committing deeper moral mistakes than its morally less active opponent. Accordingly, it is difficult for me to condemn these moralistic mistakes, which are basically a phenomenon of doubt. But this doubt contains suicidal consequences. Those who never have experienced these temptations have no reason for moral self-satisfaction. The real productive path does not end in these doubts, but begins when we have learned to confront them directly. One can reduce the moralistic problem of morality to a simple formula of which intellectuals would normally be ashamed, because of its simplicity: In the end the final basis of human social life is love and not morality. Morality is the next-to-the-final basis.

6. Anxiety

Do we really live in anxiety? The answer is "Yes," but is that not highly peculiar? Should we not be ashamed of our anxiety? Prosperity is greater now than ever before. What is now material "necessity" was certainly a luxury earlier. Life expectancy is longer than that of earlier generations. We have laws, we have free speech, we can travel without weapons, and we can cross most borders without a visa. There has been relative peace for forty years, and we plan as if peace will last forever. This is our material reality, and look at us. We live with anxiety.

Are these fears not an ingratitude toward those who have worked for what we enjoy, an ingratitude toward destiny? Should we not admonish each other to get rid of this unnecessary anxiety?

Yes, we should do that. That is the first partial answer.

But while we are admonishing, we must not repress the fact that at the same time billions share our world who do have cause for concrete fear. There is anxiety about possible war in the Middle East, and there is anxiety about hunger and the possibility of not surviving this or the next year, certainly throughout the Third World. There is anxiety about not belonging to the victorious party, as in Czechoslovakia since 1968, in Chile since 1973, in Vietnam and Cambodia since 1975. What emotions are awakened in us by the television images that show us scenes from these horrors? "Should one help there?" or even more: "What if that should happen to us?" In any case these images play on the screen of our conscious and unconscious anxieties.

But we ourselves, do we really live in anxiety? The second partial answer is, "Yes, more than we generally know." Whoever is aware of the anxiety in his own soul receives, occasionally perhaps, proof through dreams. I have, next to the other dreams that are deeply rooted in my unconscious, three characteristic dreams of anxiety that infrequently but obstinately return year after year to disturb the quiet hours of my early morning sleep: (1) Hitler is again in power, democratically elected, and has begun his war again, which he will lose again. (2) The Communist secret police send me to Siberia, and I will never come back. (3) On the bright horizon a tiny cloud appears, the first atomic mushroom of the beginning Third World War. These are typical traumas of my generation, and one cannot understand the politics of this generation if one does not know its fears. Actual anxieties can be recognized by all of us from political terms of abuse such as "Communist" or "radical." They remind us that our prosperity and our liberal constitution, which are at the same time class and property arrangements, are not self-evidently secure. Anxiety is expressed in the aggressiveness of political terms of abuse. Every television image of an unreally distant reality gives us the dull feeling that it may be our own situation that is unreal. Aggression makes this discomfort somewhat easier to deal with in that it attributes the threat to others, to the "guilty," rather than ourselves, and thus relieves our conscience. And then come confirmations by way of bombings and kidnappings by political and terrorist groups. And how greatly they effect us when they are happening near by!

Anxiety is greater perhaps in Germany than in other countries with a similar level of prosperity and a distorted relationship to it through our hidden present. If this is the case, perhaps it is caused by the knowledge that we are, after forty years, still repressing a feeling of guilt, and this repressed guilt causes anxiety and other related symptoms. Just as others have their problems, this problem is ours.

I will not dwell on a description of the anxiety of everyday life, of love, or of fear of the void and of meaninglessness. But these anxieties exist.

Are our anxieties justified? And if they are justified, why? What is the cause of this condition of anxiety? I attempt an answer: "Yes, they are justified." The cause that justifies our fears lies in the fact that we all act out of anxiety. Anxiety itself creates the conditions and the events about which we are justifiably anxious. The system of anxiety stabilizes itself.

Fear is the emotional response to a definite danger. Anxiety is a seemingly causeless general mood related to fear that one cannot adequately name by reference to concrete situations, one that does not disappear despite understanding and consolation.

The reason for fear should be first acknowledged. The system based on fear stabilizes itself. Every partner fears, with reason, the behavior of another who is also acting out of fear. It is certainly permissible, in the initial attempt, to develop a general theory, basing it on one's own experiences. I would like to elaborate on this theory with two examples with which I have been occupied professionally, and still am. The first example is the debate about nuclear power, and the second is the problem of the prevention of war.

In the debate about nuclear power, there exists an apparently great fear on the side of the environmentalists. It is fear about destruction of the environment and the possible extinction of some or all of the species, beginning with changes in the climatic effect caused by the use of large power plants and continuing with the possibility of radioactive pollution of air and water. Whoever has fear themselves can observe the motives of opponents only with distortion. It is important to recognize that among those who support nuclear power there is also deep fear, and that they are not motivated by the so easily denounced profit motive or by the fetish of economic growth for growth's sake. Their fear is that our economy will not be able to compete internationally in the future unless new sources of energy are made available to insure continued economic growth. The issue for those concerned with the economic future is also connected to the question of how hunger and poverty could possibly be eliminated in the world without continued economic growth.

An empirical study of this issue reached the conclusion that those who are prepared to risk conflict are, in general, those who have the least economic disadvantages to fear from the result. Those who support nuclear power will probably in the end be able to silence their opponents, without resorting to direct repression, arguing that the opponents' own jobs will be threatened unless new sources of energy are available. But also the pronuclear side sees the motives of its opponents with distortion. The technocrats refer to antinuclear motives as being "emotional." Of course, this deprecation of motives of the opponents to nuclear power has been made easier by the lack of special knowledge on their part, causing them to defend their deeply felt position by relying on unprovable lines of reasoning.

At first glance, the contemporary reality supports the fears of both sides. The structure of our economy is such that without continued economic growth that is dependent upon new sources of energy, there exists the possibility of deep economic crises. On the other hand, continued unlimited growth of energy consumption is climatically insupportable. Also, the issue of the security of the continued construction of nuclear power plants has not been adequately and factually discussed, given the politically dangerous times in which we live. But with a second look, meaning further intellectual pursuit of solutions, it might be that the objections of both sides could be very easily overcome. There is no metaphysical reason why a rational future economic use of energy should not be possible. There are technological solutions for most of the technologically caused problems.

I am concerned here with the human factor. In regard to the people-caused dangers there is, in the end, no technical solution, only a human one. Why has our economic-technical system developed so that it produces the double dangers of crises and destruction of the environment?

The basis for growth from the economic perspective, and also the dangers of continued growth, can be attributed to the system of competition that is called market economy by its supporters and capitalism by its critics. Also, the reference to technical progress as the motor of economic growth itself refers us back to the competitive system. The reason is that this system has been responsible for profitable technological growth and innovation, much more so than the inventiveness of private or individual researchers, or the earlier mercantilistic system, or the present socialist system with its centralized state planning. The competitive system demands continued growth because it is necessary for the survival of every participant to innovate and invest continually in new technology. In analyzing the psychology of the individual entrepreneur or manager, it is not adequate to attribute to this class the symptoms of the competitive system and the profit motive. A much deeper and much more rational motive for the successful manager is the palpable fear of losing out to competitors. The fear is rational for every single participant in the competition by knowing that those who are successful are so because they continually act out of the same concerns. In this sense, the system, from a psychological perspective, stabilizes itself through fear of the consequences of another's fear. From this comes systems growth and survival power because the rationally controlled application of this fear of another is a powerful motivator. From this thought come also dangers, because *who* represents the general public interest that is not represented by private interest, such as the protection of the environment?

The second example, that of the prevention of war, is one that I will merely mention. We recognize in it the same structure, only here the competition is not that of economic groups, but rather of sovereign states with their military potential. It is the classical rational foreign policy of every great power to want to be more powerful than the other great powers out of the same justified fear of the other that drives economic competitors. The result is periodic power testing of the other, and that means war. The deeply rooted anxiety about a Third World War is certainly well founded.

If, though, fear legitimizes fear, and if fear stabilizes a system through fear, is there an exit from this vicious circle? The answer lies in dealing with the theme of social structure. The opinion is widely held that a socialist change of the existing social systems would be able to eliminate the vicious circle of competitive interests and their rational survival fears. Is this hope justified? At least in the past, whenever revolutionary socialists have come to power, the result has been a secret police that personifies the anxiety of the leadership. The controversy as to whether or not this is a necessary and decisive attribute of revolutionary socialism refers us back to anthropological arguments, arguments about the nature of humans as social beings.

What does anxiety have to do with the human condition? I can again subdivide the response into the separate concepts of anxiety and fear. Fear is the emotional perception of a danger. Anxiety is the fear of our own incapacity for peace. I introduce here two new concepts that need further elaboration: perception and peace.

Any contemporary theory about humankind must know, as background information, about the evolution of organic life and about animal behavior. What form does the perception of a danger take? Every organic form is threatened. This is something different from the transitoriness of inorganic things. A stone lies for a thousand years in one spot and disintegrates; other stones take its place.

Organic life rests on a discovery of nature, the discovery of forms that show a relation between self-reproduction and self-preservation. Self-preservation can fail. Therefore every living being can be threatened. Self-preservation *must* fail, for evolution proceeds beyond all of its previously achieved phases. In organic life certain goods are always scarce. Successful evolution makes them scarce, and their scarcity pushes evolution along.

The perception of danger such as a human being is capable of is related to the capacity of imagination. One can perceive "something as something," danger as danger. One can even perceive danger when it is not present, and this is the basis for the capacity for human fear. Fear itself is not a rational act; it is emotional. But it is sensible. It has, if I may again use another figure of speech, the rationality of the irrational. The structure of the power system is connected with the limited rationality of fear. Imagination permits us to accumulate means for defense. This accumulation is reasonably limited against the dangers of nature. But my human competitor can accumulate as much power as I. This compels me to further accumulation. Such power is essentially tragic because the result is that every single step in rational increase increases the danger for everyone.

Fear and its corresponding power systems are, however, not the final word in community life. They are only a specific condition bound to the human rationale. I would like to discuss the mysterious phenomenon of anxiety in connection with the perception of this danger we all live with internally, the inexpressible fear that does not know of what it is afraid. I have earlier called it the fear of our incapacity for peace. I would like to use a third mental image to express what I call the embodiment of truth. I designate as a truth a perception that is at the same time the positive counterpart of a fear, the perception of a reality that makes human life, above all community life, possible—in brief, perception of the possibility to live. The embodiment of a truth should be called the realization of this possibility. Every perception is incomplete, every human truth is only a partial truth. Therefore, I speak of "a" peace as the embodiment of "a" truth. Human history as we know it is the history of struggle between truths, struggle between successive periods of peace. The contemporary problem of peace in political terms is the problem of world peace. The struggle between competing truths destroys, again and again, older possibilities for peace. New anxiety unavoidably results from this process.

I have tried to explain anxiety in the context of the contemporary social realities that correspond to widely held perceptions of these same realities. But it also has very much to do with the capacity of the individuals themselves, with the capacity to live together with others, or with the peace of an individual that is reflected in the psychological mirror known as identity.

One certainly learns about oneself by learning how to live together with others, by finding love through them, learning language through their language, and finding one's sense of order in their social customs. In this respect we are fundamentally social beings. But maturity only occurs in the individual. Nothing that another does for you and for me, nothing that you and I do for another can release us from the task of becoming ourselves.

One cannot offer what one does not have, including oneself. In this sense, anxiety is most of all the perception of the danger that one is not able to be at peace with oneself—thus, the danger upon which one's own existence is dependent, the danger of not being able to perceive oneself. Almost the same is the danger of not being able to embody self-perception, and thus to be obligated to fear or hate oneself.

We are afraid of each other and of our own incapacity for peace. Peace is the requirement. But how will we be capable of realizing it? Morality requires it. But does not morality, if we mean to act earnestly in accordance with it, lead us only into confusion? The social revolutionaries are morally motivated. Is it mere chance that their creation of new power systems comes about only after much blood has flown? There are times in which we must rightly concede that change is necessary in the historical struggle between competing ideologies, times when one must recognize that the new power system is different in a decisive nuance from the one it has replaced. But it is the tragic nature of power that it leaves unchanged what it originally wanted to change, a system maintained through fear.

I would like to quote a few passages from the New Testament to remind us that it speaks to these questions. "These things I have spoken unto you, that in me ye might have peace. In the world ye shall have tribulation: but be of good cheer; I have overcome the world." (John 16:33) Here anxiety and peace are dealt with in the same verse. As a more precise translation the word *thlipsis* that Luther passed on as "anxiety" means constriction or affliction, similar to the word *stenchoria* used by St. Paul. In Luther's language, anxiety meant precisely a constriction. It is the constriction that belongs to the condition of the world that has not received the light by which it was created.

A second passage concerning the conquest of the world says, "For whatsoever is born of God overcometh the world: and this is the victory that overcometh the world, *even* our faith." (1 John 5:4) A third passage reads, "Now faith is the substance of things hoped for, the evidence of things not seen." (Heb. 11:1) If I read the original Greek text in the context of the then predominant intellectual concepts of Greek philosophy and jurisprudence, then I must translate this passage as follows: "But it is the belief of the substance of things hoped for, the critical proof of things that one does not see." It means here the *hypostasis*, the substance, the essence, the thing itself. *Elenchos* means the legal and articulable proof, the test of resistance.

I will attempt a brief elaboration of the above. The world forces us to be anxious. Anxiety is not a weakness of judgment, but rather a correct perception. "I have triumphed over the world," says the incarnated Logos, the Word of God that has become flesh as it is expressed there in the Gospel according to St. John, the Logos through which everything has been created that exists, the substance of the world as creation. Incarnate does not mean an abstract metaphysical concept of theology, but a human being among us, real life in the world. This person is the first born among the many siblings. This life is the possibility of life also for us all. This possibility is grasped through belief.

Belief, first of all, is not an attitude, and certainly not something unreasonable: It is content, it is what we believe. It is the substance of the exaltation, the reality of the possibility. One can only test reality when one engages oneself with it. There is no critical test of the possibility of life without "testing" it with the possibility of failure. Belief is the test of the thing that one does not see. It brings the truth to the fore in that it practically engages itself with peace. That means that the soul becomes real.

These texts and their interpretations may appear to many of us as if they were written in a symbolic language to which we are missing the key. One can make the same experience more meaningful through an examination of the three levels of the Sermon on the Mount. The first level is the universal ethic of the golden rule, "Do unto others as you would have them do unto you." That is the condition under which a just society alone is possible. It is the condition for external peace in which we can live free from the fear of each other.

But do we really want that? Don't we think, "I want that, but the other does not?" That is the psychological mechanism of projection: I need an "object" for my own evil thoughts. Therefore, we have the second level, that of the command of the moral upon the entire person, not just on the visible external deeds of the person. It is not the one who first murdered a sibling who is guilty before the court, but whoever thinks the murderer does not regret the death. This is the condition of inner peace, the maturity of the personality, that alone can bear inner peace. But who is really capable of that? The recognition of that which should be leads us into the constriction, into an anxiety of doubt about ourselves. For whatever harms another is something we cannot permit in ourselves with good will. Maturity undergoes an experience of death. "Verily, verily, I say unto you, Except a corn of wheat fall into the ground and die, it abideth alone: but if it die, it bringeth forth much fruit." (John 12:24) The third level is that of the Beatitudes, to which we referred earlier. Blessed are the peacemakers. Blessed are the poor in spirit. They are blessed here and now. The constriction has opened itself. There is the experience of the reality of peace that goes beyond the requirements of morality. It does not discard morality but fulfills it in a way different from what any moralist had thought.

But what use does any of this have for us? It is not worth much to talk about this if our own transformed essence does not radiate peace. These claims are not especially reserved for the Christian church. If one shows the Sermon on the Mount or the Gospel according to St. John to an aware Hindu or Buddhist, he or she will reply, "That is true. That is what the Enlightened One said." But whoever sees that human maturity is the meaning of anxiety and its truth, must not wonder that anxiety cannot be overcome without maturity, no matter how much progress might have improved the rest.

7. Beauty

Viens-tu du ciel profond ou sors-tu de l'abîme, O Beauté? wrote Baudelaire. Do you come from the depth of heaven or do you rise out of the abyss, oh beauty?

We humans, finite beings, stretched between the two immensities of heaven and hell—to which of these two shall we give thanks for the overwhelming power of beauty?

To hear voices, such as Baudelaire's about beauty, one must return to the lost bourgeois century, to the age preceding the disillusion that began with World War I. Our time mistrusts the beautiful. We do not want to allow ourselves to be overwhelmed, we do not believe in its blessedness.

Criticism of tradition is one of the great traditions of Europe. Likewise, the mistrust of beauty had its antecedents in Western thought since the time of the Jewish prophets, the Greek philosophers, and the sobriety of the Romans. We know at least four criticisms of beauty from our tradition: Beauty is not useful. Beauty is not just. Beauty is not true. Beauty is not pious.

Beauty is not useful. The lazy enjoy the magic of beauty, the industrious produce goods for their own and others' use. The value of beauty is only subjective; it depends on an irrational feeling.

Beauty is not just. There is a deep gap between esthetic and ethic. The rich subsidize festivals while the poor go hungry. The members of the ruling class recognize each other with esthetic criteria. Art that today wants to be valid must be ugly.

Beauty is not true. Art is beautiful illusion. Beauty is not blissful, it is limestone and brass, it is a document of hand-made culture. The work is not blissful. The perceiver who loses his way in the quest for truth by getting lost in esthetic pleasures enjoys his loss of reality only as a temporary state of bliss. Poets do not show humankind the reality, said Plato, but rather they show us the image of an image.

Beauty is not pious. Lucifer was beautiful, and for this reason he fell from God. Beauty is the idolatrous perfection of something worldly. It kindles a seductive fire from a spark loosened by the divine, and it is fueled by instinct, leaving behind only ashes when it has burned itself out. It is the final crossroads at which the highly gifted leave the road to heaven to turn to the road to hell.

These four objections appear to me to be important partial truths. They can be reduced to one assumption, namely, that beauty is not truth. If the sense for beauty were an ability to recognize reality, then it could be useful, even economically useful. If the sense for beauty were valid, then its unjust consequences would be perceived as ugliness and be corrected. If the sense for beauty were situated in truth, it could not separate itself from God.

Nevertheless, I maintain that beauty is a form of truth: The sense for beauty is a sense, that means a special perceptive ability to see reality. However, those who designate beauty as a form of truth, do they not claim an objectivity of the subjective, a rationality of the irrational, of emotions? My answer is, "Yes, that is exactly what I want to maintain." There is a rationality of the irrational. Or, said more exactly, a reason of the emotions, in which the subjective, precisely in its subjectivity, proves itself as objective, as knowledge.

But what is perception? Before I refer to the highly differentiated perception of beauty, I would like to give the simplest example, that of direct perception by the senses. What is perception by the senses? There are many senses, and I want to look at four examples.

I am driving fast at dusk on the highway. Suddenly, I see another car approaching me on the wrong side of the road. "I see" is visual perception. After a steep ascent, I finally lie in the sunny alpine meadow and hear the buzzing bees. "I hear," is auditory perception. "I taste the marmalade— ah, strawberries!," is taste perception. And the fourth is, once again, visual: In the Vatican I see Raphael's *School of Athens*. I see two teachers, in conversation, leaving through the doorway. One of them is Aristotle carrying a heavy book against his hip with his left hand and pointing with his right hand towards the fullness of reality, and the other the old man, Plato, gently raises his index finger to point to heaven.

So what is perception by the senses? The usual analysis differentiates between three aspects, pure perception of the sense organ, judgment that interprets this perception, and emotional reaction that results from the judgment. I see a red shape looming larger as it approaches me, and I think, "A car on the wrong side of the road." I am frightened by the danger. I hear a sound. I think, "Bees." I enjoy the peacefulness of nature. I taste something sweet. I think, "Strawberries." I desire more. I see patches of color on the wall. I think of Plato and Aristotle. I live in the artistic representation of classical philosophy.

But this division into perception, judgment, and emotional reaction does not lie in the phenomena themselves, it is the product of the subsequent analysis. The phenomenon is described much more directly if I say, "I see the danger; I hear the peaceful sounds of the mountain meadows; I taste the enticing strawberries; I see *The School of Athens.*" And the emotional reaction is not the end of the unity of the act of perception. Perception and action cannot be separated. Regarding the danger, I have already grasped the steering wheel. From the buzzing in the meadow, I have already relaxed. With the taste of strawberries, I am taking another bite. Looking at *The School of Athens*, I sense the beauty of truth.

The research of animal behavior teaches us that the unity of perception and action is original, simple, and understandable. In contrast, the capacity to separate perception and action proceeds from a high level of development. It first permits us to substitute active action for reactive action. It allows us not to be obligated but to want. The storage of past perceptions in memory permits the making of free decisions, verified by inhibited reactions that are known as emotional states, based upon mental images of nonperformed actions that are known as concepts and judgments.

In this highly differentiated mode of experience there is also rooted a phenomenon that I would like to call the related perception of higher levels. This related perception, if I am correct, is the sense for the beautiful. We humans receive, with every sensory impression, with every single judgment, with every emotional state, at the same time the true, higher universality that makes this impression, this judgment, this emotional state first possible. But often we can barely distinguish the higher from the individual, causing perplexion if we should say, "What, then, is this related higher perception?" In every true sentence, we perceive the phenomenon of truth, in every required good deed, the moral order, and in every beautiful impression, the mysterious reality of the beautiful. What are these other perceived realities?

One should not expect to find simple answers to such questions. They are questions concerning the basis of human culture. But human culture is not simple. If we come to know a foreign culture, we often recognize a completely different order and designation of principles. Let us take the ancient Japanese culture as an example, as we are talking about beauty. The Japanese culture, to this day, is still the most esthetically oriented culture of all. No sensitive European who visits Japan can escape this impression. But perhaps we Europeans designate falsely what we perceive there if we label it with our own concepts of the esthetic that are so easily associated with something almost noncommittal, unserious, and untrue. How is beauty in Japan connected to the ritual and the rational? Is the ritual of Japanese politeness that often annoys the European rigorists of veracity not just a strict, esthetic stylization of manners, a way of making them endurable? Is not the sense for esthetic harmony in all East Asian thought and feeling really a mediator of integration, a feeling for the whole, a possibility of perception, for which we Europeans, with our troubled reflections that we call reason, cannot find an equivalent, so that we continually and painfully offend the delicate Asiatic refinement?

But as different as cultures are, the possibility of dialogue between them should not be ruled out. This may be the greatest promise of our times. The principles of the utilitarian, of the ethical, and of beauty are, at the same time, plateaus to which human perception and action adjusts itself again and again. In every culture, these plateaus are related differently to each other, but still one can recognize that they exist. Perhaps nobody has yet been able to describe cultural structures with universal validity. So I consciously now return to the narrow horizons of Western tradition, and ask once again about its meaning of beauty.

I will venture make a second assumption: Beauty is a manifestation mode of the good, and certainly a manifestation mode of the good in indirect perception. What does this mean? I introduce a new word, "good." With this I do not only mean the moralistic good. I mean good as in a good shoe that does not pinch, a good sportsman who wins, a good researcher who makes a discovery.

Plato has indicated the highest principle to be the good. His index finger in Raphael's painting points to the good. One talks now, not with more understanding but usually less reflectively, of values. The basic phenomenon of the good might consist of this: that we do not always merely perceive how something is, but enjoy the related perception of how it indeed should be; and since we have this related perception of how it should be with everything, a shoe, a sportsman, a moral act, then we also are perceiving the comprehensive phenomenon of the good itself with it. We thus see the phenomenon that there is, apparently for everything, also the possibility that it is the best, the good against which we can measure its manifestation.

There are directly related, perceived forms of the good. I would like to add to them the utilitarian and the ethical.

Let us begin with the utilitarian. We call useful that which is good for us. Earning one's daily bread is useful because one wants to live. If I am hungry, then I immediately perceive in a piece of bread what it is good for. In the concept of bread its usefulness is given through direct perception. Education is useful because it makes earning one's daily bread easier, makes life easier, allows us luxury goods, even the luxury of the beautiful. But is the easy life, is luxury, is beauty, really useful? One can say these are absurd questions. The useful is always a means towards an end. The first end is the good. That survival is good seems to be self-evident. Is comfort good? Luxury? Beauty? Is something that serves a perhaps questionable good of true value? Do I then know my own true interest?

There is a way to answer the question about the true value, the true interest; it is the way of the moral, of ethics. Its guiding motif is the elimination of the egoistical concept of the utilitarian. In reality what is useful for me is not what is useful for me alone, but, on the contrary, what is useful for others, the community, society. This process leads to the second level, to the principle that is known to us as the right or the ethical. The living nerve of the ethical exists in a qualitatively different experience from that of the utilitarian, even if it, too, has social usefulness. If I recognize humanity in others, then I lose the barriers of the ego. This experience permits me the recognition that the ego is a boundary and the source of unending suffering. The core of the ethical is an experience of release, release from the blindness that is known as the ego. Therefore, I should not attempt to assert my own egoism against others nor should they attempt to subject me to theirs. Rather, I should strive for a release together. I should seek the ethical.

Why is the naked ego blind? A backward glance at human history will give us a clue. The ego is our animal heritage, although it was the human race, above all Europeans, who, using its many facets, developed the tool of power to the highest degree. In organic life, there are three principles at work: perservation of the individual, preservation of the species, and further development. The presevation of the individual has apparently the earliest but not the highest priority. It is a precondition but not the goal of preservation of the species, not to mention its further development. Preservation of the individual is secured by the instincts of hunger and fear. The ego, as mental phenomenon, is the embodiment and the guide of the psychological processes that serve to preserve the individual. Nothing, however, is as certain for the individual as death. The human being is the animal that knows it must die. Thus, the experience realm of the human ego is limited by a quiet, or an explicitely present, perception of futility. The blindness of the animal ego is that it does not know through reflection that it must die. The blindness of the human ego is delusion, the compulsion to look away from futility. Therefore, the release from the interests of the ego is an experience of gaining sight.

The ethical is not the final principle. It is a satisfactory lesson in a mode of perception, but it is not content. The categorical imperative remains a formal principle. The real problem, the problem of our true interest, is a problem for the community just as it is a problem for the individual. I speculate that the sense for beauty, inborn and then culturally developed, is a perception of certain manifestations of the whole, especially of those manifestations that are important for life but that are outside direct judgments about the utilitarian.

Beauty is related directly to the perception of life's necessities, but in an indirect manner, without the solemnity of necessity. We will first look at the elementary interests of life, which our technological age has only now begun to be aware of—let us hope, not too late. If I am lying in my meadow, what do I perceive? I said, "A buzzing, no, the bees, no, the peace of nature." Is this emotional state of peace merely subjective, or is it the perception of something real? It is a perception. What it perceives is what contemporary science calls ecological balance. More than a hundred million years ago, evolution had already led to the simultaneous development of two organic forms that depended upon each other: the flowering plants that entice to pollination, and those insects that live from pollen and nectar. Much later, humankind got involved in this balance and, as gatherer, farmer, and animal breeder, became dependent on these plants or the animals that eat these plants. If one perceives this balance as beautiful, then one perceives the harmony, as shown in the example of the alpine meadow, as a sensual harmony without which one cannot live.

A humanity that neglects and destroys the ecological beauty as economically meaningless is demented. It thus commits nearly always an economic mistake that is only recognized as a mistake when it is too late. Of course, I am not saying that humankind should not alter nature. That would be absurd. But the sense of beauty has been given to us so that we can measure our own work against another standard than what is considered useful by a blind ego. How beautiful are the old civilized landscapes! When I returned from North America the first time, a place that I admire and love, I was moved to tears by the beauty of the landscape on the Bodensee or in Umbria, where every tree and house has stood for centuries where people with a sense of beauty have wanted it. The contemporary crises of America are also the crises of the puritanical contempt for beauty.

Viens-tu du ciel profond ou sors-tu de l'abîme? When Baudelaire asks that, does he not mean the harmony of the landscape and only by echo the beauty of art? He means the overwhelming power of material beauty, the beauty that compels to the passion of love. Now, love is also inherited from the animals, and animals are decorated for the sake of love with colorful garments and baroque ceremonies, garments and ceremonies that for the preservation of the individual would be useless, even harmful. As biologists we think we can actually grasp what is good in this beauty. Sexual love *must* be overpowering and splendid for it requires that the individual take an essential step away from his behavioral pattern of individual self-preservation, a step that is necessary for the preservation of the species. Once in its life, the animal must become crazy from the perspective of its self-preservation. But for humans, erotic love has become, next to morality, a second and completely different kind of release from the ego, and in a different way moves the ego toward maturity.

Common to both, despite all the differences of how they are experienced, is a quality of sensation that one could perhaps call bliss, the overwhelming bliss of erotic ecstasy and the quiet bliss of the good deed, more exactly, the good will. Perhaps what they have in common is that both steps originate in the blindness of the ego and teach us to see something entirely different. For the core of reality, as the Indians say, is the trinity of being, consciousness, and bliss.

But whatever is beautiful appears to be blissful in itself. Art is the conscious depiction of the appearance of things we call beautiful. Kant, who was certainly not an artistic man, had, with his own precise and profound view, designated the beautiful as the object of a necessarily recognized impartial pleasure without concept. "Necessarily recognized without concept," is what I have called the rationality of the irrational, the affective perception. Kant calls interest the pleasure we connect with the existence of an object. An impartial pleasure therefore desires nothing from existence. More crudely put, it desires nothing from the possession of an object.

There are things in nature—for example, the grain of wood, the inside of a shell—that are not made to be readily seen, but which are no less beautiful than a butterfly wing or bird feathers. Perhaps it is the omnipresent hidden mathematics of nature that is the real basis of all beauty.

At this point, the question whether art must be beautiful or if it, to be valid, must be ugly, proves itself again to be an illusory question that stems from the most superficial understanding of the word beauty. Whether a work is academically beautiful or expressive ugly, in either case there is a difference between the superficial glance, which judges with the pedantic standards of the academic, and an inner appearance that is not seen, but which conveys a perception of reality.

To return to a much more comfortable subjective language: The inner blissfulness of beauty says that it does not depend on us. It means the release from the demands of the ego. But what about the criticism of beauty with which we began this chapter? Wherever the existence, or the possession, of beauty becomes an interest, there is danger. Lucifer, the beautiful, did not want to be a reflection of the only good, he wanted himself to be the center of all. Therefore, beauty sometimes seems to come from heaven, sometimes from the abyss. Beauty is true and not true. It releases us from the blindness of the concept, but it should not be played off against reason that learned to see from it. The gap between esthetic and ethic should not be closed. We must always be reminded that the beautiful in itself is not ethical, that the just in itself is not human. And we must return from beauty as presence to the firm ground of the utilitarian. But while we are working for our daily bread, the aching bliss of a melody by Mozart should still remain with us.

8. Death

A. *De mortuis nil nisi bonum*

Can one dare talk about death? Will whatever I say be valid, given my own death? Is it valid in the light of the death of my neighbor? Is it valid in the light of death that everywhere surrounds us and for which we often have more responsibility than we are willing to admit? But then again, can one dare *not* talk about death? Can we really speak of life if we do not look death in the eye?

Buddha was the son of a king. It is said that his father raised him in the palace and in the gardens of the palace far away from awareness of suffering. The prince already had a wife and two children when his request was granted for the first time to visit the city. We know that in such oriental streets there is immediate confrontation with human misery. Buddha saw a sick man. "What is that?" he asked his companion. "A sick man." "Must I become like that?" "Yes." He saw an old man. "What is that?" "An old man." "Must I also become like that?" "Yes." He saw a funereal procession. "What is that?" "A dead man." "Must I also become like that?" "Yes." He saw a wandering monk whose face was beaming with the peace of awareness. "What is that?" "A monk." "Can I also become like that?" "Yes." The prince returned to the palace. That same night he left behind all of his possessions, his father, his young wife, and his children, and became a wanderer. After years of difficulty, he finally became enlightened. Then he taught for fifty years for the salvation of all and for the release from suffering and from want through enlightenment.

We do not need to go to the Orient to learn how to think about death. From the farewell speech of Socrates we learn that to philosophize is nothing more than learning how to die. In the parables of Jesus we hear about the rich man who wanted to build a new barn for his harvest so that he could say to his soul, "You have provided for yourself now for many years; now be at peace and eat and drink and be merry." But God said unto him, "Thou fool, this night thy soul shall be required of thee: then whose shall these things be, which thou hast provided?" (Luke 12:20)

Probably never before has humankind been so confused about death. Certainly, the answer of all great religions to the question of death was alien to the daily consciousness of humankind in all ages. It was mythologically adorned to make it endurable. But in our time even the language is alien to us. Modern consciousness does not understand the adorned or unadorned answer. But we must begin with this current consciousness if we do not want just to say friendly, or even truthful, things about death, but want to say something *bene*, that is, to speak in a nice way, and sincerely. The hard core of modern consciousness is science, and as a scientist I want to say three things. First, science also has something important to say about death. Second, there is the perspective of our spiritual heritage, the treasury of experience that we have received from all religions, not just our own Christian tradition. And third, in a philosophical way, we do not merely list experiences one after the other, but rather make an attempt to find a systematic connection between them.

B. Where Does Death Come From?

Contemporary science knows a little more about the answer to this question than was known in earlier times. Expressed another way: The ego and death are two mutually dependent and meaningful aspects of organic life.

The framework of historical facts that have been outlined by science is now generally well known. We humans evolved from the animals, and the animals evolved from protozoa. All of us, humans, animals, plants, single-cell organisms, consist physically of molecules. The first forms of life probably evolved from molecules following the formation of earth together with its central star, the sun, from a cloud of dust approximately four and a half billion years ago. The sun is one of a hundred billion stars of our galaxy, the Milky Way, which is one of a hundred million galaxies that wander through the space that has been penetrated by our instruments. The known cosmos can only have existed for scarcely more than ten billion years. The beginning is veiled in hypothesis.

Even more philosophically important than the framework is the structure of the history of nature. All forms in the universe exist in time. Their common attributes are possibility, actuality, and transitoriness. We speak of certain forms as being possible: A star and a quartz crystal are possible agglomerations of material. Out of these formal possibilities controlled by natural law, there must arise real historical possibilities: this is a cloud of gas out of which a star can be created; this is a molten mass out of which a quartz crystal can be formed. The historical possibilities precondition what can become. The gas cloud and the molten mass must already exist. All that becomes actual is transitory, for if it were not so, there would be no possibility for the new. The cloud of gas becomes, for the most part, stars, the molten mass hardens or flows into larger fusions. Possibilities are based on the interplay of actuality and transitoriness. If one ventures to designate the historical possibilities as life, and the transitoriness of things as death, then death is a precondition of life. The sentence "Death is her means for creating more life" in Goethe's hymn to nature becomes applicable in this quite formal sense. Its rather enthusiastic sound is, according to science, no more and no less justified than the gloominess of the sentence "Everything that lives, lives only to die." In the real sense of the word, though, there is no death in the transitoriness of the inorganic.

The transitoriness of everything that has developed is familiar to all ancient religions and philosophies. What is new in science is the empirical determination of evolution, of an ever advancing creation of always new and always differentiated forms. There has also been evolution in inorganic nature. Newton still thought that it was possible to comprehend the solar system only as the work of a planning intelligence. We are now convinced that all forms of inorganic nature, in accordance with natural laws, are continuing to separate from each other and, accordingly, proceed to greater and greater differentiation. The belief that the so-called blind law of probability can only create ever-increasing chaos is false. I can summarize here the results but not the arguments of the conceptual proof of these questions in the following three theses: (1) In a physical system that is far enough distanced from statistical equilibrium, an increase in the number of different forms, accordingly an increasing differentiation, is to be statistically expected. (2) The established equilibrium does generally not destroy the forms, but rather terminates their proliferation; the so-called thermal death does not leave behind a mush but rather a site of skeletons. (3) Only closed systems reach equilibrium; the universe in its entirety is, we assume, not a closed system.

The core of the phenomenon of evolution is that with the continuation of evolution the number of possibilities increases. It is true that with the realization of a possibility everything else that could have been realized becomes excluded. But that which has newly become actual contains within it the possibility of leading to something that previously was not. Through the increase of the abundance of forms, what has become actual does not entirely disappear. A record of its having been remains in that which it becomes.

The most meaningful evolutionary invention of nature has been organic life. This is the way this thought has been put in the personified language that scientists use in their everyday work, in a seemingly light vein. With conceptual caution, one can call organic life a possibility that has realized itself in a phase of natural history. The metaphor of a "new invention of nature" is to imply that it does not just refer to the possibility of a new special form, but to the possibility of new possibilities, of forms that contain within themselves the principle of the creation of ever new forms. We have no empirical basis to assume any laws other than the normal laws of physics and chemistry. In biology today, it is, furthermore, the fundamental hypothesis of the Darwinian theory of evolution that if organic life has developed once, its further development will occur with statistical necessity ("with probability approaching certainty") in accordance with recognizable principles, and that evolution, again in accordance with these principles, would be sufficient to lead us to an understanding of the factually developed forms of life if we would only be able to think through the entire complicated processes.

I must now weave into this presentation a thread of the confrontation with the opinions of classical philosophy. I admit that I view the currently widespread emotional distrust of Darwinian theory to be a philosophical misunderstanding for which, however, the undifferentiated popular philosophies of many biologists are partially responsible. Darwinism is the challenge for a still unwritten philosophy of time. Classical Western philosophy places the transitoriness of formed things in the context of the eternity of the forms themselves. The idea of the idea is, according to Plato, the idea of the good. From the perspective of the transitory thing, the idea of which it is a part is its best, its highest possibility. Ideas are eternal, and thus the highest possibilities of all transitory things are always the same. In my opinion, Plato, against a background of mathematical as well as ethical and mystical experience, dared to join together the experience of the transitory with the experience of the eternal. Time is for him where the eternal remains unchanged, to where the many continuing images must ever return—a circular motion approaching the eternal. It is the beauty of the Platonically understood world that there is nothing new in it, for if that possibility existed—a blasphemous thought—then the eternal good would not be possible. This way of speaking has had its impact in the history of thought.

How are we to think now about the possibility of all possibilities, the good, if there is evolution? In the philosophy that is closest to us, the possible appears to be related to the future. It would be a rather abstract notion to attribute timelessness to the single conceptually mirrored idea. The real possibilities come first with the becoming of their predecessors. The emotionally connotative concept of chance only says that we must not see necessity in the possibilities of the future. We speak scientifically about chance if, in situations that we conceptually characterize as similar, *de facto* differences occur in different single events. Our conceptual aids only allow for the relative frequency of the occurrence of different possibilities, thus the prediction of probabilities. The physical laws are nothing other than the general rules in accordance with which the human subject can make its prognoses possible. We must consider now the theory of biological evolution in the light of philosophical questions.

A theory of evolution must explain three empirically established prin-

ciples: preservation of the individual, preservation of the species, and evolution of the species. The central principle is preservation of the species.
The Latin word *species* is a translation of the Greek *eidos* and comes from
Aristotelian philosophy. Aristotle was a heterodox interpretor of Plato.
The Platonic idea is for him the *eidos*, the form *in* the things, whatever
the metaphor "in" might mean here. The eternity of ideas for him is
realizable in the never interrupted presense of things, in which exists the
same *eidos*. The physical derivation of like from like ("a human creates a
human") is the most beautiful model of this thought. No individual is
eternal, but the *eidos* in the individual, the species, is. This philosophical
thought is, at the same time, outstanding empirical biology. Modern scientific biology began in the eighteenth century as it established the universal
validity of the physical descent of all individuals of one species from individuals of the same species, consequently, the principle of Aristotle. The
slow variation of a species that is the basis of evolution is, in accordance
with contemporary biology, only a small correction of the principle of the
species as a constant. Every explanation of evolution must begin with the
explanation of the species as a constant, hence the central importance of
the long-sought discovery of the double helix of amino acids. But the
philosophical theme of Aristotle was turned upside down through the discovery of evolution: The species, too, are not eternal. The beautiful, too,
must die to make room not just for the individual but also for the form.

One must realize that evolution has first created death, and has done so
with progressively increasing severity. According to contemporary conceptual models, organic evolution began with molecules that reproduce
themselves. Organic evolution begins with the reproduction of a species.
There were originally no provisions for the preservation of the individual.
Molecules have only their normally limited chemical stability. But now
begins the competition of different and increasing species for the limited
available resources. The first step of evolution accordingly produces the
new phenomenon of the "struggle for survival." Rapid proliferation is first
an advantage, an economic utilization of food resources. Those species
that are efficient in such operations will gain over the others. This creates
a "selection advantage" for certain kinds of behavior and therefore for
further development. Accidental or possible mutations are almost always
harmful, but they can still lead to new efficient species, which are then
successful. Thus, the first principle, the self-reproduction of a species, leads
to the second principle, the further development. In this development
follows a chain of "inventions of nature" that are mainly the result of the
principle of self-preservation, thus of the active behavior of the individual
for preservation of its own existence. This includes the superior efficiency
of individuals that possess metabolism, whose chemical processes are necessary for growth and mobility. Advantageous for higher organic chemistry
is a substance that is itself organic. This allows consumption of other or-

ganisms, therefore animals that live from plants and predators that live from other animals. Individuals now become threatened by other individuals, and self-protection through durability, poison, weapons, size, and mobility brings advantages. Evolution thus produces a pattern for individuals as the last of its three principles. Only individuals that have adapted to self-preservation can really die. For them death is an occurence because they are equipped to protect themselves against it. Thus evolution produces death.

Darwin was influenced in his theory of selectivity through the pessimistic economics of Malthus who taught that living organisms such as humans would continually multiply until they reached the minimum means of subsistence. This thought is a glance into an abyss that was always concealed in the European tradition. In Christian Aristotelianism, God appears as a gardener or head of a household who provides enough for all of his dependents. From the perspective, though, of the individual, Buddha saw much deeper. Even the early Christian tradition, which saw the world itself and the masters of this world as evil, was more perceptive. Those indignant about Darwinian theory are defending an idealized image of the world. Darwinian theory, too, contained an optimistic belief in progress, but tended to ignore the fact that the development of species and their ecological equilibrium proceeds over the bodies of individuals. One must belong to the victors to be content with the existing beauty of the world. In my opinion, the realism of Darwin contains within it also a challenge for a deeply penetrating philosophy and theology. The opposition of finality and causality is only an apparent opposition. It is, first of all, a tenet of the theory of selectivity that the finalistic description of the behavior of organisms is justified as a phenomenology by explaining the origins of *purposeful* organisms. This reciprocal explanation of the initial and final causes, this foundation of the possibility of becoming, is not un-Aristotelian. But it has new weight in the infringement of the boundaries of the constancy of species. The theology, though, of a God who sets purposes appears to me to be an anthropomorphism that, because of the religious teaching of God's omnipotence, is just as difficult to agree with as the philosophical belief in God's omniscience. Purposes are decidedly human orientation signs whose conceptual meaning contains within it the possibility that they will not be realized. Objectives are concepts of possibilities, therefore anthropomorphic. Whoever makes God directly responsible for the objective must also make an opposing God responsible for the unending profusion of failure and suffering, and is consequently compelled to theological dualism.

Death is the result of evolution in a still sharper sense than I have previously spoken of. An "invention of nature" is the structure that accelerates evolution. Of two somewhat equally endowed species, the one that develops faster will have the advantage. "Experimentation" with many mutations belongs to this process. Most probably, sexual reproduction, as opposed to the much simpler principle of cell division, is one of such evolution-accelerating structures. It mixes continually new recessive characteristics and endows each species with a bank of latent hereditary factors that give a chance to adjust to changes in the environment. To maintain this continued reproduction, the most powerful behavioral regulator is certainly required, namely, copulation. Thus, we can understand the world-mastering force of sexual love. But one who copulates has already taken the first step to make oneself superfluous. A certain female spider begins to eat her male partner while still copulating. The deep experience of the connection between love and death is not an esthetic error.

The death of the individual is still the immediate requirement of evolution. The short life span of the individual is a selective advantage for the species because it accelerates experimentation of successive generations. The aging of the individual is certainly not accidentally a compulsory process, a genetically progressive sickness. We conceal from ourselves this fact through naive beliefs that the process of aging is perhaps merely an avoidable result of the wear and tear of our physical components. Why should virtually immortal individuals be physically less possible than virtually immortal species? The process of aging is actually the process of ontogeny adapted to individual development. The short-lived fly can die after just one reproductive day. The human being lives longer because its children need it for a longer time.

C. What Does Death Mean in Our Human Life?

The human being is the creature that knows it must die. Animals have, perhaps, a perception of the proximity of their own death in fear or a release from their own instinct of self-preservation. But the human is the first creature that has the reflective awareness of its own death. Perhaps no other awareness has penetrated into human consciousness and thus opened the way to self-perception more than the knowledge of our own death.

The human situation in confrontation with the knowledge of our own death is paradoxical. The manifest bearer of human knowledge is the ego. The ego is the self-perception of the individual as individual. Without reflection, the ego is the steering center of the self-preservation instincts; with reflection, it is the conscious center of all perceptions and knowledgeable decisions; thus the ego is the human instrument of self-preservation, its first servant. The human being is the animal that can say "I." But the individual is the real victim of death. By attaining reflective knowledge, the ego attains the knowledge of its own necessary death.

Let us go one step further. The human being ruptured the animal unity of perception and action through the possibility of imagination based upon language. He can imagine that which does not exist, in fantasy, words, and ideas. He can anticipate various possibilities of the future. The science whose language I employ is the result of the human capacity to conceive of the future; concepts are possibilities. The capacity to think possibilities, also means the capacity to think of dangers and to prepare defenses against them. It means precise fears and the unlimited accumulation of power. Especially the ego of modern Europeans, through the triumph of our civilization of modern humanity, experiences the accumulation of power as knowledge and as capital, as weapons more powerful than possessed by any earlier form of life. It is exactly that foresight that has given us all the power on earth that recognizes the boundaries that lie in the death of the self. What will become of what you have accumulated?

The most common form of human association with one's own death is repression. If this were not so, why would we need the Biblical reminder? The physical mechanism of repression is in itself a necessary requirement for survival. Screening and filtering of information is one of the highest accomplishments of our sensory apparatus. It is a precondition for conceptualization. Among what must normally be repressed belongs the deluge of distant dangers that do not require immediate action. Repression is an important guardian of mental health. But its correct use is a task. The more conscious we become, the more essential it is for us to control our own repressions. Truth becomes, for us, a matter of life and death. In this sense, peace is always the embodiment of truth. Our capacity to live with the repression of death is thus an important criterion of our capacity to live, our capacity for peace.

Let us look next at the moment when I do not just know that one dies, but that I myself must now die. At the moment of birth an arrow is shot at each person: it flies and flies and reaches him or her at the moment of death. What if I hear the whizzing of this arrow? Our medicine has a problem here. The religious practice has been not to leave one in ignorance of the last hour. The person receives the consolation of knowing what the doctor, the priest, the relatives know, that death is nigh. In contemporary medicine, there is the contrary doctrine that it is the human commandment not to make the dying conscious of their own imminent end. There is even the practice now of convincing the dying of the contrary. Certainly, one cannot expect of people who have learned to repress the thought that life means learning how to die, that in the last moment they can make up for a lifetime of neglect. But even these perceive something that they can understand if one is prepared to help them with it. Often, the physician is the one who is at a loss, or the technical and commercial apparatus of medicine prevents the physician from doing the possible. Many experiences give testimony of the perception of the nearness of one's own death even if this cannot be fully understood by the conscious mind. It does not just accompany the limitation of the ego's range of consciousness as the life force recedes. On the contrary, it is the potential of a heightened and liberated sensitivity.

One of the greatest forms resulting from the confrontation with the shadow of death may be the style of the late works of artists. I have the impression that the style of an artist is often more influenced by an awareness of death than by the mere passage of the years since birth. The quartets of the fifty-five-year-old Beethoven are of this maturity, as are the paintings of the sixty-year-old Rembrandt and the ninety-year-old Titian, or the development of the character of Prospero in Shakespeare's *The Tempest*, or the last music of the not-yet-thirty-year-old Schubert and the thirty-five-year-old Mozart. I do not know if I can define the formal attributes of the mature artistic style: a diminishing sense of the obligation and the ambition to be classicial, the unbelievable concentration of self-distanced directness—"When I became seventy, I could follow the rules of my own heart," said Confucius.

I would like to try to give to dying and becoming a meaning that I can unite with evolutionary thought. Sobriety is required. Blissful desire should not be mentioned except by the wise. For almost everyone, the fear of death and the early desire for death are two variations of the same emotional state. They are, as emotional states so often are, omitted acts, perceptions of an incapacity to live. The religious answer to the problem of death where it is clearest always contains an inner sobriety. It is clear in its symbols. In the Gospel according to St. John, Jesus speaks of it when he says, "Verily, verily, I say unto you, Except a corn of wheat fall into the ground and die, it abideth alone: but if it die, it bringeth forth much fruit." (John 12:24) He says this to Greeks, and there are commentators who believe that he was referring to the Elysian mysteries. In any case, as in almost all of his parables, he speaks from the experience of life in the country and in nature. The corn of wheat, as an individual, must die in order to produce many corns of wheat. What does that mean in human life?

Development does not usually proceed in small, even increments but, rather, in steps. I would like to call this a development from plateau to plateau. Between two plateaus, the development usually goes through a crisis, through the death of a form. In organic life, the species is a plateau. In the environment to which it has adapted itself it is capable of harmonic life, it exists in the world in relative peace. Mutations occur frequently, but they are nearly always harmful in this environment and are eliminated because of their failure. However, changes in the inorganic or the organic environment, or improbable new "inventions," offer other mutants a better chance. In a crisis, which could be fatal, new forms of life appear, as additions to the existing forms or replacing them. This description, like every description, is simplified; there are always transitions, almost un-noticed crises. But the phenomenon of the plateau is quite universal. Also those comprehensive forms of organization that I at the outset called "inventions of nature" can be designated as plateaus, such as self-reproduction, cells, sexual reproduction, animals, vertebrates, and intelligence.

Also the cultural, social, and political history of humankind shows such plateaus. We now designate crises between them as revolutions: the neolithic revolution that invented agriculture, the rise of urban civilization, the empires, the great religions, the sciences, the political revolutions of modern times, and the industrial revolution. In scientific history, the concept of scientific revolution has recently been used successfully. That the human cultural history in its single steps is presumably not primarily the consequence but rather the cause of actual biological changes, makes the structural relationship between biology and the processes of cultural evolution even more striking. The reason for this relationship lies, in my opinion, in the structure of time itself.

Finally, the biological development of the human individual also goes through plateaus and crises, and here the crisis is often feared and experienced as death. Here is the ego's dying and becoming. Decisive maturity is not reached without experiencing a kind of death. Now I have listed five objective principles that designate such plateaus: the useful, the just, the true, the beautiful, and the holy. I have labeled them as manifestations of the good. They are methods by which humankind perceives that which makes life possible—truths whose embodiment can be human peace. Every one of these principles designates a quality of experience that was hardly anticipated in the preceding qualities, which penetrate with violence or gentleness into the seemingly already closed world of experience. In each of these transitions, a reevaluation takes place of what the ego had previously known, a release, a death of gods.

The ego triumphs only over the instinct of the moment in favor of planning for the future self-preservation. Use and power are accumulated possibilities that serve the ego, they are information. And still something of the ego dies in the discovery of the useful, a childlike state that was more lovable than happy. In the ethical and the just, the ego finds the possibility and the demand to radically exceed itself. In truth, humans become aware, above all, of the human will, independent of prosperity and adversity, a releasing sobriety. The beautiful is a reality beyond self-defense, a blissfulness. In approaching the holy, the ego pushes against a boundary that cannot be crossed. But step through the gate, and you find that there never was a boundary.

Now a word about the experience of death in politics. Politics is the planned structuring of human coexistence in society. As such, it has its share of the necessary and the useful-ethical.

Politics was previously practiced overwhelmingly in the form of domination. In the struggle between domination and freedom, a kind of use-fulness results that we call power. Power is a plateau of human life. It is, as possession, cumulative and almost without limits. It is, as a structure, self-stabilizing. The only effectiveness against power is almost only power. It is, as self-protection, tragic because of its limitlessness. Who lives by the sword, dies by the sword. If the victor dies in bed, the successor must tremble. War is the previously never-eliminated *ultima ratio* of power. Wars are fought continually on earth with a Third World War a probability. Politics is, almost by necessity, accompanied by a form of the lie: Whatever is useful for the party is presented as the just. Exactly because of this, the truth could be actually a healing principle of politics. But who can hear the truth? Who is mentally capable of wanting to hear it? Anxiety, the unendurable perception of one's own incapacity for peace, is what makes power tragic, for it eliminates seeing and hearing exactly where they would be most necessary. Also the screamer does not hear, except one's own scream. It seems that one must have suffered through the coming war in the depths of the unconscious in order to be able to show those who unknowingly are preparing it, gently and unmistakably, the small turn in the path that must be taken to avoid the next catastrophe.

In human maturity, we die many deaths. The realized death is the way to a new life, the veiled death is banishment in death. In the end, the flying arrow always reaches the bodily ego.

D. Where Does Death Lead Us?

This question pushes us from the known into the unknown. The ego consciousness does not know what is beyond its end. It has believed, nearly through all of history, in the religious answers to this question. The ego is not the entire reality of the mind. Religious experience mirrors a reality that transcends the ego. But in the conceptual language of the ego, this experience cannot be expressed as it is. It remains a secret within the ego. In the mythological form in which it has determined the universal history of cultures it is already colored, colored by the receptive limitations of the listener, and colored through the historically determined imaginative ca-pabilities of the religious personalities themselves. A consequence of these multiple colorings is the multiplicity of notions about the hereafter that religious history teaches us. We will briefly examine the most important of them.

In most primitive religions, there is a presense of the dead on the other side, especially of ancestors. Many primitive religions, and even more so the early high religions whose political cultures are rooted in kingdoms of this world, know a kingdom of the dead. There is a notion that the ethical world order, which is the responsibility of the king of this world, will be brought to completion by the king of the hereafter. Judgment of crime and punishment is eventually made on the other side.

As a countermovement to all of these thoughts appears the religion of Israel, as it speaks to us in all but the newest levels of the Old Testament and still determines the characteristic aspects of Judaism. Here, the life of humans with God or against God is on this side. It is decided in the light of day. To really live means, in the language of the prophets, to live here and now with God. To really die means to be separated here and now from God. The ego cannot flee with expectation of fulfillment on the other side, nor does it need this expectation. Abraham ". . . gave up the ghost, and died in a good old age, an old man, and full *of years*; and was gathered to his people." (Gen. 25:8) The ego does not stand alone on this side; the decision for or against God is always made anew by the people collectively. It is the realization of the ethical as a commandment of the holy. Thus even modern engaged intellectuals find genuine access to its ethical side. But the ethical without the holy is not capable of life; it is demand without possibility. The self-consuming effort of mere morality cannot help to become evil or doubting even if it remains true.

The Jewish light of day is a gift to humankind, but it is not the complete reality. Late Judaism incorporated many of the notions of the hereafter from the surrounding peoples. In early Christianity these notions converge with the eschatology of the expectation of the second coming of the messiah. To the approaching kingdom of Christ belongs the resurrection of the flesh. This teaching says that what matters is not the abandonment of the body, but rather its resurrection. The immediate expectation was not fulfilled, and Christian theology turns to the entirely different philosophical message of the immortality of the soul. I believe that the Christian historical expectation in its essential core is the anticipated sign of a still not completed transformation of human history. The question, "Where does the death of the individual take us?" remains a secret also in the Christian tradition.

The most powerful worldwide notion of the status of the dead is the teaching of the reincarnation of the soul in ever new bodies. Coming out of India, this belief conquered the greatest part of Asia and appeared in ancient Greece as Orphic-Pythagorean doctrine. American and European intellectuals on a religious quest are more receptive to this view today than to any of the other teachings about the hereafter. According to it, judgment for crime, and its punishment in the beyond, is eternally lived on this side. Good works lead to good reincarnations, bad lead to bad. Thus we pay for the acts of our past lives in each current life. In this notion of karma, the ethical world order operates like a natural law. But if enough has been done to satisfy the requirements of karmic justice, the question of its meaning must be asked with special emphasis. To what purpose is the eternal thirst for eternal involvement in actions and their consequences?

When the future Buddha left his home behind, he was not just concerned about the suffering in this lifetime, but with the unending suffering of unending lifetimes. He awoke from this cycle. It is not the chain of continual reincarnations but the awakening that is the core of the Buddhist and Hindu experience.

From the critical perspective of the Enlightenment, the very multiplicity of these notions about the hereafter deprecated each one of them. They appear as projections of the wishes and anxieties of this side. In light of the classical Greek Enlightenment, classical Greek philosophy and, above all, Plato, asked the question, "What was the true content of the images?" Life, we learn from Socrates in *Phaidon*, is learning how to die because death releases us from the chains that bind us to earthly desires. The soul is immortal to the extent that it participates in the knowledge of that which has not subjected its existence to time—the idea. The emotional part of the soul is, according to Plato, mortal. The reasoning part is immortal because it is part of the eternal reason. But almost everything that Plato says in the dialogues about these things belongs really to antecedents of philosophy. Did he really believe in the cosmologically depicted myth of the immortality of the individual soul in its journeys through the heavenly cycles and earthly bodies? Or was this for him only a metaphor? The souls in the hereafter choose, *themselves*, the body for their reincarnation, thus their emotional states and their destinies. This is a profound teaching, but who is really the subject of this choice?

The teachings about immortality are brought into a different light by the theory of evolution just as much as other traditional teachings. Science is not capable today of addressing this question, not because it is impossible, but because of its culturally limited perspective. It operates exclusively with objective attitudes. It describes objects as they appear to human subjects without reflecting on subjectivity. But I am convinced that science cannot be made consistent if it excludes what we philosophically call the subject. Hegel's sentence, "substance is essentially subject," exactly expresses this concern, but Hegel's titanic philosophy is not empirical enough. As long as our observations do not include the subjectivity of nature, our science is not completely science.

What would these observations show? The Cartesian duality of opposing substances, of consciousness and corporeality, is not valid when confronted with the physics of this century. Matter is, for our physics, that which obeys the so-called physical laws. But these laws define what the subjects can experience. The subjects, however, we ourselves, appear in the world where we make experiences. As children of evolution, we are organs of nature. It seems as if we must say, "The reality perceives itself through the eyes of the children of evolution, through the organs that have produced it, in respectively different gradations." Who is the subject? In the observation of evolution, the ego itself appears to us to be a tool. Must one speak as if there is only *a* self? Science leads to the threshold of an experience that is open to meditation but not to reflection. This is understandable. Conceptual thinking can comprehend that it cannot conceptually designate the foundation of its possibility.

Therefore, an essay about death does not conclude with a conceptual statement about where death leads us. Thinking is an activity of the ego that can filter, clarify, and lead to the threshold of experience. Death is a threshold.

Let me conclude with a sentence that I cannot justify through thought: Work, not bliss, lies beyond death. Bliss exists in that deep region of reality that also has created death.

Part II
A BIOLOGY OF
THE SUBJECT

1. Who Is the Knower in Physics?[5]

Western thought in the first thousand years of the Christian era was mainly theological. Its conceptual equipment was derived from Greek philosophy, predominantly in its Neo-Platonic interpretation. This was essentially a philosophy of unity. In the second thousand years of the Christian era, Western though gradually immersed itself into plurality. Three main steps may be distinguished. First, medieval scholasticism replaced Platonism with the philosophy of Aristotle, thereby opening up the field of empirical knowledge. Later, experimental mathematical physics taught us, in Galileo's words, to "dissect nature." Finally, the industrial revolution actually replaced the grown structures of nature by a huge and ever increasing system of artifacts.

This development seems to have been initiated by fruitful tensions in early Greek and Christian thought. There can be no doubt that it has brought us an extreme increase in actual knowledge and a high development of the human faculty for discernment and understanding. Yet this progress is ambivalent. It implies a loss in the faculty of perceiving unity, and hence, even within the field of plurality, a loss in harmony and wisdom. It implies danger.

Now there are forebodings of a reversal of this trend. If well understood, such a reversal will not mean the loss of all that has been acquired in positive knowledge during the past thousand years but rather its more adequate understanding. Yet a skeptical reaction to such pronouncements is natural. Similar pronouncements have been made in earlier centuries, most forcefully perhaps by German idealistic philosophy around 1800. Today the view is universally held that this and similar philosophies have always broken down under the impact of ongoing scientific research, historical scholarship, and sociological criticism. One might argue, however, historically that idealistic philosophers like Fichte or Schelling understood a fundamental truth that they were not able to present adequately in the state of evolution of their time's scientific thought. I concentrate instead on one particular but central systematic problem: the unity of the subject of knowledge. I propose the view that a philosophy that is opposite to the modern Western tradition of plurality is the consequence of present-day physics, and that this view offers the only possible solution to the seeming paradoxes of quantum theory.

A brief philosophical essay is not the place where such an argument can be presented in a strict, scholarly manner. I confine myself to indicating the main problem within the context of the evolution of Western philosophy and modern physics.

One might say that the threefold step toward plurality, namely scholasticism-science-industrial revolution, asks for a self-correction in reverse time order.

Industrial revolution seems at first sight only to offer pragmatic problems. It has destroyed one kind of unity and is producing another. It has destroyed the unity in which families, tribes, nations have lived with their environment, that is, the unity of humans with nature; a more penetrating historical analysis, however, teaches us that this particular kind of unity has been a product of human history itself, and also that modern technology may do more radically a work begun by the Neolithic agricultural revolution. The industrial revolution is producing an economic and informational unity of all humankind and thereby posing the problem of its political unity. The philosophical problem behind the political is that humanity can no longer rely on a unity with nature that is unconsciously producing itself. Political unity must be consciously articulated. Who is the subject of this consciousness? It cannot be a world monarch, even if at some time there might be such a monarch. There must be a common understanding of human beings on their common task. Democracy and socialism have made this problem apparent, but they have not solved it. This is the pragmatic aspect of the unity in the subject of knowledge.

The technological revolution is made possible by science. The central science is physics. The central discipline of physics is quantum theory. Quantum theory has been forced to discuss explicitly the role of the observer, that is, of the subject of knowledge. I try to show that this implies a criticism of Descartes' classical description of the relationship between the subject and the object of knowledge. Descartes' philosophy, however, had its presuppositions in the Aristotelian ontology, which he tacitly took over from medieval scholasticism. Hence we will have to criticize this ontology as well. It was meant to replace Platonism. Our starting point must thus be a recollection of Plato's philosophy.

II

Plato's philosophy can be represented as a movement of ascent and subsequent descent, according to the simile of the cave. This ball is round.

It has the shape of a sphere. The sphere is a mathematical form. A form has the characteristics of form, which are: to be, to be understandable ("true"), to be perfect ("good"), to be one. Seeing the ball as round I have a concomitant awareness of the sphere. I understand the sensual thing by my implicit awareness of the form of which it partakes. Mathematical thought means to gain direct awareness of this form. The same step is repeated on a higher level, the level of philosophy. In being aware of a form I have a concomitant awareness of the characteristics of all forms, ultimately of unity itself, of the One. The consummation of the philosophical ascent is the direct awareness of the One. The One is beyond being, since to predicate being of the One would mean to introduce duality into the One. Being, on the other hand, presupposes unity. Thus the one being already contains the fundamental duality of One and being, which irresistibly leads toward the plurality of forms and of the sensual things, which partake in the forms (and which actually are plural forms). To explicitly think this production of plurality is what constitutes the philosophical descent, which finally explains what we had only believed before the ascent. The production of plurality is motion. It originates in the world soul that moves itself and all things. Knowing is the highest form of motion, it is partaking in the one divine intellect. The highest motion is remaining within itself, in this sense staying within unity. Its spatial image is the circle, its temporal image is eternal recurrence. The highest knowledge is knowledge of the unchanging. The perfection of the world is that there is nothing new in it. Science is therefore the understanding of those eternal mathematical forms in which all physical events recur. Astronomy is the highest science, and its consummation is the Platonic year.

Christians who used this philosophy in articulating their theological thought had to take exception to its description of time. They thought of the history of the world as a finite series of events between creation and Judgment Day, with the incarnation of Christ as its center. This description of history was not just an unphilosophical myth. It described the experience of irreversibility. One may say that nobody has promoted history as much as the Christians, who hoped for nothing but the end of history, and their secularized modern successors. This experience was not included in Platonism, and hence the philosophical problems of being and time, and of the unity of time, were not adequately expressed in this philosophy. This is why, I think, Platonism could not remain the philosophical language of Christianity.

The next choice of an authority for the school was Aristotle. Historically, he had been a critical interpreter of Plato's philosophy. The most profound root of his criticism can be found in his assertion that the One cannot be beyond being, and that it must be possible to speak about unity and being as logically as about all other concepts. This leads to a reshuffling of the entire philosophy. Things have their being no longer in the form in which they partake and hence in the One, but in themselves. Every thing is a substance. The divine intellect now becomes a separate highest substance, the one substance not containing matter, that is, not containing unactualized potentiality.

Christian scholastics were forced by the adoption of this system to invent the distinction between philosophy, including natural theology, and revelation, implying the theology of revealed truths. Actually, philosophy was Aristotle, revelation was the Bible. But now such a profoundly philosophical idea as that of trinity (compare Plotinus' triad of the One, the divine intellect and the world soul) was expelled from philosophy into the theology of revelation. Scholasticism gained by this distinction the open field of empirical research on the multitude of substances treated by philosophy. Irreversibility of history, however, did not yet belong to this realm. In the form of the history of salvation, it remained reserved to the theology of revelation.

III

Revolution eats its own children. Thus Aristotelianism was rejected a few centuries later by classical physics for not being empirical enough. Historically this was an error. Aristotle was rather more empirical than Galileo, but Galileo's Aristotelian contemporaries were not. Galileo's real case was the introduction of theoretically preconceived experiments instead of an empirical acceptance of observed natural phenomena. The intellectual tool of the theoretical questions that guided the experiment was mathematics. Galileo agreed with Plato when he said that the book of creation is written in mathematical characters. The philosophical problem of modern science was this: How can the truth of a mathematical theory of nature be justified? This is the stirring problem behind Descartes' philosophy of the subject and the object of knowledge, a philosophy to which we now turn.

Besides God, Descartes distinguishes precisely two substances, *res cogitans* and *res extensa*. This distinction is methodologically founded in the argument of doubt. Once in a lifetime I must cast doubt on everything I believed to know. Will any knowledge resist this doubt? Not the sensual knowledge of the outside world; it may be a dream altogether. Not even the intellectual knowledge of structures, like mathematics; a malicious demon might have created me in such a way that I must constantly believe two times two to be four while in fact it is not so. But no demon can make me believe that I doubt while I am not doubting, that I think while I am not thinking, that I exist while I am not existing. In thought I am aware of my existence. I am a thinking thing, *res cogitans*.

Much as can be said against the accompanying interpretation of this train of thought as expressed in Descartes' wording, nobody can deny that it contains a fundamental insight. There is a knower.[6] Who is the knower?

In Descartes' philosophy it is René Descartes who knows himself, and another knower is any other person who recognizes himself in following Descartes' example. This is a philosophy of a plurality of egos. They are the thinking substances. Aristotle's philosophy of a plurality of substances is here tacitly applied to the knowing subject.

How does Descartes remove the doubt of the existence of other egos and of the material world? He proceeds via a proof of the existence of God, and via a proof of the existence of all we perceive clearly and distinctly because God is veracious and hence will not deceive us. Both proofs rest on the definition of God as the most perfect possible being, as distinct from other less perfect beings, hence again on an Aristotelian concept of a substantial God. The ego that lacks some knowledge and hence is not perfect, has the idea of a most perfect being. This idea, Descartes maintains, depends causally on the true existence of the most perfect being. And God's veracity is an aspect of His perfection. Yet what do we perceive clearly and distinctly that is distinct from ourselves? Only mathematical structures. Hence matter exists insofar as it is defined by a mathematical property, that is, by extension. In this philosophy, matter as extended substance is defined by being knowable. The knower, the ego, knows two things, oneself and the extended knowable. They are distinct since they are defined by different properties, that is, by knowing and by being knowable, respectively.

IV

The details of Descartes' description of subject and object have not withstood the scientific, psychological, and philosophical development of the succeeding centuries. Yet implicitly his view on their relationship is still guiding nearly all modern thought. But his philosophy is too consistent for admitting such a half-hearted acceptance. I will argue that the necessary criticism of its details reveals the impossibility of its very foundations. This can be most clearly seen in the field that he himself had wished to root in unshakable ground, in mathematical physics.

For a complete argument it would be necessary first to criticize Descartes' description of the object, of *res extensa*. His ontological identification of matter and space is an *a priori* description of matter, founded on the epistemological identification of a clear and distinct understanding of things with the special mathematical discipline of geometry. Since Newton's time, physics has rejected the ontological identification. It strictly separated space and matter. In our century, Einstein reintroduced the idea of their close connection. But in the meantime the primitive epistemological identification has broken down. Mathematical description of experience is no longer confined to geometry. It is my personal view that the mathematical structure of quantum theory rests on the simplest, and hence most abstract, description of possible knowledge as formulated in temporal logic. If this view could be defended, one of Descartes' fundamental ideas would turn out to be justified, but in a rather Kantian setting, that is, the mathematical laws of physics would express the way in which plural thinking subjects can have conceptual knowledge at all.

It is impossible to expand on this topic in the present essay. I shall concentrate on the even more fundamental question of how the knower himself is described or presupposed by quantum theory.

V

In very simplified and abstract language one can present the quantum-mechanical description of experiments as follows. Certain facts are known to the observer. They enable one to predict possible events, and to assign probabilities to them. There is then a choice to make an observation in which some event E may possibly happen. The observation is made, and either E happens, and then is a fact, or another event happens, producing the fact that E has not happened. If, however, the observer does not observe at all, it is not, in general, permissible to say that E has actually happened or not, but that it is not known which was the case.

In this description, an event is always an event for an observer, either actually or at least potentially. Those physicists and philosophers who, like Einstein, stick to the Cartesian separation of matter and mind consider this description unacceptable. But they have not so far been able to propose another that would fit the known facts. The present essay takes the opposite view. It fully accepts the quantum-mechanical description and tries to analyze its meaning.

A Cartesian question that is often raised reads, "How is the event actually produced in the observation? Is it produced by the observer's mental act of perception or by his bodily interaction with the observed object?" The correct answer is that the question is wrongly put; the event is produced by the unity of mental and bodily acts. To see this, one must analyze the two alternative answers: (1) It is produced by the bodily interaction without an act of cognizance. (2) It is produced by the mental act of making cognizance distinct from bodily action.

The second answer would go beyond existing physics, which describes only material interaction. This is sufficient to rule out this answer in the first place, not because such a purely mental interaction would be impossible but because the question is a question on the immanent meaning of the physics we actually possess. If answer (2) were correct, physics would essentially presuppose processes that transcend its own scope. In an analysis of an existing science, such an answer would only be admissible as a last resort when all attempts at an immanent interpretation have failed. I should add philosophically that this answer would not overcome but precisely establish the dualism of matter and mind while at the same time making the functioning of material processes immanently incomprehensible. If this were the answer of quantum theory, Einstein's rejection of it would be philosophically well justified.

Answer (1), however, is wrong within quantum theory. If no cognizance is taken of a material situation S, be it in the object of observation or in the body of the observer, then, under the presupposition that quantum theory applies to the situation, the theory predicts probabilities for later events that would be wrong for an observer who has observed the situation S. I refrain from presenting this statement in more technical terms.

In practice, quantum theory evades the problem by replacing the observer with a measuring instrument. But the problem is thereby only removed to an observer who observes the instrument.[7] Let us call the object A, the instrument B, and the observer C. Let us introduce a theorist D who communicates with the observer. How does D know that C observed something, and what was observed?

C will tell D what was observed. Here they rely on communication, effected by physical acts like speaking and listening, writing and reading. Even telepathic communication, if it were to be taken into consideration (which it has not so far been in physics), would probably prove to be testable by physical observations on the bodies of the persons involved. This is at least the assumption with which an immanent interpretation of physics would have to begin as an hypothesis. Physics offers no objection against D's describing C like an ordinary physical object, just the way C describes the instrument B. But at the same time, C and D are partners in life, both belong to the scientific community, they may be friends.[8] D can only describe C in terms of physics if he can also describe himself in terms of physics. Present-day physics certainly does not know whether this might be possible. But the current analysis proceeds on the assumption that it is possible. There is nothing in our existing physics that would exclude this assumption. If the mathematical laws of physics really express the way in which plural subjects can have conceptual knowledge at all, then this assumption would only formulate that there is a degree of conceptual knowledge that we can have about our own being, including one's own person. This is the assumption I try to elucidate throughout this essay.

In quantum theory one might specify the assumption on the following lines. When D describes himself, he will speak of facts in himself that are documents of events that have taken place in himself, and he will speak of possible events in himself that may or may not happen in the future. He will assign probabilities to these possible events out of his knowledge of the facts. What does "in" himself mean? Since we are no longer using the Cartesian distinction, it will mean in his mind and hence in his body; the two answers will only be two different ways of expression. Finally, the distinction between "in his body" and "outside his body" will also break down when we realize that in fundamental physics events are never strictly localized. An event is an extended process, and, in ultimate elementary particle physics, space will probably turn out only to be a "classical" approximation.

Thus far we may be guided by an analysis of quantum theory.

VI

But where then is the knower? I see my own hand. How do I see it? My eye sees it. Materially speaking, my eye is the knower. But there is a unity of the person. I also perceive my hand in feeling warmth, pressure, and pain in it. This perception is called proprioception. Eye and hand are mine. The unity of the ego is physically established by the unity of the body. When my hand is cut away in a surgical operation, it is no longer my hand. A hand is a hand through the unity of its function. The perceiving ego equally is an ego through the unity of its function. It is, so to speak, the unity of the function of the body. If I say that the eye perceives, then I can also say that on a higher level of integration the ego perceives. If I prefer to say that the eye is but an organ of perception, I will be forced to say, by the same argument, that the ego is but an organ of perception (and of volition and something more). Who, then, is the subject? Who is the knower? It seems we have two different ways in which we can speak of perception and more generally of knowledge, one pluralistic, one monistic. In pluralistic language we may call the eye perceiving. We can call the ego perceiving, due to the bodily unity of function. We can call a societal group perceiving, due to the dependence of individual consciousness on the societal interaction in which the ego learned language in the first place, hence concepts, the concept of an identical ego. Perhaps we might say that humankind or life perceive, due to the ultimate unity of history. The monistic way of expression would call all these examples organs on different levels. Is there a way, in this language, of speaking of a knower whose organs they are?

We have now gone very far in criticizing Descartes' conception of the ego. In both ways of expression the ego is not a substance but a function, or rather the unity of some function. This criticism can be combined with critical remarks stemming from empirical psychology. It was a profound philosophical idea that doubt, being an act of thought, cannot draw the fact of thought into doubt. But in Descartes' way of expression this idea was mixed with an acceptance of many aspects of everyday self-observation as certain that may very well be subject to doubt. Modern psychology speaks of subconscious thought and of self-deception that can be revealed as being self-deception by a new step of self-awareness. I have not proceeded far enough to be able to offer a modern anthropology along the lines of such ideas. I rather try to say what remains to be said by referring to some problems in the interpretation of another classical philosophical view of the problem of the knower. It is the view of Kant, which can be introduced in the form of a critique of Descartes' view of the ego.

VII

Kant distinguishes the logical or transcendental subject—both expressions describing the same concept—from the empirical. The empirical subject, "I," is in the way in which I am perceived by myself. The empirical subject is perceived as being in time. Time is the ultimate form of all appearance, while space is the form of appearance of those things that the subject can understand to be different from itself. The empirical subject is "I" who is known, the logical subject is "I" who knows. Logical or transcendental subject is Kant's name for the knower. But how is this theory to be understood? Is it pluralistic? Are there many knowers? This question may admit three ways of interpreting, and finally transcending, Kant's philosophy: (1) The true subject is what Kant calls the intelligible ego, which is the subject of moral decisions in the philosophy of practical reason. (2) The logical subject is logical in not being a real subject but the concept of subjectivity that describes what we mean by "subject" when we speak of the empirical subject. (3) There is one true self who is God. In (1) there would be many nonempirical subjects, in (2) many empirical subjects and no nonempirical, just a concept, in (3) one true subject.

VIII

Kant's theory of the intelligible subject in the *Critique of Practical Reason* seems to be the result of a metaphysical difficulty produced by classical physics. Practical reason in Kant's sense rests on the categorical imperative, which commands the universality of moral principles. Universality here, as in the theoretical field, is the index of reason. An imperative presupposes freedom. No command can be meaningfully given to one who is not free to decide. Freedom can never be empirically tested. Moreover, the empirical subject, according to Kant, is subject to classical causality, which renders its acts necessary. Hence freedom must be a quality of a nonempirical subject. Since I apply the imperative to myself, I deem myself to be free. Hence there are at least as many nonempirical subjects as there are living persons.

This theory runs into insoluble difficulties since it uses my empirical knowledge of myself for defining my nonempirical self. Kant's own ultimate struggle with these difficulties is seen in his late book *Religion within the Limits of Pure Reason*. I confine myself here to saying that imperatives are meaningful precisely within the empirical life of persons, that is, in time. They are a way of defining and limiting possibilities, that is, the future. Self-interpretation of personal freedom is a behavior with respect to my future. It is nonempirical in the sense in which the future is not past, and the past does not reveal that other possibilities than those that have come to pass were real possibilities. Hence I shall not pursue the path of the *Critique of Practical Reason*.

IX

Let us assume the logical subject to be the concept of a subject. This concept then must be a "true" concept. A true concept would be a concept describing a structure of reality that actually exists.[9] The structure that thus corresponds to the concept one would call the Platonic form, whose mental picture is the concept. In this sense the logical subject is not really the concept of a subject but the form of "subject." It is that structure of reality that makes subjects possible.

But if we interpret physics as we did above, abandoning Cartesian dualism, there is no difference of substance between the empirical subjects and the empirical objects. Whatever can be empirically known, can act as an organ of empirical knowledge, hence as part of a unity that can be called a subject. In this sense the ultimate structure that makes subjects possible is being itself. Physics, staying within plurality, will have to describe the multitude of empirical subjects. In this enterprise it will have to presuppose that being is such as to make empirical subjects possible in the form of functioning units in time. Physics cannot explain subjectivity, but we have learned that it must presuppose it. Then physics can describe the functioning of subjects as far as this can be described in the language of concepts.

We said that the transcendental subject is the form of subject and that this form is being itself. We are thus led back to the question in which philosophy such statements are meaningful.

Kant calls the self-distinction of the subject as knower and as known the ultimate of philosophy, beyond which thought does not penetrate. One may add that this distinction produces time and number, which belong together in Kant's and Brouwer's view.[10] If the knower is understood to be one subject among others, he is brought into the realm of what is conceptually known. This reduces him to the empirical subject. Facts, constituting the past, are what can be known. They are the basis of possibilities, that is, of knowledge of the future. Concepts are generalized possibilities. This is how the known makes knowledge possible, how the knower may know himself as factual (memory) and possible (anticipation). But the plurality within which concepts are meaningful presupposes a unity, of which there is a concomitant awareness in every concept of which we are aware as being a concept. This unity is depicted in physics as the unity of time.

This philosophy is not Platonism insofar as historical time—as described by the difference of facts and possibilities—is not thematic in Plato's essentially cyclical understanding of time. Still, we are led toward the same problem field that Plato treated in his own way. The dialectic of Plato's *Parmenides* is reproduced in the modern situation. There is a concomitant awareness of unity in every concept, but unity itself cannot be directly described by concepts, since this would make it dependent on plurality, while plurality, as described in concepts, rests on the concomitant unity.

Quantum theory goes even beyond this ancient Platonic argument. Plurality is not basically true. The concept of a separate object is only an approximation in quantum theory, and even a bad one. Mathematically speaking, the Hilbert space of a composite object only contains a set of measure zero of states in which a particular division of this object into parts is real. In the language used in this essay we may say that separate objects are defined by facts. Facts are the facts they are by way of the possibilities they constitute. Facts are irreversible, but irreversibility in a separate object is only lack of knowledge of the coherence (the "phase relations") of reality. If there is an ultimate reality, it is unity. From the point of view of this unity, objects are objects only for finite subjects (that is, for subjects lacking some possible knowledge), and finite subjects are finite in existing under the conditions that define objects (that is, they are minds under bodily conditions). Objects and finite subjects are such for finite subjects only. This does not seem far from what the Advaita doctrine calls *māyā*.

X

The self is beyond plurality. The considerations of this essay constitute a few steps on a ladder of ascent. They tend to show that the ascent is not necessarily promoted by leaving the questions of physics aside, but rather by unswervingly pursuing them.

There is a tendency in human thought, and especially in Western thought, to take the human person as an ultimate reality. This is not always egoism. It is also the attitude of fundamental ethics that does not permit taking anything more seriously than the other person. It can be a venerable attitude. Yet Christians, like Hindus, are rightly told that we cannot truly love our neighbor if we do not love our neighbor in God. It can be said that ascent is *eros* and descent is *agape*, but one must add that ascent will be *agape* craving its own possibility. I dedicate this essay to Sri Chandrasekharendra Saravati, Shankaracharya of Kanchi. I once had the honor of seeing him, and I shall never forget the silent, knowing look of his eye.

2. The Reflection of the Back of the Mirror

A. The Ontology of Science

Konrad Lorenz wrote: "Still the realist looks only outwards and is not aware of being a mirror himself. Still the idealist looks only *into* the mirror and turns his back to the reality of the external world. Both perspectives prevent them from seeing that the mirror has a nonreflecting back, a side that puts it in line with the real things that it reflects: The physiological apparatus whose task is the recognition of the real world is not less real than the world itself. This book is about the back of the mirror."[11]

For the biology of the subject, we are decisively indebted to behavioral research, especially that of Lorenz. Before we use this information, we should ascertain the philosophical perspective from which we read it. This philosophy differs from that of Lorenz in only one, certainly decisive, additional thought. Fundamentally, it also holds that science regards the back of the mirror as an image seen in the mirror. The biology of the subject is made by subjects, and is subordinate, under all conditions, to its subjectivity. This thought is so simple that it seems impossible to substantiate or elucidate it through further arguments. Even a biologist cannot deny it. The philosophical problem concerns only the conclusions to be drawn from it.

First, I indicate which conclusion I do not intend to draw from it. It will in no way be the basis of a mind-body dualism. This should be evident already from the thoughts in the chapter on the knower in physics. I will only indicate why I agree with the monism of biologists, at least in the sense of a working hypothesis that is eminently plausible to me. Foremost is the historical fact of the extraordinary achievements of biology as a science. This fact presents a twofold philosophical challenge. There is the question if there exists a simple and conclusive philosophical explanation for such achievements. We are also urged to examine philosophically the philosophical objections raised against such an extensive hypothesis, against its "reductionism."

Is there a philosophical explanation for the striking success of biology as a science? Methodological considerations such as those employed in contemporary scientific theory are manifestly unable to do so; they also make no claim of doing so. An ontological hypothesis that attempts an explanation is scientific monism, which is often called materialism by its adherents, and usually by its adversaries: Everything in the world, even the organisms, even we, consist of *one* kind of substance. The laws that this substance follows are formulated by physics. Therefore, everything in organic life can be described according to the laws of physics. Lorenz also adopted this view, and because he is aware of its hypothetical character (in the sense of the word "hypothetical" that is still subject to critical examination), he terms it hypothetical realism. This ontology places before its own philosophical problem only one other, the problem of body-soul, which is certainly in its framework an unsolvable problem: "The great hiatus between the objective-physiological and the subjective experience" cannot be bridged over with a better knowledge of evolution, it is "in this regard another kind in that it is not conditioned on a gap in our knowledge, but rather *a priori*, the basic incapacity to know that results from the structure of our cognition apparatus." This position, though, is confronted with two philosophical objections, one rather metaphysical and the other resulting from the theory of cognition.

The metaphysical objection sees the higher reduced to the lower, spirit reduced to matter, it sees the natural scientists appearing in the human realm as "colonial masters." I consider this objection as the weaker of the two, actually only a misunderstanding. The difference between the higher and lower structures is phenomenologically a reality (in Lorenz it appears in the form of Nicolai Hartmann's "layers"), but it is formulated in a theoretical information concept of physics, and is familiar in contemporary systems theory, which in its rudiments is also "reductionist." Lorenz himself describes the transition from the conformities of one layer to those of a higher layer through the merging of several specific systems into one comprehensive system as "fulguration," the lightninglike emergence of a new structure. Somewhat different is the relationship between spirit and matter. Here many adherents of physical reductionism enter, with pleasure, into conflict with the fundamental Platonic experience of ascension. Through "a transformation of the entire soul," according to Plato in the *Republic*, humans should free themselves of the illusion that the shadows on the wall are reality. Spiritual reality is to be striven for; material appearance is a delusion. Lorenz's anti-idealistic fervor is directed against the customary understanding of this ascent, which he considers to have been Plato's opinion, too. Vice versa, without the fervor of those who desire this ascent, the origins and existence of dualistic philosophies could probably not be understood at all.

Just because of this, it is worth the effort to realize that Plato himself, in any case, was anything but a dualist. The shadows on the wall of the cave are the sensory perceptions, and the first turn that leads back to the real objects in the cave is exactly the turn of science to the not directly perceived objects of physics, including the back of the mirror. Plato begins like Lorenz. These objects, it is true, are not what the materialistic scientist considers them to be, they are, actually, mathematical forms, almost like those in contemporary theoretical physics. The mathematical forms, in turn, are actually what Plato calls ideas. Now begins the descent, the theory of ideas in the strict sense. The ideas first make clear what mathematical forms are, these, what physical bodies are, and those, what sensory impressions of things are, thus always further into ideas released into multiplicity. The reason this philosophy appears as a conceptual notion lies in the difficulty in understanding the metaphor "in the cave," the ontology of ideas, their way of being. "We," especially the average twentieth-century mind, are familiar with mathematical forms and ideas only as contents of human consciousness. Accordingly, Lorenz is seduced by the fantastic speculation that Plato had considered all real things as mere contents of human consciousness. The subject that thinks ideas, if there is such a subject, is not the empirical human ego, but, at least in neo-Platonism, the divine *nus*. It is not the intention of these observations to defend Platonic metaphysics, but only to assert the argument that metaphysics drafted in the spirit of the greatest metaphysicist do not need the dualistic criticism of monistic science that Lorenz represents. Plato can tolerate Lorenz. He could even accept him.

The theory of cognition presents more difficult objections. In the science of our century, particularly in theoretical physics, we have learned to mistrust questions whose principle unanswerability is obvious and to ask if such questions make sense at all or are merely the consequence of vaguely defined concepts. I find this suspicion, for instance, in Lorenz's version of the body-mind problem. Lorenz himself, whose phenomenological instinct is often better than his philosophy, points out with good reason that what he postulated as the "impenetrable partition between body and mind" exists "only in our mind and not in our feelings." "In spite of all rational reasoning, we are unable to doubt the fundamental unity of body and mind." It is a reasonable assumption that it is not our "mind" but a philosophy that we have learned that draws this partition against what we are feeling. But, for the time being, let us leave it at that. More important is the objection against Lorenz's concept of reality.

Lorenz evidently believes that there are realists and idealists and that the realists consider the outside as real while the idealists consider it mere idea. Because there is obviously no empirical decision possible between two such defined positions (the decisive empirical fact would for the realist again be real and for the idealist mere imagination), Lorenz terms his realism a hypothesis. In science, however, a hypothesis is usually at least subjected to empirical controls. I suggest instead that the words used here, "real" and "reality," are meaningless words whose complete elimination changes nothing whatsoever in all positive findings of science. This should become clear if we consider that reality of which we can know is reality for us, and that reality of which we cannot know can, per definition, not exist in our knowledge. If we talk about reality in a meaningful way, then *we* are talking about reality. If no one talks about reality, then reality is not being discussed. If awareness is a mirror, then we know the back of the mirror, only mirrored. This does not mean that things are only ideas, because we can very well distinguish between a thing only imagined and one that is observed or observable. The reason for the embarrassing impression that is caused by arguing about these apparent trivialities is that behind them are unresolved, nontrivial structures awaiting clarification. And here Lorenz's questions are again fully justified.

The popular version of "idealism," therefore of philosophy, emphasizes the subjectivity of all knowledge and believes, therefore, that things that I know are "as such" unknown to me, but that I myself am known to myself. In truth, however, one has then to learn from Kant that also the ego does not empirically know itself better than it knows the things, just in accordance with its perceptual forms and categories. But with that, the boundary between the empirically known subject and the empirically known object loses its metaphysical status. They are dependent upon each other (Kant's "Refutation of Idealism" in the second edition of the *Critique of Pure Reason*). It is thus completely legitimate to state that one learns to understand the ego better if one understands it as a material entirety (Kant in *Opus Postumum*). That means that the way to Lorenz's entire complex of questions is then open. Only the misconception that the empirical ego is the irreducible center of knowledge prevents us from taking this direction.

But the actual power of this consideration becomes evident only if we question once again the previously assumed ontological explanation of the universal validity of physics. If we examine the assumption of a universal substance with the same skeptical theory of cognition, then it does not appear anymore as a hypothesis, but rather as a tautology. We cannot characterize the properties of "matter" except by the laws of physics that it obeys. Therefore existence of a universal matter and universal validity of physics are two synonymous assertions. The first does not explain the second but, on the contrary, repeats it. Can we make the universal validity of physics comprehensible, or do we simply have to believe it? I follow here Kant's thinking that the basic laws of physics formulate the conditions of the possibility of experience. Lorenz also uses Kant's thoughts, but in another sense than I. The two applications of these thoughts do not exclude but compliment each other. Lorenz proceeds from Kant's observation that we have knowledge *a priori*, which we obviously cannot have obtained from individual experience. The most important example for him is our perception of space, that is, our capacity to have geometric understanding *a priori*. Kant concludes that we gain *a priori* knowledge obviously not through the affection of the objects, that it, therefore, cannot teach us anything about how the objects as such might be constituted. Lorenz points out that this argument is not conclusive. Kant postulates here a naive empirical theory of cognition and refutes only this one. Whoever knows modern evolution theory has no difficulty in attributing to species innate ways of behavior that have been learned through adaptation.[12] (What is meant by "learning through adaptation" will be explained more precisely in section B of this chapter). But one must then expect that the selection has led exactly to the survival of behavior that is well adapted to reality, to "things as they are as such." According to Lorenz we do not know much about the "objective outside world," namely, all that possible knowledge that had not given selective advantage to our ancestors in the struggle for existence; but what we know, especially what we know innately, we can surely trust, because if this knowledge were not trustworthy, then we, the descendants of victors in the struggle for existence, would not exist at all. This argument is powerful and will not be challenged here. There is no use in basing the objective validity of physics on the conditions of the possibility of experience; we should, instead, base our capacity to have experience and, therefore, our belief in physics, on the objective validity of physics, on the structures of the "real external world." It is thus an anti-Kantian application of the Kantian *a priori*.

My tendency in philosophical thought remains closer to Kant. If the logical train of Lorenz's thought is all there is to say about Kant's *a priori*, then the laws of physics could have any arbitrary form. If they are valid as laws, therefore always valid, then the organisms will adapt to them and acquire a corresponding innate knowledge. I am trying to emphasize those conditions without which we absolutely cannot imagine any experience, and to determine from them the contents of the laws of physics. What is presupposed here is essentially the structure of time in its various modes—present, future, and past—and the possibility of conceptual thinking in general. What results is a still not completely fixed version of the quantum theory. For the quantum theory, as it is described in the preceding chapter, the subjectivity of all knowledge is fundamental. The "objective external world" that is independent of the subject is seen in the quantum theory as only the so-called classical extreme case. We have no reason to be surprised if it becomes apparent that organisms have innate knowledge precisely about this extreme case, because "objective" in the sense employed here is exactly that upon which several subjects can agree.

According to this concept of physics, an image of what we call reality can only be drawn, if at all, in a circle. Nature is older than humankind, humankind is older than science. Humanity, the child of nature, owes its origins to adaptation to nature; Lorenz describes these under the heading of the back of the mirror. Through the human being's adaptations and its cultural inventions, it practices science, through science it reflects nature. Even concepts like "nature," "reality," and "knowledge" make sense only within human knowledge. These mirror concepts (reflection concepts) were necessary to be able to form, at all, concepts like "adaptation," "mirror," and "back of the mirror." In each of the two semicircles, the results of the other semicircle were used previously in an abridged form only. The quantum physicist, just as the transcendental philosopher, presupposes the nature of the cognitive subject to be such as he knows it in educated people and in the culture of modern Western civilization, and observes subtly what kind of knowledge can be possessed by subjects that are thus constituted by nature. The biologist and behavioral scientist presupposes the knowledge of nature that supplies one with essentially classical physics that has not been philosophically reflected upon, and studies in all details how the animal and human subjects have learned to adapt themselves to this nature. This book, too, is not yet able to join the two semicircles. The theme of this book is not a description of nature on the level of quantum theory and transcendental philosophy. It studies the human being as a child of nature, and in doing so presumes a concept of nature that is deliberately vague. In this manner, I have no difficulty in applying the mode of thought used in behavioral research.

Finally, one has to examine if the mind-body problem, with this method of thinking, is as impenetrable as it is to Lorenz. First, no new positive knowledge is contributed, only a philosophical principle. If we now enter the circle at the place of transcendental philosophy, we start with the assumption that there are, in any case, cognitive subjects, humans, and we maintain that for them everything of which they have objective experience, everything that is conceptual experience in time, has to obey the laws of physics because these laws are the conditions for possible objective experience. What obeys these laws is what we call matter. From the nature so described, human subjects have historically emerged. As much as they can obtain from themselves objective experience, they can describe themselves as objects of physics. But this does not eliminate, at any time, their knowledge that they are subjects, thus conscious. Lorenz has stated, phenomenologically exactly, in the above quoted sections that our spontaneous knowledge cannot let go of the identity of "body" and "mind." What happens in detail when conscious subjects develop through evolution, and how the image of their environment and of themselves emerges, is still unknown. This is exactly what we now want to begin to examine. In any case, the two Cartesian "substances" are only methodical positions. They are reality seen once as "subject" and once as "object." And the quantum theory teaches us that both positions describe merely approximations. The old metaphysical rule that nature is spirit in a form that does not recognize itself as spirit describes a horizon within which everything that science has previously been able to recognize has a place—a place that it did not previously reach with its positive knowledge. Each plateau of progressing knowledge is a plateau limited by questions that are formulated by its concepts but remain unanswerable with these same concepts. The mind-body problem may be such a problem to the thought patterns of classical physics and, therefore, to biology as Lorenz understands it.

B. Evolution As a Process of Cognition

Lorenz titles the first chapter of his book, "Life As a Process of Cognition." I have chosen here a title that is more reticent, but merely with respect to method. I compare evolution only with those processes that we designate as cognition in the specific sense that pertains to the most highly developed organisms.

One can define cognition as the formal acquisition of information. The philosophical question is, then, what we mean by "information." To be able to answer this question better, it is necessary to describe, in some detail, the formal structure by means of which the acquisition of information through evolution coincides with cognition in a narrower sense. Here we cannot follow, step by step, the presentation of Lorenz without writing another book. Popper[13] has recently given a brief and challenging sketch of this structure, which we can use to orient ourselves. I quote a few passages.

Popper proceeds from "the notion of *instruction* and of *selection*": "From a biological or evolutionary point of view, science, or progress in science, may be regarded as a means used by the human species to adapt itself to the environment: to invade new environmental niches, and even to invent new environmental niches . . . We can differentiate three levels of adaptations: genetic adaptation, adaptive behavior, and scientific discovery, the latter being a special case of adaptive behavioral learning . . . My main thesis asserts the *fundamental similarity of the three levels* as follows. On all three levels—genetic adaptation, adaptative behavior, and scientific discovery—the mechanism of adaptation is fundamentally the same.

"Adaptation starts from an inherited *structure*, which is basic for all three levels: *the gene structure of the organism*. To it corresponds, on the behavioral level, *the innate repertoire* of the types of behavior that are available to the organism, and on the scientific level, *the dominant scientific conjectures or theories*. These *structures* are always transmitted by *instruction*, on all three levels: by the replication of the coded genetic instruction on the genetic and the behavioral levels, and by social tradition and imitation on the behavioral and the scientific levels. On all three levels the *instruction* comes from *within the structure*. If mutations, variations, or errors occur, then these are new instructions, which also arise *from within the structure* rather than *from without*, from the environment.

"These inherited structures are exposed to certain pressures, or challenges, or problems: to selection pressures, to environmental challenges, to theoretical problems. In response, variations of the genetically or traditionally inherited *instructions* are produced by methods that are, at least partly, *random*. On the genetic level, these are mutations and recombinations of the coded instruction. On the behavioral level, they are tentative variations and recombinations within the repertoire. On the scientific level, they are new and revolutionary tentative theories. On all three levels we get new tentative trial instructions or, briefly, tentative trials.

"The next stage is that of *selection* from the available mutations and variations: Those of the new tentative trials that are badly adapted are eliminated. *This is the stage of the elimination of error.* . . . Thus we may speak of *adaptation by 'the method of trial and error'* or better, by 'the method of trial and the elimination of error.' . . . It operates on all three levels."

Popper discusses only the manifest differences between the three levels and then turns to his main theme, the rationality of scientific revolutions. Scientific theory does not lie within the scope of the present book. We observe only those points that he draws from the comparison of evolution with science, because, in the reverse explanatory direction, they are a contribution to comprehending the cognition formation of evolution. "All this is part of the critical approach to science, as opposed to the inductivist approach; or of the Darwinian or eliminationist or selectionist approach as opposed to the Lamarckian approach, which operates with the idea of *instruction from without*, or from the environment, while the critical or selectionist approach only allows *instruction from within* the structure itself. In fact, I contend that *there is no such thing as instruction from without the structure*, or the passive reception of a flow of information that impresses itself on our sense organs. All observations are theory impregnated: There is no pure, disinterested, theory-free observation." "A new revolutionary theory functions exactly like a new and powerful sense organ."

His thesis that theories can empirically be falsified only, but not verified, was originally based on logical arguments. A sentence that has the logical form of the universal is empirically contradicted if there is an opposite example, but is empirically proven only if all of the possible single examples can be demonstrated, an impossible undertaking. Now Popper brings a biological, even empirical, argument that structurally strengthens the thesis. The question is how both of these arguments relate to each other in their cognition-theory valence. In the usual hierarchical order of science, logic is primary. Popper says: "What is true in logic, is true in psychology" (as quoted by Lorenz). This simple rule leaves out the other half of the circle, namely the question of what truth means in logic, and how it, from the historical-anthropological perspective, can arrive at something like logic. That one can also attack this last question as a scientific question, through application of the already existing logic, does not justify the hierarchy. Rather, it is only an example of Popper's previously mentioned thesis: Logic is also a kind of powerful "sense organ," a "closed theory" in the sense of Heisenberg, that teaches us to see phenomena and, at the same time, is aware of its eventual replacement by an advanced future theory.

Popper's new points appear to me now to amount to the following. His old argument made use of the historical fact that science presents its convictions in the logical form of the universal. Why does it to do this? Could it not more simply just tell of the experienced? On the contrary, one could always say that it has then no prognostic power and, accordingly, no practical use. This can be formulated more precisely. If there are instructions from within, then every cognition apparatus has to prepare the form, a definite structure that can react to the previously mostly unknown environmental stimuli. It has, therefore, logically observed, its essence according to the form of the universal. That applies, logically speaking, not only to judgments, but also to concepts. Therefore, science without the form of the universal could not tell its experiences because it explains them with concepts.

In this section on evolution as a process of cognition, we do not yet select evolution as a means to elaborate on human cognition; rather, we select cognition as a means to elaborate on evolution. Cognition accomplishes, in accordance with the classical definition of truth, the adaptation of consciousness to the facts (*veritas est adaequatio intellectus ad rem*). Hence, we find a rule about evolution that can be generalized: Organic evolution is the adaptation of the genetic code, and of the behavior made possible through it, to the facts. In this objective sense, evolution is acquisition of information, and the acquisition of information was our original definition of cognition. The only questions now is: What do we understand by information, truth, and adaptation when extending these concepts from subjective knowledge to objective behavior?

C. Information, Adaptation, Truth

For a philosophy that would explain these three concepts with precision, this entire book is only propaedeutic, only a collection of anthropological materials. Even for an adequately broad exposition of the philosophical problem within the framework of evolution theory, I have to refer the reader to other essays. From these, I will here include and specify only a few formulations.

First of all, information exists only for humans. Shannon's definition of information emerges from the theory of communication systems, especially the telegraph. This system relays messages from human to human. Only for a person who can read does the telegram contain the information that is quantifiable according to Shannon's rule. For example, only a person who can read will identify the letter *e* in each word as the same letter. For a fly wandering around on the printed telegram, these spots of printer's ink contain completely different information values.

The modern concept of information, however, contains the tendency of objectification, of detachment from the subject. The first step is the observation that the theory of communication systems is not concerned with the understanding of a single subject but with the communication between several subjects. The same sequence of letters contains, for everyone who can read them, the same quantity of information (on the syntactic, not necessarily the semantic, level). The second step then is to replace the already exchangable subjects functioning as sender and receiver with apparatuses. Now that means: Information exists for a sender *or* receiver. In the third step, one can then attempt to apply this concept of information to organisms that are not apparatuses constructed by humans. The receivers that receive environmental information and, in communication between organs or organisms, also the senders, are now organs. Their emergence is described selectively. With that we are at the evolutionary formation of knowledge.

In this a difference is to be observed that is not emphasized by Popper, but that plays a decisive role in Lorenz's statement. It is the difference between permanent acquisition of information through the creation of new structures and acquisition of temporary information that cannot be stored. Many important organs react to unstorable temporary information. Also, for example, the telegraph, to which we owe the concept of information. It processes continual information without changing itself structurally. That the printed telegram is also storable is not essential to the telegraph, which could also just give accoustic signals. The emergence of organs that achieve exactly this is, in itself, already a relatively high achievement of evolution. The evolution of the first, preorganic, complex molecules and of the primitive DNA-protein synthesis in the most elementary organisms can be interpreted as acquisition of information without the existence of organs for the actual processing of the information. But for a more precise definition of the concept of information we must observe, through models, the organs that receive, but do not necessarily store, the actual information, such as the sense organs combined with the innate motor reactions to the impulses received by the sense organs.

Information thus exists *for a receiver*, or for a sender-receiver pair. Sender and receiver may be organs or apparatuses. What does the word "for" mean in this context? We assume the receiver has no awareness, or at least no reflection. But we can say that information exists *for that receiver*. The scientific justification for *us* saying that there exists information for that receiver can be indicated in the statement that information exists only through a concept. This applies certainly to information for humans. The same telegram text contains completely different types of information depending on the possible concept by which we understand it, as a sequence of letters of the Latin alphabet, as a sequence of words of the English language, or as a report on the results of a presidential election. The same chromosome contains different information depending on whether one looks at it as an organic chain of molecules or as a gene carrier for a species. It is the same with the information for an organ. This is only defined after *we* have specified the *function* of the organ and can thereby determine the quantity of yes-no decisions relevant to this function. Then we can specify that the organ represents exactly the concept of this function objectively, independent of our judgment, through its structure and its thereby produced results. Organs are, if I may express it this way, objective concepts. This observation, of course, leads us to the question of whether, in the phenomenology of our own process of cognition, we actually know what we perceive to be a concept.

Information for the really functioning organ exists only as long as it lives *as* an organ. The functioning organ exists within a context of functions. One may say then that it is never only a receiver but, on the basis of received information, also a sender. In that way we can justify the statement that *information is only what produces information.*

What does all this have to do with the concept of truth? Information exists only through a concept. When an organ sends the information, then *we* can translate the objective semantics of this message into *our* language in such a way that we claim the organ had communicated: "An example of my concept occurs." Or, to say the same thing differently: "An occurrence has taken place that falls within my concept." "My concept" is therefore the concept defined by us through our understanding of the function *of* the organ. In that way we allow the organ to speak metaphorically of *its* concept. The message of the organ, therefore, has to be expressed in *our* language, in the form of a judgment, a statement. The perception itself has a predicative structure. This last statement, however, exceeds the preceding one in that it claims at the same time to indicate the logical form of the opinion, a thesis that we do not apply for the present. Statements can only be true or false. The above quoted definition of truth, which ultimately originates in Aristotle, is about the truth of statements. Thus, the message of an organ is something that *for us* can be true or false. For us it is a judgment.

This evaluation of the organ's message as a judgment is an achievement of our reflection. Here we compare the message of the organ with certain achievements of which we ourselves are capable. The organism is not capable of reflection. It normally cannot judge the messages of its sense organs as true or false. In the overwhelming majority of cases even we cannot judge our own sensory perceptions and conclusions in respect to their truth or falseness, we merely accept them. We accept them, so to speak, spontaneously as true. The German word *wahrnehmen* (to perceive) expresses this nicely: It means, literally translated, "to accept as true." Nevertheless, there exists an objective sense in which the messages from the organs prove themselves as true or false also *for the organism* or for the species, namely, by its success, its selection value. What is thereby examined objectively is, however, not the individual message of an organ, but the unit of actions to which it belongs as one part of a chain. A pragmatic concept of truth can attribute the predicates "right" and "wrong" only to entire actions. There are two important divergences from a concept of truth referring to individual statements. First, the individual action is not right or wrong just because it is successful or fails, because its success or failure can be caused by accidental circumstances. What is right or wrong is the scheme of action the animal follows again and again, thus something universal. Secondly, the action is not an *image* of the environment, but its adequacy according to the facts is an adaptation, a fitting like that of a key in a lock.

Human action and thinking distinguishes itself from this simple scheme mainly through the capacity of conception, of symbolic representation, which receives its extraordinary reinforcement through language. I dare assume, however, that exactly these two above-mentioned divergences from the usual description of the truth of the individual statement survive in human thinking. If thinking in its origins is an acting of conception, then it is the primarily universal, thus conceptual, and therefore supplies primarily no image of the reality, but an image of what we do with reality, an image of our acting. The conception of reality as being "as such," just as the perception of the individual *as* individual, is then a further superior achievement of thinking, an artifact, a product of culture.

3. The Rationality of Emotions

A. The Concept of Interest

What leads us to inquire about the rationality of emotions? Perhaps, at first, skepticism about the usual view of their irrationality. This view likes to pair the concepts of rational-irrational.

What do we mean by that? If one says about people that they behaved rationally, one means, perhaps, that their behavior complied with two conditions: (1) One can give fairly accurate information about the causes of one's behavior, and (2) in view of one's own interest and of the interpersonal values, one can feel somewhat compatible with one's own behavior. In Habermas' diction, it could be defended in a practical discourse.

Condition (2) contains two criteria: personal interest, and interpersonal values. Common and perhaps even dominant, however, is a rational pattern of behavior in a limited sense. People acting with complete consciousness realize their own interests even in opposition to interpersonal values of which they are aware and which they do not oppose. We could call this mode of behavior "rational interest." It is not completely rational insofar as it contains the pending conflict between our interests and established values. One can even maintain that a function of the public acknowledgment of interpersonal values is, at first, at least to maintain this conflict and not always to give in to private interests. The conflict is also a conflict of the personal interest with itself because the interpersonal values reflect the interests of the community whose well-being is a condition for the well-being of the individual. If the individual thinks rationally, one has to modify one's understanding of one's own interests to adjust to those of the community interest. Here we see the bottomless nature of a purely empirical concept of interest based on the opinion of the individual. Its contents depend upon a judgment that might be modified after further reflection. The question arises as to what is the real interest of both the individual and the community. Even if the individual convinces himself, as is usually the case, that pursuit of one's own interests serves as well the common interest, he argues with a concept of the real interest of the community.

If one observes the real effects of rational interest behavior, including the destruction of the environment, and wars caused by powerful interest groups, then it does not seem an exaggeration to speak of *the irrationality of the rational*. Perhaps one should more precisely state that the practical mind needs this practical rationality, this conceptual thought of interest as a perception of whole that first makes recognizable the real interests of the individual and the group. In the light of this analysis, condition (1), above, reveals its meaning. What criterion do we have for determining if we understand the reasons for our own behavior?

One direction in conflict research finds the reason for conflicts, or at least their insolvability, in the irrational motives of our actions. These motives, such as aggression and fear, are certainly important. But one can understand their importance only if one recognizes that they are deviations from sensible behavior. One could term the next goal of understanding in this context, 'the insight into *the rationality of the irrational.*' Sensible "irrational" behavior can be called a perception of reality without concept. Animal behavior is certainly like this. But in human culture, conceptless perception of reality plays an even greater role of which interest rationality is aware. The rationally unavoidable perception of self-interest is a good example. But also the rational rationalization of individual interest as the real interest is based on a highly differentiated conceptless, or not fully conceptualized, perception.

At this point, a brief look at a contemporarily neglected range of experience might be useful. The most explosive interests may be identifiable by the fact that we work hard to control them. The most obvious and most symbolic renunciation of interest is probably that of the mendicant friars. The three monastic vows are: poverty, obedience, and chastity, or renunciation of property, of domination, and of sexuality. Of course these are also the most explosive interests.

B. Place and Action (Possession, Domination, Power)

The human being is a living being. Every living being is a body. Every body is a place. A person needs at least one place.

Life is a process. To this process belongs at least metabolism, consequently nourishment. The higher animals get their nourishment by moving within a territory. A human also has to move. We call his movement action if it is meaningfully coordinated. One's place is not only one's respective place of residence, it is also the necessary territory for one's activities.

Higher animals usually live in societies. The absolute minimum requirement is temporary socialization of the sexes necessary for mating. Society is fundamental for humans because we owe to society the wealth of behavior that we exhibit in language and customs, without which we could not live. For social life this treasure of behavioral patterns in respect to other members of the species is fundamental. This first gives the individual a "place" in the society that is also territory for acting. Because of this analogy, I entitle this section with the abstractions of place and action.

The elementary *possession*, which already exists in animal societies, is itself a place; the ecologist would call it territory. Behavioral scientists have shown us that a fish bravely defends its territory, and they inform us that the male nightingale sings so that others know which is its territory and refrain from entry. It appears fundamental that evaluation of the human grasp at possessions must include a very long animal prehistory of territorial possession.

Territory possession is the animal habitat. Territoriality, however, is not universal with animals; but it is a usually acquired behavior pattern. The territory commonly does not belong to the individual but to the social group and sometimes, in a distinct sense, to its leader. The readiness for territorial behavior is always present in humans. The transition from the cultural forms of gatherer, hunter, nomad, farmer, urban dweller only give different forms to the disposition of land, as does the varying size of the group that participates in the possession. It is rather a simplification when some social theories assume that at one time the most powerful divided what had been common to all into private property. The historical process vacillates between both tendencies. Especially at the highest levels of culture, and accordingly individualization, there is recognition of property held in common as an achievement of a society that imposes on its members a high standard of asceticism. I believe that humankind's ability to renounce landed property is possible only if one has another home, an unquestioned place in the society, or a spiritual existence.

The second form of property, that of things, has only minor precedents in animal life. In humans it is related to the capacity for methodical action. The first tangible possession of things is a means to an end: food supplies, tools, weapons. What is fundamental here is not habitation, thus existence, but ability. To be able means to be able whenever one wants, accordingly power. With power, probably the most important ambivalent attribute enters the picture. I pass over the "territorial" relationship that extends also to one's own tools, to one's own furniture, as well as the dominant power function of real property as it exists in advanced power structures. I rather seek to approach the phenomenon of power in a direct and abstract way. To do so, it is first necessary to differentiate between power and domination.

Social hierarchy among members of the same species and domination over members of the same species is as common among higher animals as is possession. One can say that these relationships of domination and subordination are fundamental to animal societies with generally individualized relationships between their members. As far as humankind has been determined by its animal heritage, this is valid for humans, too. It is again an optical illusion of certain social theories to maintain that domination and hierarchy are the result of power that is contrary to nature. Through nature and custom, the human being has been conditioned to secure his or her social standing exactly by knowing who is above and who is below. It is an extraordinary historical effort and achievement, where it succeeds, when people indeed recognize each other as equal. Later we must ask how this achievement is possible at all.

Animal societies, and also human societies to the extent that they have similar dominant traits, I will call simple societies or actual societies. Let us imagine someone who knew only such societies and who was then introduced to the realm of power. He would find himself confronted with completely strange phenomena not deducible from his previously existing knowledge, and with a new level of behavior. Despite the continual quarrel over hierarchy and possession, they existed within the narrow limits of the actuality of being and having. Now, though, one is confronted by the essentially unlimited realm of ability or power. I use the term power here as discovered potentiality. Potentiality is never completely and definitively realized. Complete realization means the end of the potential. Power is principally understood as the ability to do what one wants to do and as not having to do all that of which one is capable. That such a realm of possibility exists at all is a discovery, and it belongs in this respect under the heading of insight, but it can be observed here already as an isolated factor.

Power through tools, hunting weapons, and habitation is, at first, power over nature. I am not referring now to the well known exterior process of humankind's seizure of power on earth, but about its effect on human patterns of behavior. Humankind must have been deeped transformed and affected at the beginning of history by the discovery of power. The fascination and horror of this transformation are still reflected in power dreams of magic and in the religious reconciliation of the powers of nature, a striving for the reestablishment of equilibrium. I quote three testimonials from classical high civilizations: the quiet command of God in the biblical text for priests to "have dominion over all the earth," the deeply troubled chorus in Sophocles' *Antigone*, πολλὰ τὰ δεινὰ, and Chuang Tzu's anecdote of the wise peasant who did not want to use the bucket wheel at the well because, "Whoever uses a machine gets the soul of a machine."

Power, though, obtains its actual explosive effect as power over others, through weapons, through superior knowledge, through the functional structure of advanced civilization. The specific phenomenon of domination that is the subject of the contemporary debate arose because of power from the traditional social hierarchy, from the natural fights between the groups and within the group in the art of war and the art of politics. At this point we are close to the source of the ambivalence of progress for the first time. Also, the power over people, once it is discovered as a possibility, is subject to no immanent limitations. If much is possible, then more is possible. Only one who wants to make the second million will make the first. Here possession is no longer territorial security, nor fulfillment of needs. It is not a means toward luxury. But it is the unlimited scope of activity, consequently of power. Therefore the requirement that profit be measured in accordance with needs completely fails to understand the principle behind profit maximization. The same applies to concentration of power in the hands of the state. It is from this structure of power that I argue that I find a Third World War probable and that I think world government is the most conservative solution. At least this solution does not attempt the colossal task of breaking the power of power.

Jakob Burckhardt says that power in itself is evil. I always resisted this statement, which gave frightened aesthetes the justification for running away from the responsibility of politics. But I was just as much fundamentally dissatisfied with the claim that power in the right hands was good, even if this often is practically the most tolerable compromise. The self-appointed "right hands" of the conservatives as well as the revolutionaries characterize the problem. Occasionally I have rephrased the thought "Power, as such, is evil," namely, power not integrated into the framework of human values. But this is merely another embellishment because its not being integrated only signifies the discovery of the unlimited potential. I would be inclined to say today that power, even if combined with good will and responsiblity, is ultimately tragic. It has to render its opponent powerless, harmless, or it will not last, and a result of power is that it produces opponents. But the victors, the successful bearers of power, discover their own deep powerlessness, their own incapacity to change by means of power the basic structure of power. Tragedy is accompanied by delusion: Whoever still fights for power will hardly notice this powerlessness.

Tragedy is not, however, the last word. I have only taken an isolated look at power. We must now come out of isolation.

C. Love

Let us imagine someone who only knew the realm of possession, domination, and power, and then meets love. One would see oneself again confronted by a completely strange phenomenon, not deducible from existing knowledge.

Possession, domination, and power are domains of the ego. Even the relations between groups in these domains are known appropriately as group egoism. Interest rationality serves interests that the ego knows. The tragedy of power is the nonfulfillment of the ego. We experience in love a rationally purposeful, completely incomprehensible fulfillment of the ego,

which is overcome, transforming all values. A science that thinks instru-
mentally can easily describe possession and domination because the very
concepts of science are in the service of such finite rationality. The limitlessness of power finds its partner in the limitlessness of knowledge. It is
almost impossible to determine love scientifically because it transcends the
very determinant. In spite of this we shall attempt the task.

That living creatures must have descendents is biologically not as self-
evident as it seems. It is also related to progress. In an eternal world, in
a cyclical time, the continuous existence of the same individuals would be
imaginable. This is the dream of personal immortality. Life that newly
emerges needs descendents to populate space. Accordingly, evolution needs
new individuals so that there can be new species. Species with a short life
span for individuals and with many descendents will develop faster, and
therefore survive in the struggle for existence. Sexual procreation, when
understood as selectivity, appears to offer the advantage of the accumulation of recessive characteristics. Accordingly, this is how this highly perplexing form of procreation *a priori* may have developed and become
successful.

From a biological perspective, the security of sexual procreation therefore safeguards an interest that goes far beyond the needs of the individual
or the individual group. Our concept of purposeful rationality, however,
is in accordance with the needs of individuals and groups. The sexual
instinct must forcefully break this world of conceptual needs. It cannot,
and consequently must not, argue. This might explain some of its enchant-
ing power. Among animals it creates the richest rituals. It luxuriates in a
manner that makes its productions akin to those of the freely playing mind.
Eroticism moves away from the sole purpose of procreation in two directions: toward a personal bond and toward purposeless beauty. The strongest nonrational force in humankind becomes the bearer of a development
that is only made possible by overcoming mere purposeful rationality.

Against this background can be seen the ambivalent struggle of all cultures with sexuality. Sexuality, even if completely different from purposeful
rational power, is a domain of the possible, too. The plasticity of human
behavior permits many different ritualizations of eroticism. But for these
ritualizations to be successful, there must be sufficient pressure for their
realization. Therefore, the expression of sexual instinct that runs counter
to rituals has to be repressed. To name a classical example, one must avoid
the polygamous tendency for the sake of the development of *one* personal
bond and the care of children. What is being repressed, however, keeps
its radiant power, and that makes it superior to all the narrower interests:
the prospective release of the ego from its own boundaries. The error is
repeated again and again that this force could even then be preserved when
it is given the status of a positive ritual. But when thus acknowledged, it
enters the sphere of interests. The test of its value is then only its con-

structive force in that sphere. Tabus, being blind and not knowing their own purpose, have exactly that in common with instinct, and to play one against the other is, at times, considered to be enlightened.

Given that, it comes as no surprise that science discovered the mechanism of repression exactly in the example of sexuality. Repression here appears as a condition for the precision of a ritualization, and sexuality is the instinct that most encourages ritualization. But to understand better the meaning of repression, obviously a fundamental process of ambivalence, we have to ask what is the conscious and what is the unconscious. However, we cannot do this until we have examined insight.

First we must remind ourselves that there exists still another completely different relationship between individuals that is also sometimes called love, the nonsexual personal bond. Because it interweaves with all communal life, we have come across it many times already without, however, it becoming a theme itself. Its quality, though, has to appear as not deducible from hierarchy, power, and sexual love. Every direct reductionism from either sexual theory or the theory of purposeful rational behavior fails to explain it. The most interesting book about its animal prehistory is, in my opinion, Lorenz's *On Aggression* (German, *Das sogenannte Böse*—The *So-Called Evil*), especially the chapter "Das Band" (The Bond), which to me is more interesting than all of the other, more popular, ideas expressed in his book. Lorenz genetically traces the personal bond back to aggression and its assimilation through ritualization, through which he sees the possibility of individual relationships within a group that goes far beyond the *first* achievement of ritualized aggression in the form of the social hierarchy. There, too, the ritual does not realize self-evident values but creates or makes possible values that are not self-evident. If Lorenz is right, then he makes comprehensible the structural relationship of various kinds of personal bonds, even if these cover a very wide area ranging from indissoluble friendship to partnership and companionship to lifelong animosity. This appears to me as one of the important contributions to the understanding of ambivalence. It is especially a contribution to the comprehension of institutions that are neither interest-rational nor sexually reducible, such as marriage.

Obviously, the personal bonding of humans, just like all other relationships and probably more so, is in its gestalt comprehensible only through insight.

D. Insight

Let us imagine someone who only knows possession and hierarchy, power, love, and individual bonding. Could this person understand insight? In a certain sense, however, we cannot imagine this person at all because to know all these things must mean having insight into them. We cannot even imagine someone completely without insight. But if one, as is customary, knows interests, instincts, and order by having adapted to them, does one not already have an insight into one's insight? And could such a person comprehend what insight is?

To make insight understood, we would need a philosophical psychology that, as far as I know, does not currently exist. The empiricists, who dominate science, do not usually see the problem, and the philosophers, who should be educated to see the problem, cannot recognize it in the thought forms of empiricism.

Insight is not self-teaching through trial and error, but rather the ability to anticipate the success of each act. It is, after all, "insight" into the processes of such successes. It might be a completely partial insight or a comprehensive awareness, it always rests on what I can only call "truth." Truth, of course, does not mean infallability. Terms like infallibility or error also lie and only make sense where it is already understood what is meant by truth, even if not reflected upon. Insight is one's certainty through some recognized truth, through a truth that has proven itself to the individual. This begins with instruments. An instrument consciously constructed and employed is not possible without insight. It continues with sociability. Social customs might be passed on and observed without insight, although I doubt that they emerge without some kind of insight. There is no personal relationship without insight. How far one can proceed with insight cannot be stated beforehand because every special insight permits further inquiry into the cause of its possibility, which, when answered, offers insight on another level.

Insight seems to cut across all compulsions of instinct, habit, "unreasonable" interests, and custom. This diagonal path is connected with its unlocking of the three related regions of facts, possibility, and freedom. I can free myself from a compulsion only when I can confront what compels me as a fact. In this sense we can say: "What wonderful things facts are." The fact, as a fact, as something that happened, is unalterable. To not see the facts, "wishful thinking," is self-inflicted bondage. To this extent, innate behavior, individual habit, and social custom are not free no matter how well they may be adapted to the circumstances. Insight into facts liberates insofar as it opens possibilities. The recognized and acknowledged fact is therefore no longer a compulsion; it can perhaps be altered, as a situation. Insight is insight into possibilities. A fact is understood as exactly this fact only by being thought of as a possible fact and thereby being acknowledged as something that happened. Thereby, however, other possible facts are set up as possibilities. These possibilities are not fantasies but "*de facto* possible" insofar as they are based on recognized facts. To have factual possibilities, however, means freedom.

These observations are philosophically abstract. One can speak concretely about insight only by speaking of the concrete facts and possibilities into which there is insight. Thus our anthropology will lead to concrete observation of history; it cannot do otherwise. First, though, we have to pursue the abstract structures a little further.

Insight not only opens freedom, it also needs freedom. This is valid psychologically. If I look at the state of consciousness of a person who experiences this state as insight, and if I understand its psychological cause, then I cancel its characteristic as insight. This is the figure of ideological criticism. If my "insight" is determined through my economic interest (or my libido, my neurosis, my tradition, or my contrariness), then this causal derivation is unmasked as not being insight. This unmasking is affected even if the "insight" concerned corresponds with the facts, consequently fulfilling the classical criterion of truth. Because this correspondence is then "accidental"; and only the ideological critic who deliberately examines it has (at least he thinks so himself) true insight. I will not pursue here the resulting philosophical problem of truth and freedom, but rather turn now to the ethical-social question.

If human life is not possible without insight, then communal human life is not possible without communal insight. This is my meaning when I say that a peace is the embodiment of a truth, truth the soul of peace. The understanding here of peace is the possibility of living together. I speak of "a" peace because there have, historically, been many forms of communal life. Of course, there is an ethical claim in this use of the word "peace." The fact of communal life can also embrace fighting, wife-beating, and, between two superpowers, the waging of war against each other. Even in such coexistence one usually can still find the rudiments of a peace, e.g., the continuing communal life of husband and wife, the framework of martial law, and the continuation of politics embracing war objectives that envision future peace. But peace always signifies, first of all, the value for which we strive and whose absense signifies the terrible misery of modern times. The peace for which we strive is not mere coexistence but what I call, in a terse sense of the word, "possibility," the possibility of living together. It is the possibility of life common to humans that opens a common freedom. This freedom requires a common insight, consequently a common truth.

One can say now that truth is common by nature. Two people who recognize the same thing are united in this insight beyond all arbitrariness: They cannot shake off this mutuality even if they wanted to. They have common facts and the resulting common possibilities. Therefore, I have stated earlier that truth as such is intolerant. Recognized truth excludes the possibility of sincere acceptance of the opposing untruth. In another sense, the orientation in reference to truth is, by nature, tolerant. The mutuality of a certain truth that I seek with my neighbor requires that he understands this truth, that it be truth for him. The mere repetition of a statement that expresses my truth is, however, not truth to him even if he thinks he believes what was said. If I want to live with my neighbor in a mutuality obtained through truth, then I have to permit him the freedom of approving this truth. That is, I have to grant him peace. In this regard, peace is not only a consequence of comprehended truth, but at the same time a precondition for its factual realization. In this double meaning, I call peace the embodiment of truth.

Obviously, in practical experience, many problems emerge concerning education, enlightenment, and advocacy. This is obvious and need not be further discussed. I only point out a kind of tension that is different from the tension existing between tolerance and intolerance. All mere factual authorities become invalid in the name of truth and in the light of recognized truth. What makes the achievement of equality among humans possible is always a common truth. On the other side, *one* authority is immanent in peace based upon truth, namely, the authority of whoever possesses insight. Truth equalizes its perceivers. Social equality in the name of truth can also go so far that it considers everyone equal and as virtual perceivers of this insight, especially if nobody claims to possess a monopoly of the truth himself as an institutional basis for power. But this equalization is false if it denies the difference between actual insight and the lack of insight. Such a fiction will be unmasked in the course of time because of the instability of the peace that is based upon it. Such a fictitious equalization makes both partners equally unhappy. For the one lacking insight, the most important insight accessible to him is the insight that he does not have the insight in question; any equalization that obstructs his access to the knowledge of his ignorance does not take him seriously as a person and as having awareness, therefore it despises him while claiming to respect him. On the other hand, the person who knows is forced, because of this fictitious equalization, to deny, to the person who does not know, this indication of respect and consequently any help the other could be given. I have never found people as free as where the authority of insight was acknowledged as self-evident.

By using the indefinite article in "a truth," "a peace," I have begun describing the factual plurality of truths and of forms of peace. Traditional societies live under a religious truth and under the peace it makes possible. The contemporary world lives with the truth of science and with the peace of the technocracy made possible by it. These two examples will demonstrate to contemporary young intellectuals the questionability of the achieved peace and the questionability of the truth upon which it is based. Does this alone not refute the entire anthropological position on truth? If there is a truth, who possesses it? If there are many truths that are obviously contradictory in their realization, what sense does it make to call them truths?

It was against this background that Nietzsche said, "Truth is that kind of error without which a certain species would not be able to live." If "to be able to live" means the possibility of communal life, or "a peace," using my terminology, then truth would be in accordance with Nietzsche's definition the error that enables peace. Let me anticipate at this point the philosophical question about truth with an abstract and individual psychological reflection.

The language of cybernetics ("adjustment to a nonoptimal, nominal value") can be used to make the point but it is not essential for establishing the basic concept of "false truth." If one understand as truth that something appears as it is, then what appears in error is not nothing: Something *does* appear, but not the way it is. At least something appears, and perhaps we can even live with it for a while or in an ecological niche. Thus the error that enables peace is an incomplete truth. Only when it claims to be obviously true does it become false. But nothing is known to us in its complete truth. Our articulated insight is always "a kind of error." Therefore, "truths" must oppose each other. It is precisely the legitimate claim made by errors to be truths that compels them to opposition. This opposition moves the historical process. The historical process can appear as a chain of successive truths. This is what dialectics formalizes. The historical process can be represented in our contemporary perspective only as an opening toward the unknown. We cannot explicitly think of world peace as the embodiment of the final truth; where this hope takes the shape of concrete thoughts, it evidently becomes unreal and tyrannical. We must seek to comprehend truth as the sequence of truths, in the truth of the process itself.

Let me add that the unlimited succession of truths is related to the limitlessness of power. Power is always based on an insight. Whoever can achieve peace is the most powerful. But the tendency to use peace as a vehicle for power is a nontruth, a perversion of peace, and ultimately a cause of conflict from the perspective of the possibility of being able to live communally. We must expect that we cannot easily get rid of the problem of power through progress.

In an interesting individual psychological parallel: Even in a person's intimacy with himself there is peace and conflict. Here, too, peace is the embodiment of a truth. Here one can see very well the limited value of limited peace. The human being learns, matures. Certain insights are more natural at certain periods of life. Goethe said, "If you are someone, do not stand still; you must move on from one light to the next." This transition from one insight to the next rarely happens when one is at peace with oneself. Crises are the usual manifestations of conflicting truths within the individual. Inner peace can result as much from the happiness of having obtained insight as from the suppression of troubling thoughts. One is inclined to call the one a true peace and the other a false peace. Are there criteria for this evaluation?

E. Values

Can there actually be insight into values? Or is there only insight into the facts of a case that we then judge as "irrational"? Is agreement about values only mutual irrationality? If not, what is the rationality of values?

This question has been dealt with *de facto* from the beginning of this book. At the outset, I proceeded with a conscious naiveté from values that I assumed were held in common by all thoughtful people in our era. Insight into ambivalence undermines the naiveté of our values. To gain insight into the cause of ambivalence, we proceeded to anthropology. The question concerning insight into values is an abstract philosophical question. I pose it here intentionally, though, in the empirical context of anthropology. The first attempt to answer it must not be burdened with philosophical considerations. How do we react—provided we have not entirely lost a certain naiveté in our own values—to anthropological material?

I have frequently emphasized that it is very easy to be certain (and consequently in agreement) about values, if their absense is experienced as an obvious lack of values, as obvious suffering. We can now say that in this regard we are not different from animals. Animals do not need to ask if self-preservation and preservation of the species are values. Hunger, fear, sexual love, mother love, speaking anthropologically, compel animals to do what these values demand. If animals were not so constituted, they would no longer exist. Humankind can question if all this is actually a value or even the ultimate value, but even for us this question is usually not raised in elementary situations, or it is met with silence if it is raised. It does not, however, become silent with necessity, because humans can question the meaning of survival. This skepticism or despair is even a natural symptom of certain crises of maturity. We also understand that human life *should not* exhaust itself in providing for basic needs. (The same goes for animal life, if we examine it closer.) We hope to secure our lives in order to make possible a good life. But what does "good" mean? This is obviously the central question in the exploration of the conditions of life.

The American Declaration of Independence lists among the rights of humans the "pursuit of happiness." This phrase seems to me to be almost a summary of all the ambivalence discussed here. It can be interpreted as simple truth or as the source of human misery. The commitment to such an ambivalent phrase clearly characterizes the self-contradiction of America and our American world epoch. Is happiness a value or even the criterion for other values?

Pleasure and pain are, from the biological perspective, indicators or signals of the advantageous and disadvantageous. In observing and judging animal behavior (which animals cannot do) according to the most simple criterion of survival, we see the resulting clear hierarchy of Darwinian values. There are, still today, individual members of species that were able to develop very quickly. From a biological perspective, progress is a higher (that is, more successful) value than the mere preservation of the individual, preservation of the individual is a higher value than pleasurability and painlessness. The lower value only expresses a condition that usually serves the next respectively higher value, but which is sacrificed (or fails in the struggle to survive) if it does not serve. Pleasure and pain, though, are a kind of value that is different from preservation and progress. On the one side, pleasure and pain can be understood as purely functional, and if something functions by itself, it does not need other value indicators. On the other side, they serve all values, not just the lowest; sexual pleasure, for example, does not serve the preservation of the individual, which it survives.

Now, using the value of mere survivability, we judge other organic life insufficiently (did dinosaurs not have a fulfilled life merely because other species won the race of evolution?). And for humankind, pleasure and pain have a completely new significance.

There has been, in the human disposition, a disintegration of instinctive constraint that considerably devaluates the indicated function of pleasure. Civilization has largely separated elementary instincts from their original biological intent. The struggle against this separation is itself ancient. What our tradition calls animal lusts (gluttony, drunkenness, fornication, even murder, should be listed here) are in reality specifically human inventions. In all of them, a pleasure that no longer serves as an indicator is structurally linked to unlimited capacity, to power. The same is true of the relief of pain through drugs. But it is especially true about the higher and more abstract forms of pleasure that domination and property provide. Pleasure is here a principle that is inherently without insight while it functions as an indicator for the animal, exactly because it does lack insight. Humankind, however, needs to control itself through insight. The pursuit of happiness, as a principle of pleasure if separated from insight, can have ambivalent, and ultimately destructive, effects.

There is a contemporary point of view that holds that the destructive effect of pleasure is only a retaliation against social repression and that if pleasure is not repressed and free to expand, it will find its limiting gestalt by itself. To me this viewpoint mixes deep insights with naive errors. It is itself an example of ambivalence. It is self-justification for experimental experiences that are probably necessary today. Its error for me is a naive optimism that is neither historically nor scientifically justified. But the positive insights are far more important for my present argument.

Again and again, in organic development and especially in human history, we see that old material can be used for completely new purposes (such as the air bladder becoming the basis of the aqualung, and aggression the basis of communication). Accordingly, the intellectually, and often esthetically, stylized satisfaction of elementary instincts becomes the embodiment of culture: eating a meal together as culinary art, drinking as symposium, living in the city and the country, a society structured according to social roles, love as play, as emotion, as partnership. In many of these manifestations, one might just as well talk about insightful happiness rather than basic pleasure. One of the highest kinds of happiness is to experience progress, to see the results of one's own productivity. Is happiness in *this* sense not the true human value? ("All pleasure desires eternity," according to Nietzsche.) And will this happiness not find, through inherent insight, its own limits where that is needed?

This concept, human happiness as a dominant value, also includes the unity of values as well as the plurality of values. This plurality is part of the structure. Humankind is happier when not always doing the same thing, people are happier together if they are not all equal (*vive la différence*). Equality is equality in freedom, freedom is the freedom to be different. But part of the structure is this mutuality, precisely this plurality of values, the solidarity in acknowledged differences. And this mutual happiness is *a* value, the dominant value, in a certain sense *the* value.

This dominant concept of value can be real only if conditions exist for the possibility of its realization. Insight and creativity are among them. None of the above-mentioned cultural stylizations of basic needs are the logical result of their biological purpose. Instinct and elementary pleasure exist everywhere as material only. What are the conditions of insight and creativity that are necessary for their realization?

We can understand happiness and suffering, to use more abstract concepts than pleasure and pain, as indicators of the success or failure of cultural processes. Perhaps suffering is the most reliable indicator. It is also the indispensible teacher and motivator. The experience of happiness has the inherent natural tendency to become shallow. If one is of the opinion that progress is also a dominant value, and the unlimited number of possible insights such as the mere concept of creativity indicates that it is, then this is be to expected, because the indicator of the experience of happiness invites lingering. The struggle between competing truths is accompanied by suffering. The positivity of ambivalence consists of the insights that result from the suffering that it causes. The danger consists of accepting partial happiness without any insight. Happiness experienced by the individual cannot be the value at this stage either. The belief that suffering is only the consequence of society's defects is naive (or a projection). How would we be capable of feeling physical and psychic pain if we did not need this indicator? Still, we will encounter the question of a painless society again.

One criticism of the contemporary world is expressed in the concept of alienation. If this means alienation from a life of fulfillment through happiness and suffering that has been replaced by one of meaningless work and functionless pleasure, the criticism is valid. But alienation from happiness would be as ambiguous a concept as that of happiness itself.

Our observations have led us back to the concept of insight as supplemented by the concept of creativity. But these concepts, other than the brief reference to cultural stylizations, have remained formal. What is the truth that guides insight and expresses itself in works of creativity?

F. The Enlightenment

The Enlightenment is, according to Kant, humanity's taking leave of its self-imposed minority and its coming of age. Kant explains minority as the inability to use one's intelligence without the guidance of another. This minority state is, according to Kant, self-imposed if the cause is not lack of intelligence but is a lack of resolution and courage to use intelligence without the guidance of another. *Sapere aude!* (Have the courage to use your own intelligence!) is thus the motto of the Enlightenment.

Kant's essay *Beantwortung der Frage: Was ist Aufklärung?* (Answer to the Question: What is the Enlightenment?), first published in 1784, was written on the special problem of freedom of expression against restrictions of the church and the absolute state. Kant's definition, however, reaches far beyond that, and following is an interpretation that goes explicitly further.

Kant uses the usual concept of intelligence, always understood, of course, in light of his elaborate concept of reason. I use here the much less elaborate concept of insight and understand intelligence as the ability to gain insight. The state of minority then is an inability of gaining insight oneself. It is self-caused if it is the result of a lack of courage.

But what does this have to do with the historical process of the Enlightenment? The intention here is that an entire society should emerge from this state of minority. Therefore, the example of the maturity of the individual becomes significant. Every person is originally immature and not yet capable of using his or her own intelligence. One must mature to reach certain insights and then summon the courage gained to shake off authority and thereby to come of age. But if we make the concept of minority mean that, then it appears to us that the concept of one's own guilt slips away. Am I guilty of being born a helpless child? And, from another perspective, am I guilty for what my parents and teachers taught me? Am I indebted to the society in which I have grown up? Is not Enlightenment to be understood more as emergence from a not-guilty minority and as liberation from a foreign bondage?

Kant's concept goes much deeper than this thesis of rebellion. He touches on a subject that is also dealt with in the attempt to heal neurosis through psychoanalysis. It mainly concerns self-discovery, which is part of the process of assuming personal responsibility for one's life. If I recognize an uncorrectable flaw, there can be no healing, no escape from the causes as long as I look outside of myself for the reasons. There is no healing if I try to find the root of what has been done to me in my parents, in society, in an inner compulsion, in my unconscious, or in my instinctual structure. All of these observations might, factually, be entirely correct. But the ability to overcome *my* flaw and not immediately regress to the same dependency all over again is that I do recognize it as my own flaw. *Mea culpa, mea maxima culpa* is not an expression of false remorse, but the clear recognition that occurs exactly when I become mature and capable of responsibility. Rebellion that is directed against the real mistakes of others contains the possibility of enlightenment, but it is not yet enlightenment, because recognition of the mistakes of others permits me still to conceal my own mistakes by projecting them onto others.

The use of my own intelligence is the search for truth. And the endeavor of this book may be seen under the title of the Enlightenment as understood by Kant. Which truth is sought? Naturally that truth that is relevant to the previously asked questions. Which is that?

Kant's thesis exists in a political context as does the entire concept of the Enlightenment in its broadest meaning. Its purpose is in answer to the mistrustful and skeptical questions of the clergy. It is an aggressive and direct defense of the concept of the Enlightenment. Beginning with the eighteenth century, the term Enlightenment designates an intellectual movement whose tendencies are exemplified in the use of the words progress and emancipation. Enlightenment is to be understood as the triumph over absolutism, and it accompanies the movements of liberalism and socialism. It is to be understood as the liberation from that political domination that maintains itself through artificial preservation of the minority status of its subjects. Its politics are essentially pedagogic. It attempts to liberate the consciousness of humankind from the thought patterns of an imposed minority status. To the extent that equality is based upon mutual insight, the Enlightenment has egalitarian tendencies. To the extent that those already emancipated want to extend the emancipation, it compels the formation of a temporary elitist structure, the avant-garde, a vanguard of progress.

This political Enlightenment contributes to the ambivalence of progress, easily detectable in the transitional attitude from self-enlightenment to the enlightenment of others. The claim to be enlightened oneself is often nothing but naiveté. The claim that one is emancipated means frequently that one is actually not changing and is stuck at the stage of projecting rebellion, a preliminary stage of development. In this book we must always make the apparently opposite movement. We must strive for self-enlightenment with the question of what has been repressed in each instance in the movement that calls itself the Enlightenment. We proceed in this manner to investigate how humankind, in the course of history, has asked questions concerning the dominant truth.

We proceeded from the problem of peace, hoping to find the criteria of the truth being sought by examining the international political problems of our time. Historical anthropology is always anthropology in the real history, that of the respectively contemporary world.

G. World Peace and Self-Realization

What must happen in the contemporary world, the world in transition to tomorrow? What has to happen? Avoiding the obvious formulation of the question, "What should we do?" What is the meaning of "we"? The formulation, "What should we do?" gives the weak impression that one has only to hear what must be done and then do it. But as we have seen, this would be inadequate for two reasons. First, because this is, in this simple interpretation, itself a formulation from the world of will and intelligence. To attempt to answer this question in a simple way encourages too easily that behavior that caused the need and perpetuates it. Basically one does not reach the point where one can act meaningfully without having gone through a period of doubting direct action. Secondly, any action that is potentially meaningful requirers a complete rethinking of all questions.

Much to my own dismay, I have often failed to reach in my own thinking the point where I could suggest the best course of action or what I myself should do. One answer I would give to the question, "What should we do?" would be: "Think!" This was one of the reasons I founded an institute instead of going into politics.

The question "What has to happen?" formulates specifically an intellectual task. Action without theory takes place anyway. We do not have further to encourage it. But what should a guiding theory of well-thought-out action look like?

In my opinion, the guiding political thought has to be world peace. It is the only thought that can integrate worldwide political activity. It is obviously necessary for the avoidance of a catastrophic Third World War and, if this cannot be avoided, for the prevention of the next one. This necessity cannot be denied, even if it fails for the time being. On the other hand, much is demanded, and it is a hard criterion with which to judge all other political thoughts. Finally, this guiding principle can be understood by everyone even if its consequences are not easily comprehended by everyone. Peace should not be tyrannical. It has to embody a truth. Thinking about this truth is the meaning of our political theory.

I consider the happiness-oriented postindustrial society incapable of mastering the ambivalence of the systems that it will tolerate in order not to be disturbed in its happiness. If it is unavoidable that the most important value for the majority of humankind is subjectively experienced personal happiness, then this fact compels an elitist structure of society. The elite, if we are lucky, are at least partially oriented towards that truth that embodies world peace as a guiding political value. For the moment, this structure exists anyway to the extent that only a minority realize the existing problems, then assume a pedagogical function for the others.

What is the essence of the values in whose context lies the truth that inspires world peace? In the course of our reflections we have come upon several key words in trying to define these values. The meaning of these words is important in the context of these meanings. I have divided some of these words into three groups. The first group could be freedom and social justice, the second group could consist of words like place, prosperity, physical and psychological health, love, partnership, and cultural creativity, and the third group could be insight, progress, coming of age, and self-realization. I have explained the contents of each of these words at the appropriate place. What is their context, their relationship to world peace, and, consequently, their political relevance?

The list is framed with the concepts of freedom and self-realization. They can be considered the most important words of its respective groups. What do they mean? Freedom is essentially the freedom of self-realization, for only self-realization is actually freedom. Therefore, all depends on what is meant by self-realization. Happiness is an indication of realized values. Suffering may provide the impetus. The indicator is not always reliable. We differentiate between true happiness and questionable, partial, compensatory, false happiness. I believe that happiness is ultimately an indication of the stages of self-realization. This realization occurs in stages, therefore terms like progress and coming of age also appear here. What was happiness at earlier stages is a means at higher stages, or it has to be sacrificed in order to reach the higher stage. The ultimately decisive knowledge of humans is the difference between the ego, with its need for happiness, and the self. The ego, in all its domains, is one of the stages leading to the self. The remaining at this stage is the origin of ambivalence. Whoever does not succeed in sacrificing this remaining, succeeds neither in self-realization of person, nor in the community of society. Accordingly, this sacrifice, and the realization made possible through it, and the resulting happiness, can only occur in stages, in the individual and, perhaps, in history.

This self-realization has been the theme of religion through the entire history of humankind. In concrete historical terms, it was the theme of religions in their plurality. The social embodiment of the achieved realization was cultures. Each such culture was a result of the relative peace of human self-realization. World peace, if it is possible, is the peace of cultures encountering each other. However, the culture that compels this now, the Western culture, compels this through an uncontrolled process of accumulation of knowledge and power that has not obtained the goal of an acknowledged truth and is itself essentially without peace. This culture in its present form is an ambivalent secularization of its own religions. World peace might be compelled, for the time being through political events, as the external coexistence of cultures. But our own culture in its present state cannot even exist with itself, let alone coexist with others. As paradoxical as this may sound from the viewpoint of a strictly political or social analysis, I am convinced that the actual process through which the possibility of a true international peace can take place is dependent upon the realization of the human self. One of its forms is the realization of religion as truth, assisted by a meeting of cultures and religions. Recognition of truth means realization of what is actually meant here, the coming of age. Political endeavors are a part and a consequence of this effort for realization.

Humankind understands very well the demand for the sacrifice of the ego. In respect to political values, this is actually everywhere their core. The unity of absolutism results from forced sacrifice of particular interests. The freedom of liberalism is essentially the freedom that I tolerate in my fellow citizen. The solidarity of socialism always demands the sacrifice of the personal in the name of common interests. There is perversion in all these values in that the ego converts them into demands made on others rather than on itself. The insight of these political evaluations is usually limited by the replacing of the egoism of the individual with the egoism of the group, in which the undifferentiated values of the immature ego merely reproduce themselves. The task is to recognize and describe the true relation of self-realization to the human community of world peace.

4. On Power

A. The School of Political Realism

The historical function of the school of political realism was to correct American historical optimism in reference to the realities of power politics.[14] I believe it has essentially contributed to the understanding of present American world-power politics. The traditional American self-interpretation held that power politics (originally the power politics of monarchies) was historically a European evil in which the immigrants in the New World, from the Pilgrim fathers to the Germans fleeing in the 1848 revolution to the Jews fleeing Hitler, refused to participate. This view left the Americans with only two attitudes toward foreign policy that were consistent with their moral self-respect (and lively self-criticism): either isolationism, or interventionism for the purpose of restoring freedom and justice. Thus came about either renunciation of power politics (outside of America) or power politics aimed at breaking the power of power politics in the world. Neither attitude has been compatible with actual American international politics as practiced over many decades. Therefore I maintain that no other imperialist power has permitted itself to be forced into the imperialist role as much as America against its own intention and tradition. The discrepancy between moral self-interpretation and imperial reality has led to many inconsistencies in American politics. At times these have been likable, at times irritating, at times terrible. Knowing that one is morally on the right side of the war to end all wars means legitimization of actions that, under any other point of view (for example, as the actions of another nation), could only be called criminal.

Political realism is, in this respect, a basic introduction to politics for Americans. It teaches them to understand how power politics functions everywhere, even where they themselves participate in it. This lesson, especially with Niebuhr, also with Kennan, contained a strong moral impulse: These Americans who were wise in the ways of the world realized the extent of the involvement of Americans in objectively immoral activities in a world whose functional laws they did not understand. I consider this an inevitable process of shaping political consciousness in this specific historical context.

But the question must be asked as to whether this demand for an anthropological foundation has not meant that historically relative incomplete insights into politics have become dogma and simultaneously an ideological function that transformed the American nation, which once naively believed it could overcome power politics. I admit that power politics, by and large, functions in the way described by political realism, but I doubt whether this can be attributed to anthropological reasons.

First, though, we will discuss the question of what is understood here by anthropology.

It is no coincidence that the foremost thoughts are those of a Protestant theologian, namely, of Reinhold Niebuhr. Kindermann quotes St. Paul: "For the good that I would I do not; but the evil which I would not, that I do." (Rom. 7:19) A basic human experience is expressed here with a precision that is almost uniquely found in Pauline Christianity. In the light of this thought, humans are initially divided into those who are naive, and ideologists who manage not to know this about themselves, and those who do know it. Each of us actually incorporates both sides. We will later discuss the anthropological theories that see this dilemma itself as a result of history and that hope to overcome it through history.

The ancient Christian myth of history also belongs to these theories, because it traces humankind's sinfulness back to Adam's fall, and believes that it will be triumphant on the Day of Judgment. To this extent the myth is not exactly "anthropological" in a strict sense of scientific laws. But, then, it is not science at all. Ever since the emergence of Christian dogmatism, meaning the self-interpretation of Christianity through the concepts of Greek philosophy, it is been under pressure to prove itself rational. I assume that all of these attempts at rationalization (including my own), as necessary as they are, remain inferior to the experience of reality transformed into myth, and thus distort it. We must now, though, follow the direction of modern scientific interpretation of this ancient experience.

At its starting point, the anthropology of Niebuhr and Morgenthau is not naturalistic and dualistic; it does not derive humans from nature, and it does not understand the tension of evil as the tension between nature and mind. It finds contradiction in the mind itself, namely, in the nature of freedom. Accordingly, it at first stands in a great philosophical tradition. But the proof that freedom by its nature has to lead to the known historical tragedies of power is not possible without intervention by a more empirical anthropology. In this context, Morgenthau develops a psychology of instinct that presupposes a division of the instincts into those of self-preservation, procreation, and power. Thus, he has to explain the emergence of the power instinct itself. After reading Kindermann's lecture, I feel that the obscurities of a causal-genetic anthropology, with which we have to deal

later, are as little clarified here as in other existing anthropological statements. We are probably on safer ground again with the phenomenological
description of what power means in contemporary international politics.

According to Kindermann, realists see power as becoming "a fundamental concept of the science of politics," comparable to the role of the
concept of energy in physics (according to Bertrand Russell). A very interesting philosophical statement has been made here. I believe that mass,
energy, information, and power, if understood with sufficient abstraction,
are, in fact, identical in essence. The statement articulating the identity of
these different concepts only makes sense if their roles can be articulated.
An attempt to do so is this verbal definition by Max Weber: "Power means
any chance of imposing one's own will within a social relationship, even
against resistance, no matter upon what this power is based." Here the
concepts of society ("social relationship"), will, resistance, and chance
(thus possibility) are assumed as understood. The question now is whether
this concept of power is sufficient to substantiate the "typologically understood characteristics of political power" (Weber as quoted by Kindermann), which I can condense as follows: (1) omnipresence in politics,
(2) omnipresence in its abuse, (3) potential limitlessness of its drive for
expansion, (4) a fundamental orientation towards gaining security, domination, and prestige, and (5) a tendency to serve its own purposes and
simultaneously to disguise this ideologically.

If there are mainly conflicting interests of individuals or groups and if
politics is defined as the arena where such conflicts are settled, then power
is indeed omnipresent in politics. Securing power is then essentially an
interest, because it is a means for the realization of interests. Accordingly,
the characteristics of (1) and to a certain extent (2) are explicable. The
other three characteristics, unlimited drive for expansion, a tendency for
serving its own purpose, and abuse and disguise, presuppose characteristics
of humankind that we know only too well from experience, but whose
origin and necessity cannot be made comprehensible through concepts like
society, will, resistance, and interest. Here we must use as explanation
something more relevant than these last-mentioned and somewhat vague
generalities. The open question is, "Are these continuing characteristics
anthropologically necessary? If yes, why? If no, how can they be historically
explained?"

And if we then inquire historically, we must also consider how valid, in
general, are these extremely "demonic" characteristics of power. The au-
thors themselves have been marked by a certain historical experience. They
are contemporaries of Stalin, Hitler, and the atom bomb; World War I
was the horizon of their youth, a Third World War is on the horizon of
the future. Is power in history always like this? They speak of a tendency
that must be continually resisted. Politics becomes immoral only where it
transforms the norms of the factual political behavior of humanity. Is not

successful resistance to this tendency the actual norm of humanity? Does the Pauline consciousness of sin understand humankind more clearly, or is it itself pathological?

The dispute about the relative importance of a tendency can hardly be decided empirically. The phenomenological position emphasizes, out of this multitude of events, a structure that is perhaps the decisive one for our own inner attitude towards history. For a more objective insight we can attempt at least to understand how it could, and perhaps had to, result in such a structure or tendency. So we take the detour of science.

B. Biological Anthropology

Evolutionist Thinking. Is a power instinct part of human nature? Initially one may try to determine the characteristics of this assumed power instinct. One has to ask, "What is understood by the word instinct: a vague desire or a structured scheme of behavior, the latter possessing an innate structure or an innate capacity to be structured or imprinted by experience?" This then leads to the question of what one wants to understand as human nature. Is it an innate system of patterns of behavior, or perhaps only the ability to acquire such patterns of behavior? Is it in the nature of humans to have a history?

What appears to opponents of biological anthropology as a biological error, namely, the establishment of an invariable "human nature" comparable to the nature of an animal species such as the nature of the wolf, is specifically already an inadequate biology. Compared with this, the necessary standard for the formulation of the question is to be found in the theory of evolution. According to it, the nature of the wolf is a stage in a historical process that is incomprehensible without knowledge of its ancestry, its ecological niche, the environmental changes caused by it, the reaction of its behavior to these changes, and so on. Humankind's manner of having a history is very different from that of animals. We can, however, conceptually label this difference only if we have understood how animals, life itself, and nature can have histories.

The constant evolution of more and more differentiated forms is not a speciality of organic life. It only proceeds much further there than in inorganic nature. The evolution of new forms results from exactly the same calculations of probabilities that also result in the second law of thermodynamics. Both are consequences of the same structure of time. Entropy and information are, according to Shannon, identical. Information is, again according to Shannon, a measure of the expectation value of the knowledge one could gain. Entropy is a measure of knowledge, similarly structured and understood, that one could have if one knew the complete microstructure instead of just the macrostructure. With a suitable form of interacting forces and sufficiently low temperatures, a state of high entropy will at the same time have a great abundance of forms. The thermal death of a closed system is then not a mush, it is many skeletons. The irreversible process, far from equilibrium, contains in such cases the continual increase in an abundance of moving forms. All of this is a consequence of the structure of time, as the condition of the existence of something like nature.

The organisms are distinguished from the forms of inorganic life by self-reproduction, mutation, and selection. The decisive achievement here is self-reproduction. Mutation is originally only a margin around precise self-reproduction. Selection is the consequence of the struggle for survival that is itself a consequence of the abundant production of forms through reproduction. Selection eliminates almost all mutants and therefore is the most important stabilizer of the species. It also favors the rare advantageous mutation through the additional influences of spatial isolation, temporal variations of environmental conditions, and so on, as described in the theory of selection. Selection favors not only particular types, but also type-forming tendencies, for example, those developing faster, such as the ability to store recessive characteristics or the relatively short life span of each generation.

There is no proof that the selection theory is sufficient to explain the evolution of organisms, and proof need not be assumed here. It suffices for now to see that there is selection pressure in favor of certain structures. We then have to examine, case by case, the relevance of such observations.

The Structure of Instincts in Humans and Animals. The usual way of speaking about human instincts is hybrid or at least thought-provoking. Let us take as an example the three basic instincts of political realism that I quoted above: self-preservation, procreation, and power. Here instinct is apparently understood as an irrational drive causing certain kinds of behavior whose purpose can nevertheless be rationally articulated. The instinct is irrational insofar as it operates without insight into its purpose and even can assert itself against the insightful decisions of the will. Instincts can, *de facto*, shake the very structure of rational purposeful behavior, or even make it collapse. This is, after all, one of the fundamentals of the Pauline experience of sin. What justification exists then to label instincts in accordance with rationally formulated purposes? By what authority are these purposes set, and what determines whether certain instinctual actions actually fulfill the purpose of the instinct? Procreative instinct is basically a *petitio principii* when one realizes how far separate the sexual instinct is from the idea of procreation. However, with procreation and self-preservation, reflection can at least recognize a biological meaning, whereas with power even this is doubtful. Freud finds stages in the unconscious that partially operate as if they were conscious. In his theory, however, these unconscious stages have explanatory value as the causes of "irrational" behavior only because the rationality of the unconscious is different from that of the conscious. Freud's great early discovery is his understanding of the significance of unconscious actions. But the utter strangeness of this explainable significance, and its methods of operation, forces Freud to search further and further for causal or structural hypotheses to explain the basically blind instincts. His later theory of instincts reads like a gloomy myth whose deepest affect is the horror of the inexplicable within ourselves. It is a great concentration of concepts that has a fascinating unverifiability. But however one might feel about it, it does make us realize how little we know about ourselves.

If we proceed from Freud's image of humanity to what behavioral scientists teach us about animal behavior, it is as if we are emerging from night into moderately bright daylight of comprehensible details. It might be that clinical cabalists perceived other phenomena than the optimistic natural scientists, but in any case the perceptions of the latter are open to rational discussion. Perhaps the most important discovery in this respect is that among animals there are not simply a few basic instincts; there is a highly complex web of many independent, interlocking, and differentiated patterns of behavior, some of which can be experimentally made to fail individually, or to be deceived by decoys, or, through new environments, to be directed toward new biological purposes. An implicit basic assumption of Freudian psychology, one that is presumably valid for the repressed contents of human consciousness, namely, that the unconscious knows what it wants, is not applicable here (unless one wants to fall back upon panpsychic metaphysics). It is obvious that the animal does not need to be aware that by eating, copulating, and breeding it is preserving itself and the species. The innate instinct can be described as being subjectively totally irrational and unknowing because it permits itself to be deceived in a manner that is easily recognizable to us but is completely senseless for biological purposes. At the same time, it has a rather admirable "objective rationality." Evidently this admirable aspect is so much taken for granted by scientists that they usually do not bother to express their fascination. I reminded Konrad Lorenz of Kant's remark about a bird's nest, "One can only kneel before it and adore it," Lorenz replied, "I feel exactly like that every day." This adoration is, however, not scientifically idle. It seeks the comprehensible causes of practicality and tries to find them in evolutionist thinking.

What can we learn from this about humankind? First we learn that an instinct can be highly differentiated, without a conscious or unconscious stage, in individuals that understand it (with the exception of the still incomplete, specifically human stage of subsequent reflection). Comprehension of our own instincts does not lie in the past where the myth makers often see it. Perhaps it lies in the future. We also learn that especially the highly differentiated, once objectively purposeful, instincts can lose their purpose merely through changing circumstances. They were, perhaps, as subjectively irrational at inception as they were later. All this takes us far away from the fervor of Freudian (and also Jungian) conceptual mythology. It is a fundamental contribution of scientific sobriety, indispensible even to someone like myself who believes very much in the relevance of myths.

The dispute with the environmental theorist begins where the behavioral scientist emphasizes the innate and, to that extent unplastic, character of instinctual behavior. The dispute, factually very interesting and relevant, and whose ideological component is evident, does not have to concern me in regard to the problem of power because I am entirely willing to define the human being through its capacity for tradition and insight, and because I understand power as a human attribute due to this capacity. In regard to a theory of insight (cybernetics of truth), the structural relationship of innate disposition to achievement that is not innate has to be studied, a disposition for which there are many simple examples in animal behavior.

But the phenomenon of the convergence of innate and acquired patterns of behavior is of the greatest importance. In evolution theory, convergence is the appearance of similar facilities in genetically independent organisms, for example, the eye lens in vertebrates and octopods. Certainly it is not by chance, given so many human achievements, that one can dispute whether they are innate or acquired. Such a dispute can only arise if innate and acquired behaviors resemble each other. This can be expected when similar causative factors are operating in both cases. The result is not only a matter of purposeful solution to the same problem, such as adaptation to certain environmental conditions (for example, the convergence of the streamline shape in fish, seals, and whales, as well as that of airplane bodies and submarine hulls). It is just as much a question of behavior patterns that are without apparent purpose or even undesired by humans, but upon which the pressure of selection is operating. One will not understand the phenomenon of power without examining such convergences.

Stabilization in Inequality through Selection. Free competition favors the stronger. There exists a continual pressure toward increasing inequality. By slightly shifting the meaning of the concept, one can talk about a selection pressure in favor of inequality. One talks about selection pressure in favor of a characteristic of an individual (for example, body height) if this characteristic favors the individual in competition. If the characteristic is inherited, then selection pressure will favor the survival of those in which this characteristic distinctly exists. This does not always mean a continuous development of the characteristic if this pressure is countered by opposing pressures. One can also talk about selection pressure in favor of a characteristic of entire societies if, due to this characteristic (for example, a higher fertility rate), they can assert themselves against competing societies. But inequality is not a characteristic but a reflective concept on a higher level. Inequality rises *within* a society, for example, if the stronger members can differentiate themselves more from the weaker ones. In this regard inequality is then a characteristic of this society and not of the individual members. But it is not necessarily a characteristic that gives this society a selection advantage over other societies; it may be the opposite. Inequality, thus sets off a consequence of selection without necessarily offering an advantage to an individual or a society.

The existence of selection pressure does not in general mean that an actual evolution in this direction occurs. Because the conditions that we can observe, at least in animal life, are somewhat established equilibriums, it follows that the equilibrium has been shifted in the direction where the pressure has an effect as compared with the fictitious example of an equilibrium without this pressure. Thus the pressure toward inequality usually does not lead to ingrowing inequalities but towards an equilibrium with established inequalities. In the ecological equilibrium of a species this means, for example, that big, small, and tiny fish live together. Within a society, it is the social hierarchy establishing itself. Where competition and equilibrium exist simultaneously, equality between competing individuals is just as "unnatural" as the extermination of the weaker by the stronger.

Therefore my thesis that equality among humans is not something natural, but an accomplishment that needs a moral postulate to be realizable. With respect to economic causalities, it seems to me to be equally wrong to expect from a market economy the preservation or establishment of economic equality, or to assume, in contrast, that it must destroy itself through monopolistic concentrations. The former is not valid at all; and as for the latter—as one is currently aware of from other sources—there is no possibility for establishing an equilibrium. Regarding human competition, one has to consider the specific human phenomenon that serves competition and is the real central issue: power.

What Is Power? I assumed above that power was identical with mass, energy, and information, an assumption that requires not only the specification of the characteristic *genus proximum*, but also that of the *differentia specifica*. Mass, energy, and information are quantities. There is more or less of each of them in comparable cases. But this is much less obvious when applied to power, though one can be more or less powerful. Specific economic power is, to a certain extent, measured by the quantity of money. But what is the essence of the thing being measured here?

I define mass as a measure of matter, energy as a measure of movement, information as a measure of form. Energy and information are as much the measure of potential as of actual movement and form. The mechanical law of the conservation of energy, for example, applies only to the totality of potential and kinetic energy. But how could one measure movement and form?

To the extent that reality presents itself to us as moving form it is actually an entirety that is stripped of its essential characteristics through every act of mental dissection. But where forms can be regarded as identical, they can be counted, and thereby the context that differentiates them is lost. It is this "regard as identical" that is the basis of the formation of a concept. Physics is based on this counting. Determining whether in a given situation a certain form does or does not appear means deciding for an alternative. A part of the entirety of reality that is lost by dissection into alternatives is found again in the form of the laws that dominate the choice between alternatives, laws that we call the laws of nature. Physics is accordingly a partial mental restoration of the entirety that has been divided into alternatives through the dissection of the real—which makes physics possible. The total of possible independent decisions on alternatives is information. The capability to make such decisions can be called power. In this regard one can state that the information available to someone is a measure of the individual's power.

There is form, and consequently information, on very different levels of integration, on very different semantic levels or under different concepts. Information on the level of the most extreme dissection we can achieve constitutes, if I interpret physics correctly, matter and energy as defined by physics. The power of a human individual or a group can be measured by the information *available* to them. This information does not affect the lower levels of integration. The power to dissolve these is usually only destructive. One can attempt to understand power as information on a level of integration specific to humankind. This, however, can and must be elucidated.

Recognition of the parallel between information and power turns a first, dim light on the cause leading to the possibility of the egocentricity of power as observed by political realism. I have said earlier that information is only what produces information. In which sense does one use these words if one formally translates this into the assertion that power is only what produces power?

I can only indicate the not entirely obvious and deeply structured levels of abstraction behind this interpretation of information. The philosophical background is a philosophy of time that understands form essentially as motion and, in this regard, as self-renewing.

Against this background stands the question of the way information relates to the recipient. To whom is it information? Whose concepts are controlling its definition in each case? Biologists have to use the concept of information objectively; the genetic information of a DNA chain shows its semantic ability in the produced phenotype. Here one has to differentiate between actual and potential information. Shannon's information $H = \Sigma k p_k \log p_k$ as expectation value of the news value $J_k = \log p_k$ of the possible event k is potential information: J_k is, if k has occurred, actual information. The thesis that information produces information contains then two very different laws in cause and application, a law of conservation and a law of growth, parallel to the two principal laws of thermodynamics. The first is connected with the operative-objective definition of information and cannot be further pursued here. The latter is a thesis of evolution: Potential information increases with time.

The thesis of evolution can now be transferred with crude selectivity to the concept of power as commonly understood. Power is only what produces power. In any power competition, the one who can accumulate power will prevail. This is the abstract core of Marxist analysis of capitalism. Our reflections show that this fact does not depend on power having here the form of economic capital. Therefore I maintain that the abolition of capitalism does not, as such, liberate us from the problem of power. If we hope ever to overcome power, then we have to abolish the "crude selectivity" structure not only in our opinions but in fact.

In which sense can I actually call power a *humanum*, something specifically human, if I connect it with energy and information and continually argue in the context of biological evolutionism? I have described power as a product of insight, of isolated or isolating insight that I understood as a *humanum*. Now I have introduced information within the framework of exactly the same kind of insight as the quantity of possible alternatives. Accordingly, I have introduced information itself as a measure of power. Thus information itself is a *humanum*: Only to human thinking in power categories is nature a structure of information. But energy, it seems to me, is information, and matter is energy. Physics and biophysics are then themselves ways of thinking about nature in power categories. A physically understood nature itself is a *humanum*. This is not a new thought. We find it in Heidegger, and in Marcuse, who probably took it from him. But in its effect it remains destructive or romantic as long as we cannot limit the scope of the validity of power thinking, employing deeper-rooted premises. There we have to reckon with a great challenge if it is correct that the isolation of recurring forms characterizes not only quantitative physics but conceptual thinking.

In summary, the subsumption of human power under information itself belongs to the method of thinking in categories of disposition or power; on the other hand, within the frame of this subsumption, power is a specific kind of information occurring in humankind and connected with the accumulation of tradition and insight.

In the chapter "The Rationality of Emotions" I connected power *and* peace with insight without specifically discussing their reciprocal relationship. I connect power there with the limitlessness of isolating knowledge; later this realm appears under the name of volition and intelligence. I define peace as the embodiment of truth; this corresponds later to the name of reason. Among the concepts used here, intelligence must be employed as the capacity for an isolating kind of knowledge, and reason as the capacity for understanding an entirety as an entirety. There is no total antagonism between intelligence and reason, only one that is supplemental or occasionally subordinate. To isolate is itself an achievement that, like any achievement, presupposes an entirety it can achieve. This accomplishment usually occurs without insight into its own nature ("Consciousness is an unconscious act"). If it is recognized, however, it is an act of reason. Intelligence thus presupposes *de facto* something that is accessible only to reason. The achievement of intelligence does not consist of dissecting. Intelligence recognizes the context of what it has isolated in laws. In physics, too, the method of formulating the problem is power, the knowledge of the law is peace.

In answer to the question of whether these thoughts have sought to establish power as a fundamental biological-anthropological concept, I would say, "Not empirically, but in a certain sense transcendentally." "Not empirically" means I do not need to assume there exists an innate power instinct comparable to the innate sexual instinct, but neither do I have to contest such an assumption. "In a certain sense transcendentally" means that power appears as the unavoidable result of the coincidence of any competitive situation and intellectual understanding. In view of the possibility of reason and peace, power is not necessarily the last word. That is for history to decide.

5. Conversation with Sigmund Freud

A. Our Theme

Freud's theory of culture is an attempt to comprehend the ambivalence in civilization. The title *Civilization and Its Discontent* indicates that. Freud clearly expresses it near the end of the essay when he draws his conclusion. At the beginning of section VIII[15] he speaks of his intention to present the guilt feeling as the most important problem of cultural development and to demonstrate that the price for cultural progress is loss of happiness through increased feelings of guilt. At the end of section VII he says that "the guilt complex is the expression of the ambivalence conflict, of the eternal struggle between eros and the destruction or death instinct." Freud's theme is the ambivalence of progress.

In his other writings (for example, *Totem and Taboo* or *Moses and Monotheism*), Freud's theory of cultural processes might seem intended as genuinely historical in that he traces, as he does in the psychoanalysis of individuals, fate-determining impressions back to concrete events of the remote past. It could accordingly seem as if the healing of the neurosis that is present throughout civilization could be found in the discovery of those original traumatic experiences. But Freud himself promises no cure for culture, but only its recognition as a necessarily ambivalent process. One must critically remark that Freud relies primarily on historical events that were the result of his own myth-constructing imagination. Freud's actual arguments are structural. They refer to the nature of humankind and, still deeper, to the nature of life or of all reality.

Freud attributes the tension in civilization initially to the opposition of the pleasure principle to the reality principle. He demonstrates this in the metapsychic triad of id, ego, and superego. While the possibilities of avoiding suffering are limited in relation to our own bodies and the external physical world, we perceive the suffering that results from our relations with people as "more painful than any other. We are inclined to view this as a so-to-speak unnecessary addition" (section II). However, even this may "not be less unavoidable by fate . . . than the suffering of our origins."

The deepest reason for this lies in the duality of our instincts, not just for humankind, but as an attribute of all life. "And now, I think, the meaning of cultural development is no longer hidden from us. It must show us the struggle between eros and death, the life instinct and the death instinct, as it has been realized in the human species. This struggle is, after all, the essential content of life, and cultural development must therefore be designated as the struggle of the human species to survive."

Metaphysics of the ambivalent naturally results in resistence from those who are not prepared to peer into the abyss. Criticism comes easily for them. They can say that Freud's theories are unprovable as a whole and are often too abbreviated or false in their details. I will soon join this criticism in certain aspects. But the ideological function of criticism of details is not to be denied. How easy they make it for us not to look where Freud's vision takes us. Technical cultural optimism and an expectation of a hereafter, expection of a change in history through socialization of the means of production or through continuing enlightment—all this is referred to in the concluding sentence of section VI: "And this struggle of giants is what our nursemaids still think they can soothe with lullabies!" If we criticize Freud, as we must, we should first determine if we really know what we are talking about.

Let me begin with a remark that W. Pauli once made to C.G. Jung and which seems very applicable to Freud, too: "Mr. Jung, you have the Midas touch. Whatever you touch becomes psychic." The Midas effect of Freud is mitigated by his sense of reality and veiled through the vulgar dualistic-mechanistic philosophy of the science of his time, which he nevertheless constantly used despite his insight into its cloudiness. The speculations about physiological mechanisms in the nervous system only serve him in his justification of causal reflections in psychology. Freud's special form of the Midas touch is his transformation of truth into inner-psychic causalities and structures.

Here one confronts a difficult philosophical problem, still unresolved in contemporary scientific thinking. In everyday terms one can define it as follows: Truth exists where someone knows something. Knowledge here may be imprecise, one-sided, without basis, and subject to the possibility of error. If knowledge can be corrected, then it is corrected through better knowledge. Whoever maintains something has already made the assumption that knowledge is possible, that it is on the "horizon of truth." Freud also moves obviously on this horizon. Each of his skeptical self-interruptions testifies to his highly developed sense of the demands of truth. The objects of his research are psychological causalities and structures. His object, the mind, is at the same time the subject of cognition. It is Freud's fundamental discovery (new for science, not so new for poets and religious seekers) that conscious mental life is not completely aware of its motives, that it is influenced through unconscious motives, often even decidedly controlled by them. The demands of the truth of consciousness are placed in question. Behind the claims of consciousness, other determining psychological causalities are visible.

For the clinical sense, for the healing success of psychoanalysis, it is important that this is not a criticism of all truths but only of the claimed truth, through a better truth. Something here becomes "visible," which is exactly the meaning of the statement "The truth will make you free." It is now accepted into consciousness and accepted as true. For example, according to Freud, "If I want to classify my future acts according to social standards as either good or bad, then I must accept the responsibility for either result. If I say defensively that what is unknown, unconscious, and repressed in me is not my real 'ego,' then I do not act according to the tenets of psychoanalysis, and I have to learn a lesson through other people's criticism, through the disturbances caused by my activities, and through the confusion of my emotions." It is a terrible misuse of psychoanalysis to shift the responsibility for our desires and actions to our parents, society, or instinctual structure. Psychoanalysis may make the self-punishing rigorist comprehend the origins of his guilt complex and make him capable of an understanding kindness toward himself and humanity. This does not change anything in one's automatic acceptance of responsibility for the knowledge that "I am all this."

We understand what is happening here by practicing it. It appears to me that Freud never fully clarified this theoretically. Neither he nor anybody else, in my opinion, has proposed a psychology of the truth. Even the philosophical problem that would require this approach is hardly even seen by psychology. Still he managed to avoid, in constructing his theoretical superstructure, in his metapsychology and cultural theories, to reduce truth to psychology. Habermas' criticism is convincing: "The theory of structural models resulting from the experiences of the analytical situation links the three components, ego, id, and superego, in the specific sense of a communication between doctor and patient, with the goal to set in motion a process of enlightenment and to make the patient begin the process of reflection. It is therefore not meaningful to describe the context of ego, id, and superego in turn with the help of the thus introduced structural model. But this is what Freud does . . . The theoretical language is poorer than the language that has been used to describe the technique . . . It means that the unconscious is transformed into the conscious, thus appropriated again by the ego, and that the repressed matter can be found and criticized . . . But in the structural model, the ego stage is not equipped with the corresponding capacity: The ego exercises the function of intelligent adjustment and the control of the instincts, but the specific achievement, of which the defensive mechanism is only a negative, is lacking: self-reflection." (*Ekenntnis und Interesse*)

Not only in relation to self-reflection, but in a certain way concerning all truths, the capacity for truth is not made explicit by the structural model. It is, so to speak, used illegitimately and without reflection where Freud's psychological-critical perspective does not deal with its genesis, for example, in the thesis that it is the ego that adapts itself to reality. I myself use the structural model to designate three "areas" of truth that are not important for Freud or which he rejects. If the id is inherited by us from animals, it remains completely obscure how animals accomplish their adjustment to reality. The human society appears as the product of the interaction of egos, beginning with a mythical prehistoric and practically nonsocial condition. One ego, the primeval father, has actually created society, and all adjustments to society became historically required of humankind. The structural—as in language—and historical priorities of the society, and thereby the cognitive aspects of our social relationships, remain obscure. This cognition is accomplished through the biographical-historical compulsion of the superego, a compulsion that is not disputed as a psychic fact. It seems to me that Freud must not take seriously the truth requirements of conscience that belong to self-reflection, because otherwise the truth requirements of religion would find a loophole. Everywhere reality becomes psyche, truth becomes causality. Midas' gold.

B. Instinct Theory

"Why do our relatives, the animals, not demonstrate such a cultural struggle?" (section VII). It is remarkable how Freud, who continually emanated one hypothetical theory after another, could admit in such sentences that he did not know. His line of questioning is of interest here.

Freud stated that the "cultural struggle" has to be understood as an eternal human form of the unavoidable conflict of all life with itself; the meaning of cultural development "lies no longer in the dark for us" (section VI). Thus the security of animals in their societies and in patterns of behavior becomes a problem that Freud consciously raises, only to resign himself to the elusiveness of a solution. Science today knows more in this respect.

Are Freud's simple fundamental structures, those based above all on the eros and death principles, more than just a fantastic superstructure built to contain a variety of meaningful patterns of behavior? Let us first give a critique of the pleasure principle.

It is merely the pleasure principle that operates in the id; only the ego constructs an adjustment to reality. The pleasure principle determines, though, the purposes of life. "And yet its program is in dispute with the entire world . . . It is generally not realizable; all of the constructions of the world contradict it" (section II). The id principle may define the actions of the still egoless human baby, but never those of a mature animal. Animals objectively experience and adapt to the demands of the reality principle with admirable ability. The entire point is that they are subjectively not aware of this and don't have to know this. Freud would respond that exactly this not knowing is what is missing in the human reality principle, and I would immediately agree. This means sole domination of the pleasure principle, and with that I hesitate to agree. Can we join together, under the title of "pleasure," eating and drinking, walking and flying, hunting and flying, nest building and care for the young, hierarchal struggles and a good night's sleep? Where these operations function most reliably, there they are often not accompanied by pleasure. Does blood circulation or the growth of hair give us pleasure? The capacity to experience pleasure and pain and to react to them appears to be a very specific achievement, as an "indicator function." Freud himself attempts to explain the lack of pleasure as stimulus blockage, and pleasure as the destruction of this blockage, as "satisfaction," and thus approaches a "nirvana theory" of pleasure. But no matter how specific the individual qualities of pleasure and lack of pleasure, it remains extremely difficult to measure them quantitatively in relation to each other.

It appears to me that the conflict between the pleasure and reality principles that we encounter profusely every day of our lives is a *humanum*, a cultural product. If we consider it as such, then we comprehend why the animals do not have any cultural conflicts. They experience, certainly, something analogous: the struggle to survive and the forces of evolution. Even the adjustment to reality by plants and animals is incomplete, and sometimes they learn from their maladies, as we do. But what learns, above all in the primitive stages, is just the mutating species or, chemically speaking, the DNA.

The question remains why, in our own lives and in observation of animals, the subject of pleasure and pain always reappears. What, then, is this common quality, and why does it exist? There might be a physiological center of the brain for pleasure (electrode research in rats). This would support the argument that pleasure and pain are actually functional aspects of the organism, and would make the "pleasure principle" subordinate to the "objective reality principle," as a kind of preliminary stage of the higher accomplishment of the "subjective reality principle" that is accomplished by the ego.

And someone with a metaphysical disposition (as Freud certainly had) could ask the question whether this accomplishment does not articulate a basic condition of all life. Striving and avoiding seem to be fundamental aspects of all behavior. Nietzsche's song comes to mind:

> . . . deep is its sorrow.
> Pleasure, deeper still than suffering.
> Pain speaks: Vanish!

Yet pleasure wants eternity,
Wants deep, deep eternity.

Such perceptions are heard when Freud depicts the unsolvable opposition between eros and the death instinct. The death instinct wants perhaps the deepest pleasure, for all life is movement and only its end seems to promise eternity in time. But does Freud even know here what he is talking about, what motivates him to theorize?

His claim is science. But what in his instinct theory is provable? Behavioral scientists do not find one or two or three basic instincts, they find, in higher animals, perhaps fifty coordinated patterns of relating to different situations. The concepts of these behavioral patterns are not organized under unified instincts such as hunger and love but in accordance with functional relationships such as the search for food and propagation. And in humans even more such behavioral patterns can be found. These serve the erection of a specific human construct, that of tradition and insight. And, exactly as Freud teaches, something inherent can very well be repressed or given new applications. Inherent behavior is material for culture.

The empirical core of Freud's libido theory appears to be his experience of the displacement of psychological energy. Therefore observations appear to show something like the preservation statement of psychological tension that manifests itself in many different forms and takes many different directions. Similarly, behavioral scientists observed already in animals the "leaping movements." I could speculate easily here about the physiological explanation for what in psychological energy can actually be seen in correspondence with physical energy or information, and to organize the libido under the parallel concepts of mass, energy, information, and power. However this basis would certainly not justify the duality of instincts, the coupling of the mythological opposites of love and hate, attraction and repulsion, life and death. But this I must leave unexamined.

Still, a few words about aggression are necessary. Freud has recognized, phenomenologically, that aggression cannot be derived from sex and eros. His astonishment about this discovery was essentially what motivated him to introduce the death or destructive instinct. Much more convincing than the quick conclusion coupling these experiences to an instinct mythology, and also more convincing than all the other psychoanalytical explanations, is Lorenz's concept of limited aggression with its validity only as a positive accomplishment of the individually structured society in relation to other species members. The threatening outbreaks of aggression such as murder, war, sadism, and aggressive enthusiasm would then only be human cultural products.

The opinion that one can educate children in such a way as to prevent aggression is, according to Freud and Lorenz, invalid. If one follows the behavior scientists' theory of culture, then one can see the use of aggression as a cultural material. Lorenz sees aggression already in animals as building material of personalized relationships. One must then give aggression its due (not just in sports, also in culture).

Only fragments remain of Freud's instinct theory. But these fragments still circulate widely in the language that Freud used to describe his cultural theories. What did he really see, what did he really construct?

C. Ego, Society, History

One can criticize Freud's theory of the history of society from two opposing sides, and both critiques are equally justified.

(1) He observes structures of society as determined either *de facto* through mythical early events or—scientifically more serious—through inherent instinct structures, which, however, are really products of history and as such are soluble.

(2) He does not see the priorities of inherent social behavior in the inherent attributes of humankind.

I will not deal again with the second criticism. The first we can handle in accordance with empirical anthropology (ethnology). This critique is at the core of the socialist conflict with Freud.

Freud attributes the ambivalence of culture occasionally to economic necessity. "The motive of human society is, in the final analysis, economic; if there is not enough food to preserve their number, than the number of members must be reduced and their energy channeled from sexual activity to work. Accordingly, the eternal, ancient, and still present necessities of life" (*Schriften*, XI, quoted from Habermas' *Erkenntnis und Interesse*). This remark is closely related to the thought that, with the progress of a technological society, permitting adequate feeding of all people, it would be possible to overcome cultural repressiveness and thus to eliminate the ambivalence, if Freud's remark is valid. Marcuse's argument in *Triebstruktur und Gessellschaft* rests on this thought.

Freud himself is not uncritical of socialist expectations. "I have nothing to do with the economic criticism of the communist system, I cannot investigate whether the abolishment of private property is purposeful and advantageous. But its psychological assumptions I must recognize as an illusion. With the elimination of private property one takes away from humans one of their tools of aggression, a strong one, though not the most powerful" (section V). This passage continues: "I believe that as long as virtue is not rewarded on earth, then ethics will be preached in vain. It also appears to me to be beyond doubt that a real change in the relationship of humans to property will bring more relief than any ethical command; however, this insight is dimmed by the socialists through a new, idealistic misunderstanding of human nature, invalidating this insight" (section VIII).

One could object that Freud has not seen the possibility of the technical elimination of the shortage of life's necessities in his last writings. But that would only show a large inconsistency between Freud's different arguments that would have remained concealed to him because he held the economic necessities of life to be as unchangeable as the aggression instinct. (This, by the way, is a widely held bourgeois opinion.) But the pathos of the unchangeability of human nature is unmistakable in his antisocialist writings. "It cannot be predicted here what new directions of cultural development can be built; but one thing one must expect is that the undestructable character of human nature will remain the same even there" (section V).

The disintegration of the instinct theories of Freud puts an end to the stringency of his arguments at this point. In spite of that, I find his pathos there, as in many other places, to be a phenomenological view that sees the connections, even if he gives an erroneous rational explanation. For me, too, the "great" socialist expectations (in contrast to a sober socialist practice) operate exactly, as they did for Freud, as a cheap regression that actually veils the depth of the problem. In contrast to Freud, I find that the problem can be resolved, but I maintain with him that the socialist theory of private property is an attempt to cure merely a symptom.

If I want to continue along this line of reasoning, then I must next ask if Freud's dualism of instincts is necessary in order to comprehend the continuation of power structures even after the elimination of economic necessity. In contrast, Marcuse views this power structure as a historical-social inheritance. This might be descriptively adequate, but it becomes invalidated through further employment of the "pleasure principle" as an explanatory attempt. My analysis of power tries to shed some light on this problem. It is not the necessities of life but the inherited behavioral patterns determined originally by the necessities of life that are the origins of the durability of power structures. For billions of years our ancestors were, and we are now, descendants of victors in the struggle to survive. We act spontaneously, as one must act, to survive the struggle. No matter how much of our behavior is inherent or how much is acquired, I am convinced that cultural forms can be developed that enable us to adjust to this struggle and reduce it to an endurable level, and even to make it productive. But this is only possible if its structure is recognized. Therefore, the central theme of political ethics is knowledge and truth.

D. Superego and Truth

Just as Freud's id does not, in general, depict how humankind is in the reality of nature and his ego does not adequately depict how humankind is in the reality of society, his superego veils how humankind is in the reality of truth. I deny the existence of the superego structure as little as I deny the existence of the other structures proposed by Freud. But here, as elsewhere in Freud, his thought remains unclear as to how much the causally depicted behavior is at the same time "in the truth." This impenetrability serves then his affect as a weapon against religion. If I wanted to criticize Freud immanently, then I would have to try to discover the basis for his affect. I believe that it is closely connected with Freud's fanatical pursuit of the truth. In this pursuit of the truth, Freud's lack of the reflective becomes especially meaningful, a lack that Habermas, in *Erkenntnis und Interesse*, criticizes as a metapsychology that does not understand itself: Freud continually seeks the truth and never asks what truth actually is, "psychologically" or otherwise.

6. Biological Preliminaries to Logic

A. Formulation of a Question

Is it not inconsistent to keep referring to the Platonic tradition of philosophy as relevant for this book on the one hand and, on the other hand, to pursue a biology of the subject? The formal answer to this question is contained in our earlier discussion of the image of the circular movement. We now seek a stronger contextual statement of what we see in the circular movement.

The fundamental thought of Attic philosophy, of Aristotle as much as of Plato, is that only the *eidos* is recognizable. The *eidos* appears in later philosophy under the term "concept." A philosophy that maintains the priority of the concept stands opposite that tendency of the medieval-modern tradition that designates itself as nominalism in logical respect and as empiricism in epistemological respect. It holds the individual fact as the primary given and attempts to understand the concept as a designation of the particular. It would be meaningless to want to decide the dispute of the argument between such vaguely characteristic philosophical tendencies. In the attempt to formulate precisely the positions, to be able to discuss the issues at all, it would be necessary to invest so much philosophical work that it would make much more sense to spend the effort on introducing new concepts that no longer need the old names. But the way to these new concepts would be also very difficult as we attempt to understand what the old concepts have meant in their assumed clearest phase. Presumably, they were clearest at the beginning, when a single philosopher introduced them to designate phenomena he saw and when they had not yet reached the stage of historical multiplicity that necessarily accompanied their introduction into different philosophical systems. Because every concept establishes its meaning only in context.

The dispute about the priority of the concept or the particular usually takes the form of the categorical judgment or, as we commonly say today, of the predicative sentence. Therefore it takes on the form of logic. The sentence "*S is P*," for example, "Socrates is a philosopher," says about a subject (Socrates) what its predicate (philosopher) is. In the so-called singular judgment, the subject is a particular (Socrates). The predicate is, on the contrary, normally not a singular thing, but a concept. The question as to the relationship between the particular and the concept is therefore, in part, a questions as to the meaning of logic. Why does the predicative sentence form even exist? What is its logically so fundamental meaning? Why do sentences, concepts, proper names exist at all?

To what authority should one turn to answer such questions? Tradition holds that logic is self-evident, that it is certain *a priori*. If that is so, the authority for our question would be this evidence, the insight that we have and owe to the certainty of logic. The search for evidence in support of authority normally leads no further than to a more precise repetition of the assertion, to an assurance that it is really so. The problem becomes more acute if we ask what kind of certainty really exists *a priori* in the case of logic. Kant has introduced the difference between analytical and synthetic judgments. He illustrates them even with the predicative sentence form. An analytical judgment is, according to him, a judgment whose predicate only states something that is already contained in the concept of the subject, while a synthetic judgment adds something to the concept of the subject. One also sees that Kant must think of the subject, too, as determined through a concept in order to be able to explain his differentiation. It appears obvious to him that analytical judgments are *a priori* certain, just as judgments *a posteriori* are synthetic. His problem is the synthetic judgments *a priori*. Let us ask now what constitutes the certainty of analytical judgments.

The new logic retains the concept of analytical truth as a concept of reflection (a concept of the metalanguage in which we speak about logic). But it attempts to separate it from the connection to categorical judgment (and from the imprecision of "a concept within a concept") and approximately defines an analytically true sentence as a sentence that is true through its mere form. If we ask, however, what sentences are true through their mere forms, we are referred to the rules of logic. If we then ask why the rules of logic are true, we are again referred to evidence. But we must assume that the rules of logic are not merely true through their form. If they were certain *a priori*, then they themselves would be the simplest example of synthetic judgments *a priori*. But the synthetic *a priori* is highly suspicious to most philosophers of logic today. This short summary has perhaps been useful to make understandable the claim that the foundations of logic are philosophically unclarified (which I would be prepared to defend in a larger context).

Perhaps it is in this situation that one can attempt the method of circular movement. What is the origin of logic in life? From what historical situation does it come? And what is its biological background?

B. The Place of Logic

The question, "What should we consider the beginning of philosophy?" is asked only after the beginning of philosophy has already been made historically. What, then, does this question mean? It concerns the systematic beginning of philosophy. It thus presupposes a systematic beginning. It concludes that from a historically given knowledge. From which? I maintain: from the model of deductive sciences. But of these there exists, historically, so far only one, namely, mathematics.

Let us leave open the question of how much the transference of the structure of mathematics is worth to philosophy, and let us ask instead about the basis of this structure. Deductive mathematics appears as a system of axioms and theorems; the theorems are arrived at with the help of logic from themselves, and finally from the axioms. The structure of deductive mathematics is therefore determined by logic. What is logic? It is a system of conclusions, of judgments, of concepts. The order of these three words begins with what is first the conscious purpose of logic, that of correct conclusions, and then proceeds to what as a component of correct conclusions becomes observable through continued reflection.

The next question must be, "How come there are concepts, and their combination in judgments and the combination of these in conclusions?" The "metaphysical" answer is the doctrine of ideas. A "positivist" answer, which first looks at the unquestionably given, finds concepts in the form of words, judgments in the form of sentences of a language, conclusions as parts of texts. Logic is then the system of rules about language, a chapter from grammar.

Linguistics today is a booming science. It discovers, in its way, the *a priori* in the form of those rules without which nothing meaningful could be said.[16] If logic formulates a part of these rules, through what, then, is it distinguished within the system of grammar?

At this point in our reflection, the question must be raised as to what constitutes the simplicity of logic? When we asked about the beginnings of philosophy, it appeared natural to assume that what determines this beginning as beginning is at the same time the simplest. But now further reflections have led us into the immense field of linguistics. Between the immensity of sciences whose contents were arrived at with the help of logic and the immensity of the grammatical structures that exist behind logic, logic itself appears as a "bottleneck" of simplicity. From where does this simplicity come?

I assume that it comes from the reference of logic to truth. Every declarative sentence must state the truth. But whether or not it is true does

not depend on its grammatical form. Logic, however, formulates requirements for the form of utterances so that they can be true at all.

A theory of logic thus requires a theory of truth.

C. Practical Meaning of the Bivalence of Logic

As a pragmatic definition of truth, I will designate its definition as the
adaptation of the cognitive process to the circumstances. This definition
does not make the claim of elucidating the nature of truth. It concerns one
aspect of truth. It grasps logic as a theory about language actions and
language actions as a specific type of activity. In its application in this
chapter it observes human activities in essentially those traits that they
have in common with animal behavior. The thus defined truth refers then
to the correctness of behavior; everything that for human truth touches on
the capacity for dialogue and reflection is ignored here. But we will see
that certain charateristics of logic that are almost always accepted as given,
such as the division into sentences and concepts and the bivalence of sentences, have their precise correspondents or precedents in the structure of
animal behavior. This correspondence is rooted in the cognitive aspects of
life procedures. One can thus speak, in a strict sense, of the biological
preliminaries of logic.

The basic fact of logic and of grammar is the sentence. It is a unity,
often complex. As unity it is characterized, insofar as it is a declarative
sentence, by having, in its entirety, a "truth value," being either true or
false. Other sentences, such as commands and requests, have mostly a
similar unity of intention. Through the sentence intention—meaning the
intention of the speaker who means the word or words as a sentence—
and, in cases of declarations, through the truth value—meaning the fact
that what is said must be either true or false—one can also differentiate
between a sentence that consists of a single word and the mere uttering of
that word.

What, actually, makes the unity of a sentence? We should ask this mostly
in regard to a declarative sentence. In the case of a theory that demands
conformity with the truth, unity would mean unity of the intended circumstances. But if one attempts to say what a circumstance is, then one encounters difficulties that may only be overcome by reversing the explanation: Circumstances are what can be said in a sentence. But with that
the unity of the sentence intention becomes all the more a problem. Circumstances that one could capture in a sentence appear continually to
merge with each other, and only the understandable but never fully articulated sentence intention picks out from the continuum something that is
usually not well delineated. For example, "It rains." Where? "Here." That
means in the vicinity of the speaker. "All humans, by nature, desire knowl-

edge" (first sentence of Aristotle's *Metaphysics*). What do they desire? What is knowledge? Do they always desire this? Do all really desire this? No, not really but by nature. A law is established to make the declaration true. Are the facts really verifiable or falsifiable? But from such sentences comes knowledge. Can one explain the unity of such circumstances, as in these two examples, other than through the unity of sentence intention?

Another problem that relates to the unity of the sentence is the bivalence of logic. Every declarative sentence is either true or false. What are the circumstances if the sentence is false? The circumstances stated in the negation of this sentence. But are there really negative facts? "It does not rain" is the only possible answer to the question "Is it raining?" or, stated pedantically, "Do the facts exist that it is raining?" Bochenski says about the negation of predicates, "The world is full of non-elephants." Negation is a characteristic of logic required for explanatory purposes, not a fact of reality. Plato saw this clearly in his *Sophist*.

I propose to understand the declarative sentence fundamentally in the sense of the pragmatic definition of truth. A declarative statement is exactly true when a certain course of action would lead to success. Precisely when it rains do we have need of an umbrella. Precisely if all humans desire knowledge by nature does it have meaning to write *Metaphysics*. Precisely if 2 times 2 equals 4 must one prepare four beds if two couples are coming to visit. Of course, these examples are simple stylizations, comparable to the uneducable primitivity of innate behavior patterns. The assertion is only that even our subtly provable declarative statements have content through the methods of their proof. But the subtlety of a pragmatic epistemology can be developed only after we know to what extent the pragmatic definition of the truth explains fundamentally the unity of sentence intention and the bivalence of logic.

Here, we could go back to a characteristic of behavior theory that is first given empirically. A behavior pattern in animals is, in the simplest cases, a sequence of activities whose order is innate and whose discharge follows in accordance with external circumstances. There is, in the simplest examples, no intermediate stage between the occurrence of this discharge, with its resultant behavioral response, and the nonoccurrence of both. If we look closer, an occurring intermediate stage can be the result of either a poorly functioning pattern or a complicated pattern in which numerous opportunities for decision exist, possibly under the influence of learned procedures. Since both of these refinements of the basic pattern do not deny its structural validity, let us remain, for the sake of simplicity, with the simplest example. Then the decision about the occurrence of the discharge in a certain time period is a simple yes-no decision. Also, it possesses the asymmetry that we find between being and nonbeing. If the discharge takes place, then the behavioral response occurs. If the discharge does not take place, "nothing" happens, and this requires an inquiry into the disappointed interest of the respective observer, to find out what it was that did not occur.

But the behavior pattern, with its all-or-nothing structure, is not yet a sentence, neither imperative nor assertive. However, we can analyze from it the structure of sentences. We, the behavioral scientists, can define "circumstances for the animal" as those factors that have caused the discharge. Uexküll's *Umwelt* consists in such circumstances for the animal. Human thinking is, then, the representation of possible activities with their consequences, be this in language or be it, for example, in visual fantasies. How this representation is possible is a highly complicated theme of a descriptive and causal theory of speaking and thinking. But it appears plausible that such represented activities have also the basic yes-no characteristic of elementary animal activities, though in a highly complex form, which yet permits a reduction to its simplest elements. A language representation for humans of such represented "circumstances for humans" would then be a declarative statement. Here the phrase "for humans" appears twice: Circumstances for humans are represented in language for humans. Our common language logic recognizes the "for humans" of the language but not that of the circumstances, and thus accepts the unity of linguistically represented possible actions and its all-or-nothing structure as the unity and the being-or-nonbeing structure of the circumstances.

In a simplification that brutally suppresses the many inherent complications of human speech and thought we can state the origins of the bivalence of logic as follows: The declarative statement represents a circumstance. Circumstances are defined through a suitable pattern of activity. The pattern of activity has an all-or-nothing principle: It can happen or not happen in a given situation, but not both at the same time (proposition of the contradiction of activities) and not *neither* of both (proposition of the excluded third possibility). The bivalence of the declarative sentence is, itself, only an insight of reflection. In "simple" statements we express the circumstances that exist. Nonexistent circumstances are not expressed. But almost all existing circumstances, too, are not stated, namely, when they are without active motivation or when no motivation exists to communicate their possible action motivations. Every simple statement is "meant to be true." But it is possible to doubt every simple statement, but not all at the same time. A doubted statement is reviewed through a process that can be expressed in a newer and in turn more simple statement. This process tests if the asserted circumstances actually exist. The original simple statement (call it p) becomes now a reflective statement. If it proves to be true, then we can designate p as true, and we can also say "I maintain that p" or "p is true." Otherwise, "I maintain that not p" or "p is false."

This depiction, I hope, also explains a number of phenomenologically known characteristics of our perception in causal respect. Logic is bivalent because it refers to activities that can be either done or not done. If we call thinking in the context of logic to be intellect and the conscious, decision-making active motivation to be will, then the correlation of both follows: Intellect can think what the will wants, and the will can want what intellect can think. The bivalence, the division of reality into alternatives, is not a property the world shows us without our assistance; it is the way we successfully grasp reality. Intellect is power-forming. But the bivalence of logic is valid only for reflective statements. Through the grasp of doubt the isolated simple statement becomes a reflective statement. For simple statements and for what is not said, the predominance of truth over falsity is valid, what Heidegger phenomenologically describes with the concept of nonhiddenness. A fringe of nondelineable possible simple statements is indispensable for every single act of doubting reflection. This fringe results from the extensive and inexpressible perception of what is given, and what can only be articulated in small pieces expressing the circumstances. This is the predominance of perception over intellect. In perception, we are already informed of the whole. Therefore we are able to act in detail toward specific goals. Perception of the whole that functions together with conceptual thinking I would like to call reason. In this respect, reason is the precondition for activities of the intellect. Emotions are then something like reason before the development of the intellect. Therefore we talk about the rationality of emotions.

We end this section with another philosophical reflection about the meaning of our selected procedure. Circumstances have proven to be "circumstances for humans." It is by no means my philosophical intention to reduce the world to our ideas. The theory of animal behavior offers a better model. Behavioral scientists know that in the "circumstances for animals" there are essential aspects of the kind of reality that he knows as a natural scientist (and which he is convinced he knows better than the animal does). Critical reflection means that we test also our own respective and preliminary knowledge for its truth contents, its conditions, and its boundaries. A philosophy like the one attempted here reflects critically not only on particular knowledge but on the form of knowledge itself. It asks why knowledge is presented in statements, and even in negatable statements. It is methodically illegitimate if it thereby refers back to empirical facts of the ancestors of homo sapiens (more precisely, of the present descendants of such ancestors). It is just as legitimate that it uses that method of knowledge whose very origins it itself studies, and that it thus articulates its speculations in statements, in statements that are negotiable. This is exactly what is meant in the "philosophical genitive" which is simultaneously *genitivus subiectivus* and *genitivus obiectivus*: "The critique of pure reason" is a critique of reason through reason. Only our essentially historical way of asking forbids the division of the contents of our knowledge into empirical and transcendental; our transcendental reflection uses empirical material with the eventual goal of finding that its empirically discovered laws are transcendentally necessary.

In this sense it is, naturally, also legitimate to ask whether the depicted discharge scheme of behavioral events has itself a basis in things, such as, for example, a selective advantage in the world as it is (whereby we furthermore describe the world "as it is" in negatable statements). Let us use the preservation of the species as the criterion for success. Something, namely the species, and in the short term also the individual, should remain preserved. Therefore, the activities must maintain, as constant, certain properties of the one who acts with a certain unambiguity or must reproduce them after a while. This maintaining happens by itself as long as the conditions are unchanged. It happens also by itself as long as the conditions change only to an irrelevant degree. Therefore, there must be a mechanism that normally does not respond, but which does respond to relevant changes of the circumstances (external or interal, for example, enemies or hunger). Finite beings such as the organisms can have only a finite number, in fact, only a small number, of reliable functioning, relatively complex active and dischargeable patterns of behavior. This plausible statement can be quantitatively substantiated through the thermodynamic conditions of reliability, namely, adequately certain irreversibility. Here we run up against the same arguments as when dealing with necessarily irreversible processes in measuring instruments according to the quantum theory of measurements. Just as classical physics presents itself to us through measuring instruments, here the unity and negatability of circumstances, thus classical logic, presents itself to us through the functional conditions of the physical object, which is expected to act in a manner that is structurally understandable.

With this reflection we have, of course, not escaped from the historical circle of our own knowledge. The finiteness of the reaction methods of an organism is the physical result of the fact that it consists of a finite number of atoms and that these have only a finite number of reproducible modes of reaction. The law describing the facts of this situation is, for us, the quantum theory. We try to derive these laws from finitary axioms, and their finitism expresses the finiteness of a thinking that is dependent on uniform sentence content. By attempting to express this in negatable propositions, we also think of the possibility of the negation of these propositions, thus of nonfinite circumstances or of a reality that is not reducible to a "circumstance." In a certain sense, future modal logic, such as quantum logic, is not bivalent.

D. The Basis of the Subject-Predicate Structure of Sentences

The elementary declarative statement of a subject predicating something, namely, either giving or denying something to the predicate, has been taught, since Aristotle, in close connection with the unity of sentence intention and with bivalence. Plato, in *Sophist*, already presupposed this structure of the sentence. But the relationship of both structures is by no means evident. We also recognize sentences as true or false that are constructed in a complicated manner from elementary sentences, as well as sentences whose simplicity does not suggest an immediate meaning in the sense of the *S-P* structure, such as "It is raining," "Fire!," "It is not raining." This means that the oneness of sentence intention, bivalence, and negatability does not result in the *S-P* structure; the latter is a limitation of the multiplicity of conceivable sentence structures. On the other hand, this structure is very widely used; and if I understand Chomsky correctly, he sees it as an indispensible element of deep structure even where it does not appear in the surface structure. Is it possible to comprehend such universality?

In the Aristotelian syllogism, *eide* are built upon *eide*. Tied to this is the clasical notion of the dominating term, of the pyramid of notions, etc. According to Detel, Plato already constructed predicate sentences. But among Snell's three examples of predicate sentences—"The lion is a predator," "The lion is yellow," "The lion roars"—this model applies only to the first. Properties and activities are only forcibly made into dominating terms. Essential to them is that they do not always or essentially or necessarily apply to the subject. "The lion roars if he is not silent" (Wilhelm Busch), and a gray lion is a lion, too. The limitation of the predicate structure to the timeless relationships among *eide* does not only exclude the fullness of the time-related language, it also blocks the way to temporal logic. We suspect today that the *eidos* structure is, on the contrary, a special variation of the predicate structure, that, for example, *eide* are predicates that have become timeless.

We find a temporal foundation of the predicate structure in Aristotle himself, in his *Physics*. Aristotle shows that if there are changes they must exist because of the operation of two or three principles, which he calls matter, form, and limitation. The bronze (matter), which is not a statue (limitation), becomes a bronze statue (form, namely material as form). Abstractly stated: Whoever wants to describe transformations must indicate something that remains unchanged (if nothing remained the same, then a conceptual description would be impossible) and something that changes. What remains the same is called matter, and what changes is its form. As form changes, it assumes two appearances: *A* becomes *B*. The usual description designates one of the two appearances as the intended form and designates the other only through its absence. In this regard, the two-principle structure of matter and form can also be understood as three-principle structure, of matter, form, and limitation. One sees here directly the relation aspect of the concept pair matter-form. In relation to a certain transformation, bronze is matter, namely, in relation to what does not change. In relation to those things from which it is made, copper and tin, it is form. Matter that is the subject of a declarative sentence is itself an *eidos* because only an *eidos* is expressible. *Prima materia* is an abstract philosophical concept, not an actual thing.

It belongs essentially to the Aristotelian concept of matter that matter means possibility, namely, receptive possibility. Bronze can be made into a statue, but it need not. The transformation is not described as a deter-mined course but as the realization of a possibility, which need not have happened. This implies neither positive nor negative prejudgment of de-terminism. It is conceivable that whoever knows all interacting causes could also know that this bronze must become a statue. But that is not the actual situation of people with insight. One needs the interrelated concepts, thus possibility: matter as possible realization of a form, form as possible form of a given matter.

In a temporal logic, it make sense to use an analogous scheme. We speak of determinable alternatives. Here we must first indicate the alternatives, that is, differentiate them from other alternatives, and then indicate what the decision is. The first step corresponds to matter, to the possibility of form itself or its limitation, and the second step corresponds to form itself. A form is only identifiable if it appears often (confirmation). A possibility is only identifiable as possibility of a form. But its being a possibility means that the form may exist or not exist in the present case (unprecedentedness).

Under this concept fall the three examples of Snell, once the concept of a constant subject has been justified. This justification, however, needs further development. Subjectless sentences such as "It rains" indicate that the phenomena do not have to show permanent subjects along with ap-plicable concepts. Methodically speaking, the subject is a permanent al-ternative (the possibility itself as form: for example, the piece of bronze). But there is, we assume, no transcendental proof that permanent individual objects exist. This may be seen through a detour to physics. Elementary particles are the simplest quasi-individual objects, but even they are no longer the original alternatives.

Snell's three examples appear to lie much closer to a world of individual objects. An object can have properties that either can or cannot change. If they cannot, one calls them intrinsic characteristics and groups them under a substantially expressed dominating term. If they *can* change, one designates them with adjectives. Change of their properties occurs usually through outside influences. The causal concept of influence indicates the determining character of temporal processes in a world of individual objects: One works upon the other.

That we describe the timeless relationships through predicate sentences is the least obvious. Negation is natural in temporal circumstances, where it expresses real possibilities. The negation of a timeless true sentence ("two times two is four"), as a real possibility, expresses only the possibility of ignorance (of error, of lie). We can disregard here this central question of philosophy.

In modern philosophy of logic, in view of the background of Aristotle's substance ontology, and strengthened through the direction of nominalism, one has chosen a construction entirely different from the one attempted here. One has presupposed or attempted to prove as immediately obvious what is in need of justification, or what has only limited truth: the existence of isolatable objects of remaining identity. Objects are designated by singular terms, by proper names. The philosophical problem then begins with the introduction of concepts, that is, predicates. The name "Socrates" designates that Athenian philosopher who was Plato's teacher and who drank hemlock. But to what do predicates refer such as "philosopher," "Greek," and "mortal"? We say they refer to a class of objects. But what is a class? Is it a totality of objects? One view in a narrow nominalist sense would be that a predicate is only a common name for all objects of a class. Frege and Russell have pointed out the difficulties that arise if one does not distinguish a class from its objects. It can be said, in proposing a temporal logic, that we can never know completely all the empirical objects that fall within a class. At least we cannot know the future ones. But we can already know the predicate that determines whether they belong to the class when we will know them. Accordingly, the concept of the predicate takes precedent over the concept of class.

Frege's and Russell's thesis, that predicates may occur as subjects of predicates of higher levels and thus form something like objects of higher levels, is sometimes designated as "Platonism," especially in English-language philosophy. But this is a historically and systemically absurd designation. This so-called Platonism accepts unquestionably the existence of elementary objects—something Plato consistently denied. It then conceives of concepts according to these objects—the second mistake that Plato tirelessly fought against. In the Aristotelian syllogism, there are no examples of singular *termini*, only of quantified predicates. It is not "Socrates is mortal," but "all Greeks are mortal."[17] In order to approach the meaning of Plato, one must first understand every singular *terminus* as a characteristic, that is, as a predicate under which an object falls precisely. In this sense I have explained above the meaning of the name "Socrates." Only then can one, like Kant in his explanation of analytical judgments, talk in the traditional way of the respective concept of the subject of a predicate sentence.

Contemporary analytical linguistic philosophy is subject to the same pressures. I paraphrase here from Tugendhaft's presentation. If we search for the meaning of a sentence in the conditions of its use, we can first explain sentences that are connected to a situation and that attribute a predicate to the present situation. Then the introduction of singular *termini* takes place to make the sentence independent of the situation. The designation of objects is connected by Tugendhaft to the spacial-temporal situation, or, as the quantum physicist must say: to the concepts of classical physics.

Keeping the logical problems in perspective, we return to the biological analysis of the perception of concept and individual case. We can say that *for us* a concept corresponds to the simple behavioral pattern of animals. *For the animal* the respective behavior may be hardly more than the undifferentiated unity of the three moments that we separate into concept, emotional state, and action. It is only where a higher degree of complication of behavioral patterns can restrict or permit a definite course of action in accordance with a higher criterion, that there can be a biological need to view this process *as a possible* process. It may be here that the separation of action and emotion begins. Emotion, in a way, is the perception of not completed activity as indicated but not yet completed. Here perception separates from motion. The concept as concept, thus the separation of concept and individual case, of thinking and perception, is an accomplishment that higher animals occasionally achieve, but which is truly achieved only by humans, articulated by language.

Here are the roots to an understanding of the philosophy—above all Platonic philosophy—of a fundamental phenomenon that I would like to call *co-perception*. It is the co-perception of the concept in what occurs under the concept, which is, in the simplest example, the individual case. "There goes the ball!" Have I perceived the individual thing that is included within the concept ball? Or have I perceived the *eidos* (the concept) ball in one of its manifestations? This manner of inquiry is wrong. I have perceived *this as ball*. If we speak of the perception of animals, we must say that they perceive concepts. If the young bird in the nest opens its beak when it notices the approach of the mother with food, but also responds the same way to the approach of a cardboard dummy: Does it confuse the dummy with the mother? Presumably not, but it reacts to the concept of the "feeding beak." It is the accomplishment of philosophy to distinguish the co-perceived concept from the individual case. The perception of the individual appears as perception in the narrow sense since the time of Greek philosophy and continues, more narrowly, in the nominalist-empirical tradition. In Plato and Aristotle, the thinking of a concept is still designated with a word that refers to optical perception (νόησις). The problem of empiricism, how special experiences can be the basis for universal concepts and universal judgments, is solved in Aristotle's theory of induction, in which he says that we perceive the universal *in* the individual case. The gathering of isolated data can be helpful but, in principle, *one* individual case is enough for induction. Here the phenomenon of co-perception is still directly described from the untroubled phenomenological view of Greek philosophy.

This task of philosophy can be depicted in the following simplified steps. If the individual case and the concept are differentiated by the reflecting perception, then in the individual case of this perception the difference between the concept of the individual case and the concept of the concept is co-perceived. The *eidos* is, described from the individual case, the orderliness that we co-perceive in the concept—in the possibility of the mode of behavior reflected in the respective concept. The co-perception of the *eidos* in the sensory object is the appearance of the *eidos*, in the sense in which Greek philosophy understands the concept of appearance. The co-perception of the difference between *eidos* and sensory object is the appearance of this difference. Philosophy, since Plato, has been the attempt to directly perceive this co-perceived difference. It is a meditation on this difference. Therefore, philosophy is theory of appearance: It is an appearance of appearance. Here one must co-perceive what is co-perceived in *eidos as eidos*, and *therefore* is co-perceived: the intrinsic elements of *eidos*. Thus, expressed in the Platonic tradition, the transcendentals: the One, the good, being, and truth.

The ascent from the cave is the path of this meditation. But it must be said again that only Plato's *descent* is constructive philosophy. It is the reestablishment of the unity of *eidos* and individual thing, disrupted for pedagogical reasons at the beginning of the ascent. It is thus the recognition of all individual things as *eide*. Because of the ascetic tradition of neo-Platonism only Plato's philosophy of ascent was welcomed, and this resulted in division, since the high Middle Ages, of the two movements of ascent and descent into two philosophies, the Platonic and the Aristotelian. This division is reflected in Raphael's *The School of Athens*, which apparently motivated Goethe to give a beautiful depiction of both philosophies in the historical part of his color theory.[18] But the separation of the schools, in the radicalization of positions, leads to unsolvable problems. Empiricism holds that the data received from sensual impressions are given as such, and it cannot reconstruct laws from them; it does not understand that sensual data, because of our biological endowment, are bound to be given under a co-perceived concept. Idealism maintains that the direct perception of the *eidos*, the accomplishment of a meditative abstraction, is an independent property that can be illustrated through experience but not taught by it; idealism's historical destiny is to dogmatize the respective steps of empirically based insight. Idealism, so far, lacks the perception of history, the co-perception of time.

7. Co-Perception of Time

In concluding this part, let me add a stenographic, cryptic note, which, if expanded, would go beyond the boundaries of this book. It refers to the last sentence of the previous chapter and points to the brief note on Time and the One (part III, chapter 5).

I start with a few formulations from Picht:[19]

(1) The past does not disappear.
(2) The number of possibilities keeps increasing.
(3) Time itself is being.
(4) Truth is appearance of the unity of time.

The past is preserved in facts. Facts are possibilities of the appearance of the past. Possibilities are based upon facts. If the past does not disappear, then the number of possibilities keeps increasing in that new possibilities constantly realize themselves as facts. The "is" in (3) must be read as a transitive verb, according to Picht. In what exists factually, being is co-perceived. Being, in turn, is possibility, which means time "is" it.

One can say that the present is the unity of time. But here the concept of the present does not explain what the unity of time is, but rather the reverse. Nor does the concept of the past explain what facticity is, or the concept of the future what possibility is, but, rather, the reverse: The past is what is factual at present, the future is what is possible at present. "At present" is in the present as in the unity of time. The factual present is what it is, as possibility of the appearance of facts. It is the present insofar as the future is co-perceived in it.

Truth is what is co-perceived in every perception that is perceived *as* a perception. Perception is presence of the perceived, unity of its facticity and its possibility, consequently of "its time." The truth of perception is the unity of time co-perceived in it.

"An observation that requires elucidation in the future." (Kant, *Critique of Pure Reason*)

Part III
PHILOSOPHICAL TRADITION

1. Platonic Science in the Course of History

Werner Heisenberg depicts himself in his memoirs, *The Part and the Whole*, as a *Gymnasium* student and, as it was then termed, a "volunteer." During the street fighting in Munich in 1919 he lay on the roof of the Catholic seminary across Ludwigstrasse from the university and read Plato's *Timaios* in the original. He read that to practice his Greek for his approaching final examinations and because it contained Plato's theory of natural science, in which he was interested. He recalls how astonished he was upon finding that Plato depicts the smallest parts of matter, what we would now perhaps call atoms, as regular polygons, tetrahedrons, octagons, hexahedrons, icosahedrons (only the dodecahedrons were not mentioned). He asked himself what it would mean that these mathematical figures were at the same time the ultimate building blocks of fire, water, air, and earth, what we term the elements. If one reads Heisenberg's book to the end, one finds, in the conclusion, observations about the relationship of his own physical theories which he had in the meantime developed, and those Platonic ideas. Heisenberg admits that basically, with his contemporary theory of elementary parts, he is actually practicing Platonic natural science as understood by Plato. Thus one can say that the greatest living theoretical physicist understands his science as science in the Platonic tradition. So I could give this entire essay the title "In what sense can contemporary science be Platonic?"

I find Heisenberg's book to be Platonic itself. It is actually the only real Platonic dialogue in contemporary literature that I know. It is a book on conversations. In these conversations, the surrounding world is very lively, and the participants are likewise. As in Plato, all the people who take part in the conversations have actually lived, and some still live today, and, as in Plato, they are characterized by what they say. Thus their opposing intellectual positions become clear. I believe that I do my teacher and friend Heisenberg no injustice if I say that the precision and conciseness of the philosophical thought in Plato's own dialogues is somewhat superior to that found in Heisenberg's, and that the level of Plato's philosophical reflection is still higher. But I must add that I hardly know of any writing in world literature about which I would not have to say the same. On the other hand, Heisenberg's dialogues have also a precedence over Plato's. In Plato, whoever speaks for Plato is right, be it the Athenian Socrates or the Pythagorean Timaios. In Heisenberg, sometimes the other is right. And that is very refreshing.

Heisenberg's theses can be clearly formulated. If Plato is of the opinion that the ultimate building blocks of fire are tetrahedrons, and the ultimate building blocks of earth are hexahedrons, etc., then he uses those "Platonic bodies" that were not discovered by him but that are now usually named after him. They have principally mathematical properties that can be represented in the symmetry of three-dimensional space in discrete form. They are geometric presentations of the symmetrical groups of space, the rotations permitted by space. All these bodies have the property that there are certain rotating operations, that their edges lead to other edges, and that the entire body finally takes up the same amount of space as before. They are in this sense regular bodies, they are the representations of symmetrical groups. Heisenberg is of the opinion that contemporary physics must, in the end, be built upon the assumption that the basic laws of nature are symmetrical and invariable, in relation to the application of definite symmetrical groups. These groups, however, are different from Plato's. Heisenberg holds that the same symmetry that was, for Plato, the fundamental of science is also, for contemporary physics, the fundamental of science, but mathematically more advanced and now assuming that the fundamental law is not that of ultimate bodies, but rather can be found in certain differential equations that give the law of transformation, of the possible states, of objects. That this differs from Plato is naturally clear to Heisenberg, and Heisenberg is certain that this difference is a progress. Progress of science cannot be denied. But Heisenberg is of the opinion that we here resume a principle that was first formulated by Plato, discounting possible Pythagorean predecessors. That is a question historically difficult to research, and I will limit myself to Plato.

Now comes the question of whether this opinion really has something to say and, if so, what. In Heisenberg, it has an outspoken aesthetic coloration. Heisenberg knows expressively that the natural laws are beautiful and that symmetries are forms in which the beauty of regularities of nature allows itself to be conceptually comprehended and mirrored. It is also doubtless that for Plato beauty occupies one of the highest places and is one of the highest values. On the other hand, one can ask if this recourse to beauty is intellectually provable. Does this mean more than the artistic impressions and variable moods of a scientist? I believe that if we pursue this question, which is really the philosophical question that concerns me here, then we must first of all ask, "Do we not, perhaps, have a completely satisfactory theory of science that explains why such mathematical regularities are valid?" I believe that it is the essential point of Heisenberg to say, "No, we do not have such a theory, one that can be offered scientif- ically." Recourse to Plato is necessary because the non-Platonic opinions that dominate contemporary scientific thought cannot explain the phenom- enon that is at work. This phenomenon, simply stated, is primarily the validity of mathematical laws, thus those laws of which I have already spoken, consequently the validity of certain laws of symmetry. Today we have, in general, a more or less empirical theory of science that undoubtedly presents correctly an aspect of science, namely, that our science is based on experience and must be proven through experience if we are to believe it. As control of the truth of our theses and as motivation to develop them further, we need to conceptualize our sense experience, something with which Plato certainly would not have disagreed. But Heisenberg indicates that the mere fact of experience, as we normally know and recognize it, does not illuminate why there should be completely simple, fundamental laws, fundamental laws that one can describe with a few simple mathe- matical concepts, although they are laws that determine an unmeasurable abundance of individual experiences. Why are the laws, supposing they exist, not as complex as those of individual experiences? What is at work here is something that one cannot understand merely with methodology because the different sciences that employ the same methods make com- pletely different discoveries. The weather is complicated, and every attempt to make a simple science of meteorology fails. But if we remove the clouds from the sky and look at the stars, we find them to be the objects of another science, astronomy, which has entirely simple mathematical laws of move- ment, discovered by Kepler as early as the seventeenth century. And yet, the basic laws of meteorology and astronomy are the same. There are complicated phenomena and simple phenomena, and this difference cannot be methodically explained. One can not imagine that there could be a science that would be simple for meteorology and complicated for a theory of the movement of the planets. Therefore, the discovery of simplicity is a genuine discovery and not just a methodical step, not just a means for easier mental formultion. What is discovered here? What is discovered if it is established that just those fundamental laws, even if one penetrates the atom, are really simple? This is Heisenberg's question, and I belie~ . that one can say with a good conscience that the scientific theory of our century does not have an answer. Does Heisenberg, does Plato, does anyone have an answer?

At the beginning of the seventeenth century, Galileo had presented the thesis that the book of nature, the second book of God after the Bible, is written with mathematical letters. Whoever wants to read it must be able to read these letters, that is, understand mathematics. Galileo thus rejected the Aristotelian tradition. His authorities were Plato and Pythagoras. Gal- ileo argued here in favor of the mathematical natural science of Plato against the qualitative natural science of Aristotle, he argued in favor of the constructive science of Plato against the empirical-descriptive science of Aristotle. In the scientific mythology of modern times, these relationships were reversed, and it has been said, contrary to the truth, that Galileo had argued here for an empirical science against a pure speculative science. He argued, in any case, in favor of experience, but of an experience that was explained through mathematical constructions, not in favor of the description of what one sees, but of the construction from experiments and the production of phenomena that one does not normally see, along with their advance calculation on the basis of mathematical theory. I will try to show to what extent the law of inertia or the law of gravity of Galileo, for example, are mathematically describing something that was not observed exactly in this form and certainly could not be observed with precision, and I will try to show that Galileo saw that his science was performing the service of proposing a purely abstract mathematical model, through which he could differentiate the essential from the nonessential in the natural phenomena, and through which the unessential, namely, the deviation from mathematical laws, could be made accessible through further mathematical analysis. For example, he postulates that the law of gravity is strictly valid only in a vacuum, something that he could not empirically know. Then the deviations of the real law of gravity from the law of gravity that is valid only in a vacuum will be accessible through a mathematical analysis, the analysis of the force of resistance and friction.

Galileo believes here in the mathematicization of natural phenomena, but he does not substantiate it; he lets the results substantiate this. The question is whether the mathematicization that Galileo postulates can be made understandable, for it is certainly not self-evident. Galileo occasionally uses theological formulations. I have referred to the "book of nature," which is a metaphor. The same theology that Galileo loosely refers to has been more clearly reflected upon by a contemporary, Kepler. Kepler further developed the mathematical empirical science of modern times beyond and, in a certain way, on the basis of what Galileo had accomplished. Let us remember that Kepler's first law of planetary motion, that the planets' orbits are elliptical, has supplanted the older view, that the movement of the heavens must necessarily take place in circles, through his attempt to describe the observations of Tycho Brahe with the highest degree of mathematical precision. He determined that the depicted orbit differed from the actual observable movement by only eight radian minutes, which is very little. Eight radian minutes is approximately a quarter of the diameter of the full moon seen from the earth. One might say that it is not really important whether Mars is where the orbital calculation says it is, or a quarter of the breadth of the full moon away. But to Kepler it was important. He abandoned the circular orbit and proposed an unheard-of elliptical orbit, a less-than-perfect circle as it appeared because one still believed in the perfection of heavenly movement. But with the ellipse he presented an exact correspondence between observation and calculation, and it was on the basis of empirical tests that he developed the new law. Kepler thought empirically, that is, he believed that experience permitted analysis with strict mathematics. And now comes the question, "Why?" His answer is directly theological. I sketch it briefly here as it is depicted in his work about world harmony: God had created the world in accordance with his thoughts on creation. These thoughts on creation are the pure original forms that Plato called ideas, and these original forms are relevant to us as mathematical forms. Numbers and figures are God's thoughts on creation because they are pure forms. God created the world in accordance with these forms. Humankind is created by God in his own image, not the physical image of God because God is not physical, but in the spiritual image of God. That means that humankind is capable of imitating God's thoughts of creation. These thoughts are physics, which, as service to God, is true. That is a very brief summary of Kepler's philosophy, which attempts to substantiate the empirical fact of the success of mathematics in science by referring to the only thing that he was convinced could actually explain things, namely, the work of God's creation in its double form as the creation of nature and the creation of humankind who knows and understands nature.

I spoke and wrote about these questions a decade ago, accentuating the Christian components in these thoughts. I must say now that I have read more of Plato and have learned that much of what Kepler said is actually not Christian but Platonic. It is Platonic to the extent that historical Christianity, in its theology, is Platonic in the broadest sense. It is Platonic, but it remains a question whether it is Platonic on the highest level. I would say that it is not entirely. Neither Heisenberg, nor Galileo, nor Kepler have completely fulfilled the philosophical reflections of Plato.

How did Plato himself understand this situation? I must admit that what I am about to say is incomplete. In order to present truly the relationship of science to Platonic philosophy, I would have to present Plato's entire philosophy. That is certainly not possible here, so I will limit myself to a few observations. What I say is in part an attempt to reconstruct certain teachings of Plato that are suggested in his writings but not fully developed. In this respect, there are Plato's remarks in the seventh letter, and there is the well-known dispute about the "unwritten teaching" of Plato. I must briefly deal with this and give my own interpretation without going into specifics. I know that I do not do full justice to Plato because there are areas of Plato that I have still not fully understood, but of which I am convinced that Plato himself knew exactly what he meant. Essentially, I will limit myself to Plato's thoughts as expressed in *Timaios*, because that is the dialogue where Plato has depicted his understanding of nature and science.

This dialogue begins immediately with a rather puzzling joke: "One, two, three, but where is the fourth?" says Socrates. He simply means that there are three conversation partners, and the fourth is still missing. And yet, if one knows Plato, one will say that this must be meant as an allusion to something else. C. G. Jung has indulged in great flights of fantasy about the beginning of this Platonic dialogue because he considered the quaternity a fundamental psychological phenomenon, and absense of the fourth and the commencement of the dialogue by three was accordingly a basic phenomenon. But did Plato actually mean that? I would say that Plato referred to a quarternity that is perhaps indicated in the linear image of the *Republic*. But I do not know that, I only say that one is aware from the first sentence of this dialogue that secrets are being alluded to that the author does not intend to reveal. When one reads further one discovers that the three talk about what Socrates had said, the previous day, regarding the dialogue in Plato's *Republic*. Not the entire work, only the first half. There are a few linguists who believe that Plato at that time had written only the first half of the *Republic*. But that is not likely. I would rather believe that Plato used a trusted literary reference: that one must have read the first half of the *Republic* to get to the place where the *Timaios* begins. And this is the teaching of a state with guardians who are actually philosophers and who rule this state on the srength of their knowledge. This knowledge, which exists partially thanks to a divine spark, is advanced, above all, through the study of mathematics and mathematical science, to the extent that it can be furthered through education. This can be found in the seventh book of the *Republic*. The *Timaios* dialogue, at least as I interpret this transition, is an elaboration of the teaching that is only hinted at in the *Republic*, namely, that one must have learned if one wants to govern a state well. For this, one must have studied astronomy. Naturally, this was as confusing for readers of Plato then as it is for us now. Why astronomy? The only answer can be that in astronomy, and in particle physics, fundamental structures of reality are made visible upon which anyone must reflect who wants to understand the extremely complicated and confusing structures of reality that manifest themselves in political struggles or in political orders. Instead of pursuing here the relationship to politics, let us return to the dialogue in *Timaios*.

The Pythagorean Timaios, a man who otherwise does not play a role in Plato's works, and about whom we basically know nothing, explains the theory because it is obvious that Socrates, the ethicist, the political thinker, the religious philosopher, himself did not know it. That is what one must assume. Consequently Timaios presents it in coherent and solemn speech. He begins with the difference between what always is, never becomes, and never passes and what never is, always becomes, and always passes. This distinction, with which *Timaios* begins, is a reminder of what the reader of this dialogue must have been familiar with for a long time: the theory of ideas. That means that science can be understood only on the basis of the theory of ideas.

We must, therefore, ask "What is the theory of ideas, and what is its role in science?" The theory of ideas, to mention something that is known, was introduced, for example, in *Phaidon* through the idea of the identical. Two pieces of wood that lie before one are entirely alike. But they are not exactly the same. More precisely, they are never the same. How can I actually say that they are not the same if I do not already know that sameness exists? At this point the myth of anamnesis is mentioned: From all of my sensual experience, from this life, in this body, the soul has already experienced sameness. Accordingly it is reminded of this through things that are really not the same but contain only a share of this sameness. This sharing, this apparent sameness, which is not yet sameness, this is the essence of the sensual that becomes and passes. But sameness itself is always the same as itself, is immortal, and is always the same. That is the "gestalt" of sameness or, to use the Greek word, the "idea."

This classical and well-known thought sequence of Plato must be interpreted if we want to see that it is relevant to the sciences. One obvious interpretation is the realization of mathematical forms. I have often drawn a circle on a blackboard in my lectures, saying: "This circle is perhaps a very beautiful circle, but it is still not a real circle." Mathematics talks about the circle itself and not about empirical, alleged circles. If science is mathematical, then it joins mathematics, which talks about the circle itself, and describes the things that we sensually perceive as sharing in the mathematical forms, and which can thus be understood by an understanding of mathematical forms, such as the circle on the blackboard and the movement of the stars. But now a problem has been formulated. What does "a part" of *methexis* in Plato mean? What does it mean that I have a figure that is a circle and is not a circle, rather a part of the circle gestalt? Does one understand what one means when saying this?

I proceed to still another example. In the tenth book of the *Republic* Plato introduces, perhaps to the horror of many who thought that they had understood the theory of ideas, ideas of things, for example, the ideas of beds or of bridles and reins. He first introduces the idea of the Greek eating couch and says that there are three kinds of these couches, the one that God made, the many that the artisans make, and the pictures of these that the painters make. The many couches that the artisans make are copies of the single couch that God made. That is the couch in heaven. And there are the paintings that look like couches but are only copies of the couches that artisans make. The same goes for bridles and reins. There is a bridle that exists only in nature, physically, known to the rider. The many bridles that are actually made are made by the saddlemaker. And then there are painters who paint them. Leaving the painter out, we see that in both examples the artisans do the same thing, but in both cases, on the highest level, something different is at work: namely, in the one case it is God, who has made the couch, in the other case it is the rider, who knows the bridle. To maintain the parallel at this point, one must conclude that the rider knows what God has made. I will add here an interpretation of this text: I maintain we must take seriously that the rider knows what God has made. Let us first stay with the rider. Let us say that Plato's talk about God is perhaps metaphorical. It is perhaps a form of expressing, in the language of the religion of the people, a philosophical thought that cannot be easily articulated. But what does the rider know? He can tell the saddlemaker that he wants a bridle that functions well. The rider knows the function of the bridle. He knows what it does. He knows the relationship between horse and human that makes it possible at all that a person can ride on a horse. To control a horse, the human being needs the bridle. This relationship is a real relationship in the world. But the relationship is not a material thing. It is something that one can understand if one understands the functional and law-determined relationships of the world. If one says that this world has been created by God, one can also say that God has made the real bridle, namely, the functional relationship that enables the human being, with the help of the bridle, to control a horse.

I want to turn to a modern version of these same thoughts by paraphrasing a contemporary author. Konrad Lorenz has repeatedly written about the greylag, as in his book on *On Aggression*. He says that the greylag as described by the zoologist or the ethnologist is a goose that can never and nowhere exist, just as those perfect circles. The greylag as described, according to Lorenz, by the ethnologist or the zoologist is the creature that optimally fills up the ecological niche, consequently the life conditions, of the greylag. Real greylags are always different from that. I repeat what Lorenz says in this connection. Greylags, as we know, are monogamous. This appears to be optimal for their way of life. But when Lorenz and an associate reviewed the many individual biographies of the greylag that he had observed, he determined that the greylag was not always completely monogamous. And this upset him. It is typical of him that he would get upset about this. His coworker then said to him he should not get so upset because the greylags, after all, were also only human. Now, "they are also only human" means that they have only a *methexis* of the real greylag. The real greylag that the zoologist describes *is* monogamous, but it does not exist. Still, the real greylags that exist, the empirical greylags, are only possible because the pure form of the greylag exists in another sense, namely, as that law that describes the optimally functioning greylag. And Lorenz is a Darwinist. According to Darwin, that form of the greylag is successful in the struggle for survival that is optimally adjusted to conditions that only the zoologist knows and which the greylag does not know, and without which there would not be any greylags. This means that Lorenz has the beautiful thought that the realization of the Platonic idea in modern science only happens because everything happens very scientifically, just as Darwin, for example, describes it. There is no contradiction here between Plato and Darwin. In any case, Lorenz did not dare to talk as Platonically as I do here. I talked once with Lorenz about this and told him I would like to give him the courage to think in this manner. This is Platonism. It is not precisely what is found in the Platonic dialogues, but it is in accord with Plato's theories.

However, with this another problem has emerged. Plato, too, may have been occupied with couches and bridles and geese, but he had especially asked what also the contemporary physicist will ask, if he thinks about it, namely, how greylags are possible at all. What actually are the underlying laws? But it is exactly by practicing this beautiful science and by remaining completely true to nature and its laws that one arrives at Plato—not by leaping too quickly into the spiritual. The greylag is, the scientists say, made of molecules and these are made of atoms. The atoms obey the laws of quantum mechanics, and these are the true laws of modern physics, of elementary particle physics.

How do these correspond to Plato? First of all, in that the basic laws of nature are mathematical. But why should they be mathematical? With this we are led back to the question of how there is, in nature, in what we call the sensual reality, somelike like circles that share in the form of the circle itself as described in mathematics. We have now entered into the realm of the theory of ideas; everything I have previously said was merely an application of the concept "idea" in order to describe some phenomena. I want to characterize in my own words the systematic step that we must take here: I have drawn a circle on the blackboard and have asked, "What is this?" and the answer was, "A circle." It may not be a perfect circle, but, then, what is a circle? This I must ask in order to know to what extent it is or is not a circle. Now I say that a circle is a geometrical location of points that have a constant distance from a fixed point in a plane. With this, I have given a mathematical definition; the circle is thus a mathematical form. Plato calls this an idea. The mathematical forms are not the highest ideas. There is a Platonic terminology according to which *mathematika* are not yet real ideas. But I will not pursue this distinction for the moment. The circle is thus an idea. I recapitulate and ask, "What is this?" "A circle." "What is a circle?" "An idea." But what is an idea? Now, how have we proceeded before? We have gone from the frequent occurence of the systematically lower to the next higher through the inquiry "What is this?" It was always the explanation through that which we would name, logically, the higher concept. This is certainly not adequate for a characterization. Because we must ask: "What is the possible higher concept through which one can determine what an idea is?" If one were to say, "An idea is this and that," and were to point to something, then we would miss the entire train of thought. Then one would have explained the explanatory principle through something that should be explained precisely through this principle. The answer to the question "What is an idea?" can initially be the attempt to characterize what properties ideas have, just as I have characterized the circle through a mathematical definition. What are the properties of the idea? The idea, as Plato says, for example, in the middle of the *Republic*, is *one* compared with many realizations. He said that God has made *one* bed. The greylag, as the zoologist says in the singular, is *one*. Because the regular relationship that is being discussed here is one. The idea is thus one.

The idea is *good*. The circle that the mathematician describes is a good, *true* circle, in distinction from inferior circles that are drawn by hand. The idea *is*, is it real. I describe that which is a thing by naming its idea, therefore I describe its being through its idea. The ideas are characterized through being, in distinction from becoming and passing.

One can understand the idea. In fact, it is the only thing one can understand, and in this sense it is nonhidden, as Heidegger translated very well, it is *alethes*, it is true. In contemporary language the word "true" is used in such a way that we speak only about sentences and not about forms. Therefore, the translation as "nonhidden" is good: If I want to understand the figure that I draw on the blackboard and call "circle," I understand it *to the extent* that I call it a "circle." Therefore I understand its idea. Deviations from the idea are difficult to understand. I could say: These are chalk molecules. Yes, certainly chalk, but what is chalk? This, again, is a conceptual designation, and if I want to state it precisely, then I arrive perhaps at something like the idea of chalk. Therefore, what I understand is always the idea. And in this lies the essence of the idea. Now I have characterized the ideas through the transcendentals one, good, true, and being. These are the classical trascendentals, and they can all be found in Plato's *Republic*.

An inquiry that is continually pursued leads from the idea to the One. In the *Republic* it says that just as the sun gives the plants and animals being and light, being and visibility, so the idea of the good that is introduced as the highest idea, as the highest *mathema*, the highest teaching, gives to all that truly is, that means to the ideas, being and visibility, *on* and *alethes* as properties. That the good that is here discussed is systematically the same as the One is never explicitly said in Plato's writings, but is transmitted by Aristotle, and I think we should accept it. The transcendentals thus do not exist in an easily disclosed context, and I characterize them now as the One, *to hen*, the unity. The Platonic theory fulfills itself, if it can fulfill itself at all, in the teaching of the One. But what is the One? The attempt to refer the One back to something else is obviously a hopeless undertaking. Then it would not be the One, but rather a second or third. I cannot explain here Plato's philosophy of the One as he presents it in

Parmenides. It is here that the real theory of ideas begins. Aristotle tells us that Plato was of the opinion that there are two principles: One of them is called *to hen*, the One, and the other has different names, the "large-and-small" or the "undetermined duality," or, as we could say, the continuum. He says Plato used these two principles in order to arrive at the ideas and at what shares in the ideas.

If one pursues this line of thought, then one must wonder how there can be a *principle* if it is more than one. A reduction leads necessarily to the One and ends there. But how can there be two principles in a philosophy that is as strictly constructed as the Platonic? On the other hand, how is it possible to derive from one principle the multiplicity in which we live? The demonstration of this tension of the unity of the principle in respect to the multiplicity of principles is one way to interpret *Parmenides*. That dialogue, after all, attempts to show that whoever tries to think the One has no choice but to think the One in this movement of unity and multiplicity.

But now we go from the ascent to the descent. Only the descent, if I understand Plato correctly, is science. Also, only the descent is politics. In the image of the cave in the *Republic* Plato shows how we humans are all like prisoners in a cave where we sit chained and look at the walls of the cave where we see moving shadows, shadows of objects that pass by behind us, illuminated by a fire that is farther back. If we do not turn our eyes while sitting in the cave, we believe these shadows to be the only reality. This is the world of the senses. In the realm of politics, this is the triumph through elections and similar occurrences. But let us remain with physics. If we describe what we sensually perceive, then we mean that the sensually perceived is the thing itself. Now an about-face of the entire mind must occur, we must be led out of the cave so that we see the objects whose shadows we have seen on the wall of the cave. When we leave the cave to see the real objects, our eye at first is painfully blinded and cannot grasp them because it is not yet prepared for them. First, we saw only the shadows and images; now we see the things themselves in the light of the sun; and finally we can look at the sun itself. And the sun, Plato expressly says, is the metaphor for the good and is the appearance of the idea of the good. Once humans have come out of the cave, they will always want to see the things as they exist. But we must descend again into the cave, if only to teach those who have remained in the cave how to see. In the descent, we pass through all stages again and we again sit on a stool and see again the shadows on the wall, but—unlike those who remained—we *know*, now, what it is that we see. I would say that the late philosophy of Plato is the philosophy of the descent, of the return to the cave, explaining through the loftiest principles what it is that we see in the cave.

Into this presentation of the descent enters, it seems to me, the theory that is developed in *Timaios*, and which Heisenberg referred to, the theory of the polyhedrons of which the physical elements consist. In *Timaios* Plato gives a number of indications that he is being silent here about certain things. He uses a few puzzling sentences that contain precise assertions, and it appears to me unthinkable that Plato did not mean these assertions to be precise, even though he does not elucidate them. I am ready to accept, although not in every detail, a thesis developed by the Tübinger School, the thesis of Krämer and Gaiser that the unwritten teachings of Plato, about whose existence Aristotle speaks, did really exist, and that an essential part of these teachings was the outline of this mathematical science. What Aristotle says about this, for example, in *On the Soul*, is just as puzzling, and if one reads such reports by Aristotle and a few others, one cannot help feeling that this is a completely confused and incomprehensible philosophy, not worthy of Plato. This resistance against such interpretations of the unwritten teachings appears to me specifically linked to the belief that one has to protect Plato from the accusation that he produced bad philosophy. But I think that this philosophy is not bad, but that it remained unarticulated because Plato knew very well that it was merely hypothetical and because he wanted to avoid pointless speculations about it.

What is the content? Among other things, the content is, according to Aristotle in *On the Soul*, that Plato taught that there is a many-leveled descent from the pure numbers, which are the ideas, from there to the lines, from there to the surfaces, and from there to the bodies. In these four stages would be found the complete enumeration of that which nature really consists. This ascent or descent, depending on the side one is coming from, I would like to interpret as follows. Let us observe the question "What, after all, is a body?" first, mathematically. Plato teaches that, for example, fire consists of tetrahedrons, thus of certain little bodies. What is a tetrahedron? Or what is a cube? It is a volume that is enclosed by certain surfaces. These surfaces are triangular for the tetrahedron. The tetrahedron has its boundaries in the triangle. *Peras*, boundary, is a Platonic term that can systematically be used where otherwise "idea" is used. The idea is what gives the thing its form, of which it is a part to the extent that is has a form. The form is understood here as outline. The boundary, therefore, of the body called tetrahedron is the essence or idea of this body, and that is a certain arrangement of triangles. But what is a triangle? This is a flat figure, characterized through its boundaries, for example, the equilateral triangle through three equal sides. These sides are consequently that what make the essense of the triangle. The idea of the triangle lies in its boundary lines. But what is a line? A line is determined by a definite number of points, in this case two. The essence of this line is given by the points that terminate it. The points themselves have no further extension. They have no further part in the extension, in the large and the small, but they still have a number. What is the essence of point configurations? It is at least their number.

Now I have made the ascent through the dimensions from bodies to number, always operating with the conceptual pair of thing and essence. The essence is the idea; therefore, I have iterated the theory of ideas three times. I would now like to believe that this agrees with the Platonic construction at least to a small extent; and if that is so, one could understand the theory in *Timaios*. Then the pointed tetrahedrons, which are so sharp that one understands that fire burns because they penetrate our skin with their points, are an attempt to make such physiologic connections understandable, but they are only the lowest level of a derivation system, as the Tübinger School calls it, that traces back the essence of fire via the triangle to the line and to the number. The number, in turn, is what is developed through progress from the One—thus, in the end, through the two principles of the One and the unlimited duality, that is, the principle of multiplicity in general. This is an attempt to represent symbolically to what an extent the sensual world is not something that is opposed in radical dualism to the world of ideas, a one has so often taught, and to show, rather, to what an extent the sensual world is where the ideas present themselves in accordance with the principle of multiplicity, of indeterminate duality. It is thus an attempt at a deductive science.

If one is then asked why the mathematical laws of nature are valid, the answer is: because they are its essence, because mathematics expresses the essence of nature. To use the language of Kepler, this means God has created the world in accordance with his own thoughts of creation that are the pure forms. The demiurge who is introduced in *Timaios*, the divine artisan who has created the world, is the symbolic presentation of this essential connection. To what extent Plato had joined to this theory the notion of a conscious, personal being, of a world soul, of a world intelligence is something that he himself has concealed behind the veil of symbolic figures of speech, and which I will not try to analyze here.

The decisive transition from the One to multiplicity is essentially related to the principle of motion. Therefore, I must say a few words about Plato's theory of motion and time. Here I also reach the point where modern science has learned more and more how to separate itself from Plato. Modern science began as a theory of the mathematicization of motion. Galileo did that. He has mathematicized the motion in distinction to the mathematicization of the equilibrium, of statics, that had been taught in antiquity. The distinction, though, is not precise because in the astronomy of antiquity motion had already been mathematicized. How does Plato conceive of motion, how does he conceive of time in which, as we say, motion is? I could say here again that this question takes us only to the gate of Platonic philosophy. I think Plato's later philosophy is essentially a philosophy of motion.

Plato gives a definition of time in *Timaios*. It is, he says, the numerically progressing *aion* abiding in the One, that is, the image of the *aion*. What does *aion* mean? We translate it as "eternity." But one can also translate it, according to Greek usage, as a meaningful and fulfilled period of time. It is a term that appears in Plato without explanation. In any case, time is the image of something else; *Chronos* is the numerically progressing image of something else. This is numerically measurable time. Immediately after this, Plato says that the vault of heaven was created by the demiurge, so that time may exist, because time is measured by the orbits of heavenly bodies. The ideas appear in Plato as motionless. But in *Sophists* he speaks of them as if they were not motionless but perhaps existing in a motion that remains always the same. This is only hinted at, and I will not explore this thought further. Time represents itself in the vault of heaven as follows: There are two circles in heaven, the circle of the equal and the circle of the unequal; we call them the equator and the ecliptic. And the day is measured by the one circle, in which the entire vault of heaven revolves around the stationary earth once in 24 hours. The planets orbit in the other circle, in the ecliptic, and they enable us, through their always changing positions to tell one day from the other. Or let us put it this way: One needs a clock and a tear-off calendar in order to measure time, something that always remains the same while revolving, and something that is different every time, so that one can know how many revolutions have elapsed. This is presented in the Platonic construction through the day and, on the other side, through the planetary orbits. But Plato connects here with a Babylonian theory, as I have learned from van Waerden, namely, the teaching about the great year or, as one also says, the Platonic year. That is the period time after which all planets are in the same position as they were before. Plato suggests at least the thought, expressed also elsewhere in the Greek tradition, that if all planets are in the same position at the end as in the beginning the world is, in principle, the same as it was then. Time is thus cyclical according to the astronomical construction, and I would say that time must be thought of as cyclical also from a philosophical and metaphysical standpoint. Otherwise how could time be an image of what abides in the One if it proceeds out of the One and then never returns to where it came from? If time should really be an image of eternity, then the numerical advance of time must be a return. I would like to use again a formula. If one thinks Platonically, then it is the splendor of the world that there is nothing new in it. If there could be something new, then there also could be times in which the world was not as good as it can be. But, as stated in *Timaios*, we are not permitted to think that the world could be other than the best and that the demiurge could have viewed a model other than the best. Thus the splendor of the world demands that there be nothing new, and that means that time is cyclical.

Proceeding to modern times, we find, of course, many deviations from this Platonic plan, and yet there is a forming effect that penetrates everything, and the question is to what extent this is realized in modern science. Let us return again to the seventeenth century, to Kepler and Galileo. To them, this Platonic plan is not really a lucid philosophical theory, rather a great reservoir of images that one can use and in which one must have confidence in pursuing science. The real strictness of these arguments had not been seen in the seventeenth century, it was just surmised. But because this strictness was not really seen, and because experiences followed one another in rapid succession, of which Plato had no idea (and which could certainly not be understood according to Plato's special constructions), science slipped down from the Platonic pedestal. For example, we find instead of Kepler's personal piety and artistic fantasy, which could not be passed on, his physical and astronomical insights that connected him to completely different philosophies, such as that of the mechanical image of the world. The mechanical image of the world explained the regularities of nature in such a way that the things of nature consisted ultimately of matter, which has no other definable property than its impenetrability, and whose laws could be explained through pressure and impact, that is, through the effect of one impenetrable body upon another. This theory strongly influenced, even dominated, modern science for a few centuries. This theory disappeared completely through nuclear physics because, for us, the so-called atoms are not little billiard balls, and certainly not impenetrable matter. We describe them through the mathematical regularities of the quantum theory and not through visual images. One can show very easily to what inconsistencies the mechanical image of the world leads, but I do not want to pursue this here.

There are, also, empirical theories, which teach that one must follow experience and that one may anticipate it with mathematical hypotheses that one then tests against experience, theories that certainly correctly describe what happens in physics, but which leave completely unexplained why it is that these mathematical hypotheses are successful.

If one proceeds with these question to the twentieth century, then one sees that physics has things in mind that have no connection to Plato—with the exception of a few great figures such as Heisenberg—but that one aspect of Platonic thought begins to reassert itself, one that since the seventeenth century had been conceived only in the form of the mechanical image of the world, namely the thought of the unity of nature. Nuclear science incorporates chemistry and biology in different disciplines, in evolutionary theory, in the theory of selectivity, in cybernetics. And we do not know how far this development towards unity can proceed. It appears now that a unified science is possible, including even organic life. Physics itself merges out of the classical disciplines into a single theory, the quantum theory. Particle physics, which is now incomplete but which one hopes will be completed, and for which Heisenberg has made plans, attempts to explain why certain elementary particles exist, and not others, and tries to explain this through a single fundamental law. This fundamental law was already attempted by Einstein in a unified field theory, in a pre-quantum-theory manner. Heisenberg and other particle physicists are attempting today, in quantum theory, to present this unity better and anew. Here, it seems, we will eventually have the outcome of the historical development of physics, namely, that physics has unity as its fundamental principle, and the question is whether this unity has essentially much in common with the unity that Plato sought to conceive.

Pursuing further Heisenberg's thoughts about symmetry, one can say that the symmetrical groups that Heisenberg simply postulates were still hypothetical in Plato and, as we must admit, not objectively explained. The regular bodies are explained by Plato as all having as boundaries the same triangles; he explains that these triangles are all the same because they all have the same sides; and these sides are of equal length because they are the realization of the principle of equality that exists at the beginning of the entire construction. Here again the poorly proven theory of indivisible smallest lines is presented, and this theory, as it were, is an attempt to subject the mathematics of the continuum to a final unity. This loses itself, though, in something that we can hardly comprehend philosophically. Let me just say that Plato attempted to explain the symmetry of these bodies. His attempt thus goes beyond that which Heisenberg actually dared to undertake. But Heisenberg, too, would not reject an explanation of these symmetries if someone were able to present it.

So it appears that our physics recapitulates the different thoughts that were presented in Plato, but with an essential difference. The essential difference, in my opinion, is our understanding of time. Time, as we understand it, is not cyclical: it has an open future and a factual past that does not repeat itself. It is the time of history. In our physics, time is seen together with space, as in the relativity theory, which has no real analogy in ancient philosophy. Therefore, one could certainly not say that we have returned to a Platonic view, and I would be misunderstood if it appears from the above that my aim is merely a vindication of Plato. What I want to say is that modern science, relying in the beginning upon Plato without fully accepting his philosophy, returns to problems that Plato saw with clarity precisely at places where it did not follow Plato, and that a completion of physics, as might be possible in the future, seems to require the kind of philosophical reflection that would be in intellectual partnership with Platonic reflection. But only via Kant, I would like to add. Because the formulation that appears to me to be essential to explain the extent to which we can believe mathematical laws must contain the sentence that these laws are conditions of the possibility of experience. Otherwise we cannot really conceptualize the connection between the empirical proof of this science and the impossibility of establishing it empirically. This thought of Kant, that the laws of nature are the conditions of the possibility of experience, must be dealt with if we want to complete our argument with the old Platonic position.

2. The Dialectic of Hegel

A. Hegel's Design

In the search for the reasons of the ambivalence of progress, we encountered the phenomenon of the fragmentation of truth in the progress of the Enlightenment. "The heroic efforts of philosophy" appeared to be an answer to this fragmentation, originally in ancient Greece and later in Germany during the period from Kant to Hegel. We find ourselves now in a conversation with this philosophy.

Accordingly, the dialogue with Hegel has a specific reason. One cannot deny that Hegel, in his dialectic, attacked the phenomenon I have previously named ambivalence. His successors, especially Marx and the more subtle Marxists, possess in the dialectic a method of thinking that gives them a methodical superiority over positivist science and over the politics of liberalism, which both are blind to ambivalence. Someone could tell me: The personal discovery you think to make here has long been made. Pay attention and join up with the dialectic thinkers! Thus this dialogue with Hegel.

If, in reading the *Phenomenology of Mind*, one begins with the chapter on sensual certainty, one soon is pulled into a maelstrom of relentless reflection that does not let go until the last page of the book has been read. What is the whirling motion of this current? It is dialectic. But what is dialectic? One can comprehend it as a systematically maintained philosophical process. This process is embodied in Western philosophy in the person of Socrates. Socrates philosophized in conversations. He accepted the positions of his partners as they were presented and asked basically only one question: "Do you know what you are saying?" This question leads, if we can trust Plato's depiction, invariably to the exposure of ignorance. But it remained so only for those unphilosophical minds that were irritated by this. Those who were capable of philosophical reflection discovered that they could only have recognized their ignorance when they could compare apparent knowledge with knowledge of true knowledge.

They discovered in ignorance a knowledge they had possessed without knowing it.

In accordance with the accepted rules of classical philosophy, this philosophical process, which was strictly adhered to, did not lead to emptiness but to a goal. If it is followed step by step, each new step explains what appeared in the previous steps as knowledge. The process leads from the respectively conditioned to its condition. There would finally be no basis for knowledge without a last, unconditioned condition. Hegel calls the conditionless the absolute. True knowledge is knowledge of the absolute and of the knowledge that is based upon or contained within it. Only this knowledge Hegel calls "science."

But we must ask a skeptical question: Is absolute knowledge really possible? Is not the absolute intrinsically unknowable? Does this thought process not contain in the wishful thinking of a *petitio principii*?

It is an essential, methodical principle of Hegel's approach not to refrain from making skeptical objections. If the philosophical process is itself the sustained skeptical question "Do you know what you are saying?" then it must also ask this question of itself. It must itself be a part of this process, especially if the counterquestion is asked: "Do you know what you are asking?" Applied to the absolute: It is because of this question that before the dialectical process in the *Phenomenology of Mind* begins, there is an "Introduction." It is a reply to skepticism concerning the absolute that I would like to phrase as follows: With knowledge it may be that an intermediary term is necessary between knowledge and the object to be known, a condition of knowledge that may require special reflection. But with the unconditioned this cannot be so. If the absolute "were not and did not want to be already in and for itself with us,"[20] then it could not be brought closer to us through any "tool." There would be no knowledge of the absolute and consequently no other true knowledge, namely, knowledge that can bear skeptical questioning. One can make this thought easier by defining the absolute for the moment as knowledge itself. All knowledge of particular objects exists under the conditions of its knowledge. But whatever is knowledge, is "in and for itself" always "already with us" if we know anything at all, and without the existence of knowledge as such there would be no particular knowledge.

This answer, however, may be questioned, too. "But science, by appearing, is itself an appearance" (II, p. 70). How can it establish its better claim against other, from its perspective untrue, knowledge? "*A* dry asurance is just as valid . . . as *another*"[21] (II, pp. 70–71). "For this reason, the appearing knowledge should be presented here" (II, p. 71). This means that the appearing knowledge should be subjected to skeptical questioning until it has been revealed *what* appears in it, namely the absolute.

The philosophy of Hegel, taken itself as a phenomenon, is a dialectical dual process, first in the *Phenomenology* and a second time in the system that starts with the *Science of Logic* and which is summarized in the *Encyclopedia*. The phenomenology leads the appearing knowledge back to its causes in absolute knowledge; the system reveals the absolute knowledge according to its internal structure.

The way of knowledge that the phenomenology traces is the way of the mind to itself. To the intellect, the object is something that is different from the intellect. In this lies an untruth, which is overcome in the dialectic process. Consciousness reaches the point where it becomes self-consciousness. "I am different from myself, and I am directly aware that this difference is not differentiated" (II, p. 137).

But reason draws all objects into self-knowledge. "Reason is the certainty of consciousness that it is all of reality" (II, p. 183). "Reason is mind in that the certainty to be all of reality is raised to the level of becoming truth and in that it is conscious of itself as its world and of its world as itself" (II, p. 335). Religion is knowledge that the mind is all of reality, in the form of idea; religion conceives of the absolute as God. Absolute knowledge is knowledge in the form of a concept that comprehends itself. "The mind, which in this element (the concept) *appears* to consciousness or, which is the same here, is created in it, *this is science*" (II, p. 61).

"If in the phenomenology of mind each element is the difference between knowledge and truth and is movement in which it is neutralized, science, in contrast, does not contain this difference and this neutralization, but the element, by having the form of idea, unites the objective form of truth and of the knowing self in immediate unity. The element does not appear as this movement that passes from consciousness or from the idea to self-consciousness or vice versa, but its pure form, freed from its appearance in consciousness, the pure concept, and its motion depend solely on its pure *definiteness*. On the other hand, to every abstract element of science there is a corresponding form of the appearing mind as such. Just as the existing mind is not richer than science, it is also not poorer in content" (II, pp. 617–618).

It may seem confusing that science is not "this movement" in which "the difference between knowledge and truth . . . is neutralized," but that, nevertheless, the "pure definiteness of the idea" gives it "motion." Why is it that not only the phenomenology of mind but science itself is—one is tempted to say: again—a dialectic process?

Logic (see logic in Hegel's *Encyclopedia*, VIII, p. 201) may be seen as a sequence of "definitions of the absolute." It begins with the most unavoidable and content-free definiteness: pure existence. This, remote from any closer definiteness, turns out to be nothingness. But nothingness, in that it is, turns out to be existence. This transition, this turning-out-to-be, turns out to be development. The chain of reflectively gained definiteness leads from existence to that which has existence, to essence, and from essence to the understanding of essence, to the concept. The absolute exists. It is existence. It is what exists: essence. It is what is understood in essence: the concept. It is itself the concept, thus the concept that understands itself: the idea.

For the transition to nature and history I will again refer to the brief outline of science at the conclusion of the *Phenomenology of Mind*. "Knowledge does not only know itself but also its negative, or its limitation. Knowing of its limitation means knowing how to sacrifice itself. This sacrifice is the renunciation in which the mind presents its development as mind in the form of the *free, gratuitous event*, seeing its pure *self* as *time* outside itself and seeing its *existence* as space. Its last development, *nature*, is its live, direct development; nature, relinquished mind, is in its existence nothing but this eternal renunciation of its *development* and is the movement that is represented by the *subject*. But the other side of its existence, *history*, is *knowing* and *mediating* development: mind that is relinquished to time; but this renunciation is, in this manner, renunciation of itself; the negative is the negative of itself. This development represents a sluggish movement and sequence of minds, a gallery of images, each of which, equipped with the entire richness of the mind, moves so sluggishly because the self has to penetrate and digest all this richness of the substance" (II, pp. 618–619).

The objective inquiries that occupy us humans concretely and which in the ascent of the phenomenology to absolute knowledge were passed through with a certain impatience unfold in this philosophy of nature and mind. The possibility of science is seen by reason because nature is objectively reasonable, because it is mind that does not know itself as mind. Even more typically Hegelian is the notion that history is objectively reasonable; it is the working of the mind that finds itself. This working is not primarily the working of knowledge and not the mere development of the individual, but concrete human life in human society. "Self-consciousness is *in* and *for itself* in that it is for something other than itself and for itself; that is, it exists only as something known" (II, p. 148). Actual human life is rule and subjection, it is public morals, estranging education, morality, it is family, society, law, and the state. All these are not contingent events or eternal order; all these are the actual way of truth. "Therefore, until the mind cannot complete itself *in itself* as world mind, it cannot reach its completion as self-conscious mind" (II, p. 614).

In a specific sense of the term, history for the first time has become the subject of philosophy in Hegel's system. The subject of philosophy is truth. Truth, from Greek philosophy on, has been seen as the eternal, in contrast to the transitoriness of humans, which was always known and which is already Homer's subject, and in contrast to the relativity of opinions, which was uncovered in the sophistic. History, transitoriness, had to appear as that which is opposite to truth or as that which shares in truth in an incomplete manner, or—which is already quite modern—as an unending approximation to the eternal truth. Hegel realized that each one of these views is unsatisfactory. He feels this also in the state of unarticulated swimming in history that is obvious in the naive belief in progress—taking into account the background of such a modern feeling in Hegel. But in Hegel this feeling is already opposed by the deep experience of estrangement, thus of the ambivalence of progress, and forces him to take the negative seriously. Hegel reflects thoroughly on the inadequacy of those views on truth; he subjects them to skeptical inquiry: How can we humans talk about truth at all if our transitoriness separates us intrinsically from the essence of truth, of the eternal? How can the absolute, in and for itself, be with us—want to be with us? These questions force Hegel to think of the truth of history as the history of truth. This is realized, for example, in the philosophy of political theory as the road to a free society, because freedom is an appearance of the existence of truth.

This thought struck like lightning into the dark contours of actual history. Even the muted thunder of his successors has proven to be a powerful political force for more than a century. We must, indeed, not overlook the fact that Hegel's philosophy undertakes something that is enormous—both from the perspective of classical philosophy and from that of the average modern awareness. Isn't it that the history of truth was precisely not the history of progressive knowledge of a truth that existed in itself, with no truth existing at all, only a sequence of successful opinons? How, then, can truth itself have a history, inner movement, development?

Hegel approaches this problem through the manner in which he thinks of the relationship between the self-movement of the concept and the absolute. "In my opinion, which has to be justified through my system, everything depends on our viewing and expressing truth not only as *substance* but also as *subject*" (II, p. 22). In the beginning of movement, the absolute is only in itself, as mere existence, but it has to be in and for itself. "Truth is the whole. But the whole is only the essence that completes itself in its development. Of the absolute it must be said that it is intrinsically *result*, that only in the *end* it is that which it is in truth; and it is in this that lies its nature, its nature of being reality, subject, or its-becoming-itself" (II, p. 24). "Therefore, time appears as the fate and the necessity of the mind, which is not completed in itself" (II, p. 613). "It is the *externally* seen pure self, *not perceived* by the self, the merely viewed concept" (II, p. 612). "This is why the mind must appear in time, and it appears in time as long as it does not *perceive* its pure concept, that is, as long as it does not abolish time" (II, p. 612). "But this substance, which is the mind, is the *development* into what the mind is *in itself*; and it is only as this self-reflecting development that the mind in itself is truly the *mind*. It is in itself the movement that is knowledge—the transformation of that *in itself* into the *for itself*, of *substance* into *the subject*, of the object of *consciousness* into an object of *self-consciousness*, that is, into a thus abolished object or into the *concept*. It is the circle that returns to itself, which presupposes its beginning and reaches it only in the end" (II, 613).

This philosophy thus knows an *end*, not out of arbitrariness but out of speculative necessity. One could say that it knows it for the same reason that it knows a beginning, which, after all, is in itself already the end. Therefore, a discussion of the absolute that is and wants to be already with us must precede the beginning of the dialectic voyage. Or, more precisely put, Hegel's concept of truth, too, as it is in and for itself, excludes time; and this is why time, in the end, must be abolished. Again, this is not arbitrariness. It is a consequence of the fact that Hegel takes truth in history seriously as truth in the only sense in which philosophy could think of truth until Hegel. Whoever disagrees with this would have to demonstrate that he can think of truth in any other sense or, which is even harder, that he can get along in truth without truth.

B. Criticism of Hegel

In the foregoing thoughts I have, I admit, passed over that skeptical inquiry at several places. If we follow Hegel's opinion that history is objectively reasonable, then we must be able to discover reason also in the historical effects of his philosophy. Among these historical effects is the so-called collapse of the Hegelian system in the middle of the nineteenth century under the onslaught of a diversity of critics. It was a veritable zoo of skeptical inquiries, mostly in the form of mindless hostility. I would like to group and articulate some of these critiques and examine their validity.

Methodically speaking, one can try to separate the critiques into external, immanent, and fragmenting. An external critique does not deal with Hegel's thought processes but criticizes their results. An immanent critique tries to lead Hegel's thoughts to a result that is different from Hegel's; it usually sees itself as going beyond Hegel. A fragmenting critique I call a critique that presumes to pursue certain thought processes immanently to new goals by cutting other thought processes off externally. Any historically presented immanent critique has eventually been fragmenting *de facto*.

Hegel's philosophy lends itself to this grouping of critiques because of its dual claim of intellectual rigor in each dialectic step and in the systematic unity of the whole. The connection between the individual steps and the whole does not consist—as superficial critics have charged—in a formalism of dialectic thought, which could be applied, so to speak, mechanically to each step. The inquiry, in each individual case, concerns the question of the essence of the respective matter; it cannot be "applied" as a procedure but must be thought spontaneously in each instance. The dialectic would lose its meaning if this requirement were overlooked. But a result of this is that Hegel, as a person, had to examine the respective matter, in each individual case—actually examine, with intellectual adequacy. The gigantic nature and dimensions of Hegel's work are the result of this attempt to fulfill these factual requirements as a single human being. Psychologically speaking, one could say that it was his tendency toward omnipotence, with philistine and professorial safeguards, that made Hegel's gigantic undertaking possible. But which professor could throw the first stone here? And one has to see the philosophical consistency of the undertaking. If a philosophy attempts to demonstrate absolute knowledge as a result, it has to realize this in each step it takes; if not, it would be criticized not to do what it teaches, it would be criticized as untrue. Any relevant criticism of Hegel's system as system should therefore not find fault with individual inadequacies or with his personality; rather, it would have to prove the intrinsic impossibility and falseness of the undertaking as a whole. For such an immanent critique of the system, criticism of details would then furnish important examples. But criticism of the system as system has usually remained external. One became accustomed to hear simply of the collapse of the system and of all systems generally and of the impossibility of any kind of systematic philosophy.

But through the external abandonment of the system all critiques of details became *de facto* fragmenting; and it was this that made it easier to interpret them, after all, as immanent. I would like to talk of three groups of individual critiques: critique from positivistic science; critique of philosophy of religion; and political critique.

Critique coming from *positivistic science* was overwhelmingly external, and it was mainly this critique that for a century conveyed the negative image of Hegel. Some of its external arguments were, in fact, good or at least plausible. I will look at this critique from the perspectives of logic, of science, and of history; the positivistic social science of our century has simply perpetuated this critical tradition.

Critique from the standpoint of logic dwells on the fact that Hegel understands dialectic as movement through contradiction. The actual contradictions he constructed have provoked ridicule on the part of modern logicians. Bertrand Russell says that Hegel's dialectic is nothing but the repetition of those logical errors that Aristotle had managed to overcome with his creation of scientific logic.

Critique from the standpoint of science is just as scathing, for example, the criticism of the young Hegel's misfortune in his justifying the number 7 of the seven planets coincidentally with the discovery of Ceres, which was thought to be the eighth planet. This relatively unimportant anecdote (who has never believed in false theories?) typified the empiricists' healthy aversion against constructions that are made at a desk *a priori*. This aversion, which is historically conditioned and, I think, only historically justifiable in its lack of reflection, created an atmosphere in which a fair examination of Hegel's philosophy of nature was impossible. But even though we are better able today to appreciate the thoroughness of Hegel's knowledge of the science of his age as well as the level of reflection of many of his thoughts, we are, I think, still far from doing justice to the great design of his philosophy of nature. I have the impression that it cannot teach us anything seriously today. Nevertheless, I consider the underlying questions of great importance.

Critique from the discipline of *history* has largely taken the form of quarrels among colleagues. It is true that here, too, the positivistic research of the nineteenth century has, in general, rejected Hegel's entire system as a structural straitjacket. Jacob Burckhardt, in the introduction to his *Force and Freedom: Reflections on History*, comments on Hegel: "He says that the only thought that philosophy *contributes* is the simple thought of reason, the thought that reason rules the world, thus that the course of world history has been reasonable, and that the outcome of world history *must* (sic) be that it has been the reasonable, necessary process of the world mind—all of which, after all, would have to be proven and would not be *contributed*. . . . However we are not privy to the purposes of the eternal wisdom and are ignorant of them. This cheeky anticipation of a world plan leads to errors because it starts from wrong premises. . . . *Our* point of departure lies in the only remaining and, to us, only possible center, that of the suffering, striving, and acting human being, the way we are and always have been and will be; so that our reflection, in a way, will be pathologic."[22] As consoling as this passage may be in its skeptical humanity, it cannot entirely escape the reproach of unexamined postulation of its own historical-philosophical premises ("the way we are and always have been and will be"). Hegel has often criticized this mistake of unexamined philosophical premises on the part of postitivistic science. Burckhardt, further, does not escape the charge of being superficial in his critique because Hegel, in the introduction to the philosophy of history, from which Burckhardt quotes, has said: "Actually, I do not have to presuppose such a belief. . . . Only a contemplation of world history itself has to show that reason did prevail in it, . . ." (XI, p. 36). Burckhardt, of course, would have thought that no imaginable serious contemplation of world history could yield such a result.

When we look at details, we see that today's historian is more likely than today's scientist to find many of Hegel's individual observations and reflections instructive and worthy of discussion. I personally find it rewarding to test any of Hegel's descriptions of historical processes whenever a concrete occasion presents itself. He nearly always touches an essential nerve of the events or, in intellectual history, of the respective thoughts. On the other hand, I practically never find that he sees the process adequately in its entirety, be it only as it would have been possible with the knowledge available to him. There is a trace of brilliant foreedness that clings to his interpretations. Occasionally, too, he sees more than one can see; he did not possess the virtue of discretion.

Of interest is the question of how we relate to his grand historical-philosophical design. His onesidedness is obvious, not only in the traditional identification of European history with world history, but also in his arbitrary choice from this history. Hegel himself has formulated the selection principle in his offensive thesis that in each era there is only *one* people that counts in world history (*The Philosophy of Right*, Para. 347, VII, p. 447). In that aspect of history where we, today, believe most consistently in truth, namely, in the history of the exact sciences, it is natural for us, too, to give priority to that trend of development that leads to truth as we know it today, and to use it to test the historical rank of everything else. Thus our judgment of Hegel's principle of selectivity will eventually depend on our interpretation of truth in history; one does not escape philosophy through flight into positivism. The two remaining groups of critiques are closely connected to this question of truth in history.

Hegel's *philosophy of religion* has been criticized from opposite directions, by nonbelievers (for example, Feuerbach) and by believers (for example, Kierkegaard). Oddly, these critiques are less at opposite ends than the standpoints of the critics. What they have in common could be called ideological reproach. Feuerbach's religious criticism that God has been made according to human image, which goes back to the sophistic of antiquity, finds a natural resonance in Hegel's philosophy. Hegel is absolutely consistent in asserting that the only thing that can be meaningfully discussed in philosophy is what is actually known. His immanent critique of certain figures in the history of Christianity under the headings of unfortunate consciousness and of belief consists precisely in saying that to these persons their own self disappears into unreachable realms in the image of an otherwordly God. The only, but decisive, justification of religious consciousness that is possible in Hegel's philosophy is that God himself, the mind itself, recognizes itself as all of reality in the human consciousness. There is just one step of fragmenting critique—common to nearly all later Hegel critics—that suffices to present this metaphysics as untenable: namely, the rejection of the philosophy of science. If nature itself is not mind, that is, if the mind has no right to comprehend itself as all of reality, then the problem of religion becomes historically immanent; it becomes, in modern parlance, existential. One may then view nature and the human being, in Christian tradition, as God's creation, or one may, in the sense of the scientific materialism of the nineteenth century, see matter as reality and God as invention—either way, in religion, the divine mind no longer thinks in itself. The human being, in religion, is now faced either with itself or with something "entirely different." To both attitudes, Hegel's view represents an ideologicalization, a flight from the actual human situation into dreams of metaphysics.

If we go, here too, into details, Hegel's philosophy of religion shows again an amazing touch of the nerve of matters in many situations, from the experience of the "essence of light" (II, p. 529) to certain traits of Oriental, Egyptian, Greek religion to Christianity, even though, again, not without forcedness on Hegel's part. This forcedness often stems from the need to classify, for example, when Hegel, despite astounding knowledge of details and apt description of many traits of Indian religion and culture, nevertheless does not consider the Indian tradition as an equal conversation partner to ours, making derogatory judgments where he should know quite well that he lacks the relevant experience. The mystical experience is alien to him. Instead there is reason as the self-aware mind, and mysticism is judged as mere feeling; the *unio mystica* appears only in the Sacrament (XVI, p. 338). I personally think that his theological exegesis of the Christian dogma is far superior to the orthodox, rationalistic, liberal, and existentialistic approaches, and yet I can hardly believe that anyone would risk his life for a Christianity that is explained in such a manner. This philosophy is a cathedral in God's honor, built out of thoughts, but it is not the live mind of God among humans. And, philosophically seen, the objection is not that the absolute does not exist, but it is the question whether the revealed unconditionalness is really only this—merely this. But, here again: Who can throw the first stone?

The coarse and superficial thesis of *political critique* consisted in the charge that Hegel glorified the goal of world history in the Prussian state in the same way he glorified the self-knowledge of the world mind in his philosophy. This criticism is external and unjust. I would like to refer especially to J. Ritter's presentation (*Hegel und die französische Revolution*, Suhrkamp edition of 1965), which shows that one gains a much better insight into Hegel's self-understanding if one looks at him as the philosopher of the French Revolution. In revolution, the freedom of everyone has become a principle, and this is the political goal of world history. W. Lübbe has pointed out that among Hegel's disciples the so-called Hegelian Right was reformed-liberal and by no means conservative. But when the Hegelian Left maintained that going beyond Hegel meant making a transition from thought to revolutionary action, then this was immanent-fragmenting critique; this is not the way Hegel thought. I am not going to examine Marx's critique of Hegel, which would take too much space here. Marx was certainly right when saying that Hegel did intrinsically not want what Marx wanted politically, although it is possible, he said, to extend Hegel's philosophy in such a way that Hegel would *have to* want the same thing. In the critique of the Hegelian Left, Hegel's philosophy of religion is seen as retreat into conservative ideology, as renunciation of action.

What did Hegel want politically, as a consequence of his philosophy and as empirical individual? As for the latter, let me derive the following picture from the description that Ritter and Popitz give in *Der entfremdete Mensch* (Europäische Verlagsanstalt, 1967): Along with his entire generation in Germany, the young Hegel felt deeply the self-estrangement of the human being in the modern world. Into this receptive atmosphere entered the decisive experience of the French Revolution. From a political perspective, one could see Hegel's entire philosophy, according to Ritter, as an effort to comprehend what thus has entered world history and in this way make its reality possible. Making possible means neither to prevent it through restauration, nor to let it slide into chaos. Both dangers are actually the same because restauration would, without knowing it, provoke the countermovement of chaos. These dangers are realized in Hegel's late writings on the British Reform Bills. Personally, Hegel sought stability, and he suffered to the end of his life under the perpetual political uncertainty. Stability, however, has to be stability of freedom for everyone. The state is the objective form of the mind that can guarantee this stability. On the one hand, classical economics is one of the great models for the working of reason in history without the individual's being aware of it; it is the opposite of Plato's philosopher kings. On the other hand (*The Philosophy of Right*, Para. 243, VII, p. 318), the industry of bourgeois society engenders "dependence and misery of the class that is tied to this work." A guarantee of freedom for all cannot be found in the free play of societal forces. "The state is the reality of the moral idea, it is the moral mind as the *obvious*, self-perceived, substantial will that thinks in itself and knows and accomplishes what it knows and in that it knows" (*The Philosophy of Right*, Para. 257, VII, p. 328).

From a biographic-historical perspective, Hegel's political philosophy is an intelligent and decent way of ordering with a good concept, for a while, the problems of his time and of his position in Europe. But such political theories are designed quite often, and they retain only historical interest after a short time. It is more rewarding to deal with the full philosophical consequence of his theory, even at the risk of making it thus appear stranger. Namely, we cannot separate it from the context of his philosophy of religion. The revelation of God takes place in the sensory reality of the unity of divine and human nature, in that the mind "*exists* as an actual human being"; "It is *really the case*" (II, p. 576). The Christian community, in the realm of the mind, lives in this knowledge. "A subjectivity that has understood its infinite worth has thus given up all distinctions of domination, of power, of social class, even of gender: All humans are equal before God. It is only in the negation of the infinite pain of love that one can find the possibility and the root of true universal law, of the *realization of freedom*" (*Philosophy of Religion*, XII, p. 313). It is in the organization of the state that the divine becomes reality, that reality becomes imbued with the divine, and that the secular becomes justified in and for itself because its basis is the divine will, the law of right and freedom. The true reconciliation in which the divine is realized in the realm of reality consists in the moral and just life of the state: This is the true role of the secular" (XVI, pp. 343–344). Thus political freedom in the state is the fulfillment of world history; Hegel himself saw the need to understand the political theme of his age as realization of the absolute.

But how can such a philosophy exist when history goes on? One could say that even today the political theme is basically the same. But I will not take this way out. Hegel certainly is not politically obsolete. But, then, with the proper arguments, the same could be said for Plato. It is necessary to resort to an emphasis of this aspect of philosophers if one tries to show that they have contemporary relevance. But we do them greater honor, and we can learn more from them, if we make sharp inquiries and find out where they went wrong. "Until . . . the mind *in itself* has not completed itself as world mind, it cannot reach its completion as *self-conscious* mind" (II, p. 614), or, more poetically: "Only when twilight comes does the owl of Minerva begin its flight" (Introduction to *The Philosophy of Right*, VII, p. 37). If I have interpreted this correctly, above, then Hegel's concept of the truth of history demands this ending. Hegel, as an intelligent representative of his age, had an open mind toward the future; but his philosophical self-interpretation could not allow that there would be anything *essentially* new in history.

C. Countercritique

In order to elevate these various critiques to the appropriate level, I have often contradicted them and have discussed them with a tone of respect and with sympathy for Hegel. However, if we now ask what Hegel can mean *to us*, it appears that the answer is disappointing. No one believes in the system anymore. The dialectic as movement through contradiction has been cast aside by logic. The philosophy of science is irrelevant to the physicist of our age. The philosophy of history contains intelligent observations and the constraints of a system to which we might perhaps be sympathetic, not through empirical experience but possibly through a systematic decision on our part. The philosophy of religion is seen, by both the believer and the nonbeliever, as ideology, as flight into doubtful metaphysics. The political philosophy may evoke partial contradiction in Marxists and proper skepticism in liberals; but it is politically outmoded and fixed in its outmodedness through its system. The grand design of understanding the truth of history as the history of truth ran aground in 1830. Hegel, today, is just an interesting subject in the history of philosophy. The owl of Minerva ended its flight long ago.

It is to this kind of criticism that I will now undertake a countercritique. It will not dispute anything that has just been said and will thus not try to lead us back to Hegel. What it wants to point out is that those critiques leave us with a fragmentation of truth for whose sake we inquired into Hegel in the first place. This outcome need not surprise us. We knew from the outset that Hegel's philosophy had not withstood the ambivalent progress. But it is also true that the positions with which this progress is being interpreted today cannot withstand a skeptical inquiry either. We must again make this inquiry the way philosophy has always done it, and the way Hegel, too, did it with the philosophies that preceded him.

In the social sciences we have today the position of the dialecticians. They make a skeptical inquiry into the supposedly objective results of the positivists, questioning theoretically the choice of isolating positions, and questioning practically the interest underlying the choice. But the dialecticians, in turn, must be subjected to skeptical inquiry. What is it that is called dialectic in this procedure? What is the strength of dialectic in the framework of sociohistorical inquiry? Is it dialectic in Hegel's sense? Does it know what it means by contradiction? What is its relation to nature? In 1962, in conversation with J. Habermas, I let myself be carried away and said that the Rhodes for the *saltus* of dialectic is not history but nature. Just as we can conceive of nature dialectically, I would be willing, I said, to grant dialectic a greater role in history, too. This does not mean that I have hopes for Hegel's philosophy of nature, but that the dialectic still has to face its toughest matter, if it still values the statement that truth is the whole. Also the retreat of the dialectic from religious concerns cannot hold up. Mere disregard of religion inasfar as it is reactionary ideology is not on a level that would be accessible to dialectic. Religion cannot be irrelevant. It is either truth or a lie.

D. Estrangement

Let us return to the question of ambivalence. How did Hegel describe this phenomenon? We find two concepts in this respect, the speculative concept of negation and the historical concept of estrangement.

The mind is only real and alive in being differentiated from itself, and this difference is negation. The directly positive is only in itself; it becomes for itself through the self-differentiation, through negation; it becomes in and for itself through the negation of negation. "The life of God and the divine knowledge may also be expressed as a playing of love with itself; this idea deteriorates to mere edification, even to shallowness, if it lacks seriousness, pain, patience, and the working of the negative" (II, p. 23). The dialectic *always* leads to something other than the intended. If reality is dialectic or can be understood only dialectically, then ambivalence is a basic structure of existence in general. In this case, ambivalence is not a disturbing aspect of progress but the essence of progress. It can end only where progress ends, in the self-realization of the absolute mind.

This answer refers us to the basis of our entire existence. If our dangerous naiveté is to be shaken up, than the implanting of ambivalence in historical existence as such must have taken place at one time. But the answer is not enough for us, for two reasons. It is too general, but it is also too much oriented toward certain doubtful traits of the Hegelian system.

The answer is too general. We are dealing with sharply outlined ambivalences to which we must relate in a practical manner: the ambivalences of technology, of liberalism, of socialism, the ambivalences of human nature, of social failures, of the ego that fights against itself. It is for these that we need counsel. And Hegel's system does not leave us without counsel here. It deals with a large number of these ambivalences under different titles, especially under the title of estrangement. On the other hand, these concrete examples take us dangerously close to the unsolved question of whether Hegel's era, or a later era, or any era could represent the end of progress as the self-realization of the mind. But it is important to face this problem directly, by examining Hegel's theory of estrangement.

The *Phenomenology of Mind* includes a section called "Mind *Becoming Estranged:* Formation." It is the center portion of the chapter entitled "The Mind," which pursues loosely the history of the West. The first portion, "The *True* Mind: Public Morals," is mainly a depiction of Greek and Roman society. Our portion looks at basic forces in modern times up to the French Revolution. The final portion, "The *Self-Conscious* Mind: Morality," includes a long discussion of Kant's ethics and, under the title of conscience, of that mode of being human that has overcome these diverse ambivalences and which, certain of itself, is ready for absolute knowledge. Then follows the chapter on religion, reaching into the depths of history, and then the final chapter on absolute knowledge.

One sees immediately that, to Hegel, estrangement is not an act or state of "structural force" that one part of society inflicts on the rest. It is true, it can assume also this role. But intrinsically it is something that the human mind does to itself, in order to find to itself, on the long road of hard work. If in itself it was already with itself, it has to become estranged from itself in order to learn to be for itself. The being-for-itself takes the form of estrangement that is, as understood in the end, necessary in order to be mind with itself and in and for itself.

I will not deal with the antiquity here. As for the Middle Ages, Hegel usually does not mention them. In modern times, we are concerned mainly with the human value of the individual that was disclosed through Christianity. The world of the self-estranged mind "is two-fold; the first is the world of reality or of its estrangement itself; the other is the world that the mind, transcending the first, creates in the heavens of pure consciousness. This, as it is opposed to that estrangement, is for that reason not free from it, but only the other form of an estrangement that consists in its having consciousness in dual worlds and in comprising both. What is contemplated here is thus not the self-consciousness of the absolute being as it is *in* and *for itself*, not religion, but *faith* insofar as it is the *flight* from the actual world and thus not *in* and *for itself*" (II, p. 376). Here we see designed as estrangement the basic structure of what later was called ideology. "But the existence of this world as well as the reality of self-consciousness is based on movement, so that self-consciousness gives up its personality and thereby creates its world, which it regards as something strange that it now must seize. . . . Or, self-consciousness is *something*, has *reality*, only insofar as it becomes estranged from itself" (II, pp. 376–377). I think that these words describe a structure of modern times that prevails today more than ever.

I will not deal here in detail with the dialectic of the forces that characterized the seventeenth and the eighteenth century. Power of the state and wealth—we would say, absolutism and capitalism—are examined in their positive and negative aspects. The irresistibility of the Enlightenment is described. "The communication of pure insight is . . . comparable to a quiet expansion and the *spreading* of an aroma in the nonresisting atmosphere. It is a penetrating infection that does not announce itself as something extraneous to the at first indifferent element into which it insinuates itself and that therefore could not be assessed" (II, p. 418). But it becomes "as insight the negative of pure insight, it becomes nontruth and nonreason . . . in that it gets involved in fighting and means to fight something *else*" (II, p. 420). What is opposed to it is faith.

In the description of the further development of the Enlightenment we find this beautiful historicodialectic sentence: "A party proves to be *victorious* only in that it breaks up into two parties; because in this it demonstrates that it itself had the principle it fought against, and that it now abolished the onesidedness with which it first appeared" (II, p. 442). The world of utility, of absolute freedom, and of terror ("the only work and deed of general freedom is therefore death," II, p. 454) are results of this development. Here we arrive at the political philosophy we discussed earlier.

In Hegel's theory of estrangement, the description of the manifold phenomena often has great clarity and brilliance. The diagnosis of the modern age as a time of estrangement is still true today, in fact, increasingly true. The hope that in this estrangement the mind would find itself is dwindling. Hardly anyone would dare today to identify specific events in recent history with the overcoming of the estrangement unless he acted under an inner ideologic compulsion, which might be merely a repression of despair. I am not asking here a content-oriented question of Hegel that far exceeds a diagnosis of our time. I am only asking which inner consequences of Hegelian thinking may be expected, to the extent that we intend to assume his thoughts.

The essentially optimistic view that estrangement, as a particular historical form of negativity, is an appearance of seriousness, suffering, patience, and the working of the mind that finds to itself, is essential to Hegel's *system*. From a Christian perspective, Hegel's view of the modern age may be understood as an evolutionist interpretation of eschatology—in the sense of Schiller's "world history is world judgment." But even though this may have been, biographically and thus in reality, a motive of Hegel, Christian eschatology does not play an important role in the inner consequence of his thinking. Rather, such a role was played by his concept of the truth of history, thus by the absolute as result. If the reality of history, in Hegel's time and in ours, does not demonstrate this reconciliation, and if we nevertheless do not want to abandon Hegel's basic thought, then there are two ways out: a postponement of the time of reconciliation to the future or the radical renunciation of this expectation.

I think that Marxism is the greatest example of the postponement of expectation. It modifies not only the time scale but the very structure of the expected reconciliation by adding a revolutionary economicopolitical step that Hegel had not foreseen. Whether this step is compatible with the Hegelian concept is a question I will not discuss here, just as I will not deal here with a dispute with Marxism in general. For the Marxist it is, of course, by no means necessary or even desirable to take over the Hegelian system. But I would like to point out that *Hegel's* belief in a reconciliation of the estrangement is intrinsically tied to his system and that without his system this belief would have appeared to him as entirely unfounded.

If we disregard Hegel's system, then the question arises whether dialectic without this thought can be a strict, viable concept at all. It is because I consider this doubtful that I have not applied the concept of dialectic in part I, using instead the concept of ambivalence, which presented itself not as something that was already known but as a problem.

3. Remembering Martin Heidegger

The first meeting was in Todtnauberg in the fall of 1935. Somebody, I believe it was the physiologist Achelis, had come up with the idea that Viktor von Weizsäcker (my uncle) and Werner Heisenberg should speak with each other, in Heidegger's presense, about the introduction of the subject in science. We were Heidegger's guests for a meeting that lasted several days. We lived in a hotel, and the meeting took place in Heisenberg's little hut high up in a mountain meadow near the edge of the forest. We sat close together, and there were seven of us, if I remember correctly, around a wooden table in the tiny room. Heidegger sat at the end of the table closest to the door, and he was wearing self-designed and fashionable peasant attire, with a pointy cap on his head—little, collected. My uncle and Heisenberg sat at either side. Next to them sat Prince Auersperg, the highly gifted colleague of my uncle, and the art historian Bauch. I, the youngest, sat on the other end of the table facing Heidegger. I do not well remember what was said, but I remember how it was said. Both protagonists spoke for a long time with each other, each interested in what the other said, but they were separated by a chasm. Heisenberg deeply felt the abyss that had been opened through the unsought discovery of the inseparability of subject and object in the quantum theory, but he knew also that one cannot live in the abyss. He held on to a precise explanation of the role of the subject as observer and experimenter. Viktor von Weizsäcker, on the contrary, wanted to see the subject as the living thing, as the partner, "introduced into medicine" and to become philosophically the pathetic bearer of the undertaking of science: "in order to understand life, one must participate in life." He did not yet see the objective observer of the quantum theory as the subject. After both of them had talked for an hour in intelligent misunderstanding, Heidegger summarized the situation. "Herr von Weizsäcker, you seem to mean the following." Then came three crystal-clear sentences. "And you, Herr Heisenberg, seem to mean this." Again three just-as-clear sentences. And the answer, "Yes, that's how I imagine it to be." "Then the context may be as follows." Then four or five concise sentences. Both agreed, "This is the way it could be." The dialogue went on, until Heidegger helped them get through the next bottleneck.

At leave-taking, Heidegger said to me, in a friendly way, that I should come again whenever I had time. After that, I visited him regularly, perhaps every other year, either in his mountain hut or in his Freiburg house where his wife always received me with hospitality. Later we also met in professional situations such as linguistic conferences in Munich and Berlin. On the occasion of a preliminary conference in Bregenz with Martin Buber and Clemens Graf Podewils, he visited my mother with me in the small old farm house near Lindau where she had lived for a long time. It remains unforgettable to me how he immediately felt at home in the hospitality of these low-ceilinged rooms. In the sixties, as an old man, he was three times my guest at my house in Hamburg, during seminar weeks with six of my colleagues. To my wife he was an especially dear, quiet, friendly, and considerate guest who left us a permanent impression with his evening readings of Hegel.

I have had read Heidegger's books with hesitation, the way I was generally able to assimilate philosophy. I bought *Being and Time* in Copenhagen in the winter of 1933–34 as I worked with Bohr (my copy still bears the name of the bookseller, "Host & Son, Bredgade, Copenhagen"). I read Kant at the same time. In both of them I experienced the endless difficulty of understanding that is rooted in the power of this philosophy itself, but I found Heidegger closer to me than any other philosopher in the unresolved problems that concerned me. The memory of the only academic lecture that I ever heard him give, while on a visit to Freiburg in the late thirties, become a symbol of this reaction. The theme was "logic," and he spoke about Heraclitus. There the little man, in his green attire, went through the overcrowded lecture hall to the podium and began to recapitulate the last hour, in Southern Schwabian dialect, formulating it concisely, sentence by sentence, as we held our collective breath. My reaction was: "That is philosophy. I do not understand a word. But that is philosophy."

Our conversations, during my visits, adhered to a loose ritual. He received me with friendliness, and asked about Heisenberg, my family, my health. Then he sat down before an almost empty work table, on which were just a few, neatly written pages, lying at right angles in front of him. I remember what my friend, and his student, Georg Picht said about him: "Heidegger is, by nature, concentrated. When he lets himself go, he is concentrated." He would ask me what I was working on, and I would talk about it for an hour or longer. He listened with quiet attentiveness, even if I spoke about theoretical physics, which he could not follow mathematically, or of the fundamentals of mathematics, or of aspects of temporal logic that I had thought out for myself. His short questions while I spoke were limited to factual matters. But what remained unclear to him in my presentation, and what his questioning exposed, was what was not fully clear to myself at the moment! And when the report was finished, I could expect with certainty that his further questions would uncover the weak spots in my construction, and either strengthen them or help them to their demise. Proceeding from physics and mathematics, we continued with inner consequence to the great intellectual issues of modern and Greek philosophy. The same thing happened when I told him in later years about my political analyses and engagement. He considered my political positions, almost always, with sympathy, and wished me success, and with a few questions he elicited from my slumbering awareness the insight into why they must be in vain.

Wide-ranging philosophical conversations followed his inquiries into my own work. Occasionally we read together a short classical text. Once it was in Aristotle's *Metaphysics*, another time a passage from Kant or Hegel. He spoke about his *Being and Time* as if it were the work of an older philosopher. He recommended that I read this or that paragraph and reflect upon it. Once during a convention, after I had missed his lecture, he read it to me alone in his room, in the Berliner Hotel on the Steinplatz. In Hamburg he read to a seminar group from his *Time and Being*. In Todtnauberg, our conversations almost always took place during long walks, and many of his formulations, including casual ones, remain to me imprinted with the surrounding nature.

Once he led me on a path that ended in the middle of the woods, at a place where water came out of thick moss. I said: "The path ends." He looked at me slyly and said: "This is the wood path. It leads to the sources. This, however, I have not written in my book."

One summer evening, we sat before his hut. The sun was setting with evening red, and over the woods in the dark blue eastern sky rose the metal disk of the full moon. He said to me: "You, as a scientist, must not say that the sun sets. You must say that the horizon rises." I answered: "No. It is enough that I know what my words mean. If I travel by ship across the Atlantic to America, and another ship from there passes us, and I stand on the deck and watch it disappear in the east under the horizon, then I know that for whoever is standing on the deck of the other ship it is our ship that sinks in the horizon. Each of us is correct with his description, namely, because he knows that it does not contradict the other's." Heidegger became pensive; he was not satisfied with my answer.

Once, during World War II, I went by foot to Todtnauberg and had to return by foot to Schauinsland. He accompanied me for a while. Before the edge of a forest I said to him that I thought I was able to understand that one philosophized as he did, and that one granted to science only a self-forgetting projection of the truth; but that it was not clear to me how his philosophy could make it understood that science can be successful at all. In the meantime, we had entered the forest, which was penetrated by sunlight. He stood still, looked at me and said: "I don't know this either."

I have never lost a certain conversational inhibition with him when the subject was his own philosophy. I always felt that I was still not ready for it. I did not want to employ the neologisms of his published work, neither in his own terms (which he certainly would have prevented) nor in casual, general language, even though I, at least in later times, did not have difficulty in explaining his work to others. His conversation, it must be said, was entirely free of "Heideggerisms," or they slipped in so naturally that they were not noticed as such. Also his Marburg lectures, whose publication has begun, are given in ordinary language. I find them to be some of the best he has ever written. I see in them the lucidity that I found in his personal conversation. When I had difficulty with his written diction, I sometimes resorted to modestly phrased foolishness, which he often responded to in an amazingly positive manner. Thus I told him, after a private reading of his speech on language, the East European Jewish story of the man who sits in an inn and, when asked why, says: "Ja, my wife!" "But what is wrong with her?" "Ja, she talks and talks and talks and talks and talks . . ." "What does she talk about?" "That she does not say!" Heidegger's comment was: "That's the way it is."

In his later visits to Hamburg, in the milieu of academic philosophy, he loved telling about his early years, mostly and not uncritically about Husserl. Actually his world of human experience was limited; besides his small provincial home, it consisted of little else but the world of continental European universities. His reactions to people, as everyone knows, could be very critical, though often strikingly perceptive. I had the luck never to be out of his favor and thus experienced his sharpness only from a distance. One summer evening, we were sitting on a terrace, in a circle of colleagues in philosophical conversation. The person sitting opposite him began a discourse on the interpretation of a certain problem from the Greeks to the present. Heidegger interrupted him suddenly and said: "Herr X, the history of philosophy appears to be completely clear to you." The man addressed, a very nice man, laughed, somewhat embarrassed, and the discourse was over. About another, younger, man whom I was praising to him for his comprehensive philosophical knowledge, he said to me privately: "He does not see anything. He is blind." With that he gave what was for him the ultimate criticism. A clever observer said about Heidegger: "Actually he is not more intelligent than many others. But he is an eye-witness." This was my own experience with him. One could learn from him not so much the art of discussions that took place in the philosophical milieu, but one could learn his *seeing*. This is why it was not possible to answer him with arguments, but only by giving something to see in turn.

I would not give a great man the honor he deserves if I passed over in silence the political errors he committed at the beginning of the National Socialist domination. I belong to a German generation of which a majority succumbed to this error, and I myself have not resisted with the clarity that today I might wish to have had at that time. My father, within his own strongly political horizon, had seen clearly here. Heidegger was silent later about his behavior in 1933. In any case, he never spoke with me about it, and I never brought up the subject with him. When I met him, this was already in the past. In the meantime, in accordance with his wish, the *Der Spiegel* interview has been published following his death. He defends himself there, justifiably no doubt, against the charge of cheap complicity with the regime. But I regret that he was not capable of conducting the interview in a stronger way than he did. Through a conscious and full acknowledgment of his error he could have established, with one blow, superiority over the level of the questions being asked. He could have opened the eyes, perhaps not of the journalists questioning him, but of many discerning readers, for his diagnosis of our times, without which his error can, after all, never be comprehended.

I would like to add here few anecdotal memories. I have heard it said that already before 1933 he had set his hopes on the National Socialists. A student from Freiburg told me that in the winter of 1933–34, "They invented the Freiburg National Socialism in Heidegger's circle. They kind of whispered that the real Third Reich has not yet begun, it is still to come." On the day of his resignation from the office of university president, Schadewaldt supposedly met him on a streetcar and asked him, "Now, Herr Heidegger, are you back from Syracuse?" The allusion to Plato's error about Dionysius has an explanatory value. Heidegger's analysis of the continuing forgetfulness of European history, later condensed in the thesis of the *Ge-stell*, should have made him expect only deep delusions from those movements of our century that considered themselves reasonable. But these memoirs are not the place to investigate the truth of this perspective. Let us assume, for the moment, that he saw correctly. Is it inconceivable that he hoped, that National Socialism saw itself as a countermovement to "Western" rationalism, as a directness toward reality that was not obstructed by an overpowering conceptual system? The unobstructed experience of reality came indeed, as the experience of accelerated self-destruction. The Heidegger I knew did not deceive himself anymore about that. That was in 1935 not different from the way it was in 1967. In 1967 we sat together, in a large group for an evening conversation, in Hamburg, after a seminar week, and the unavoidable subject of the student movement, the New Left, came up. Great expectations were expressed. I agreed with the expectations only under the condition that the undeniable benefits of liberalism must be preserved. The debate was long and heated. Heidegger sat there in silence. Finally I turned to him: "Herr Heidegger, what do you say to all this?" He hesitated briefly, then he said only two sentences: "You all add up the bill without asking the innkeeper. Only the deity can save us now."

Heidegger in his later years suffered through his times, but he lived, if I have observed correctly, not in a mood of hopelessness. If he, as philosopher, was obstinately silent about God, it was not out of disbelief but out of respect for a reality that our metaphysics was no longer entitled to speak about. It seems to me that he respected naive talk about God when he encountered it. As for *thoughtful* talk about God, he perceived its tenuousness. In the poetry of Hölderlin he found the tone he could trust. He said to me once that the purpose of his philosophy was to make Hölderlin's poetry retroactively possible. But he never made me feel obligated to follow him in this view, which was like a private religion. He noticed something here that was on the very edge of his capacity or perception and which was beyond the perceptive realm of almost all who felt it necessary to criticize him. He told me, in the sixties, of the deep impression that visiting Japanese Zen Buddhists had left him with. Zen could say crucial things without metaphysics; it was as if a door had opened for him. It remains unforgettable what he once said to me, in Hamburg, in a soft and hesitating way, about his *Time and Being*: "Sometimes this text appears to me so strange that somebody completely different, whom I cannot understand, could have written it. Then, other times, it is completely obvious to me."

My last visit to him was in the fall of 1972, in the little garden house that had been built for him in Freiburg-Zähringer. I was told not to stay longer than half an hour, because of his health. But he kept me more than two hours, and he examined and tested me as always. I had to tell him about the way I dealt with time in physics and logic, and he told me to read a section in *Being and Time* that I had not thought about. He was warm, as always, and his eyes were sparkling. An old man is not different from the man of his youth, just more himself.

4. Heidegger and Science

A. Introductory Remarks

"Science is a way, a decisive way, in which all that *is* presents itself to us.

"Therefore, we must say: The reality within which humankind today operates and tries to maintain itself is increasingly codefined by what one calls Western-European science.

"If we think about this process, it becomes obvious that science has acquired, in the West and in the course of Western history, a power found nowhere else on earth, and that it is in the process of extending this power over the whole world." (Heidegger, "Wissenschaft und Besinnung" in *Vorträge und Aufsätze*, 1954)

Our century is a century of science. In our century, science seems to be the hard core of the modern age. If one were to name one philosopher as the philosopher of our century, one is compelled to name Martin Heidegger. But Heidegger was not a philosopher of science. Science was neither the starting point nor the goal of his thinking. How can these statements be reconciled? The Heidegger sentences quoted above indicate the path to an answer. Heidegger recognized the decisive role of science in our time. He suffered under this time, under our, his time. In his early years, this suffering expressed itself as a demanding criticism, and in his later years it became a deeply concerned reflection on fate.

So far, science has not understood what Heidegger had to say to it. Heidegger, on the other hand, was unable, it seems to me, to penetrate to the fundamentals of science. This two-sided unfulfilled task is my theme when reflecting here on Heidegger and science. I will proceed in three steps. First, under the title of *Das Ge-stell*, let us look once more at the historical role in which Heidegger saw science and technology in his later years. Then let us reflect on the ontologic problem that determined the early Heidegger's perspective on science. And finally I will undertake a physicist's answer to Heidegger.

B. *Das Ge-stell*

First, a brief comment. It refers to two of Heidegger's statements on science. The first is the lecture "Die Zeit des Weltbildes" (of 1938, published in *Holzwege* in 1950), cited below as "ZW." The second is the two lectures "Die Frage nach der Technik" and "Wissenschaft und Besinnung" (of 1953, published in *Vorträge und Aufsätze* in 1954), cited below as "FT" and "WB" respectively.

The first of these lectures begins with the sentence: "What happens in metaphysics is a contemplation of the essence of that which is and a decision on the essence of truth. Metaphysics founds an era by giving it the basis of its essential form through a certain interpretation of that which is and through a certain perspective of truth" (ZW, p. 69). The era in question is the modern age. Heidegger sees modern times as determined through metaphysics, thus through a decision on the essence of truth, but in a way that is different from the first appearance of metaphysics in Greek philosophy. Heidegger lists five manifestations that are essential to modern times: science, technology, aesthetics, culture, secularization. We will limit our subject to modern science. In contrast to the *doctrina* and the *scientia* of the Middle Ages and to the Greek ἐπιστήμη, modern science is essentially research. Research in any area of that which is, for example, of nature, presupposes a design of the essence of this subject that *is*, in this case, of the processes of nature. Contemporary physics is mathematical through "the design of that which is henceforth to be nature for the pursued knowledge of nature: the closed motion context of spaciotemporally referred points of a mass" (ZW, p. 72). In the later lecture (WB, pp. 60–61) Heidegger sees the mathematical pre-design as maintained throughout all transformations of modern physics up to the object criticism of quantum theory.

That is the purpose of the pre-design? "The facts must become . . . objective. Therefore, the process must present the changeable in its changing, bring it to standstill and yet let the movement remain a movement . . . The constance of change in the necessity of its process is the law. It is only in the realm of rule and law that facts become clear as the facts that they are . . . Only because contemporary physics is essentially mathematical physics can it be experimental" (ZW, pp. 73–74). Behind these sentences there is an insight in the essence of a physics that has gone through Kant and which is related to Einstein's statement that "Only theory decides what one can observe." This pre-design makes it possible that science becomes operation. "The scholar disappears. He is being replaced by the researcher who works in the context of research systems" (ZW, p. 78).

"Which knowledge of that which is and which concept of truth determine that science becomes research? . . . In the pre-calculation one postulates nature, in the historical post-calculation one postulates history . . . This objectification of that which is takes place in a conception whose aim it is to present the respective 'that which is' in such a way that the calculating human being can be sure of that which is and thus know it for sure. Science as research is reached if, and only if, truth has become certainty of conception" (ZW, p. 80). Only under the rule of conception is a world conception possible—hence the title "Die Zeit des Wetbildes" (the age of world view, or world conception). "World conception, properly understood, thus does not mean a conception of the world but the world understood as conception" (ZW, p. 82). "The basic process of modern times is the conquest of the world as conception. The word conception now means: the construction of a conceptualizing production" (ZW, p. 87).

The lecture "Die Frage nach der Technik," written fifteen years later, continues the connection with technology that is indicated here. He sees technology not as applied science but as a separate mode of truth that determines science, or, as Heidegger now says, a separate mode of unconcealing (FT, pp. 20–21). "Technology exists in the realm where unconcealing and unconcealmeant, where ἀλήϑεια, where truth happens" (FT, p. 21). "The unconcealing that is active in modern technology is a challenge to nature to furnish the energy that can as such be produced and stored" (FT, p. 22). Now Heidegger, in the style of his later years, plays on the word related to placing. "The thus placed has its own stance. We call it the sub-stance" (FT, p. 24). "Who brings about the challenging placing, through which that which one calls the real is unconcealed as substance? Obviously it is the human being . . . But there is one thing the human being cannot control, and this is the unconcealment in which the real shows itself or in which it withdraws . . . Only insofar as the human being is already challenged to produce the natural energies can this placing unconcealing take place" (FT, p. 25). "The challenging claim that it is the human being who is to place the self-concealing as sub-stance, we will now call—the Ge-stell" (the com-posite) (FT, p. 27). "Contemporary physics is the harbinger of the Ge-stell, a harbinger of still unknown provenience" (FT, p. 29).

I would like to assume that the reader of this chapter will not try to cope with his or her astonishment through the convenient dismissal of Heidegger's linguistic mannerisms. It may seem appropriate to trace the strange line of these thoughts carefully in conventional language. It is a familiar thought, today, that science and technology make nature available to modern humanity in the form of a conceptualization, in the form of availability. Technocrats think in this manner: We rule because we know, we know in order to rule, knowledge is power. Social critics and environmentalists reverse the same thought: The form of this knowledge is determined by the will to power; the untrustworthiness of such science is often claimed and justified through its destructive effects. Both versions, with opposite evaluations, follow the same pattern. In both the human being appears as the doer, as the author of the events, namely, through human knowledge. The beneficial character of true knowledge is presupposed; it is for this reason that science is seen as true by the technocrat, but is viewed with suspicion by the social critic and the environmentalist.

Do Heidegger's thoughts belong to one of these two versions? No one would think him to be among the technocrats. Does he perhaps belong to the group that I have called here, somewhat loosely, social critics and environmentalists? It is obvious that his personal reaction to the world of technology was a feeling of horror, even enmity. One could refer to a sentence from his lecture on technology: "Thus wherever the *Ge-stell* prevails, there is imminent danger" (FT, p. 36). However, Heidegger then adds a quotation from Hölderlin: "But where there is danger, the saving element grows too." This means more than just the hope for the unknown rescuer. But not only in the *Spiegel* interview, also during an unforgettable conversation at my house in Hamburg, Heidegger said: "Only the deity can save us now." The combination of truth, danger, and rescue, however, is of inseparable immediacy to him. "The essence of technology, as fate of the unconcealing, is danger" (FT, p. 36). "Fate," here, is a term for history, for a history whose author is not the human being who believes to be free. The unconcealing is truth; and thus the sentence means, in conventional language: "The essence of technology is danger because this essence belongs to the history of truth."

In this statement there is something that is astonishing in two ways. Epistemologically: The essence of technology is not application of truth, it is truth itself. Historically: Truth itself is danger. It is also salvation. "The acting element that in this or in that manner aims at the unconcealing is as such the saving element" (FT, p. 40). "As long as we think of technology as an instrument, we remain caught in the desire to master it. We drift past the essence of technology" (FT, p. 40). "The essence of technology is ambiguous in a lofty sense. Such ambiguity points to the secret of all unconcealing, that is, of truth" (FT, p. 41). "The irresistibility of the placing and the restraint of the saving element pass each other like two stars in heaven. Alone this passing is the hiddenness of their nearness" (FT, p. 41).

I will not comment here on these sentences. Even in the stylization of the language of his later years, which is a sign of increasing loneliness, Heidegger is precise in his statements and precise in his allusions and his silence regarding those things that he could not say anymore.

C. Ontology, Logic, and Truth

The dialogue between Heidegger and science does not depend on isolated texts of his later years. These texts belong to the final phase of a lifetime of work. However, the decisions about his attitude toward science took place early in his career. They had been made before the first sentence of *Sein und Zeit* (*Being and Time*) was written. It is only today that the immense intellectual work of his early years becomes known to the general public, with the publication of his Marburg lectures. In these lectures his language is still that of science and traditional philosophy. In this language he conducted a dialogue with the kind of thinking that, precisely, has been adequately expressed in it. In great detail and with lucidity he exposes the foundations of this thinking and of its unresolved questions. His decision to create his own stylized terminology in his published works, beginning with *Sein und Zeit*, was the result of this critical analysis of language, that is, of the thinking of tradition. And it is through this that he breaks off the direct discourse with traditional thinking; from now on, anyone who wants to understand Heidegger's published thoughts has first to accept his language and thus his intellectual position. Science, however, does not take part in the transition to Heidegger's new language. For this reason, the conversation partner of science is the early Heidegger, the Heidegger of the Marburg lectures. Only after such a conversation is it meaningful to return to the texts in which we have read above.

His collected works, as published so far, include only two volumes of lectures: volume 21, *Logik: Die Frage nach der Wahrheit*, and volume 24, *Die Grundprobleme der Phänomenologie*. Phenomenology here means ontology. Science is not a subject in these volumes. In order to initiate a dialogue with science, may I, therefore, make an excursion into the final section of this chapter by giving a sketch of what I see as the relationship between science on the one hand and logic and ontology on the other.

The development of science proceeds toward a systematic unity. The multiplicity of disciplines is no obstacle; on the contrary, it contributes to an acceleration of the systematic progress that has brought it about. It becomes obvious that the same fundamental laws prevail in all fields that can somehow be called "nature." Physics is the science that formulates these fundamental laws. In the realm of the anorganic this development has been manifest for a long time. In the realm of the organic it has made rapid progress in the last decades. The least we can say is that physicalism, that is, the hypothesis that the laws of physics are the sole fundamental laws also in the organic, is heuristically successful and nowhere contradicted. Furthermore, there is no generally acknowledged dividing line that would allow to see the human being or certain aspects of human existence as exempt from the subsumption under the concept of nature; but this is a problem—unresolved in the scientific awareness of our time—to which I will return later.

Physics itself has developed toward a systematic unit. The central discipline of this unit is the quantum theory, which was given its final shape by Bohr and Heisenberg in precisely those years—now remote by half a century—in which Heidegger gave his Marburg lectures and in which he wrote *Sein und Zeit*. One could describe the general or abstract quantum theory as a nonclassical theory of probability. The term "nonclassical" denotes here, in a formal sense, a multiplicity of possible events that lies behind the evaluation of probability, as different from the theory that can be derived by applying classical propositional logic (Boolean algebra). Occasionally one speaks of a "quantum logic." The foundation of this nonclassical logic can be seen in a deviation from classical ontology, a deviation that physicists have not worked out, it is true, only circumscribed in words. In quantum theory, a possible event can be defined only in relation to a possible observer. For the first time in modern physics, the subject-object relationship becomes thematic.

I do not intend here to analyze quantum theory further. What I have said will be enough to show that Heidegger's analysis of the foundations of ontology and logic, when applicable, is of immediate importance to the core of all science. Of course, Heidegger himself was fully aware of this, even before he became acquainted with quantum theory.

In the first part of the lecture *Die Grundprobleme der Phänomenologie*, given in summer of 1927, shortly after he wrote *Sein und Zeit*, Heidegger discusses, in four chapters, basic theses of traditional ontology. These are:

1. Kant's thesis that "being is not a real predicate,"
2. the Scholastic-Aristotelian distinction between essence and existence,
3. the Cartesian confrontation of *res extensa* and *res cogitans*,
4. the logical characterization of being through the copula in the predicative sentence.

From the four chapters I will choose a few points that are relevant to our subject.

In the introduction Heidegger states, along with the problem, also the solution that he proposes. The ontological difference, "that is, the separation of being from that which is" (p. 22), focuses on the question of being. "Being is the genuine and sole theme of philosophy" (p. 15). "Being, as *a priori*, precedes that which is. So far, we have not clarified the meaning of this *a priori*, that is, the meaning of the earlier and its possibilities . . . The earlier is a determination of time, but one that is not within the temporal order of the time that we measure with the clock . . ." (p. 27). "The being of that which is is encountered in the understanding of being. Understanding is what first opens up something like being, or, as we say, makes it accessible" (p. 24). "Being is only if there is nonhiddenness, that is, if there is truth . . . Being is only if there is truth, that is, if existence exists" (p. 25). Ontology itself cannot be justified purely ontologically. Its own realization is referred back to that which is, that is, to an *ontal*: to existence" (p. 26). "Ontology has an ontic foundation," as already in Aristotle's sentence "The first science, the science of being, is theology" (p. 26). "If temporality constitutes the being sense of the existence of humans, but if understanding of being belongs to the being state of existence, then this understanding of being can become possible only against the background of temporality . . . The horizon out of which something like being can become understandable at all is time. We interpret being out of time" (p. 22).

The first chapter then anticipates the second in that it interprets—in Kant's thesis that being is not a real predicate—being as *existentia*, and the real predicate as a component of *essentia*. The ontic, namely, the theological, basis of classical ontology becomes obvious in that Kant develops his thesis in the course of his critique of arguments for the existence of God. Kant's explanation of being as position indicates a relationship of the object to the capacity of knowledge, thus to the ontic foundation of ontology in the knowing subject. From this Heidegger proceeds to the phenomenology of intentionality: "Apperception is freely permitted encounter of what is on hand" (p. 98). Being as being on hand is a conception of being that requires further explanation.

The second chapter deducts from the theses of Scholasticism, from Thomas Aquinas to Suarez, that "the problem of the distinction between *essentia* and *existentia in ente creato* depends on whether one orients, at all, the interpretation of being in the sense of existence toward realization, toward creating and producing" (p. 138). "If created being is to be possible as created, then possibility must be joined by reality, that is, both must be different in actual fact" (p. 139). Heidegger pursues this line of thought back to Greek ontology. The "guide in their interpretation" is, to him, "the consideration of production." "The potter makes a pitcher from clay . . . The thing is made in consideration of the preexisting mental image of it. It is this anticipated and foreseen appearance of the thing that the Greek mean ontologically with the words εἶδος, ἰδέα. The thing that is formed according to the image is the exact likeness of the image" (p. 150). But the Greek consideration of production does not let everything that *is* appear as produced. The thing is made from available matter. "It is in producing that we encounter that which precisely does not require production" (p. 164). Therefore, however: "What does not require production can be understood and discovered only in the being knowledge of production" (p. 163). "The concepts of matter and material originate in a being knowledge that is oriented toward producing" (p. 164). But can all that which is be "understood as something that is on hand"? (p. 169). Least of all the human being. This leads to the modern distinction between subject and object.

The third chapter deals with the difference between person and thing as expressed essentially in Kant's practical philosophy. "Thus the being mode that is specific to the moral person is free action. Kant once said: 'Intellectual is something whose concept is an acting.' . . . The ego is an 'I do,' and as such it is intellectual" (p. 200). "Intelligences, moral persons, are subjects whose being is an acting" (p. 200). Heidegger's farther-reaching critique of Kant begins with this thought: "There is in Kant a curious omission in that he did not succeed in determining the primary unity of the theoretical and the practical ego" (p. 207). "Kant treats the existence of a person like the existence of a thing . . . In the concept of the thing as such, be it recognizable in its whatness or not, there is already determined the traditional ontology of the being on hand" (p. 209). This would lead us to an examination of Heidegger's ontology of existence as being-in-the-world, an examination that we will not undertake here.

The fourth chapter begins with an interpretation of the copula in Hobbs, Mill, and Lotze. It is painful to realize that the early Heidegger, while encountering this tradition and Husserl, did not occupy himself with the central figure of modern logic, Gottlob Frege.[23] A Heidegger critique of Frege would have been the Rhodes of his leap through the cold fire of logic. Heidegger's special problem in this chapter is the indifference of being in the sense of the copula toward his interpretation in accordance with the classical ontological distinctions of essence or existence, of person or thing. I will not try to answer the question of whether this view of Heidegger is logically tenable. Essential to us is the concept of truth that he uses to explain it. "The primary character of the presupposition as proof must be maintained. It is only in this proof aspect that the predicative structure of the proposition can be determined. Predicating is thus primarily an analysis of the preexisting, that is, a defining analysis" (p. 298). "The proposition if uttered is communication . . . In communication, an existence and another, namely, the addressed, enter together into the same being relationship to what the proposition deals with, to what we talk about . . . From all this it becomes clear that the proposition does not have a primary knowledge function, only a secondary one. That which is must already be revealed if a proposition about it is to be possible" (p. 299). From this follows: "The 'is' may be indifferent in its meaning because the differentiated being modus is already determined in the primary understanding of that which is . . . The indifference of the copula is not a shortcoming; it only characterizes the secondary character of all predicating" (p. 301).

Heidegger also established a ranking list. The declarative sentence as proof is primary in relation to its components. The concept must be defined as possible component of the sentence, not the sentence as a composition of concepts. The nonhiddenness of that which is is primary in relation to the proposition. Truth as unconcealment is primary in relation to truth of the sentence. Sentences may be true or false, and it is only through this binary structure that logic as a science is possible; the theory of correct deduction presupposes the possibility of false deduction. Truth as unconcealment, however, is a prerequisite of the dictinction between true and false. "Existence exists in truth, that is, in the disclosure of itself and of that which is, to which it relates. Only because it is, existing, already essentially in truth, it can as such go wrong and there is hiding, disguising, and withdrawal of that which is" (p. 308). And the return to the ontic foundation of ontology: "Truth, disclosing, and disclosure can only exist if, and as long as, existence exists" (p. 313).

I will not trace here the path that led Heidegger, with inner necessity, from these decisions via *Sein und Zeit* to the philosophy of his later years. But how is a contemporary physicist to respond to these decisions, a person who follows willingly the section of the metaphysical path that the Heidegger of the later years describes? What do truth and that which is, danger and salvation, mean to this physicist?

D. A Physicist's Answer

So far, physicists have not understood what Heidegger had to say to them. It is for this reason alone that I cannot speak in the name of physics, only as a physicist assuming personal responsibility. Also, I am no longer speaking here as an interpreter of Heidegger, because I do not believe that he was capable of thinking deeply enough about the reality of physics. Thus, in regard to Heidegger, too, this answer will remain risky.

It seems to me that Heidegger had a clearer notion of the historical role of science than have had its followers as well as its critics. He sees that science determines our fate because science, in modern times, is the true form of truth. Only during the course of his life has he come to see this with clarity, although this insight was a consequence of the decisions he had made in his Marburg lectures. This may have contributed to the fact that his later phase has so far been less valued by academic philosophers than his early phase. In his early years he still shared the traditional, erroneous view that science is a regional field of knowledge. This view, after all, is not merely a superficially convincing and plausible position of the theory of science, but it was (and largely still is) a defense strategy and defense position against the interpretation of reality by classical physics. Among the positions that this line of defense tries to protect are, for example, the vitalist view in biology, the attempt of the Dilthey-Rickert era to establish the humanities as independent in essence from the sciences, Husserl's regional ontologies, and, in radical simplicity, the Cartesian dualism. In the early Heidegger one can find certain peripheral points of agreement with some of these positions, which were prevalent in his academic

surroundings. However, the main thrust of his critique was basically opposed to all of them from the beginning.

He leaves some hope for the establishment of positivist sciences that
avoid a reduction of reality as found in the classical-physical design, such
as a vitalistic biology or knowledgeable humanities, at least he leaves this
hope on the periphery, in the presupposed regionalization of that which
is; but he destroys this hope at the core. All these fields of knowledge
present that which is, which they study, as the object, even where the
intention of the individuals aims at the opposite; see the above-quoted
passage from "Die Zeit des Weltbildes" in regard to the science of history.
They are forced into this position through their pretense at being scientific,
that is, at certainty. They do not think that the subjective collaboration in
science is founded *de facto* through a being-in-truth shared by scientists;
but the communication of scientists on their shared truth is rooted in the
pretense at objectivity of the results of research.

The early Heidegger considered also the regional ontologies as merely
peripheral beside the grand design of the fundamental ontology. He still
sees the latter as scientific, phenomenologic philosophy that takes seriously
the ontological core of the Cartesian question, the differentiation of the
existing being from the being as being on hand, of the existential from the
category. This, too, is still a strategy of regionalization. Now the fundamental ontology could be seen as that science which does not objectify.
The compromise character of this position is taken into account in that
Heidegger does not publish the second volume of *Sein und Zeit* and that
he does not claim scientific status for his later works. Only the philosophy
of his final years, which no longer seeks to occupy any place in the realm
of science, gains an open view of science as a unified form of truth, central
to the modern age.

The price for this great advance, though, is a serious loss; it is not without
reason that much of Heidegger's later thinking is an experience of failure.
As a physicist, I would describe this loss from the perspective of science:
It is the loss of the possibility to inquire after the basis of the factual success
of science. In the Marburg lectures, being as being on hand is the ontological design that makes science possible. It is, in turn, founded ontically,
in the being state of the human being as a producing being. This being
state appears as *a priori*; the physicist would say it is known from pre-
scientific experience. The fundamental ontologist seeks a fuller existential
determination of the human being; in this quest he has already overcome,
so to speak, the disclosed realm of producing and availability. This is a
research situation, not an answer. One might hope that when the structures
of existence are disclosed the place of production can be better determined
in them. But Heidegger's later philosophy sees the human being in a history
that is interpreted as fate, and in which the last, still recognizable step is
the unconcealing of that which is in the *Ge-stell*. It is this fate that does

not let us see how this truth relates to other modes of truth. The talk about the event that is still hidden by the *Ge-stell* remains a prophetic note.

As a physicist, I believe that one of the reasons for this hiddenness is that the path of science has not been pursued to the end. This obligates me to indicate what I mean by the failure to have pursued this path to the end. I will do so in language that is immanent to science, continuing from a comment I made earlier.

The development of science proceeds simultaneously toward a systematic unity of laws and toward a limitless multiplicity of disciplines. The possibility of this multiplicity is the logical consequence of the conceptual form of the fundamental laws. For example, the fundamental laws of a certain, supposedly penultimate, step have the mathematical appearance of differential equations. A differential equation has, in general, an infinite number of solutions; thus it characterizes a class of possible functions. The individual disciplines can then be seen as theories of certain subclasses of the totality of all solutions, or of certain approximations to solutions of a subclass. To pursue the path of science to the end does not mean to exhaust the richness of a scientifically describable reality, which would be impossible; it means to discover ultimate fundamental laws. In axiomatic mathematics we see how little a field of science can be exhausted through the statement of fundamental laws. The axioms of Euclidean geometry can be listed on a few printed pages; the abundance of geometric forms and their relationships is an inexhaustable richness. The basic laws, if they exist, are, in turn, not the ultimate truth of being. Heidegger, in a passage quoted above, has made clear that the concept of law already presupposes a design for a being mode of that which is as something that can be conceived of in the sense of Heidegger's terminology. What we want to know philosophically is whether fundamental laws of physics exist, and what they define. In order not to prolong this argument, I will assume here that they do exist. What they define is not a region of that which is but a manner of understanding that which is. How is this manner determined?

The hypothesis that I personally follow concurs with Kant and holds that the fundamental laws of physics express only the conditions of the possibility of objectifiable experience. They are not only regulative principles of pure reason, but the kind of positive laws that Kant sought to find in the metaphyical beginnings of science and in the *Opus Postumum*; the problem of irreducible special laws of nature is superseded by the systematic unity of science. The abstract quantum theory is a general theory of probability. Probability is quantified possibility. Possibility is here a predicate of future events, thus a temporal modility. Experience, too, is a temporal concept; experience means to learn from the past for the future. Objectifiable experience is experience that is subject to logic. Logic means distinction between true and false. Logic, applied to experience, requires that experience is formulated in decidable alternatives, in yes-no decisions in the sense of information theory. The hypothesis thus means that the fundamental laws of physics formulate nothing but the logic of objectifiable experience.

In this respect, the hypothesis fits smoothly, if I am right, into Heidegger's way of thinking. But it has three universal properties that explicitly transcend Heidegger. First, it holds that the necessary systematic unity of science has a philosophical basis; it breaks with the methodological separation of positivist science and philosophy to the extent that philosophy remains conceptual. Second, it would explain why it has been impossible to justify clearly a regional delimitation of science. Science as discussed here is supposedly coextensive with conceptual empirical thinking generally. A substantiation of this thesis would, however, require a new analysis of conceptual thinking, thus of the essence of the concept. From this follows a third, farther-reaching, observation. The thus defined science does not stop with the human being, insofar as humans can be dealt with conceptually. The continuity of humans and nature has become a component of science anyway, through the theory of evolution. In this situation, phenomenological and empiricoscientific knowledge of the human being cannot relate to each other in accordance with the traditional scheme of *a priori* and *a posteriori*, as they did in the erstwhile phenomenological formulations. The reflecting or phenomenological self-knowledge of the subject can be supported or corrected through scientific causal knowledge. I merely justify here—against untenable philosophical defense positions—what has actually been happening in the science of our time.

The question about the basis of the possibility of science thus joins intimately the question about the basis of the possibility of conceptual thinking in general. Contemporary science permits here an explanation of the ontic foundations of ontology through the insertion of the human being into nature, and the insertion of human history into the history of organic life. The three-step hierarchy we discussed above, that of unconcealment-sentence-concept, has a precursor in animal behavior. Animal behavior has its own truth and falseness. The measure of animal behavior is whether it succeeds or fails, but it is not identical with this. Rightness of behavior is *adaequatio actionis ad rem*, adaptation to the conditions of the ecological niche. Rightness or falseness of behavior does not depend on whether it is successful or fails in individual instances, but whether it is basically adapted to the situation or not. *Adaequatio*, here, is not the congruence of pattern and afterimage, but the congruity of key and lock. Right behavior that is thus characterized is the precursor of the universal proposition. The dissection of the sentence corresponding to the unity of action into concepts that, in turn, are general, is only a human accomplishment, mediated through the capacity for conceptualization; it represents the step from the ability to act to power that can be accumulated. Conception, at first, is not conception of existing things, but of possible acts. It is in this sense that

Heidegger, in *Sein und Zeit*, places the being at hand before the being on hand. The individual case, that which the empirical epistemology sees as given, is genetically a later phase of knowledge; actually, it is merely the specialized concept. Genetically speaking, there are initially sentences ("Fire!"), then concepts ("the fire," "to burn"), then proper names ("the conflagration of Moscow"). But unities of action exist only in a previously disclosed environment. This nonhiddenness is beforehand and unexpressed, it is not presented and not in need of being presented. To become aware of it is not the same as conceptualizing it.

At this point I would like to make a personal remark. The attitude reflected in this answer deviates fundamentally from the one that Heidegger has shown in each phase of thinking. In the four decades of our personal acquaintance he could not have deceived himself about this. He never tried to change my position, but he has forced me to think more clearly about it by asking questions that were right on the mark. This presentation of a position that without him would have remained unclarified is a way of giving thanks to a great man. If I believe I can see more than he in a few places, I am aware that in other, central places I have no doubt been unable to perceive what he has divined, seen, and expressed.

I am convinced that in his later years he has seen correctly the signature of our age in one decisive point. The *Ge-stell* is the dissection of reality into conceptual acts of apperception and the attempt to reconstruct the whole as the sum of interactive elements. This conceptual reconstruction of the whole is called systems theory today. This is the unavoidable world conception of the world of will and intellect that, as a possible societal mode of behavior, had begun latest with the modification of nature through agriculture, and possibly even with the era of the hunter. This thinking, in the same action, through the same characteristics, is truth as revelation of structures, and deadly danger. This truth is at the same time untruth because the components that are presented as independent—be they atomic objects or atomically functional units—are themselves products of the concept, they are reality mirrored in a mirror that is unconscious of itself; they themselves are not real. The saving element already exists, intangible, amidst this world of tangibles. To seek and enter dangerous paths is plannable and possible and therefore duty. The confidence in safety through planning, the planners' so-called pragmatic optimism, is a means of denying entrance to the saving truth. Heidegger's later suffering about our world was a present he gave it. For with that he did not evade it.

5. Time and the One

A. Theory and Practice

We are witnessing today a quarrel among theoreticians, especially among social critics, about theory and practice. The theory of our traditional theory assumes precedence of theory over practice. One could say that the practice of contemporary practice, in contrast, has developed and is still developing in the context of a precedence of practice over theory. These contemporary theoreticians assert the precedence of practice over theory in that the major portion of what I have called practice in the preceding sentence is, in their view, not practice but merely technological or pragmatic action. In this they employ Aristotle's theoretical distinction, who considered practice that life which contained its own purpose, in contrast to making, to *poiesis*, of something whose purpose lies outside, and which we usually call technology today. Thus practice is, in contemporary terms, action that is itself a value. But according to Aristotle the supreme value is the pure contemplation of truth, the theory, the *vita contemplativa*. In this respect one could say that for him theory is the highest practice. But this is what those modern theories contest. Why?

An intermediate link in this dispute is contemporary science. It has its own theory—a largely mathematical one—and its own practice—a largely technological one. It plays a key role in our age. It is mainly through science that the modern-Western culture is different from all other cultures. Its theory is oriented toward practice or technology insofar as it sees experimental or empirical proof as the theoretically accepted criterion of truth. And its practice is oriented toward theory insofar as theory is the goal of empirical experience, in the prevailing thinking of scientists. In science, there is a mutual challenge between theory and technology (in the sense of useful applications). The twentieth century, with its theory-induced applications, permits the thesis that theory is the most radical practice. This represents a modification of Aristotle's thesis insofar as radicalism is a *terminus* of world transformation, and contemplation is a *terminus* of world preservation. Therefore, the representatives of classical culture, whose concept of theory is determined by contemplation, often do not see scientific theory as theory, but as a strategy of technology; this is what lies behind C. P. Snow's concept of the two cultures. On the other hand, the great theorists of science have often felt very much akin to the theory of the Greeks (Plato, Archimedes).

However, contemporary theoreticocritical theory sees in the traditional concept of theory a refusal to take part in world transformation. To this contemporary theory, world transformation is a central value of practice. It sees in the model of science in the primacy of theory an ideology that veils the dependency on a technology that is controlled from the outside and tied to special interests. With the claim of the primacy of practice its adherents try to advance a crucial concern, a concern that, in my opinion, they have so far been unable to articulate adequately, be it theoretically or practically.

They are actually what I have been calling them here with obstinacy: theoreticians. Sociologically speaking, they belong to those people who, under the cynosure of theory, are trained and paid to perpetuate and apply the theory. They themselves know best that they are not free by simply ridiculing their chains. One of these chains is the traditional concept of theory. In putting emphasis on the sociotechnological function of this concept of theory, many among them arrive at plans for a social revolution. Insofar as such a revolution is program, thus theoretical thought, whose practical application requires a strategy, it is an example of the thesis that theory is the most radical practice. Contemporary revolutions are almost entirely determined by theories and made practically possible through theories.

Do these theories see themselves as theoretical? I don't think so. I will now skip all intermediate steps that are required for an actual consummation, and proceed directly to what I think is the final theoretical decision that is intellectually accessible to us today.

B. The One and Time

Contemplation appears in two forms that are essentially different and yet interrelated: reflecting contemplation and meditative contemplation. This is related to but not identical with the difference between theoretical and mystical contemplation, because theory in its fullest sense, as Aristotle understood it, contains, in practice, meditation as well as reflection. Theory is intellectual intuition—intellectual, that is, advanced and controlled by reflection; intuition, that is, interiorization through meditative devotion to what is observed. Mysticism, on the other hand, is contemplative practice, which can be life-threatening if not intellectually controlled, but in which an intellectual control concerns more the meditative process than the reflection on content. I will not examine here why reflection and meditation exist at all, how they are to be defined, what is the root they share and what makes them different, and how theory differs from mysticism—questions that would have to be the subject of meditative reflection. There are cultural differences, too. Western culture is determined more by reflection, the Eastern cultures more by meditation. Sometimes I think that their encounter is the historically most important event of our century. But let us remain here within the framework of Western tradition.

In Greek philosophy, theory has risen to the level of the One. This, precisely, is where the mystical experience leads us. (Hence the great closeness of Platonism, Buddhism, and the Vedanta.) This theory is speculatively compelled to think of the representation of the One in a cyclical time. Belief in progress on principle would be blasphemy in this theology; it would deny that the world is as good as it can be. There is only return to perfection from a world that has fallen from it. The highest practice is to think this perfection; its perpetually returning creation or approximation in time depends on its being contemplated spiritually. Theory is healing of practice.

The other tradition of the West is the Judeo-Christian. In the pure appearance of the Old Testament and in essential aspects of the New Testament this tradition knows neither theory nor mysticism but a way of life under the spoken word of a God whom one cannot approach through direct contemplation. The time in this practice is not cyclic; it is, in the beginning, the natural, open time in an everyday sense. In the great believed imagery it becomes the passage from creation to the coming of the messiah, the second coming of Christ. Faith is not belief that something is true (thus an imperfect theory), but a trust existing in practice.

This contrast has been strongly emphasized by contemporary Protestant theologians mainly, who thus resume Luther's onslaught on Greek theology. In this they are siding with the primacy of practice. But I think that they, too, do not understand themselves theoretically. They remain theologians, which is a concept of the Greek theory, and they are trying, in fact, to express their understanding in concepts. It is entirely obscure how a concept could be understood in any other way but in an understanding of the Greek theory. Modern theory of science makes use of the characteristics that the concept has in the framework of Greek theology, but without this framework, and therefore it discovers only its self-contradiction, whenever it is pursued honestly and intelligently. Recent German philosophers, from Kant to Heidegger, have concerned themselves with precisely this problem, and what I am saying here would be impossible without this philosophy.

These thoughts take us as far as to the concept of the open time. This does not absolve us from having to deal with the One, as many theologians and many adherents of the primacy of practice think it does. Because reality would otherwise break down into incoherent pieces, into a conceptless chaos of sparks. Picht defines the connection of the One with time through the formulation of the unity of time. In this unity the iterating articulation of temporal *modi* becomes possible, such as the future of the past, the present of the future. What was seen as eternal presence in the theory of the One is modified in this unity of time. The immortality of the idea reappears in the deathlessness of what is past and in the facilitation of the future through the presence of the past. Through the openness of the future the realm of ideas becomes a growing realm whose positions remain and simultaneously change their meaning.

In the real history of organic life, truth can first be thought of as adaptation of behavior to the living conditions. In this respect, "living conditions" is, incidentally, an immediately truth-related concept. The essence of this concept of truth lies in practice. The higher, that is, differentiated, steps of truth are conceptualization, reflection, and meditation. At these steps, truth as idea or intuition appears as theoretical truth, and conceptualizing, reflecting, and meditating appear as modes of practice. It is here that the naive contrast of theory and practice comes to an end. One cannot explain this truth with the traditional concepts of theory and practice; one can try to define concepts of theory and practice against the background of this truth. Picht sees the thought of the unity of time itself as one of the highest steps, facilitated only from the future.

To this way of thinking, world transformation is an ineluctable process. Here, the will to change the world is meaningful not as protest against a preservation but only as selective will in a conciliation with the process that modifies by preserving and preserves by modifying. Radically conservative and radically revolutionary positions are here equally possible because the process—through the necessary stabilization tendency of any complex form—occurs with necessity in continually revolutionary steps whose justification cannot be taken for granted but must be proven in each individual case.

The decisive process, in my opinion, is the transformation of the religious experience through knowledge of the open time. In this respect, the traditional religions remain, on the one hand, in a now impossible preservation of a concept of the One and its order and, on the other hand, in a surrender of their substance to the positivity of history, which, if isolated, leads to chaos. I have now said as much as I can with the use of reflection. But reflection is futile without meditation.

Part IV
THEOLOGY AND
MEDITATION

1. Notes on the Relationship of Physics and Religion

The general position of contemporary physicists concerning religion appears to be agnostic, but open. Conscious antireligious convictions by physicists occur less seldom than with biologists, and much less seldom than with sociologists. This might stem from the fact that the dispute between physics and the church lies farthest back in history. It remains to be seen what this historical succession might mean.

Freud speaks (in *One Difficulty of Psychoanalysis*, 1917) of the three offenses against human self-consciousness committed by Copernicus, Darwin, and psychoanalysis. We had to learn that our planet is not the center of the universe, that the other creatures are our brothers, and that "the ego is not master of the house." The third offense is the deepest. If we separate this observation from its special connection with psychoanalysis, then it can be said that the sobering self-knowledge through science continually advances closer to the human personality core.

But one must see that this continuing disillusionment means continuing conflict with religion only if one thinks of religion, from the beginning, as representative of the glorification of the human ego. On the other hand, one could also see in the disillusionment about the ego an approximation to the core of religious experience. Should not religion make us humble? But the contents of this scientific disillusionment have not, so far, been religious, and the ego finds compensation for the offense in that it itself has become the bearer of knowledge.

But physics has a doubly positive access, at least to the question of religion. The one access might be exemplified by people like Kepler. In the mathematical laws of nature an unforeseeable majesty is revealed. Kepler interpreted this experience, one shared by many physicists, through Christian Platonism. The world is created in accordance with the creative thoughts of God, that means, it has been constructed in mathematical harmony. The human being, created in the image of God, can imitate these thoughts. Science is worship of God.

The other access was opened by the physics of the first third of our century. The image of the world of classical physics was objectivistic, deterministic; consciousness was outside of the thus described nature. The quantum theory can only be interpreted if one takes into explicit consideration the relation between the objectivizing description of nature to the observer. Thus the primitive ontology of classical science was shaken. Philosophical questions have been asked that still have no answer.

The conclusion of the dispute between physics and the church (the "revision of the Galileo verdict") does not appear to be the most important aspect of today's situation. Scientists and Christians can do each other a service if they continue to ask each other critical questions.

Christians must ask the scientists whether what they do to the world is not, perhaps, criminal (destruction of the world through the consequences of objective knowledge). Questions, not accusations. Only self-accusation opens the sources of grace; one can and may defend oneself against the accusation of others. Objectively, not subjectively. The redeeming experience of sin begins where we learn to identify with our actions, although the subjective intention was perhaps not evil. A science that went through this experience might find itself. A science shielded from this experience becomes objectively evil.

Scientists must ask Christians whether they have consummated the modern consciousness. Much of this consummation has been caught up with in Protestant theology in the last decades. Here modern consciousness had often been too simply accepted as truth. But as the deconstruction of an untenable (and fear-conditioned) self-assertion of the church, this process was necessary. Perhaps the same applies to the necessary experience of the church, *mutatis mutandis*, as for the necessary experience of science. It is neither a disgrace nor dangerous to admit that the intellectual problems between religious truth and modern consciousness remain unresolved.

2. Levels of Christian Theology: A Comment on Luther

I have written in these essays about plateaus. In scientific history they are Kuhn's paradigm, Heisenberg's closed theories. In the organic evolution of species, for human beings I have designed in this manner the useful, the just, the true, the beautiful, the holy. Plateaus do not have to alternate historically, as the last examples show; they can, if they are different enough, coexist. But they can also repress each other in an inner necessity in the historical process, just as general theory explains the more specific and thus makes it relative and represses it "as truth." The word "level" is the same geographic metaphor as "plateau."

A recent reading of Ranke's *Deutsche Geschichte im Zeitalter der Reformation* (German History in the Age of the Reformation) made me realize the importance, for Luther, of the Leipzig debate with Eck (1519). In his negotiation with Miltitz, Luther had been honestly prepared to restrain himself on the issue of papal authority. But the factual strength of Eck's argument forced him, for the sake of truth, to proceed, beyond all earlier restraint, to consequences that he only then became fully aware of. Luther proved to Eck that the authority of the pope is not found in the Bible but is the result of historically raised claims, by referring to the Greek Church, with its many church fathers and saints, which, although it does not recognize the pope, is seen by the Roman Church not as heretical but only as schismatic. Eck thus forced Luther *de facto* to an outright rejection of papal authority. Luther wanted to support his argument by reference to the councils. But Eck proved to Luther that the recent councils, including the Council of Constance that had condemned Hus, had asserted the papal authority. Now Luther was compelled to say that even the councils could err. This forced him to his real position: The only unshakable authority is the Scriptures. How difficult this step was for Luther is demonstrated by the state of shock into which he fell in his intellectual follow-up work in Wittenberg. Only now did he recognize that the papacy was a system that in a consistent manner expanded its power and sacrificed to it the truth. To the question of how God's holy plan could have permitted this perversion of his church, he saw only one consistent answer: The pope is the prophesized anti-Christ. One has seen this equation as evidence of excess in Luther's opposition. In reality it was just a recognition of the character of the papacy as a genuine historical level, formulated with one of the poor concepts for historical events that the Christian teaching of the history of salvation offered him.

Any child of the Enlightenment will recognize immediately that Luther's position of scriptural authority is just as untenable as the authority of the pope or the councils. In contact with enlightened contemporaries, such as in the dispute with Zwingli about communion, he encountered factually the next historical level: reason. Critics of the Bible discovered, in later centuries, as many contradictions in its text as in the history of the church. On another level they justified one of the Catholic theses against Luther: The text itself is a part of history. If the Holy Ghost could dictate unerring Scriptures without error, then it could just as well lead the church through infallible popes or councils; if it had not done the one, why should we believe that it had done the other?

So the level of enlightened reason criticizes the levels of Christian theology. But mere emancipation is never a real understanding of that from which one emancipates oneself. A degree of historical delusion is part of the psychological conditions of emancipation. Maturity assumes an understanding of our ancestors of which neither they nor the rebel desiring emancipation were capable. This is the ("Heisenbergian") ideal example. In the history of religion as, in general, in cultural history, Kuhn's image of paradigms is more appropriate than in physics. The levels of Christian theologically preserve traditions that are invisible and untestable on the level of enlightened reason.

An enlightened theory of evolution can, to some extent, do justice to the levels of Christian theology. It can explain why in church history, too, there are levels, perhaps these intellectual levels. The Christian community knew itself from the beginning to be led through a living truth: "The Holy Ghost will lead you into all truth." This is an evolutionary process. As in all evolution, it proceeds through trial and error, through advances in different directions and the resulting struggles between these directions, the victory of the triumphant direction, integrating unification, and unhealable divisions that lead to separate evolutionary directions. Here levels of decision are possible, just as in any other intellectual and political development. According to the ideal of leadership through truth, there is an ongoing unification process growing out of the community. In order for this to be successful, one of two conditions must be fulfilled. Either the community must be so small that its members know one another and the continuation of the true agreement of the social group can be continually tested; this is the principle of sects, now most visible among the Quakers. Or the truth must have such an obvious superpersonal power that even a widely scattered human group can be certain that this truth will be realized again and again. Of this, contemporary science is a model, in which new knowledge has continued to be established through active agreement of the scientific community, with the peripheral phenomenon of the continual dying of those that are not convinced. The Christian church has claimed a similar power of convincing through its truth, mediated through its preaching and the ever effective presence of the Holy Ghost. It would not have survived two thousand years without some justification of this power (this is an argument for the papacy that Luther could only eliminate through the equation of the papacy with the anti-Christ). However, the sociologically and politically educated observer recognizes in the history of the church more obviously than in the history of science the supporting constructions that have led to the authority of the pope, the councils, and the text. The principle of authority arises wherever unification through an immediately convincing truth is not successful. Authorities may be living or historical. Living authorities are either monarchical or corporate, that is, either episcopal or presbyterian. If the Catholic preservation of the church is to be guaranteed through living authority, then a central power becomes necessary because of the enormous expansion of Christianity, thus the papacy. The principle of corporate authority can seldom be practiced in the ccumenical framework, thus the councils. The immovable authority is a once and for all definitive text, thus the canon of the Scriptures. It is evident that mere knowledge of this mechanism, as it appears to enlightened reason, is enough to make all three authorities relative, even if one is prepared to continue accepting the authority for pragmatic reasons and out of respect. Thus Luther was prepared to respect the councils and even the pope, until Eck forced him to opt for the truth. It is perplexing to the contemporary reader that Luther continued accepting the authority of the Scriptures, as the next level he could have doubted; he saw the whore "reason" as the counterpart of the anti-Christ pope. Such confusion concerning a level always shows that we have understood the levels only as stabilizing means, and that the content that makes this stability possible has remained unnoticed.

The Enlightenment symbolizes its own levels through a half-truth, the belief in progress. It was an enormous historical step that placed in opposition to the generally ruling absoluteness of tradition the free search for truth and the belief in a better future under the principle of reason. But even within the domain of rational knowledge, the mere belief in progress has something one-dimensional. It often does not recognize the content validity of older knowledges that spanned epochs. Here Kuhn's scheme of scientific history is illuminating. Normal science does not question its own dominant paradigm. It is because it applies it without question that it does not really understand why it functions. In the great scientific revolutions, science is forced to philosophize. Einstein understood Newton better than the eighteenth and nineteenth centuries had understood him.

He could relativize him because he did him justice. But no one who comes later will *fully* do justice to the earlier one. The great gift I received from my teaching the history of philosophy was that I learned to see to what extent the entire modern philosophy, though pointing beyond Plato, has not fully understood Plato. But the veil that covered Greek philosophy was precisely its role as authority. Where this authority was still valid, it remained as misunderstood as a dominant paradigm, and where it was no longer valid, it was as forgotten as a paradigm of the past.

Christianity has never questioned the authority of Christ. It has made his divine nature sacrosanct through dogma. This authority, too, was a veil hiding his reality. Thus the ever-recurring forms of conflict of the inner revolutions of the church. Whoever raised the veil a bit had to see himself as returning to the origins, to the real Christianity, and had to see the believers in existing authority as enemies of Christ, as inciters to sacrilege. Thus it was for Luther. The principle of the Scriptures meant to him the overwhelming source of living water, which was also present in the oldest great theology, the Pauline, and in the tradition of Christ himself. The issue, as so often in a new paradigm, was a single thought that reorganized everything else: justification through faith.

This thought is already so far removed from our age that one can hardly explain it to people today. (I know what difficulty I had as a youth in trying to understand what Luther spoke about; only after I had analyzed it, in the light of intellectual history, did I begin to have more than a sporadic feeling for him.) Compared with the rationalistic paradigm of reason and of good will, jutification through faith contains in fact two opposing components. On the superficial level it is emancipating, and without this level it would never have had such historical force. On a deeper level, though, it denies precisely what the Enlightenment had believed: the immanent gift of human nature for moral and rational progress. With the deeper level I mean deeper knowledge, even if Luther's form of this knowledge is no longer appropriate to our rationality. Although we know that it remains inadequate, let us try to find a modern language for this knowledge.

It is emancipating to recognize that we do not owe our identity to the fulfillment of an externally given command. The concept of identity resulting from emancipation stands for the preemancipatory concept of justification. The externally given commandment stands for what Luther, following St. Paul, calls the works of the law. But St. Paul was philosophically educated. He could, in Hellenistic version, think the thought that Kant has most clearly formulated in modern times: The law in its core is a law of reason that the emancipated human, because of reasoned knowledge, is compelled to apply to himself. He who thinks in this manner, may say "identity" instead of "justification." But St. Paul, and with him Luther, criticized exactly this central thought. Experience teaches me that I cannot do the good that I want or, if we look deeper, want the good that I concur with. Let us not consider here how Kant, who saw this problem, tried to solve it; the Enlightenment, by and large, was not able to see the problem and has repressed it with the psychic instrument of optimism. The punishment for this repression is the "dialectic of Enlightenment," the always threatening collapse of the entire modern civilization.

Where the rationalism of the Enlightenment becomes aware of the problem, it usually blames the irrationality of the emotions. This stylization of the human being, the division of the mind into a rational and an irrational part, is itself a level of anthropological theory, a paradigm, that in our Western tradition stems from the Greek philosophy, from an interpretation (an imprecise one) of a Platonic image. Cultural critique as well as the science of our time destroys this smooth solution and reveals its false elegance. Cultural critique urges us to speak about the irrationality of the rational, of the destruction of the environment through technical and political activity that is understandable if viewed from a particular interest and which the optimism of the Enlightenment thinks is reasonable. The minimum that must be philosophically accomplished here is the differentiation of intelligence as the capacity to think conceptually from reason as the capacity to perceive the whole. But how can reason be made accessible? Science, however, specifically ethnology and the psychology that came from it, teaches us the rationality of the irrational, the reason of the emotions. Emotions are perceptions without concepts; their disorder indicates only the disorder of the controlling ego.

The experience that drove Luther to a monastery and then out of it, the one he found expressed in St. Paul, was—in modern terms—that the ego itself is the origin of evil, not the emotions that are attached to it. Freud penetrated into this realm of experience, though with completely different preconceptions. Freud's relationship to Luther's problem can be indicated in three ways. First, no doubt, sexual problems had a key role for the young Luther, and thus for his entire life. One may see this in the face of the young ascetic as well as in that of the corpulent paterfamilias. This does not diminish Luther's greatness if one has understood, with Freud, the universality of the sexual problem. The frightening feeling of anxiety and the smoldering feeling of guilt without apparent cause are, according to Freud, phenomena of sexual repression. Luther could never do justice to a monastic form of life because it symbolized to him a false solution of this problem. One may wonder if his later depressions were not connected to the realization that marriage, too, was not the whole answer. Second, Freud taught that the ego should be seen not as master but as a relatively small organ of the psyche. However, Freud thereby descended into a labyrinth in which he, too, lost his way, especially because his conceptual tools, coming from his contemporary physical image of the world, were not suitable for his purposes. Third, most importantly: As Freud saw it, the cure of a neurosis depends upon my acceptance of the acts of the unconscious as acts of one's own will and on my accepting responsibility for them, even if I did not previously know that I had wanted them. This is the realization of Luther and St. Paul: I am the one—not my emotions (I cannot become their master)—I myself am the one who wants the evil that I must condemn. How that happens may be puzzling, but this is the experience. In the symbolic language of religion: There is forgiveness only for the repentant sinner, not for the one who does not admit to his own sins; and it is within his power not even to *want* repentance.

This experience of *servum arbitrium*, in various cultural manifestations, is the departure point of all religions that speak of salvation. In Buddhism and in Hinduism, despite all their differences, salvation is like an awakening. In important traditions, one speaks of an awakening to the true, divine self. In Christianity salvation is divine grace. Luther, who in accordance with his own personal experiences was especially mistrustful of every possessive claim of the ego, also of the claim of grace or of divine participation, found in faith salvation: the form of the relationship to God that he described as justification. With this he came close enough to the existing beliefs of Christian civilization that his own experience could serve as an example for and could result in historical consequences for the world.

It is thus not the principle of the Scriptures that characterizes Luther's theological level but their decisive content: faith. The opponent is not the pope but the principle of reason that prevailed from the scholastics to the Enlightenment. It might be Luther's heritage that German politics has never entirely realized the Enlightenment, has never followed it uncritically. Despite modern efficiency, Germany remains a country of brooding conservatives. Luther could not think of his experience in another rationality than that of the traditional interpretation of the Bible. No level of the historical church or theology could be based on his actual experiences. The Protestant church finally became the hostile brother of the Catholic church, a promoter of the Enlightenment. Only in our own century has the Enlightenment affected the entire earth, transforming all cultures. Its superiority to all traditions is obvious; its incapacity to solve the problems it causes is also obvious, and should not surprise us. Today, completely different spiritual levels are necessary than all traditional levels of Christian theology. But it will be a criterion for them whether they can teach us to comprehend what this traditional theology was all about.

3. Thoughts of a Nontheologian on the Theological Development of Dietrich Bonhoeffer

Dietrich Bonhoeffer was a political martyr. Through his life and word he revealed the Christian faith in resistance to German National Socialism. In World War II, he joined the circle of secret resistance within the German leadership that eventually attempted the assassination of Hitler on July 20, 1944. He was executed, along with many others of this group, by National Socialist justice.

Bonhoeffer was a highly gifted, conscientious, intellectually clear, and unwaveringly progressing theologian. The stations of his theological development have had a tremendous influence, in the decades since his death, on the German-language and the ecumenical theology. Where would he stand now, if he lived? In any case, we study this theology because it is relevant to our own problems.

These are a nontheologian's thoughts about Bonhoeffer's theological development. The word nontheologian is to designate here a member of the church who had no formal theological training and holds no theological office. It designates especially someone whose intellectual work takes place primarily in fields that traditional Christian theology considers to lie outside of theology: science, philosophy, long-range politics. I cannot and will not avoid seeing, from the outside perspective of my knowledge, Christian theology and the church itself, which is my home, in its total cultural conditionedness. I believe that this perspective belongs to what Bonhoeffer called in his last period "religionless Christianity" as a possible development, a somewhat ambiguous label. I come from the same social milieu as Dietrich Bonhoeffer, and am only six years younger than he; but unfortunately I never met him in person. I have met many of his followers and friends, mostly after the war.

I

Bonhoeffer's presuppositions, the influences that formed him, can be loosely grouped under four headings: his family background, Harnack, Barth, ecumenism.

Dietrich Bonhoeffer was one of those *homines religiosi* whose decision to place their own lives in the service of God comes early in childhood, unnoticed by others. There were some theological ancestors in his liberal, scholarly, upper-middle-class family; the well-ordered but easy-going family still included the children's evening prayers, even if they did not go to church on Sunday. To the circle of eight brothers and sisters, the firm decision of the youngest brother to become a minister seemed rather unusual and not entirely understandable. A child can have a silent and intense life with God, without doing violence to his natural child development, where the environment offers him only the cultural forms in which he interprets and unfolds his inner experience. It seems to me that Dietrich Bonhoeffer's childhood was such an experience—a source of life to the end of his existence, but perhaps never fully revealed to others.

His family also gave him something that was important for his later intellectual development: modern consciousness in the form of a tradition. Modern consciousness: The dominant member of the family was, until the end, the father, who was a psychiatrist at the University of Berlin, a scientifically trained physician. Unmistakable, in his written remarks, was the wise, cautious, self-critical, and yet sure style of this man. There was also the oldest brother, Karl-Friedrich, the leading physicochemist of his generation in Germany, and there was the world of liberal-constitutional politics of his brother Klaus and of his brothers-in-law Schleicher, Dohnanyi, and Leibholz. Many theologians of our century have never fully assimilated the modern consciousness. Others had to acquire it as a rupture in their tradition with the resulting pain, tension, and doubt. Still others, perhaps, never even knew any kind of spiritual tradition in their childhood but grew up in the reduced dimension of the self-satisfaction of secularism, encountering our tradition only later, almost like a foreign culture. Dietrich Bonhoeffer never had to experience a break with his family, and it was in this continuity that modern thought was natural to him.

The choice of the religious way of life, for the son of a bourgeois, academic, Protestant family, meant the study of theology. The first of the theological influences that affected him was Harnack. Adolf von Harnack was a Berlin colleague of Bonhoeffer's father, and a Grunewald neighbor of the family. He was the most famous and most important of Bonhoeffer's personal theology teachers. His name may be understood here as representing the world of scholarly theology in the sense of historical and philological research. This research into biblical textual criticism, this critical church history, and this putting the history of church traditions in the context of profane historical description were the result of the application of modern consciousness to theology. The dogmatic position of this school is known in the theological tradition as "liberal." In fact, the rational analysis of the past liberated thought from the norms of the positive, from the burden of having to believe what was said merely because it had been said. Harnack's history of dogma taught that the classical Christian dogmas must be understood as formal means of resolving debates that resulted from early Christian tradition, but which could only be understood in the language of Greek philosophy as the conceptuality of the culture of late antiquity.

Bonhoeffer, with his great receptivity, absorbed the rationality of this theology as a self-evident body of knowledge. But his own scholarly interest in theology was not historico-philological but, rather, what protestant theology calls systematic. The philosophical system concept that resonates in this word does not really express the actual concern, especially Bonhoeffer's. Simply stated, what mattered to him was not who did or said what, but rather what was true. This sought-after truth was for him, from the beginning, never the form of a statement, but that of real life. I see him as someone who, though a conscientious student of what was expected, made from the beginning his independent quest for reality. The liberating impetus at the beginning of his journey was the theological awakening of that decade that is best represented by the name of Karl Barth, notwithstanding a polyphony of other names.

The strength of liberal theology lay in the exposure of the profanely knowable in Christian history. In its questioning about religious reality it walked intellectually near an abyss. If rational thought leaves the classical self-interpretation of the Christian belief behind, does a better interpretation of this belief remain, or does belief disappear along with its old forms? If you were enlightened and remained a theologican, you had to hope for the better interpretation. Where this interpretation was not intellectually flat and thus ephemeral, it could not avoid conceptual borrowings from philosophy, no longer from the original Greek forms, but rather the modern. What seems to have survived amidst the multiplicity of opinions has proven to be the recourse to the subjective, to the manner in which religion is to be experienced, from Schleiermacher's feeling of absolute dependency to Bultmann's reservation of the existential for faith confronting nature, the latter attitude being easily devoured by the objective sciences. This theology furnished to the church in the bourgeois period a self-interpretation corresponding to its social role. The church was seen as a necessary member of a *de facto* pluralistic society, as an essential and yet relatively noncommittal guarantee of meaning; the theology of subjectivity was flexible enough to make its demands on the spirit broader or narrower, without having to perceive itself as dishonest. The liberal state had problems only with the Catholics and a few Calvinist fundamentalists who did not have a theology of feeling.

According to Barth's own admission,[24] it was a political shock that freed him from Schleiermacher. As he was a leftist Swiss bourgeois, his eyes were opened, from the beginning, to the moral insupportability of the public identification of the leading German theologians with the pompous jingoism with which the threatened Germany of Kaiser Wilhelm concealed its fear at the beginning of World War I. He read again the Reformers and the Epistle to the Romans, which for Luther had been the decisive text in the New Testament canon. He discovered for himself the "vertically descending" word, the word of God spoken through and in Jesus Christ to our subjectivity, that is, a revelation that cuts through all our general philosophical concepts, brought by a unique human being. After the war, the Protestant churches of continental Europe were receptive for this seed. How could Bonhoeffer not have been influenced by it? How did he react to it?

The fourth influence on Bonhoeffer, I said, was ecumenism, in the original sense of the word, concerning the entire populated world. As were many others, Bonhoeffer was liberated through the ecumenical experience from a provinciality that had been the result, for almost all churches, of schisms, of nationalism, and especially of the factual irrelevancy of the thinking of the church as a consequence of the Enlightenment. Or perhaps he sought the ecumenical experience earlier than most of his religious contemporaries because, as a modern man, he had been stifled by provinciality from the beginning. He sought not only the universal reality of the church and the multiplicity of serious beliefs in the churches of the world united by the ecumenical movement. He was interested in the profane and social reality of the countries where he stayed. He went to Rome to learn about the Catholic Church at its center. What would have happened to him if he had been able to make his long-dreamed-of journey to Asia, if he had been able to speak with Gandhi, if he had been able to experience the reality of Hinduism and Buddhism, with his perceptive organs?

II

I must proceed a bit further in my thoughts on the formative influences. In all four aspects, family background, Harnack, Barth, and ecumenism, what was at work was the contrast between Christian commitment and modern consciousness. The biographical and historical situation in these two realms was such that the Christian commitment was the given and the modern consciousness appeared as the environment, or influence, or partner, in the dialogue. As a nontheologican I would like to make a methodical inquiry and reverse the direction of the questions. One cannot understand the modern world or the development of Christian theology of the last decades, and Bonhoeffer's influence, if one is not prepared to accept modern consciousness as the given, and the Christian commitment only as an element of an almost forgotten earlier history and possibily an initially confusing and perhaps disturbing partner in the dialogue.

It seems quite obvious to me that the modern consciousness of Dietrich Bonhoeffer came from the fact that his family life included emphasis on science, even if neither he nor his later surroundings had particularly scientific interests. Science is the hard core of modern thought. But consciousness of science has not been the leading factor in modern intellectual history, as this may have been the case for certain culturally limited phases of the seventeenth, nineteenth, and twentieth century. Yet science is the most resistant intellectual product of modern times, its hard core. One could say in an inquiry into historical materialism that the laws of science are the objective background of the economic and the economy-dependent cultural progress of modern times, even where this reason remained concealed or seemed unimportant to the subjective consciousness of the bearers of this progress. Where would the dominating and artistic subjectivity of the renaissance person have been without the urban culture made possible through the late-medieval technology? Where would the idealism and romanticism, as well as the deliberate realism, of the nineteenth century have been without the bourgeois way of life made possible through the technology of the industrial revolution? And on the theoretical level, the father of strictly subjectivistic philosophy, Descartes, reflected upon the *res cognitans* in order to comprehend how he could think about nature as *res extensa*, that is, with the help of the concepts of mathematical science. Those who, like Dietrich Bonhoeffer, have lived with scientists, know something of the unswervingness of modern intellectual progress.

The historico-philological theology was part of the second great scientific advancement of modern times, the discovery of a historical way of thinking or, in a more general sense, of the humanities. The accomplishment here is the ability to understand alien individuals, even alien cultures, by *not* identifying with them. This is an enormous expansion of our intellectual horizons.

It was actually only since Wellhausen that the Old Testament was rediscovered in its unbelievable richness and intensity and its relevance for our own decisions, that is, since Old Testament scholarship taught us to see the cultural and social conditions that prevailed in Israel three thousand years ago and to which the old texts correspond with immediate liveliness and without any Christological reinterpretation. I dare say that the confusing state of New Testament exegesis—confusing in comparison with Old Testament scholarship—will not change until one learns to accept that pivotal texts like the Sermon on the Mount were addressed to people who lived like mendicant friars. Anyone who is familiar with the teachings of

Buddha or remembers how directly St. Francis of Assisi was able to read these texts knows what I am talking about.

All three theological examples that I have referred to above should force us to cross the threshold that separates the peaceful science of Harnack from the unrest symbolized by the early Barth. Contemporary humanities mostly achieved their enormous expansion of horizons through a neutralization or, even worse, a trivialization of its own value judgments. The so-called cultural Protestantism, the justification of Christianity through its contribution to the obtained cultural plateau, includes some very good historical insights, and yet it is a trivialization that ignores the abyss along the edge where enlightened theology proceeds. If Christianity is justified through its cultural contribution, then every cultural criticism, every world reform, be it social-Darwinist, or technocratic, or Marxist, will let the Christian faith sink further into forgotten and remote history. Barth knew exactly that if he was right in following Christ in his life, Christ must be more than all these world reformers and, in particular, more than the world that permits itself to be so changed. I said to Karl Barth, in the one very long conversation I had with him, at the beginning of the fifties, that I saw the direct path leading from Galileo to the atom bomb and that I was confused by the question of whether I could continue, with this knowledge, to pursue my beloved physics. He answered: "Herr von Weizsäcker, if you believe what all Christians avow and almost no Christian believes, namely that Christ comes again, then you may, you must, continue with physics; otherwise, you must not continue." That is how he had to talk. He also said to me, when we came to talk about Gogarten. "He may find my way of speaking too mythological, I find his too philosophical." I trusted in the truth in Barth's mythology and have never given up physics.

But after this agreement with Barth's position, the nontheologian is now obligated to voice all possible skepticism. It is astonishing enough that the biblical texts are still able to speak so demandingly to enlightened persons today. But they reach, almost only, people who were still educated in the language of the church, with dialectical theology remaining a subject for church intellectuals. The nonintellectual members of the church keep falling away in our century, decade by decade, at least in the old Christian nations, for the apparent reason that also the intellectual bearers of modern consciousness in these countries distance themselves more and more from Christian content. The church has not been able to overcome its provinciality in contrast to the openness of modern consciousness. It appears to me to be structurally clear that it cannot overcome this through orthodox insistence or through a modern version of apologetics. The questions of content that present themselves here have, it appears to me, determined not only Bonhoeffer's theological development but also his theological legacy.

III

To the extent that I have been able to survey the secondary theological literature of the past decades about Bonhoeffer, I see that it interprets his theological development as immanently theological, that means, referring to the testimonial power it has for other theologians. For example, this is true—despite the width of their historical horizons—of both Bethge's biography[25] and Ernst Feil's theological monograph.[26] I cannot, and do not want to, compete with these thorough and penetrating studies. I follow Bonhoeffer's theological development only in loose reflections. I said that I find his development to be a journey to reality. It is the reality that would prove itself to be the basis of the church, beyond its provincialism.

Let us proceed now to Bonhoeffer's five books, *Sanctorum Communio*, *Akt und Sein* (Action and Being), *Nachfolge* (Imitation), *Ethik* (Ethics), and *Widerstand und Ergebung* (Resistance and Surrender). The first two were written for the acquisition of academic degrees and could be called philosophical works; the next two are works in ethics, and the last contains the letters written in prison, which I see as Bonhoeffer's breakthrough to his own origins. This division corresponds somewhat to Bethge's division of the phases of Bonhoeffer's life into "The Magic of Theology," "The Price of Being a Christian," and "Participant in Germany's Fate."

Bonhoeffer's first writings, which were hardly noticed at the time, anticipate the fundamental thoughts of his last period. The dissertation *Sanctorum Communio* is, in two ways, the beginning of the journey to reality: beyond the liberal theology and beyond Karl Barth. It is a systematic, I would even say philosophical, work in the field of theology. Its contents include neither concepts of individual religious behavior such as the concept of belief nor concepts of religious metaphysics such as the concept of God, but its theme is the concreteness of religious existence in the social role of the church. And methodologically speaking, it does not deal with theological postulates but proceeds from the profane science of sociology and attempts to prove the theology of the church as the actual, the only, enduring fulfillment of the sociophilosophical teaching about community. "Christ existing as community" is the formula of this fulfillment. His professorial qualification thesis, *Akt und Sein* proceeds directly from the contemporary philosophical controversy about the tension between the understanding of the ego, of the human being, as a transcendental subject—expressed in the title as "Akt" (action)—and the ontological understanding of the human being as "Sein" (being). He sees both ways of understanding failing in their isolation and finds their possible unity, again, in the church.

The young Bonhoeffer accepts the contrast—prevailing in his time—of a phenomenological-apriorist social philosophy and empirical social research, the empiricism supposedly based on the results of the phenomenology. He identifies the *a priori* seen structures of the community (different from those of society) with the Christian-theological concept of the original condition, in contrast to which exists the real historical community, in the shadow of the destructive force of sin. The church, Christ as community, is historically the only possible way to live as a community under the aspect of sin. Today hardly any social philosopher would dare place a phenomenologically provable *a priori* before the social experience. The historical conditioning of all social forms is only too well known to us, and thus the anthropology that lies behind this history has become an unresolvable problem. The equating of philosophically ideal types with the original state of humans before the fall as told in the Bible may be an effective thought in the history of Christian reflection. But one can make it understandable only historically, through the two sources of Christian theology: Greek philosophy and the Bible. The word "theology" itself comes from the religion of Greek philosophy and indicates the core of this philosophy. The opposition between theology and religion as two separate spheres of knowledge results from a later period of Christian thought, medieval Scholasticism. It is an attempt to determine the reciprocal relationship of the two religions, the biblical and the philosophical, that converged in the intellectual history of Christianity—an attempt whose conceptual apparatus came from one of the two, namely, from philosophy. The systematic distinction between theology and philosophy exists, to the best of my knowledge, in no world culture except that of the second Christian millennium, that is, the medieval-modern European millennium, which is now coming to an end.

In my subjective opinion, the young Bonhoeffer is not to blame for not seeing the historical relativity of his problem, and perhaps even consciously repressing it. He had to defend himself against another temptation of contemporary Protestant theology, in which the influences of Harnack and Barth work together, namely, the tendency to eliminate Greek philosophy and thus, *de facto*, the philosophy that comes out of the self-understanding of Christian belief. What would remain, if this attempt could be successful, could no longer be labeled theology. This opinion rests on my conviction of the nontrivial continuity of philosophy.

If Bonhoeffer had remained an academic theologian, it seems to me that he would not have been able to resolve the problems he dealt with. In a free decision and in reaction to historical necessity, he chose a way that is more real. As a result of Hitler's seizure of power, the Protestant church in Germany came out of its condition of irrelevance and entered one of distress. Bonhoeffer proved that he meant what he said when he made the church the central concept of his theology. He soon became one of the most decisive protagonists of professing Christians of radical orientation. This cost him his academic career and brought him to the experience of the living community, first with the young theologians in the Lutheran seminary in Finkenwalde and later with their successors in Eastern Pomerania.

Bonhoeffer's life from now on did not proceed, as tradition and talent would have had it, into the wide world, but rather from the wide Atlantic world back to Germany, from the university to a minister's seminary, from there to the temporary hospitality of the monastery of Ettal and, after a brief excursion into the highly secretive community of political conspiracy, to prison, and, after a waiting period of two years, to his death. In the first eight of these twelve years, one has also seen, not without reason, a certain theological contraction. The professing church, and with it its supporters, shows a certain intransigence. And the theology of "imitation" speaks a biblicistic language. I believe, though, that Bonhoeffer in both ways followed his inner voice towards reality.

In 1933 I was too removed from church organizations and too unpolitical in my actual awareness to perceive what I discovered forty years later in Bethge's book, with a kind of horror: how the majority of the leading clergy in Germany initially were taken in by Hitler's national-conservative rhetoric, or how they at least thought it necessary to pretend that they were. If at least they had been impressed by Hitler's revolutionary tone! Actually they were, as were most of the conservative bourgeoisie, useful idiots in support of Hitler's real intentions. Bonhoeffer, thanks to the political horizons of his earlier family life and his sophistication, was compelled to assume an opposing position. The political horizons of many of his colleagues in the clergy, it is true, were no wider than those of his opponents.

The Bible-exegete theology of "imitation" was given form through the National Socialist experience, but it was not triggered by it. If the church was "Christ existing as community," then it had to ask, "What, after all, does Jesus want from us?" Bonhoeffer, in distinction to many theologians, did not hesitate to interpret the central text of the Gospels in a direct understanding. He was educated and intelligent, but more important for him was to see and speak about reality so simply that it becomes binding. Thus his breakthrough to the Bible did not occur in the highly intellectual Epistle to the Romans but in the unbearable-merciful simplicity of the Sermon on the Mount.

If we ask what Bonhoeffer has understood of the abyss that this text conceals, we see that his exegesis is not consciously learned but almost delivered as sermons. The place for these sermons is first the preaching seminary, whose members prepare themselves in a church that is persecuted or close to persecution. This framework is close enough to the condition of Jesus' disciples to overcome the almost insurmountable hesitation about a literal interpretation of this text and to make a spontaneous understanding possible. Bonhoeffer had not hesitated to urge his coeval candidates for the ministry to assume certain ancient and earnest rules of monastic life, such as a regular daily routine, organized prayer, liturgy, and even some meditation. If he could accomplish this in opposition to deeply entrenched Protestant preconceptions, then I see this as exactly the same courage in dealing with reality that we find in his later theology of engagement. His fate should demonstrate that the Christian life can only become more worldly as it becomes more spiritual, and only more spiritual as it becomes more worldly. Both of these steps amount to the elimination of the protection against one's fear of one's self.

Bonhoeffer's courage to relate every word of the text as a liberating commandment to his own life has unlocked this text to him, and to all who read him, far beyond the customary reading. In this he encountered an unavoidable ethical problem, actually a problem of becoming conscious that everyone faces upon reading the Sermon on the Mount with the sincere will of imitation, without being able to assume the living conditions of mendicant friars—be it that one cannot do this or does not want to do this or must not do this. It appears to me that Bonhoeffer, in this period, did not have the right access to an entire layer of this text, nor—as far as we can tell from his written testimony—did he ever gain it later. On the level of ethical positivism, the insight of "imitation" lead to pacifism, under the influence of his friend Lasserre. But it was his political thinking that separated him increasingly from the political thinking of his church, even from close associates. The social reality of the Protestant church in the bourgeois era permitted almost only the choice between agreement and alienation in regard to official politics, two politically unenlightening modes of behavior. What I have called Bonhoeffer's sophistication led him from these narrowing horizons into active political participation. If we compare passages of his *Nachfolge* (Imitation) with the conspiratorial political activity of his last years in regard to the questions of truth and worldly goal setting, we may not be able to reconcile them fully. He has lived as ethical conflict the conflict between the positive ethics of professing imitation and the positive ethics of political conspiracy, and finally decided in favor of politics. After that, he never wavered. His political action and his suffering in prison, which resulted from it, opened without doubt a new dimension of reality to him.

The first phase of the development of this consciousness of reality is reflected in the fragments of his *Ethik*. The difficulty is not the insight into political reality, which was always clear to him; what is difficult is not to lose the Christian reality through immersion in political action, but to understand it in an even deeper sense. Within this experience he would probably not have written at the beginning of his *Ethik* (6th edition, 1975): "The knowledge of good and evil seems to be the goal of all ethical awareness. The primary task of Christian ethics is to do away with this knowledge . . . In Christian ethics, alone the possibility of the knowledge of good and evil represents the fall from the original state. In the beginning, the human being knows only one thing: God. It is only in the unity of his knowledge of God that he knows of other humans, of objects, of himself; he only knows everything in God and God in everything. The knowledge of good and evil points to the earlier deviation from the origin" (p. 20). The rediscovered unity speaks in every transmitted word of Jesus (p. 29); Jesus refuses to be drawn into wordly conflicts (p. 31); "do not judge so that you shall not be judged" because judging itself is apostasy (p. 35). Now Bonhoeffer's ethics turns from the last things to the "next-to-last things" (p. 134). "Christian radicalism, be it fleeing from the world or trying to improve it, stems from hatred of creation. Radicalism does not forgive God for his creation" (p. 137). "Thus the concept of the natural must be found again through the Gospels" (p. 153). Bonhoeffer's ethics turns to concrete details of life and, in history, to the real sequence of eras ("Legacy and Decay," p. 94). "The world remains the world *because* it is the world that is loved, judged, and redeemed in Christ. No human being has the mandate to transcend the world and turn it into the kingdom of God" (p. 247). At that time, Bonhoeffer may have regarded *Ethik* as his final, fulfilled theological task. That this work remains a fragment cannot only be seem as a consequence of his political activities. The lacunae in his *Ethik* point to the missing step, the one he took in prison.

The breakthrough, as we can see in his letters to Bethge, occurs after his first year in prison; it happened with the force of a landslide. Judging by style differences, I would say that the last scales had fallen from his eyes; he now sees the reality that he had always felt. "We are facing a completely irreligious age; humans, the way they are, just can no longer be religious" (April 30, 1944). "I often ask myself why a 'Christian instinct' frequently attracts me more to the irreligious than to the religious, and not with missionary intentions but in a— I'd like to say—'brotherly' way . . . When others begin talking in religious terminology, I become almost totally silent" (April 30). "The attack of Christian apologetics on the emancipation of the world are, in my opinion, first meaningless, second undignified, third un-Christian" (June 8). "Barth was the first to consider it wrong . . . to set aside a space for religion in the world or against the world . . . but he has not given concrete directions for the nonreligious interpretation of theological concepts . . ." (July 8). "I will write to you about the Song of Solomon when you are in Italy. I would really like to read it as an earthly love song. This is probably the best 'Christological' interpretation" (June 2). Bultmann's essay on the "demythologization of the New Testament" did "not go 'too far,' as most readers think, it did not go far enough" (May 5). "God is beyond in the midst of our life" (April 30). About W. F. Otto's book on *Die Götter Griechenlands* (The Gods of Greece): "Do you understand that . . . I—*horribile dictu*—find the so represented gods less objectionable than certain forms of Christianity, and that, yes, I almost believe I could claim these gods for Christ?" (June 21).

I am touched to see that from my book *Zum Weltbild der Physik* (The World View of Physics) he quoted the thought "that we must not think of God as a stopgap for our incomplete knowledge" (May 29), and that he added: "if only a spiritual exchange were possible" (May 24).

Bonhoeffer saw. The manuscript that he began on these thoughts is lost, but I doubt he would have been able to work out the interrelated concepts of "religionless Christianity," "nonreligious interpretation," and "arcane discipline" (May 5) in such a way that his thoughts would have done justice to his vision. Bonhoeffer's final phase is important to the church as a destruction of a defense position, not as the basis of a theology. In a mysterious way this phase has the characteristics of a work of old age: an opening up in the nearness of death, which indicates in words the steps that the speaker has done intuitively, although in the world in which he has lived one is not able to do these steps.

IV

What does religion mean to us?

First: How does religion face modern consciousness? Let us take back, before we go on, the critical restriction of the word "religion" that Barth and Bonhoeffer have employed. Let us open our eyes to the richness of phenomena that can be seen under the general concept of religion.

Religion as cultural element, even as the bearer of a culture, this is what Christianity has been for these two thousand years. Religion as bearer of a culture shapes the social life, groups eras, determines or justifies morals, explains anxieties, gives form to joys, consoles the helpless, interprets the world. It is the traditional form of this religion that is slipping from modern consciousness.

Religion as foundation of radical ethics is critical and is therefore often persecuted in its culture. Wherever the Sermon on the Mount or at least the Ten Commandments have been taken literally, religion was the basis of radical ethics.

Religion as inner experience is, in a way, each subjective experience of the two foregoing aspects of religion. It is conscious living in faith. But it is, especially, prayer, meditation, mysticism.

Religion as theology is the attempt at understanding the experience of the other three aspects in a conceptual way. The thoughts we are sharing in this chapter are a part of theology.

If we want to define a general concept that comprises these different phenomena, then we could say: Religion is a human behavior toward the divine. This definition seems to sacrifice the neutrality with which we described the four aspects. In fact: If we include in a definition the concept of the divine, how, then, do we define the divine? Formally speaking one could answer: This is the philosophical circle from which no fundamental reflection can escape. A definition of truth claims to be true, a definition of philosophy is itself philosophy, a definition of religion is theology as the attempt to understand the experience that we call religious. The formal answer, however, is to lead us to a fertile answer concerning content. This precisely is the amazing and reflection-provoking phenomenon: that the entire human history is overshadowed by a mode of experiencing and thinking that can interpret itself only as human behavior toward a divine reality.

Let us now turn to the various manifestations of religious criticism. There is a philosophical religious critique that today is often considered scientific. The rationality of traditional religion is no longer convincing. The question about the basis of the possibility of religion either presents the historical appearance, the role as culture bearer, the experience of religion as mere dressing in the face of the arguments of rationalistic metaphysics, or reduces all religious experience—through radical skepsis—to the status of self-deception or deceit.

The political pathos of religious criticism did not originate in theoretical philosophy, but in morality, in radical ethics that is independent from religion. *Tantum religio potuit suadere malorum,* says Lucretius in *De rerum natura,* about the many evil deeds that religion can make us do. The classical attack by the Enlightenment against religion aims at its role as element of a culture, that is, as bearer of its relationships of power. It is not the absence of faith, it is morality that is the determined enemy of religion. Anyone who does not take this seriously does not understand the history of the Enlightenment. This opposition exists also, in latent form, in the compromises—such as the rationalistic metaphysics of the seventeenth and the eighteenth century—that established, after the religious wars, a natural right that is denominationally neutral. The compromise disintegrates in the course of history, and the Marxist phase of the Enlightenment considers it to be the domination ideology of the bourgeois era.

The religious criticism of the old Asiatic cultures is characteristically related and yet different. Confucianism does not see itself as a religion but as rationalistic morality that bears a culture; and this is the reason why it appealed to the European rationalists of the eighteenth century. But Confucianism, too, is a conceptual compromise of morality and the religion of the heavens and stabilizes the domination in a system of deference; Mao's critique of Confucius radicalizes morality as egalitarianism.

In the great meditative teachings of Hinduism and Buddhism, the religious outside that bears their culture is merely a reflection of the truth proper through the anthropomorphic, psychically conditioned representation of deities. Religion is recognized here as an element of culture, but on a lower level. On this path, radical ethics, often heightened to asceticism, is required, though not as a law as such but as an ineluctable purificaton stage in the receptivity for decisive experiences. The theology of these schools is an interpretation of what is gained in meditation.

Where is our own position between religion and morality? To contemporary consciousness this is an anthropological question, a question of human understanding. If we are to gain understanding, then we must not play down this contrast; we must see the sharpness of what is ideally typical here. Enlightenment, understood as self-enlightenment, departure from an incapacitation that we brought on through our own fault, this is a respectable way to begin. The theoretical pathos of the Enlightenment meets with morality in the virtue of truthfulness, whose core consists in not lying to itself. Lucretius blames religion for *suadere*, for persuading; truthfulness makes Bonhoeffer become silent when others begin to talk in religious terminology. When the autonomous ethics wants to be truthful, it becomes radical. To do this, no abstract conclusion is needed; a realistic look at human society is enough. The problems of justice, of neighborliness, even of survival remain unsolved as long as each individual, and even more each social group, applies the ethical demands to the others rigorously and to itself only loosely. The result is the chain of catastrophes that are called political history. Our human behavior in this history is not basically evil, it is, above all, beneath our own intellectual level, it is stupid. It is hard to imagine a conflict of human interests that could not in principle be resolved through reason. The stupidity that prevents a solution stems from a lack of good will, and this lack is a consequence of fear. Any morally sensitive individual who notices this in himself has to hate himself. But every failure of our alertness, of our truthfulness, lets us project this hatred onto others. For this reason the struggle for justice is accompanied by the pathos of hate. With this, however, the fighter for justice justifies the opponent's fear and hatred. This affective entanglement between humans becomes stabilized through mutual fear. It can be overcome not through rational thought but only through a purer affect, through love. The experience that love is possible is the religious basis of radical ethics. The possibility of a reconciling love is experienced as grace. Unreserved orientation toward this grace is faith. The traditional religious expression of this experience is that we can truly love our neighbor only in God. The commandment "Love your neighbor as you love yourself" cannot be fulfilled in autonomous morality because I cannot think of myself as loving myself but in God; the more sensitive I am the less I should forgive myself for being the way I am.

Thoughts like these can then point the way to the door of religious experience, but they do not extend this experience. The people of Western culture have gained this experience in relation to Jesus, to closeness to him, to the attempt of imitation. This experience at the same time is bliss and the sword. It lets us see the employment of religion in the service of the special interests of the prevailing culture. The radical ethics' critique of religion does not become false just because radical ethics is possible only on a religious basis.

From this insight stems the need to apply different names to the different aspects of religion. Barth chose the name "religion" for that element of religion that is the subject of religious criticism; for the rest he chose words like "Christianity" or "faith." He knew that he, precisely as a theologian, had taken on an immense task. How could faith express itself without right away becoming again "religious" through the concepts of its language? In my conversation with Barth I remarked, in a questioning intonation, that the Gospels are a rather short text but that their dogmatics are long. He replied, with a smile: "Indeed, if we were as simple as the Gospels, then our speech could be brief, too." He added that in the dogmatics he had only tried to work out the large amount of misinterpretations of the Gospels. But I believe that this problem demanded more than the means that Barth was able to employ. Why did he choose the term "religion" for all that was doubtful in Christianity? The reason may have been that in theological scholarship of the nineteenth century "religion" was the general concept that included "Christianity" and "faith" as particular concepts. Instinct told him that the phenomena were hidden here behind the conceptual pyramid that originated in logic. Indeed, who—having tried to communicate an experience to theoreticians—does not know the certainty with which theoreticians detract attention from the experience by classifying it in their conceptual framework? Barth wanted to deter the influx of the religion of Greek philosophy into Christianity. But one must say that his theology, too, could not do without the use of concepts, and that he did not accomplish a clarification of the relationship of theological concepts with concepts in general, thus a philosophical reflection on the kind of philosophy that was implicated in his way of thinking.

Bonhoeffer's last statements, too, fell short of the true, content-related problem. He may make it appear as though the "emancipated" consciousness of the modern world were a way of thinking that has internal consistency. If this were true, then I could hardly imagine an interpretation of the old faith within the concepts of this way of thinking. Bonhoeffer's hints at an "arcane discipline" "through which the *mysteries* of the Christian faith are protected from desecration" (May 5) point in another direction, as does the claim that "The emancipation of the world . . . is now being better understood than it can understand itself, namely, from the viewpoint of the Gospels, of Christ" (June 8). In this line we find also Gogarten's late theology, which saw secularization—not the same as the phenomenon that he called secularism—precisely not as the fall from faith but as realization of God's will in history. Of all these positions we must ask how they manage to move within the circle of understanding Christianity in modern consciousness while understanding modern consciousness from the viewpoint of Christianity.

The designation of the modern world as "emancipated" is misleading when we go beyond the parallel to the legal emancipation from parental authority. It is true, modern culture is no longer subject to the control of the church. In regard to the development of consciousness one could, at most, speak of a special phase of the maturing process, perhaps of the formation of the interrelated faculties of will and intellect, whose common tool is the conceptual thinking. But in the biography of a person as well as in the history of a culture, phases of the maturing process usually mean that certain abilities are repressed when others take their place. This applies especially to phases of emancipation, which for this reason often take a dramatic course. Emancipation is not an end in itself, not the attainment of an equilibrium, it is a transition, a release of contained forces. Contemporary emancipation has become ecumenical. It has stretched to all cultures of the world. However, it does not have the moral rules necessary to shape the liberated world. This is especially true if the thoughts about radical ethics that we discussed were correct, because modern emancipation aims at autonomous morality. Therefore, we must expect that the greatest, worldwide, political conflicts do not lie behind us but are yet to come. And one must fear that right—the right that at first seemed to be so clear—will eventually be with neither one of the fighting parties.

In this situation the church preserves the knowledge of the only thing that can heal, the love of one's neighbor across the battle lines, which is possible only through God. The church does not preserve this knowledge if it persists in a claim it used to have in the past, before emancipation; if it does, it only adds its own battle line to the others, a line between the church and the world. Part of such a battle line is that against non-Christian religions. Here the task is not to love the enemy but to understand the brother. Most Christian theologians, including modern generations like those of Barth and Bonhoeffer, perpetuated the error that the other religions were just "religion," in contrast to Christianity. This attitude was a defense line around the belief in the uniqueness of Christ, a defense line that, like all defense lines, has made understandable what is important in Christ's words. The old church, in incorporating the religion of Greek philosophy, was wiser in this respect.

These are some of the landmarks along the way of theology to modern consciousness, a way that Bonhoeffer considered to be open before he died. Had he been allowed to live, he would have traveled with us on this way.

4. A Dialogue on Meditation

(A conversation with Udo Reiter. It was taped, without preparation, for a radio broadcast, and was published in Udo Reiter's *Meditation—Wege zum Selbst*, Mosaik Verlag, Munich, 1976.)

Reiter:

Professor von Weizsäcker, I would like to begin our conversation with a personal question: When you talk about meditation, you are not just dealing with theoretical reflections, but with your actual experience. May I ask what importance meditation, meditating, has had in your life?

Weizsäcker:

Yes, you are asking an important question that I cannot really answer in a traditional manner. First, you are right: Meditation interests me mainly as something one does—not for any theoretical reasons. Personally, I have never had any formal training in meditation, the way it is available and the way we should have it if we take the matter seriously. What happened was that as a youngster I simply began something that people who are versed in this told me later was meditation. So this was quite spontaneous in the beginning and really began in my childhood. Later I learned about a liturgically structured daily Christian routine. True, I never participated in this on a permanent basis, as member of a group, but I have occasionally been a guest of people who live in this manner. They were the Protestant Michael Brotherhood, and from them I received a great present, namely, the knowledge that a structured way of life can make deeper inner layers accessible to us and can let these layers speak to us. I acquired the habit to keep silent for a while each morning, to keep still, and through this a lot made itself heard. Later, I also encountered Eastern kinds of meditation, and it was an Indian meditation teacher who told me that my childhood habit was already a form of meditation.

Reiter:

To give our readers a proper understanding of this subject, let me ask right away the central question, the question about the nature of meditative experience. What really is it that is experienced in meditation? Is it possible to define it in regard to content? Can it be circumscribed through meta-phors?

Weizsäcker:

What I should say immediately is that anything one could say about this is wrong, because this experience transcends the realm of concepts, the realm of what one can ordinarily convey in language. If we nevertheless deal with it through language, it depends on whom we talk to; either we talk to someone who has had these experiences, and then we understand each other almost without the use of words, or we talk to someone who has not had these experiences, and then the other one will find everything we say bizarre, or we find that our partner misinterprets what we say. This is one of the problems, but it is a problem that we find with any kind of experience, not only with meditation, but perhaps it is especially strong with meditation.

If you insist on an answer—the kind of answer a psychologist might give—then I would say this: It is a quieting of the conscious mechanism; and something that has always existed now appears. Generally, in medi-tation one does not become someone else, but one becomes the one that one has always been. And this becomes manifest in that what we ordinarily call consciousness begins to notice this and then becomes changed through it.

Meditation, throughout history, has existed mainly in religion. We can, therefore, try to approach the matter with concepts of religious meta-physics. And what we experience here is, indeed, closely related to what we call "prayer" in the religious language of the West; but if we say it is an experience of God, then this is just as misleading as anything else we could say—except when we experience it. When we experience it, it is no longer misleading at all, it is so obvious that there is no need to commu-nicate it.

Reiter:

Despite this difficulty, let me try again to talk about the substance of this experience. After all, meditative experience reaches a point that in our language is usually called an experience of enlightenment. You once described such an experience, and you wrote this sentence: "The knowl-edge existed, and half an hour later everything had happened." For clar-ification, let me ask bluntly: What knowledge was there? This being an experience of wholeness, isn't it that, in Christian language, the individual feels suddenly safe and secure "in God"? Does this thought go in the right direction?

Weizsäcker:

You see I hesitate to answer immediately, and this hesitation is almost the most important part of the answer. I could say: When Christians report they have experienced that they were safe and secure in God or have had a glimpse of God, then I am ready to believe they had such an experience.

But that sentence of mine that you just quoted: I *wrote* it, that is, I considered well what I wanted to say, and I knew exactly why I wrote "the knowledge" but not *which* knowledge. The passage you referred to concerns something I experienced in India, at the grave of a great Indian sage, the Maharishi, in Tiruvanamallai. And I believe I will speak clearer when I remain apparently unclear and say: At that moment, standing in that place, in half a second, I knew: "Aha!"—and this "Aha!" is something that must be experienced. If one talks about it—and I have, after all, begun to talk about it, and I am ready to use all the words at my command to explain how this relates to our philosophy and our physics and our psychology—in short, if one talks about it, it will turn out that all these words are misleading, and with them we would probably mislead more than if we simply had remained silent.

Reiter:

Can we conclude from all this that meditation is not primarily concerned with some kind of content or even some new insight into the nature of the world or of existence, but that any content has only a subordinate role; that what counts in meditation is not the cultural background or the kind of knowledge one brings into meditation; that the Indian guru, the Japanese Zen master, the Christian monk, and perhaps even a German physicist meet somewhere at an ultimate point where content ceases to play a role?

Weizsäcker:

If I were compelled to answer the question of whether they do or do not meet with a mere "yes" or "no," without being allowed to add another word, then I would say: Yes, they do meet. But if I am permitted to add something, then I say: This "yes," too, can only be understood if the meeting has really taken place, and this "yes" is not at all meant to justify a relativistic or syncretistic denial of differences where differences still exist.

For example, in the history of culture and religion we see that visions do exist but that, ordinarily, the member of a particular culture or religion encounters in these visions precisely those forms that are customary in the respective culture. And a skeptical psychologist would then say: Of course, it is obvious that what the individual sees are the subconscious cultural contents. And it is precisely from this that the skeptical psychologist would conclude that what the individual encounters is not what he thinks it is. What he sees is not the Holy Virgin or what he sees is not some corresponding Indian figure—what he sees is his own culture. But when I say—which is what I believe—that he nevertheless encounters reality or is "in the reality," then the way I must explain this to myself as a scientist is that this being-in-the-reality happens to his consciousness with the means that are accessible to his consciousness because of its particular formation. Seen in this light, the differences should be taken seriously.

Reiter:

When we talk, here in the West, about "reality" or about "truth," then we usually mean truth that can be proven scientifically-empirically. Is it possible to explain how this Western scientific truth differs from the truth of meditation?

Weizsäcker:

I am constantly tempted to answer to your questions that one must not ask questions in this manner. But this is just a temptation, and I will not really yield to it.

First I would say: A fundamental experience of mysticism, a fundamental experience that is the aim of meditation and which is already approached in the most basic and the simplest steps of meditation, is the experience of unity, of the One. What "one" is can ultimately not be asked, because a second thing would then be added, namely, the explanation of what it is. Also, the experience of unity makes it ultimately impossible to say how it distinguishes between the experience of science and the experience of meditation; because then we would not have an experience of unity, we would have multiplicity. But if I operate on the level of multiplicity, then I can express in the language of science that science cannot express this unity—cannot express it as science—although it is the same reality. My personal opinion is that the reality that the physicist studies, the reality that the historian studies, the reality that the psychologist studies, perhaps even the reality that the mathematician studies is precisely the reality that is—perhaps—ultimately experienced in meditation, because otherwise it would not be reality.

But, to get to the core of your question, we are able to say what our science can and cannot do. Science proceeds conceptually, and the concept is based on differentiation and eventual integration. When I say: "This animal is a cat," I have distinguished it from dogs, birds, and everything else, but I have integrated it in the existence of all cats. This method of using the concept to dissect the reality and then reintegrate it seems to me to be the basis of any scientific process, whereas the kind of training that we have come to call meditation is basically a training for a different mode of behavior, a behavior that does not proceed from dissection in order to reintegrate but that, I would like to say, proceeds from an acceptance of the nondissected, and thus forgoes the achievement of integration; because achievement is precisely what is not the issue here.

Reiter:

You may have been critical of my way of asking questions, but I have the impression that the result shows I was on the right track, and with your permission I would like to continue in this vein. You said: In meditation one becomes *the one that one has always been*. If we view this statement in a positive light, then it is based, in my opinion, on the idea that in the innermost core of the human psyche there is something like a pure, genuine self that exists in itself in eternal identity, and which has merely to be cleansed of all change, all accidental, all unessential to emerge as the core of the personality.

Ever since Sigmund Freud, however, we have come to see things differently. It is difficult still to believe in this absolute core of the personality; rather, we tend to see in the innermost core of the human psyche a hard-to-define chaos of impulses and motivations, which overlap and reinforce or cancel each other—and the result of these motivations is then the very fragile and changeable product that we call personality or ego or self.

Against this background, let me ask two questions: Are you nevertheless willing to maintain the fiction of an original self, "the one that one has always been"? And the second question (if you share my reservations): Is it really good and thus desirable to shed light on—and I phrase it deliberately this way—*that which one has always been*?

Weizsäcker:

Well, I don't want to say at all that your question is not asked the right way. Earlier, too, I did not really say that your questioning was not right; what I said was that one must not ask in this manner. But one does ask questions, after all, and we have to live with this paradox, and we somehow manage to get by.

As for your question, it is very complex. First, Freud. As you brought him into the picture, let me tell you what I think about Freud. I have not met him personally, but I have read him attentively and I have had, and still have, many close contacts with people who think in his tradition. It is my impression that Freud had a genius for seeing phenomena, that he saw phenomena that many others did not see. At the same time, he often was a somewhat stubborn adherent of certain scientific views of the nineteenth century. What is generally accepted of Freud today is, unfortunately, primarily that which is not good about him. What is good about him would be learning to see in his manner. But learning this is so difficult that the people who use Freudian concepts notice very rarely that they are unable to do so. Therefore, I have the greatest respect for Freud and yet great reservations about citing him in support of an argument.

Let's apply this to your question: As for all these theories of ego and id and superego, I am willing to go along provided we say that what Freud called the ego is a product and not the whole. I am inclined to say it is an organ. And if I may use the very common word "psyche" to denote the entity whose organ is the ego—a usage that psychologists sometimes permit—then I would consequently say: The ego is a psychic organ, and this organ, like many other organs, is either good or not so good, but, at any rate, it is not the ultimate, it can be derived from something else. If I have said that one becomes the one that one has always been, then this means, in the language of a psychology that employs Freud's ego concept, that the total relativization of the ego becomes manifest in the experience that lies behind these words. The ego suddenly realizes that it is not absolute, and through this it becomes aware—intuitively aware, not conceptually aware—that it is an organ of something much greater, and it knows that it has always been this organ alone and nothing else, and that it does not have to defend, after all, its identity against that which Freud calls the id, if it is content to be an organ and not the thing itself. And so it suddenly sees it has become that which it has always been, but now *knowingly*; and then the ego, in a way, is suddenly no longer merely the organ because it is the organ that knows it is an organ, and it is this quite complicated situation that I express by saying that it becomes that which it has always been. And this is a deliberately paradoxical statement, which, by the way, corresponds to a thought that we find somewhere in Western tradition. I believe we find it in Nietzsche, but, then, Nietzsche is much more traditional than he pretends to be—at any rate, this thought is: Become the one that you are!

Reiter:

To this statement I would like to add a question on a somewhat different level. What you have just explained means also, psychologically-mecha-nistically seen, that in meditation many things may emerge that one would not necessarily like to come out?

Weizsäcker:

Yes, this is something I failed to deal with, but, as I said, your question is complex. First I would say: The well-known principle that one should meditate under the guidance of a guru, to which we have a Western analogy in Freud's strict requirement that only a person who has been analyzed is allowed to analyze, this principle, this practical rule exists because in med-itation, if we take it seriously, things can happen that destroy the person-ality, things that can take us along a path of which we later would say: Wish I had not taken this path!

One can convey the same by saying that out of the subconscious or whatever we prefer to call it, out of the realm of the id or of the demons, there emerge contents and behavior patterns that are ordinarily, and jus-tifiably, suppressed, and which a truly wise person may want to face so that such a truly wise person would let all this emerge; but anyone who does not have this true wisdom and does not have a teacher who could save him is in danger of not being able to exorcise the spirits he has conjured; that what has emerged does not let him see the ego as the safe organ of the greater self but only as a tiny boat on high sea, no longer capable of resistance. I have learned this, for example, from Indians like Gopi Krishna, whom I came to know quite well personally, and who de-scribed his experiences in his first book, *Kundalini*, and if one would show this to a Western psychiatrist, he would say: This, of course, is mental illness. At the same time, however, this is the Kundalini experience, be-cause, as Gopi Krishna says himself, in his current state, a good portion of what we call "mentally ill" is of course such experiences that turned out badly.

Reiter:

You describe dangers that are possibly connected with meditation; so the simplistic equation "meditation = the good" must be seen with caution. In this context I would like to bring up a phenomenon that I have encountered in many devotees of meditation, namely, an almost limitless optimism; it ranges from the possibility of one's inner development to the lowering of the crime rate of a society to evolutionary progress that is supposed to manifest itself even biologically (if we think, for example, of Aurobindo). Is it that such expectations are merely the customary sectarian hopes of salvation as we have seen them throughout the centuries, or is it that you think they have a solid core?

Weizsäcker:

I am ready to see a solid core in them. But if I am to talk about this further, I must first admit that much of what presents itself in the form of this optimism seems to me to be more or less naive, especially if we disregard here the further development of the human species and look simply at the individual. I can understand very well that people who have meditated, who have experienced what is beneficial in meditation, are so to speak inundated by it and suddenly see it as the sole and supreme fulfillment. From the perspective of the individual's life this is understandable and to a certain extent perhaps justified. Also, it is possible that an individual who has had such experiences progresses constantly and truly becomes a sage, a knower, along the path that you have called "optimistic." But I have the feeling that this could happen only in a cultural setting in which what he experiences is considered of highest value; and even then one must assume that the advanced experiences that are made along this path are immensely complex and difficult.

So this voyage is not easy, and therefore I think that what I have just called "inundating," the inundation with this experience, will usually turn out to be a naive preliminary stage. This applies certainly to our Western culture, and I assume it also applies to Indian or Japanese culture if understood in an appropriately broad sense. In the real world, one must remain open to science and to plain reason and to common sense if one wants to demonstrate that what one has experienced is not merely regression—psychologically speaking. Maturity, after all, shows itself not only in having certain experiences more and more often, but also in being able to cope with the problems of our fellow humans and the world.

But after these preliminary thoughts I would say: I do, indeed, believe that this road makes experiences accessible that have been accessible to few people in the past. A large part of religion seems to be merely the acceptance of these experiences by those who have not had them personally, but who were sufficiently impressed by them to understand that they are real. I could imagine that these experiences are now becoming accessible to a larger number of people than in past ages, and that this may also contribute to a change of society and perhaps of human character in general. But I would not want to see this tied in with proclamations of grandiose visions for the future. I always feel very keenly that it is now that we live, think, philosophize and that the future is not within our reach, even though it might occasionally seem to reveal itself in an allegory, an allegory that we may understand only after it has come and gone.

I would rather reverse the argument: As you know, I have been very actively involved with the problems of peace keeping and economic development, of overcoming class discrimination and poverty and preventing environmental destruction, or whatever the problems are that are in the background of day-to-day decisions although the problems themselves are entirely concrete. And in regard to these problems I must share the opinion of people who are called critics of our system, namely, the opinion that the current systems of the modern world are not solving these problems. With this I mean particularly the capitalist system; and the systems that call themselves socialistic are, I think, merely a new edition of the same mistakes.

And I now ask: Why don't they solve the problems? It is not that the problems are unsolvable. With simple reason—yes, with common sense—one could state what would have to be done to solve them. So what is needed is not a particularly intelligent person who can solve complex matters of management and control; this is not the issue; the problem is eventually that our mental attitude is such that each one of us, at one place or another, and some of us at many places, reject the only thing that is salutary because each one is afraid of what might happen to him if he did make this concession, which, however, is the only one that would save him.

And this structure of the anxious self-protection of the ego can be overcome if the ego does not see itself as the final reality that must be protected at any price, but—as I have said—as an organ. And therefore I believe that in connection with the experience we talked about there is a chance that human beings cease to act in the fearful and self-destructive way that we see almost everywhere today. In this sense I could agree with the people who have those great hopes; but first we must get that far.

Reiter:

This is really the old question about human changeability. After 2,000 years of Christianity, one has to look at this prospect with a certain skepticism. But this is something that you yourself have done indirectly?

Weizsäcker:

Yes, but here, too, I would prefer to reverse the argument. What I mean is this: Suppose one happens to read the Sermon on the Mount. I did this when I was a child; I read the Sermon on the Mount when I was eleven, and I felt immediately: If it is true what it says here, then all of our life is

wrong, even the life of those who were close to me and whom I adored.
I soon learned that it is almost impossible for humans to change this life.
And yet, I never thought for a moment that the Sermon on the Mount
could be wrong. This means: When Jesus spoke those words, he must have
known that people are not going to do this. If you read the New Testament
with this in mind, or also the prophets in the Old Testament, then you
find many passages from which this becomes entirely clear.

But one does not refute Christianity by showing that people have not
acted like this in reality. The text of the Sermon on the Mount could not
have been written if there had not been someone who really lived through
this, who wrote out of his real experience, not out of some abstract principle.

This means: It is not true that the human being cannot change at all;
one can. But this is possible—to use Christian language—not through one's
own good deeds but through the divine grace one receives. But this grace,
to speak again in Christian terms, is bestowed only to him who has shown
through his own efforts that he cares. There is also the kind of grace that
is given against all reason, but grace, in general, is linked to a response.

This is the second aspect. The third aspect is that I would simply dispute
those that say that Christianity has not changed the world. On the contrary,
I think Christianity has changed the world very rapidly. Animal species
change over the course of hundreds of thousands of years; two thousand
years of history are just a fraction of a second in comparison with the
preceding history. If humanity can change in such a way that something
new happens approximately every thousand years, then this is tremen-
dously fast, compared with animal life. The reason for this is that humanity
can accumulate experiences, that it has language, that it can create tradition, that it can argue with the past and the present, that it has reflective
thought. And considering the pace that can possibly be expected from
historical changes, I maintain that Christianity has changed the world greatly.

It has been my personal opinion, for some time, that modern culture is
largely a secularization of Christian contents, and I am using the word
"secularization" the way it was used by the Protestant theologian Gogarten,
namely, as concretization of that which was merely demanded before. But
secularization always contains the danger that one forgets something else
that was related to the demand. For example, social justice: This was one
of the demands of Christianity, a demand that was not fulfilled in the
ancient world, and which was not fulfilled in the early Christian world, but
to which we have come—we can say optimistically—closer and closer. But
the demand for social justice does not release us from the other demand,
the demand of charity, of love for our neighbor. This is something quite
different . . .

Reiter:

. . . to which we have not gotten any closer?

Weizsäcker:

Oh yes, we are coming closer to it, too. But we would move away from it if we thought that we could eliminate the people whom we see as the obstacle for the demands of social justice. Isn't it that the essence of charity is also expressed in the sentence "We are all sinners"? But the people who work on social progress, while doing something laudable, are often of the opinion that only the others, the political opponents, are sinners. And whoever does not know that he himself is a sinner will commit crimes. This cannot be helped. Self-righteousness is the root of all really serious crimes, and in the secularization of Christian contents I see the danger that one may forget this, and whoever forgets it will destroy everything. "We are all sinners, and we lack the sense of justice that we should have"— to put it again in Christian terms. You could also repeat the same thought in another language, even in atheistic language, as Buddhism seems to do it. I am not concerned here with employing a Christian tradition. But if I express myself in this tradition, it is because it is the one in which I grew up, and in which I express myself with ease.

Reiter:

I would like to ask another question about a concrete aspect of meditation. For a long time, there had been little talk about meditative experiences in the Western world. But this changed radically a few years ago. We have witnessed a sudden interest in the teaching of meditation, above all among young people, which has looked for a while, and still looks, like a boom. What do you think are the reasons for this sudden yearning?

Weizsäcker:

It seems to me that once in a while a new reality is discovered, probably at a time when it is urgently needed. Some aspects of this boom may have taken on absurd dimensions and may have given opportunities to people who do not deserve them, but basically I think this boom is an awakening, an urgent need.

I welcome it because I think that the correct insight that we must make progress in regard to social order becomes self-destructive if it is not combined with the experiences to which successful meditation can lead us. And I have the feeling that the disappointed social critics are the ones who would profit most from having the meditative experience.

Reiter:

This may be related to the phenomenon that our scientific way of approaching solutions has led us into a crisis that threatens all human existence today. Meditation seems to be seen here as some kind of fundamental alternative. Do you share this impression?

Weizsäcker:

This, too, is a very interesting question. I tend to believe that any science that destroys the world is bad science. This means: The dissecting and reintegrating of concepts, which I mentioned before, is of course correlated to a dissecting of the real world, to a physical dissection, a destruction of something that perhaps can never be reconstructed, where unity is lost forever. In this respect, science is certainly full of dangers, as we can see in many examples.

There are many people today who for this very reason are strictly antiscientific. But I think that one could demonstrate here—scientifically—that in each such instance the "dissecting" takes place in a way that is still outside that part of reality that is truly understood scientifically. So I really believe that the issue is not primarily to replace science with something else but to bring science to its proper level.

But I think, from a historical standpoint, that the scientific training in conceptual thinking, which has been developed mainly in the West, but also in the East, and the training in meditation, which has been developed mainly in the East, but also in the West, are alternative paths. What they have in common is that they are training; what is alternative is their aim. And I believe: In an ultimate kind of reality, in the unity, of which we get a glimpse in meditation, both lead exactly to the same goal.

Reiter:

To look at the actual situation, here and now: A young person who feels the need for meditation finds the scene that you have described, but also sees an odd kind of Asian exoterics, and with a commercial element. What advice do you have for this person?

Weizsäcker:

Although I am afraid I will get a lot of mail on this, which I will not have the time to answer, my answer would be that I would look at each person individually and perhaps give each one a different answer. I cannot give a general advice to meditate. Nor can I simply say not to do it. No guru can do this either, he can only look at the individual, and only after understanding the particular need can he say to follow this or that path.

The Western belief that one can give generally valid advice, a belief that is related to bad science, is wrong—such as the advice that everyone should do this or that, for example, that everyone should use a certain toothpaste.

But there is one thing that I would say in a general way: One should not indiscriminately or in a surge of enthusiasm respond to a charismatic figure and become flooded by feelings that remain unexamined. One should never abandon one's alertness, one's rational consciousness, one's intellect in this situation. I have seen enough accidents happen when this was not observed.

Reiter:

I would like to go back to one aspect that you briefly mentioned earlier. Opponents of meditation often maintain that meditation is flight from reality, a withdrawal from the demands of this world, from human requirements, a retreat to one's own inner world. How would you counter this kind of criticism?

Weizsäcker:

I would like to give the same answer that I once heard from Gopi Krishna, whom I mentioned before. This was at my institute, when a young man asked practically the same question. Gopi Krishna looked at him in a very friendly way and said: "The more I hear Europeans talk about meditation, the more I feel like advising them against it. They just don't understand what it is all about. Read your own Holy Scriptures, and you find the same as in ours: Love your neighbor; love God; love your neighbor in God. And the rest does not count. Nowhere does it say that you should meditate. But if you want to love God and your neighbor and discover as a great truth that meditation can help you in this and may be decisive in achieving it, then you should meditate, and if you do not make the discovery of this need, then you should not meditate."

So this is not flight into one's own inner world, but it is a shield against those innermost inhibitions that prevent us from facing our neighbor and reality. And there is something else: A large part of what is thought to be an active facing of reality is actually nothing but a flight from the facing of oneself.

Reiter:

I began our conversation with a personal question, and I would like to end it with one. Professor von Weizsäcker, it is not at all common that a physicist, a man of the exact sciences, treasures meditative truth side by side with scientific truth, today, in this kind of society. And, as far as I know, you have been attacked for this, or dismissed condescendingly as a guru or mystic. What has been your reaction? And what was the experience that made of the physicist Weizsäcker an adherent of meditation?

Weizsäcker:

Well, let me say this: There will always be criticism; unfortunately I do not often get to hear it; but this doesn't really matter.

Even as a child I was in love with science, and at the same time I lived in a way that I later learned had a meditative basis. When I was twelve years old, I was already very much occupied with the problem that these two realities had to be the same reality, but that I just did not have the intellectual means to comprehend this. With this extended background, I would say today that the unity of nature, which we have learned to see through the development of science, is basically a mirror image of the unity that we seek in meditation. So my answer has to be that I don't see a difference. I see a difference in methods, in cultural traditions, in the concepts we employ, but I do not believe there is a difference in substance.

Notes

1. Th. S. Kuhn. *The Structure of Scientific Revolutions*. Chicago: University of Chicago Press, 1962. German edition: *Die Struktur wissenschaftlicher Revolutionen*. Frankfurt: Suhrkamp, 1967.
2. Erik Eriksen. *Insight and Responsibility*. New York: W. W. Norton, 1964.
3. See note 1, above.
4. René Thom. *Stabilité structurelle et morphogénèse*. Reading, MA: Benjamin, 1972.
5. Published in: T. M. P. Mahadevan, ed. *Spiritual Perspectives. Essays in Mysticism and Metaphysics*. New Delhi: Arnold-Heinemann, 1975.
6. In German I wrote here, *Es gibt einen Wissenden*. The word "knower" originates in the English interpretation of Vedanta philosophy. In the German heading of this chapter I use the corresponding term *Subjekt*. But I must add that in European philosophy the notion of "subject" (*Subjekt*)—criticized by Kant—always implies the notion of "substance," namely, the basis, *res cogitans*. Such an implication is avoided in Vedanta philosophy.
7. Following Bohr we say that it must be possible to describe the instrument in terms of classical physics. I have tried to analyze this statement in another paper ("Classical and Quantum Description," in *The Physicist's Conception of Nature*, edited by J. Mehra, Reidel, 1973). The objectivity of the classical description rests, I think, on irreversible processes in the instrument. But in strict quantum theory this irreversibility is only a subjective description resting on a loss of information that is in principle always the information for an observer.
8. This is the problem known as "Wigner's friend," from: E. Wigner. *The Scientist Speculates*. Edited by I. J. Good. London: Heinemann, 1962. (p. 284)
9. In a pragmatic theory of truth this structure would be called the ecological niche of the concept. It would be that structure due to which propositions using the concept can be successful speech acts or mental acts.

10. L. E. J. Brouwer. *Consciousness, Philosophy, and Mathematics*. Proceedings of the International Congress of Philosophy, vol. I, fasc. II, edited by E. W. Beth, H. J. Pos, J. M. A. Hollok. Amsterdam: 1949.

11. Konrad Lorenz. *Die Rückseite des Spiegels. Versuch einer Naturgeschichte des menschlichen Erkennens*. Munich: Piper, 1973.

12. The difference between *a priori* and innate, made explicit by Kant, is dropped by Lorenz, but that does not change, in principle, anything in Lorenz's arguments. He says only that *ideas* are not innate, but that this does not apply to the "core in subjects . . . that makes it possible that the conceived ideas originate this way and in no other way, and that they can be related, in addition, to objects that are not yet given." This is exactly in Lorenz's sense. But Kant, in the *Critique of Pure Reason*, objects against "a preformation system of pure reason" where the categories would be "subjective thinking modes that had been implanted in us by our Creator in such a way that their use coincided exactly with the laws of nature in accordance with which experience takes place," so that "in such a case the categories lack the *necessity* that is essential to their concepts," thus obviously the insight in their truth that was given with them. The *experience* of their necessity appears to be easily explicable in the way that Lorenz took; the *truth* of this necessity is made into a problem by science as it progresses.

13. K. R. Popper. "The Rationality of Scientific Revolutions." In *Problems in Scientific Revolution: Progress and Obstacles to Progress in the Sciences*, edited by Rom Harré. The Herbert Spencer Lectures 1973. Oxford: Clarendon Press, 1975.

14. I am deeply indebted to: Kindermann. *Hans J. Morgenthau und die theoretischen Grundlagen des politischen Realismus*.

15. All quotations translated from the German edition of Freud's work by Fischer-Bücherei.

16. I am indebted for essential information to: E. Tugendhat. *Vorlesungen zur Einführung in die sprachanalytische Philosophie*. Suhrkamp Taschenbuch Wissenschaft 45. Frankfurt: Suhrkamp, 1976.

17. J. Lukasiewicz. *Aristotle's Syllogistic from the Standpoint of Modern Formal Logic*. Oxford: Clarendon Press, 1951. Also: G. Patzig. *Die aristotelische Syllogistik*. Göttingen: 1959.

18. J. W. von Goethe. *Materialien zur Geschichte der Farbenlehre*. Hamburger Ausgabe XIV. Hamburg: Christian Wegner, 1960. (pp. 53–54)

19. G. Picht. "Die Erfahrung der Geschichte" (Part VI, 1958). In *Wahrheit, Vernunft, Verantwortung*. Stuttgart: Klett, 1969. Also: G. Picht. "Theorie und Meditation 1973." In *Merkur* 4 (1974).

20. G. W. F. Hegel. *Phänomenologie des Geistes*. Vol. 2 (p. 60). All quotations translated from the German edition of Hegel's work by Glockner.

21. All italicized passages in Hegel quotations are Hegel's own emphasis.

22. Jacob Burckhardt. *Weltgeschichtliche Betrachtungen*. Kröner, 1935. (*Force and Freedom: Reflections on History*.)

23. Heidegger had read Frege in his youth. Compare: Martin Heidegger. "Neuere Forschungen über Logik." In *Literarische Rundschau für das katholische Deutschland* 38 (1912). I am grateful to Winfried Franzen for this reference.

24. *Schleiermacher-Auswahl*. With postscript by Karl Barth. Munich and Hamburg: Siebenstern Taschenbuch, 1968. (p. 293)

25. Eberhard Bethge. *Dietrich Bonhoeffer. Eine Biographie*. Munich: Christian Kaiser, 1970.

26. Ernst Feil. *Die Theologie Dietrich Bonhoeffers*. Munich: Christian Kaiser; Mainz: Matthias Grünewald, 1971.

Index